# Career Paths in Psychology

# Career Paths in Psychology

## WHERE YOUR DEGREE CAN TAKE YOU

**THIRD EDITION**

*Edited by*
ROBERT J. STERNBERG

American Psychological Association • *Washington, DC*

Published by
American Psychological Association
750 First Street, NE
Washington, DC 20002
www.apa.org

To order
APA Order Department
P.O. Box 92984
Washington, DC 20090-2984
Tel: (800) 374-2721; Direct: (202) 336-5510
Fax: (202) 336-5502; TDD/TTY: (202) 336-6123
Online: www.apa.org/pubs/books
E-mail: order@apa.org

In the U.K., Europe, Africa, and the Middle East, copies may be ordered from
American Psychological Association
3 Henrietta Street
Covent Garden, London
WC2E 8LU England

Typeset in Meridien by Circle Graphics, Inc., Columbia, MD

Printer: Edwards Brothers, Inc., Lillington, NC
Cover Designer: Naylor Design, Washington, DC

**Library of Congress Cataloging-in-Publication Data**

Names: Sternberg, Robert J., editor.
Title: Career paths in psychology : where your degree can take you / edited
  by Robert J. Sternberg.
Description: Third edition. | Washington, DC : American Psychological
  Association, [2017] | Includes bibliographical references and index.
Identifiers: LCCN 2016011718 | ISBN 9781433823107 | ISBN 1433823101
Subjects: LCSH: Psychology–Vocational guidance.
Classification: LCC BF76 .C38 2017 | DDC 150.23/73–dc23
LC record available at https://lccn.loc.gov/2016011718

**British Library Cataloguing-in-Publication Data**
A CIP record is available from the British Library.

*Printed in the United States of America*
*Third Edition*

http://dx.doi.org/10.1037/15960-000

10 9 8 7 6 5 4 3 2

# Contents

# III

## *Specialized Settings*   245

# Contributors

**Jane Annunziata, PsyD,** private practice, McLean, VA

**Natalie M. Anumba, PhD,** Assistant Professor of Psychiatry, University of Massachusetts Medical School; and Forensic Psychologist, Worcester Recovery Center and Hospital, Worcester, MA

**Mary S. Barringer, PhD, LSSP,** Cypress-Fairbanks Independent School District, Houston, TX

**Colonel (Retired) Paul T. Bartone, PhD,** Professor and Senior Research Fellow, Center for Technology and National Security Policy, National Defense University, Washington, DC

**Anne E. Beall, PhD,** CEO, Beall Research, Inc., Chicago, IL

**Laura E. Berk, PhD,** Distinguished Professor of Psychology, Illinois State University, Normal

**Hilary Bertisch, PhD, ABPP-CN,** Rusk Institute of Rehabilitation Medicine, New York University School of Medicine, New York, NY

**Judith S. Blanton, PhD, ABPP,** Blanton Consulting, Pasadena, CA

**Bruce L. Bobbitt, PhD, LP,** Senior Vice President, Behavioral Health Quality, Optum, Eden Prairie, MN

**Marc H. Bornstein, PhD,** Senior Investigator and Head, Child and Family Research, *Eunice Kennedy Shriver* National Institute of Child Health and Human Development, Bethesda, MD

**Joel Brockner, PhD,** Phillip Hettleman Professor of Business, Management Division, Columbia Business School, Columbia University, New York, NY

**Wayne J. Camara, PhD,** Senior Vice President of Research, ACT®, Iowa City, IA

**Joseph E. Comaty, PhD,** Clinical and Medical Psychologist–Consultant, Adjunct Assistant Professor in Psychology;

and emeritus faculty, Southern Louisiana Internship Consortium, Louisiana State University, Baton Rouge

**David B. Coppel, PhD, FACSM, CC-AASP,** Department of Neurological Surgery, Department of Psychiatry and Behavioral Sciences, Department of Psychology, and Director of Neuropsychological Services and Research, University of Washington Sports Concussion Program, Harborview Medical Center and Seattle Children's Hospital, Seattle, WA; and neuropsychologist for the Seattle Seahawks of National Football League, Seattle, WA

**David M. Corey, PhD, ABPP,** police psychologist, Corey & Stewart, Portland, OR; and faculty fellow, Fielding Graduate University, Santa Barbara, CA

**Paul L. Craig, PhD, ABPP-CN,** Department of Psychiatry and Behavioral Sciences, University of Washington School of Medicine (WWAMI Program), Anchorage, AK

**Janet Davidson, PhD,** Department of Psychology and Faculty Director of Advising, Lewis & Clark College, Portland, OR

**Sally S. Dickerson, PhD,** Associate Provost for Sponsored Research and Professor of Psychology, Pace University, New York, NY

**Shantina R. Dixon, PhD, LSSP,** Coordinator of Special Education, Bryan Independent School District, Bryan, TX

**Timothy R. Elliott, PhD, ABPP,** Department of Educational Psychology, College of Education and Human Development, Texas A&M University, College Station

**Elissa S. Epel, PhD,** Professor, Department of Psychiatry, University of California, San Francisco

**Christine H. Farber, PhD,** independent practice, Glastonbury, CT

**Rebecca A. Ferrer, PhD,** Program Director, Basic Biobehavioral and Psychological Sciences Branch, National Cancer Institute, Rockville, MD

**Adam D. Galinsky, PhD,** Vikram S. Pandit Professor of Business and Chair of the Management Division of Columbia Business School, Columbia University, New York, NY

**Kenji Hakuta, PhD,** Lee L. Jacks Professor of Education Emeritus, Stanford University, Stanford, CA

**Puncky Paul Heppner, PhD,** Distinguished Curators Emeritus Professor, University of Missouri–Columbia

**Gregory A. Hinrichsen, PhD, ABPP,** Department of Geriatrics and Palliative Medicine, Icahn School of Medicine at Mount Sinai, New York, NY; and Department of Psychiatry and Behavioral Sciences, Albert Einstein College of Medicine, Bronx, NY

**Michele J. Karel, PhD, ABPP,** Mental Health Services, VA Central Office, Washington, DC

**William M. P. Klein, PhD,** Associate Director of Behavioral Research, National Cancer Institute, Bethesda, MD

**Ann T. Landes, PhD,** Department of Veterans Affairs, Malcom Randall VA Medical Center, Gainesville, FL

**Jennifer S. Lerner, PhD,** Harvard Kennedy School, Harvard University, Cambridge, MA

**Sam Maniar, PhD,** Sport Psychologist, Cleveland Browns, Cleveland, OH

**Malia F. Mason, PhD,** Associate Professor, Management Division, Columbia Business School, Columbia University, New York, NY

**Antoinette M. Minniti, PhD, CPsychol,** Associate Executive Director, Office of CE Sponsor Approval, American Psychological Association, Washington, DC

**Marc Nemiroff, PhD,** private practice, Potomac, MD

**Ira K. Packer, PhD,** Clinical Professor of Psychiatry, University of Massachusetts Medical School, Worcester

**Aric A. Prather, PhD,** Assistant Professor, Department of Psychiatry, University of California, San Francisco

**Rebecca M. Puhl, PhD,** Deputy Director, Rudd Center for Food Policy and Obesity, Hartford, CT; and Professor, Department of Human Development and Family Studies, University of Connecticut, Storrs

**Joseph F. Rath, PhD,** Rusk Institute of Rehabilitation Medicine, New York University School of Medicine, New York, NY

**Jennifer K. Robbennolt, JD, PhD,** Alice Curtis Campbell Professor of Law and Professor of Psychology, University of Illinois, Champaign

**Henry L. Roediger, III, PhD,** Department of Psychological and Brain Sciences, Washington University in St. Louis, St. Louis, MO

**Pamela Rutledge, MBA, PhD,** Director, Media Psychology Research Center, Newport Beach, CA; and Media Psychology Faculty, Fielding Graduate University, Santa Barbara, CA

**Marlene B. Schwartz, PhD,** Director, Rudd Center for Food Policy and Obesity, Hartford, CT; and Professor, Department of Human Development and Family Studies, University of Connecticut, Storrs

**Lonnie R. Sherrod, PhD,** Executive Director, Society for Research in Child Development, Ann Arbor, MI; and Distinguished Lecturer, Applied Developmental Psychology, Fordham University, Bronx, NY

**Rosemarie I. Sokol-Chang, PhD,** Publisher, APA Journals, American Psychological Association, Washington, DC

**Barbara A. Spellman, JD, PhD,** Professor of Law, University of Virginia School of Law, Charlottesville

**Robert J. Sternberg, PhD,** Professor of Human Development, Cornell University, Ithaca, NY; and Honorary Professor of Psychology, University of Heidelberg, Germany

**John P. Sullivan, PsyD,** Clinical Sport Psychologist and Sport Scientist, National Football League, Providence College, University of Rhode Island; and Founder of Clinical & Sports Consulting Services, Newport, RI and Washington, DC

**Gary R. VandenBos, PhD,** Publisher Emeritus, American Psychological Association, Washington, DC

**Melba J. T. Vasquez, PhD, ABPP,** independent practice, Austin, TX

**Sean W. Wakely, BA,** Founder and Principal Adviser, Academic Author Advisers, San Francisco, CA

# Career Paths in Psychology

*Robert J. Sternberg*

# Introduction

F ew fields of study offer more career opportunities than does psychology. This book is about those career opportunities and how you can take advantage of them. The opportunities are diverse, challenging, and fun. And for the most part, they pay well. They are also flexible: People can switch, often fairly easily and with a minimum amount of adjustment, from one career within psychology to another. Moreover, even within a single career, the variety of challenges and activities will interest even the most easily bored individual.

This is the third edition of this work. The first edition was published roughly two decades ago. The second edition was published roughly one decade ago. When 10 or so years have passed, the time is ripe for a new edition, simply because the opportunities for psychologists change so much within the course of 10 years. This book contains 12 more chapters than the second edition did, and that edition in turn contained 5 more chapters than did the first. You can see that opportunities in psychology, unlike in many fields, have

http://dx.doi.org/10.1037/15960-001
*Career Paths in Psychology: Where Your Degree Can Take You, Third Edition*, R. J. Sternberg (Editor)

been constantly expanding. All of the chapters in this book are new. Some are revisions of early chapters, but even the revisions reflect the changing nature of the job market in the field of psychology.

Psychology is not only one of the most interesting fields of study but also one of the most diverse: Few fields offer a greater number and variety of career opportunities. College students who decide to major in psychology, therefore, open up a world of possibilities for themselves. Graduate students can be confident of diverse kinds of careers, and practicing psychologists often can change the kind of work they do or the setting in which they work while remaining with the field of psychology.

Psychology is one of the most rewarding fields a person can enter. Psychology can be fun. It helps people, advances scientific and clinical understanding, and pays relatively well. Most psychologists earn well above the median salary for the United States. Few earn stratospheric wages, but some do—generally highly successful psychologists in private practice, organizational psychologists, or writers of textbooks or books for the popular press. Realistically, chances are you will neither go broke nor live in a palatial mansion if you choose a career in psychology. What you will do is help people improve their lives, help students learn to understand themselves and others, and perhaps advance the state of the field's knowledge—and have a great time while you are doing whatever you are doing.

This book will help you start on a career path in psychology, or perhaps continue on one or even change the path you are on. The chapters in this book tell you about 30 different careers in psychology for those who have obtained a terminal degree (usually, a PhD, EdD, or PsyD). Each chapter discusses the nature of the career, how to prepare for the career, typical activities people pursue while engaged in the career, the approximate range of financial compensation for the career, the advantages and disadvantages people typically find in the career, personal and professional attributes desirable for success in the career, and opportunities for employment and advancement in the career.

The authors of the chapters were chosen for their distinction in their chosen careers. They all have achieved a level of prominence and a depth of experience that any budding graduate student should seek to emulate. They were asked to write about their careers not only because of their stature in their respective fields but also because of their ability to convey the excitement of their careers to readers of this book.

A book of this length cannot cover every possible career, but the careers that are covered are fairly well representative of the range of work psychologists do and the range of careers that a substantial proportion of psychologists have chosen.

The book is divided into three main parts: academia; clinical and counseling psychology; specialized settings. This organization of chapters is but one of many possible arrangements, but it does seem to capture a way in which at least some people organize the field.

I hope readers find in this volume a series of examples that will both inspire and enthuse them. Psychology is a field that offers many possibilities, and I wish you well on your journey of discovery.

# ACADEMIA

Henry L. Roediger, III

# Psychologists in University Departments of Psychology or Psychological Science

1

W riters of this book make one fact abundantly clear: Psychologists work in many different settings at many different occupations. Virtually all were trained in colleges and universities, and therefore almost everyone in the field is familiar to some degree with psychology in an academic setting. Most students reading this book are also in an academic setting and so have some appreciation for what their professors do. However, my experience from talking with students over the past 35 years indicates that whereas they understand some of the prominent aspects of careers in academic settings, they do not

Henry L. Roediger, III, PhD, is the James S. McDonnell Distinguished University Professor of Psychology at Washington University in St. Louis. He received his BA from Washington and Lee University and his PhD from Yale University. Roediger previously taught at Purdue University, the University of Toronto, and Rice University before moving to Washington University in 1996. His research has been concerned primarily with human memory.

This chapter benefited from the comments of Lyn Goff, Jane McConnell, Kathleen McDermott, John Nestojko, Kerry Robinson, Rebecca Roediger, and Dave Schneider.

http://dx.doi.org/10.1037/15960-002
*Career Paths in Psychology: Where Your Degree Can Take You, Third Edition,*
R. J. Sternberg (Editor)

know about parts of the profession that are less apparent from their own vantage point. I discuss some of these more hidden features in this chapter.

Writing about the academic career in psychology is difficult because academia affords a number of different types of careers. The psychologist teaching in a community college, for example, may be a part-time professor who has another job outside academia. Professors in liberal arts colleges may devote much of their time to teaching, often three or four courses a semester. Whereas the teaching loads in community colleges and other liberal arts colleges may leave little time for research or other activities, faculty at larger universities with graduate programs (often called *research universities*) are expected to conduct research and publish it in scholarly journals. Typically, faculty at these institutions teach one or two courses a semester at either the graduate or undergraduate level.

Although the careers in academic psychology are different in the various academic settings, all share certain features, such as teaching and counseling students. This chapter covers the common features while also touching on aspects of the job that vary among academic settings. I draw on my experiences in teaching at Purdue University, the University of Toronto, Rice University, and Washington University and my own education at Washington and Lee University and Yale University. All of the schools at which I have taught are research universities, but two (Purdue and Toronto) are public (i.e., supported by government) and two (Rice and Washington) are private (i.e., supported largely by privately raised funds). Enrollment at these schools varies widely, from around 33,000 students at Purdue (when I was there) to about 4,000 at Rice.

## The Nature of the Academic Psychology Career

The nature of one's career in academia depends, as noted, partly on the kind of academic institution. The most obvious characteristic of a career in academia is teaching, the common thread at all institutions of higher learning. Anyone devoting his or her life to an academic career should have a love of teaching as well as a love of learning and a desire to instill that love of learning in others. Teaching, in its broadest sense, occurs on many levels and may take place in several settings. In addition to teaching formal courses, professors interact with students in small seminars, private consultations, research meetings, and sometimes (depending on the school) settings outside the classroom, such as dining halls.

One of the most delightful benefits for faculty members of being in an academic setting is the opportunity to learn from students. Students new to psychology often have different and interesting viewpoints. Also, faculty learn new information when students pick novel topics for term papers or research papers or when they do an outstanding job reviewing what is known.

It is wrong (or, at best, only partly right) to think of a college professor as someone who learned about his or her field in graduate school and who then went out to teach that knowledge. Education only begins the process of learning, which continues throughout the career of teaching in academia. Professors must continually keep up with their fast-changing fields to keep their courses current. Of course, no one can master all aspects of every field one teaches, but being a professor causes one to keep up with at least the broad sweep—the main ideas and major new developments—in the topics one teaches.

In sum, the primary features of devoting oneself to an academic career are the love of learning and the desire to instill that love in others. But what does one do in academic settings besides teach? I turn to this issue next.

## Activities of College Professors

What do professors do besides teach? Lots of things. They conduct research, write, and serve on committees, to mention but a few activities. College professors often are criticized because, the way some outsiders see it, they teach so little. What people mean by that is that the number of hours professors actually spend in the classroom is relatively small when compared, say, with high school teachers' hours. This difference in time spent teaching does not mean that teaching at the college level is not a demanding profession or that these professors do not work hard. They do. But most people outside the profession are unaware of the range of demands professors face. The illustrations in the following sections are somewhat personal because I do all these things, but all professors perform most of the same activities at some point in their careers.

### PREPARING COURSES

Before a professor actually walks into a classroom, he or she has undertaken a huge amount of preparation. Preparing for a lecture that lasts an hour may take several hours of background reading, note taking, preparation of slides, or other activities such as arranging a classroom demonstration. The professor not only must know what is in the assigned text but also must consult other books and research articles in preparing the lecture because the lecture usually goes far beyond the text material. Students sometimes complain about the workload or amount of reading in a course, but typically the professor is doing much more, especially the first time a course is taught. College professors who are just beginning teaching often spend most of their time in course preparation. Beginning professors often teach large lecture courses, and preparing material for 40 or so lectures for each course over the period of a semester takes huge amounts of time. Even experienced professors who have been teaching for years must update their material continually. And if they decide to teach a course on a new topic, they must begin preparation from scratch. For professors who teach three or four courses a semester, course preparation may take virtually all their time in their early years in the profession.

Recent advances in technology have changed course preparation somewhat. Many publishers of college textbooks offer supplemental packages that include aids for teaching (e.g., online tutorials, PowerPoint slides, and links to TED talks or to blogs). These aids can be wonderfully helpful in making large lecture courses more interesting, but in a way, they increase the demands placed on the professor to learn more about these new technologies, to preview the materials, and to integrate them into the course.

## TEACHING

Professors may teach in lecture courses, in small seminars that combine lecture with discussion, or in reading groups in which everyone has read the material and discusses it. Although the lecture method of teaching has been under attack for years, it is probably still the most common form of teaching. However, much has been written to instruct professors on converting standard (i.e., noninteractive) lectures into experiences in which the students participate more fully (e.g., small breakout discussions among groups, class exercises or experiments, demonstrations). Everyone reading this book knows that there are huge individual differences in teaching: Some people are gifted teachers because of some combination of personality, knowledge, eloquence, humor, and skill in presentation. But probably everyone can be a more effective teacher by working at it (see Bernstein and Lucas's 2004 chapter "Tips for Effective Teaching").

As noted previously, the time professors spend in the classroom often appears to be limited. During much of my career, I have taught two courses a semester, usually one undergraduate and one graduate course, so I spend about 6 hours a week in the classroom. I usually work 60 to 70 hours in a typical week, however, because my time is occupied with all the other activities listed in this section.

## MAKING AND GRADING TESTS

Composing and grading tests is part of teaching but is separate from course preparation and time spent in class. Depending on the number of courses taught, the number of students in the course, and the type of tests and assignments given, these activities can take large amounts of time. Multiple-choice tests (and other objective tests, such as true–false or matching tests) are easy to grade, but they often require considerable time to compose. Designing essay and short-answer tests is often quicker, but these tests take much longer to grade.

My own philosophy in giving tests has changed greatly over the years. I used to give three or four tests per course, along with a few other assignments (depending on the level of the course). I have now changed my policy so that students in all my courses are given an assignment for every class. They are supposed to do the reading before class and, depending on the size of the class, either writing a brief essay based on the reading or taking a brief quiz at the end of the class. The reason for this practice is that the process of answering questions—retrieval practice, as it is called—is an important memory enhancer (Roediger & Karpicke, 2006). Having continual assessment in a course requires students to be engaged in the material, grapple with concepts in writing the essays, and attend class regularly (for more on benefits of regular testing in classes, see Roediger, Putnam, & Smith, 2011). Lyle and Crawford (2011) showed that students taking statistics in sections in which there were daily quizzes received markedly better grades than students in regular sections without quizzes when all were assessed on the same tests. Regular assessment leads to greater learning.

What types of quizzes and tests should one use? I do not give only objective types of questions (multiple choice, true–false), because evidence indicates that these sorts of tests cause students to focus on learning isolated facts rather than drawing material together to see the larger picture and the overarching themes (e.g., Schmidt, 1983). So I prefer to give tests that require students to write essays to encourage them to look for interrelated themes when studying. The types of tests I use depend on the class size, the level of the course, and other factors. I have taught introductory psychology with class sizes ranging from 150 to nearly 500 students. Then, because of grading demands, most of the tests and exams are objective items with only one essay question. Teaching smaller undergraduate courses permits me to use essay tests in addition to daily quizzes. I always require a cumulative final exam to give students spaced review of the material in the whole course, because spacing of review is much better than concentrated (or massed) learning (Roediger & Pyc, 2012).

Teaching a small graduate course is quite different from teaching introductory psychology. When I teach graduate courses, I usually require the students to write shorter essays on various topics for class session during the course and then to write a long paper reviewing a body of research pertaining to any topic of the course that they find of interest. At the end of the paper, they are required to write a proposal for future research that would add to knowledge in the field.

I have spent quite a few paragraphs on assessment—something I would not have done when I was just starting out in my career—but I am convinced that a careful plan of assessment is critical to teaching and to student learning. You might wonder whether those of us who use frequent assessment get clobbered in teacher ratings—after all, college students might rebel at being quizzed in every class. My own experience and that of colleagues who follow similar practices is that this problem does not arise. One student wrote on a course evaluation: "I thought I would dislike having a quiz every class, but it turned out to be helpful. This is the first course I have ever truly kept up with since I've been at the university."

## CONSULTING WITH STUDENTS

Most professors enjoy meeting with students outside of class. Depending on the type of institution, students feel varying degrees of freedom to visit with faculty and to talk about problems in a course, ask for advice about courses or careers, learn more about the material, or discuss ideas. For universities with graduate programs, a considerable amount of faculty time is devoted to advising graduate students on their research and discussing research with them. I estimate that I spend 4 to 5 hours a week consulting with graduate students and undergraduate students about their research projects. In addition, once a week, I hold a lab meeting that includes both students working directly with me as well as others who also want to attend (even though they primarily work with another professor). The lab meeting functions like an informal course, but the topics shift across a range of topics from week to week. Advising students is a critical part of the life of a college professor. Keep in mind that you often are shaping young lives with your advice when they ask, "May I work in your lab?" or "Should I think about going to graduate school?"

## CONDUCTING RESEARCH

Many faculty members conduct psychological research. This activity is especially common in research universities, but psychologists in all types of schools have programs of interesting and important research. Planning this research takes time, although it usually occurs in the natural course of other activities, such as consulting with students, reading articles, and writing proposals for research. Research may seem to be a mysterious process at first, but it is the lifeblood of every academic discipline because the discoveries and advances in every field all come from new research. Scientists know the state of knowledge in their fields, and their curiosity about the unexplained leads them to push forward the frontiers of knowledge. The motivations for future research are many—exploring unexplained past findings, testing implications of theories to see whether they hold true, seeing whether findings obtained in one setting generalize to another, and many others. The researcher usually works from a theory to generate hypotheses and then collects data to evaluate the hypotheses. When students first come into a field, they often wonder about the source of all the ideas that generate the research they are reading about and about whether they will be able to generate their own ideas. Later, after being immersed in the field, most researchers lament the lack of time and resources to conduct all the research they would like to do.

When students first enter graduate school, a professor often guides them in their initial research projects. No one expects students just beginning in a field to design and conduct cutting-edge research because the process of becoming a researcher is gradual. Collaboration is critical as the student learns to conduct research. Typically, students who are beginning to work with me will take on part of a project, which already might be ongoing, to get their feet wet and to immerse themselves in the problems and procedures of the field. Throughout the 4 or 5 years that I work with the student, however, he or she gradually becomes more independent and begins designing, conducting, and writing about research, needing less consultation with me.

Students often learn about conducting research in one-on-one meetings with their major professors. Students who work with me meet in our weekly lab meeting. Sometimes a student will present his or her research or plans for future research, but often I select a recent research article or chapter for all of us to read and to discuss. Many ideas for future research come out of these meetings. (I cover other aspects of research elsewhere in this chapter.)

## WRITING LETTERS OF REFERENCE

Surely, you might think, writing letters of references does not deserve a separate section in this chapter. But, yes, it does. During certain times of the year, writing letters of reference takes a great deal of time. Undergraduate students need letters of reference for applications to graduate school and for jobs. Graduate students need employment letters of reference, perhaps for 20–30 (or even more) applications. Former students and colleagues in the field need letters for jobs to which they apply. Also, as one becomes more senior in the field, other universities request letters about candidates being considered for promotion and tenure. (Tenure is the award of lifetime job security to faculty so that professors may investigate any topic freely, without fear of reprisal for investigating taboo topics or taking unpopular stances.) Often these requests are accompanied by a selection of the candidate's relevant writings, a statement of his or her research accomplishments and plans, and curriculum vitae. Processing all this information before writing the letter can take several hours. I estimate that in a given year I write letters of reference for 10–15 students and colleagues (and these need to go to many places), as well as 5–7 candidates for promotion at other universities. All these letters take time, especially during the fall and winter. Writing letters of reference is seasonal labor.

## ATTENDING FACULTY AND COMMITTEE MEETINGS

A university is, among other things, a large organization with a hierarchical structure. Organizations need the various groups that deal with particular matters to run smoothly. Within the typical psychology department, there may be any of the following:

- A space committee to assign research space to people
- A committee for subject use to oversee proposals for testing human and animal subjects
- An animal care committee to oversee the care and housing of animals
- A promotion and tenure committee composed of senior professors
- A graduate committee to oversee the graduate program
- An undergraduate committee to perform the same service for the undergraduate program

An individual professor might be assigned to only one or two of these committees, but the assignments do take time. In addition, professors attend general faculty meetings of the department and of the university faculty as a whole.

Professors also attend committee meetings for students. In undergraduate programs with honors degrees, a professor may be a part of a two- or three-member committee that advises and examines the research of an honors student. In universities with graduate programs, each student typically has a committee both for the master's degree and for the PhD. Professors may meet with students to discuss the proposal that deals with the research the student is planning and how it is to be carried out. Then, eventually, faculty must read the thesis or dissertation that the student has written, and the student must defend it at another meeting. Some universities also require preliminary or qualifying examinations of students before they embark on the PhD, which necessitates faculty attendance at other committee meetings. Many universities require an outside member to sit on dissertation committees, that is, someone from a different department from the student candidate. I have served on dissertation committees for anthropology, education, and philosophy students over the years.

Professors attend other committee meetings in addition to those listed thus far. Professors may need to staff search committees when their department is hiring a new faculty member; these take a large amount of time—first to review the numerous applications, then to interview three or four candidates, and then to decide whom to recommend for the position. Professors also may be involved with any of the other committees that exist for the entire university, such as search committees for a new dean, provost, or president. Most universities still have other committees to advise on such matters as athletics and admissions. At certain times during the academic year, committee work can require considerable time. Sometimes it is not fascinating work, but it is critical to the overall good of the department and the university.

Serving on professional committees also can take large chunks of time. Every national and regional organization of psychologists has a program committee, an executive committee, and often many other committees. University psychologists frequently are asked to serve on these committees.

## COMMUNICATING WITH OTHER SCHOLARS WITH SIMILAR INTERESTS

One curious fact about universities is that individual faculty members may be intensely interested in one topic, whether it is the history of ancient Rome, the poetry of Wordsworth, the stars of the Orion nebula, or how people form and change beliefs and attitudes. Often, no one with your particular scholarly interest exists at your university, and yet you want to maintain contact with others in the specific field to share ideas and to learn of late-breaking developments. A century ago, scholarly communication was largely confined to reading others' books and articles, when they appeared, or writing letters. Communication is much faster now, and e-mail (and blogs and social media for some researchers) permits people to stay in constant contact and to learn of new developments almost instantaneously, either through informal contact or through formal means like posting journal articles quite quickly after they have been accepted by a journal. Many professors now find themselves glued to their computers, communicating with others with like interests. Many research collaborations blossom by e-mail; this mode of communication can especially aid professors at smaller colleges and universities by allowing them to communicate with almost anyone in the field. Although fascinating, this activity takes time, and it seems likely to become increasingly important.

## ATTENDING PROFESSIONAL MEETINGS

Professional meetings are another activity that permits academics to keep pace with their fields. People attend professional meetings to present their own research findings by giving papers or displaying posters and to hear about cutting-edge research by many others in their field. In psychology, there are national meetings of large organizations (e.g., the Association for Psychological Science and the American Psychological Association), of regional groups (e.g., the Midwestern Psychological Association), and of more specialized groups interested in particular topics (e.g., the Society for Research in Child Development). Many years ago, the big national meetings dominated the scene and they still play an important role, but many professors now choose to attend more specialized meetings concerned with research in their area of interest. Some professors do this in addition to attending national meetings, whereas other researchers do this instead of attending the more general meetings. The meetings usually last 2 to 3 days but can be longer. Attendance at such meetings is optional; some professors go to many, and others go to practically none. And attending talks and posters at the meeting is also optional. Attending at least some meetings is a good idea because it allows academics to become acquainted with people who have similar interests. Networking is important in academia, as in other spheres of life.

## WRITING

For psychologists active in research, technical writing is a critical skill, one that must continually be honed. The greatest research ever conducted would never become known if it had not been effectively communicated to others in the field. Psychologists in research universities must be skilled in writing research articles to communicate their findings clearly. Professors also have opportunities to write chapters for scholarly books (like this one), and some professors write monographs (treatises written by one author, usually on specialized areas of learning) to communicate their research to interested scholars. Technical and scholarly writing can be difficult skills to learn, but several useful guides exist (see Bem, 2004; Sternberg, 2003). In addition, researchers seeking support for their research usually write grant proposals to federal agencies and to foundations.

Some professors write textbooks in their areas of interest (e.g., developmental or social psychology) or general textbooks (e.g., on research methods or introductory psychology). Writing textbooks can be lucrative and is also a critical part of the education process. An outstanding teacher at one university, no matter how brilliant, has a limited impact: He or she will affect only the students attending those classes at that campus. But a professor who writes an outstanding textbook can help teach literally an entire generation of students about a given topic and entice those students further into this field of study. It is curious that textbook writing often is not rewarded professionally within university settings; colleagues and administrators do not see this kind of publication as the scholarly equal of other kinds of works (Roediger, 2004). With the great emphasis on the importance of teaching now reinvigorating universities, perhaps this attitude will be relaxed. After all, a textbook writer is a teacher of thousands of students, and the text is the main course contact for many students. In my own case, I have coauthored two textbooks—*Research Methods in Psychology* (Elmes, Kantowitz, & Roediger, 2006) and *Experimental Psychology: Understanding Psychological Research* (Kantowitz, Roediger, & Elmes, 2005)—that have both gone through eight editions and have been used in courses for several generations of students. In addition to the satisfaction I have obtained from having these books used widely over the past 25 years and from educating many students, I have learned much about psychology while researching material for the books.

## REVIEWING AND EDITING

Another task in academia that can take significant amounts of time is the evaluation of scholarly publications. Publishing in scholarly journals occurs by a process of peer review. If I submit an article for publication to a journal, the editor sends it to several experts in the field of inquiry (the peers), who are asked to read the article and to write evaluations of the research, answering such questions as, Does the paper deserve to be published? Does it make a significant contribution to knowledge? Do flaws exist in the reasoning or the methods or the statistical analysis of the results?

Serving as a referee on an article entails considerable work. Every manuscript deserves a careful and thoughtful reading and a fair and unbiased review. Reviewing a manuscript properly can take hours, and some researchers are called on by several journals and therefore receive many manuscripts to review. This activity can place a large burden on already overworked researchers, but there are rewards. A person learns about the latest findings in his or her field by reviewing manuscripts. In some cases (usually after a trial period during which the editor of the journal finds the person's reviewing especially good and insightful), reviewers become consulting editors for a journal. As the name implies, the editor then will send that reviewer more papers for consultation.

Psychologists who serve as editors or associate editors of journals make the final decisions about the publishability of articles in that journal. The reviewers make recommendations, but it is up to the editor to make a decision. Some journals receive hundreds (even thousands) of manuscripts a year, which means that editors must find time to read the articles, read the reviews of consultants, and then write letters of acceptance or rejection to the authors. The editorial process is critical in every field and requires great amounts of time from editors and reviewers.

Other types of reviewing may be required of the academic psychologist. For instance, textbooks are reviewed by many teachers both before they are published and during the revision process. In addition, many scholars evaluate books in book reviews published in scholarly journals or in the popular press.

## CONSULTING

Some psychology professors consult with organizations in industry or in other arenas (e.g., lawyers) about their areas of interest. Human factors psychologists may consult on the design of equipment to make the product easier to use. Industrial and organizational psychologists may consult with companies on personnel selection or on ways to improve the morale of the organization. Clinical and counseling psychologists in academia may have a small private practice. Cognitive and educational psychologists may advise companies and schools on instructional practices. Indeed, virtually every area of psychology has something to offer some industry or occupation. Psychologists in academia often step outside the academy to offer advice on more practical matters of the world.

## PERFORMING COMMUNITY SERVICE

Psychologists also may be called on for various kinds of community service. For example, they may be asked to educate the general public through lectures to civic and religious groups. In addition, they may work with community groups, such as Alcoholics Anonymous or a local crisis center, on various social or personal problems. Some psychologists appear on radio and television programs to explain psychological issues to wider audiences. Academics differ widely in how much time they spend in community service, but it can be rewarding because the teaching involved extends the traditional forums.

## SUMMARY OF ACTIVITIES

The dozen or so activities listed in this section include most of the activities in which psychologists in a psychology department might be involved, but the list is not exhaustive. Professors can and do participate in other activities, but this sample constitutes a reasonable range of the usual activities. After reading the foregoing account, your opinion might have swung from "College professors don't do much; they only teach a few hours a week" to "How can anyone do all these things?" Keep in mind that this section includes activities that occur over the course of a year; not all are done every day. One important feature of being a professor is that there is considerable time (i.e., summers and holidays) when teaching requirements are reduced or absent altogether. Yet these are not times of relaxation for professors. Most professors work as hard or harder during the summer months and vacations, but they work on different activities from those that occupy their time when classes are in session. These tasks include writing research reports, conducting research, attending meetings, and preparing courses for the next year, among others.

## Academic Settings

Psychology departments appear in all kinds of institutions of higher education. Almost every city or town of any size has a community college to—as the name implies—serve the members of the community. Professors in these settings usually devote most of their time to teaching (rather than research). Hundreds of relatively small private and public colleges and universities in the United States also offer undergraduate education in psychology culminating in a BA or BS degree. Each of these colleges and universities has a psychology department. Larger public and private schools provide both graduate and undergraduate education in psychology, so usually they have larger departments with faculty who specialize in various fields in psychology.

Students aspiring to an academic career in psychology may seek a position in any of these types of schools or in others, such as the independent schools in clinical psychology that give graduate degrees. Each type of school has its benefits, and all can be attractive places to work. For example, community colleges often have adult students who have worked and experienced more of life before they decided to return and further their education. Often these students are eager to learn and appreciate the opportunity to learn in a way that 18- to 21-year-old undergraduates may not. Other professors love teaching in small liberal arts colleges. The student-to-faculty ratio is often low, which promotes good interactions with students. Similarly, faculty at larger schools or research universities may enjoy interacting with graduate students, conducting research, and publishing in scholarly journals. The demands and rewards of the various academic settings are different, and some may appeal more to one type of person than to another. If you are considering a career in academia, you should consider carefully which type of setting might suit you best.

## PREPARING FOR THE ACADEMIC CAREER

The standard preparation for a career in a psychology department is usually fairly straightforward. Typically, a person should have an undergraduate degree in psychology or a degree in some related field, such as biology, anthropology, or neuroscience, and a considerable amount of psychology coursework. Next, a student interested in an academic career should apply to graduate school. Students do not apply to graduate school in the general area of psychology, but rather to a specialized field in which they are interested (e.g., cognitive psychology, social psychology, clinical psychology). If you intend to pursue a graduate degree in psychology, you should find out from your advisors and from other sources which schools have good programs in your area of interest and then apply only to those schools. Be sure, however, your passion lies in that area and in gaining a graduate degree. Graduate school is a long and sometimes hard road, and too often, undergraduate students seem to want to attend graduate school because they do not know what else to do.

Graduate school training usually takes from 4 to 6 years, although longer periods are not unheard of, depending on what other duties a student may have (e.g., heavy teaching requirements, a part-time job for financial support). Typically, students receive a master's degree in 2 or 3 years and then begin working on a PhD. Students receiving a PhD in clinical psychology need to complete an internship if they want to be licensed to practice, which most do. Students receiving PhDs in other areas may take a postdoctoral fellowship following completion of their degree to further their research training.

While in graduate school, the student learns about the subject matter of psychology in general and his or her field in particular. Doing coursework, reading, attending talks and colloquia, and participating in discussions with advisors and other faculty are the usual means of learning. Students usually receive their research training through an apprentice system in which they work closely with one or more faculty members to learn how to conduct research. Many other professional aspects of psychology are learned almost by osmosis (or observational learning) and from watching how successful people in the profession operate. Two books that help people prepare for academia are *The Complete Academic: A Career Guide* (Darley, Zanna, & Roediger, 2004) and *Psychology 101 1/2: The Unspoken Rules for Success in Academia* (Sternberg, 2017). Again, graduate education in a field should be considered only the beginning. Psychologists continue learning their entire lifetimes, and in academia, they do so from continual course preparation, students, research, reading, and professional meetings.

## FINANCIAL COMPENSATION

I am writing this in July 2015. The range of salaries for full-time university professors in psychology is quite great. For those interested in evaluating the salary ranges of psychologists, the American Psychological Association publishes figures based on surveys of its membership. Salary differences occur between types of schools, geographic regions, small-town versus large-city location, and the various specialty areas within psychology. The 2013–2014 figures shown in Table 1.1 are from a report by the Research Office of the American Psychological Association (Wicherski, Hamp, Christidis, & Stamm, 2014); the mean salary for all ranks at universities with doctoral programs was $80,983 for that year.

Psychology professors will never be accused of entering their profession to become rich. Professors usually can live comfortably but not opulently. Professors can augment their academic salaries by consulting, writing textbooks, reviewing textbooks for publishers, obtaining research grants (which pay summer salaries), and doing extra teaching (e.g., during summer sessions or at night). In addition, most colleges and universities offer good benefit packages in the form of health care and the like as well as good retirement programs. So although no one is likely to become wealthy by teaching in a college or university, professors usually can afford a comfortable lifestyle.

## ADVANTAGES AND DISADVANTAGES
## OF THE CAREER

Some people contemplating a career in academia consider the range of salaries the major drawback. A person could probably make more money over his or her lifetime by becoming a lawyer or engineer or by obtaining a master's degree in business administration and going into business. If you definitely have personal wealth as the major goal in life, then an academic career may not be appropriate for you. But most professors have other goals in mind. The benefits of an academic career are many, but they have more to do with the quality and style of life and less to do with money. First, professors have considerable freedom and flexibility in arranging one's time. Besides giving classes and attending some mandatory meetings, individuals are often free to manage their time as needed, so long as the work gets done.

For example, I am writing this section of the chapter after 11:00 p.m. I am free during the day, however, to attend to personal matters, if need be. I sometimes play squash during my lunch hour, which is stretched

## TABLE 1.1

**2013–2014 Salaries for Full-Time Faculty in U.S. Doctoral Departments of Psychology by Rank and Years in Rank**

| | Median | 10% | 25% | 75% | 90% | Mean | SD | N |
|---|---|---|---|---|---|---|---|---|
| **Full professor** | | | | | | | | |
| 24 or more years | 138,875 | 93,600 | 110,142 | 175,055 | 206,199 | 146,031 | 49,681 | 309 |
| 18–23 years | 126,000 | 86,052 | 102,432 | 159,398 | 188,435 | 132,959 | 41,416 | 243 |
| 12–17 years | 115,360 | 84,480 | 96,773 | 142,900 | 169,981 | 123,484 | 37,505 | 295 |
| 6–11 years | 108,592 | 81,920 | 93,080 | 132,173 | 164,864 | 117,282 | 35,100 | 380 |
| 3–5 years | 105,423 | 78,749 | 89,128 | 125,056 | 148,676 | 110,787 | 31,684 | 212 |
| Less than 3 | 92,035 | 74,077 | 81,341 | 108,271 | 140,004 | 100,520 | 30,054 | 267 |
| Not specified | 108,002 | 84,000 | 100,014 | 125,000 | 140,403 | 112,637 | 21,941 | 22 |
| All years | 111,889 | 81,188 | 92,932 | 143,052 | 180,000 | 122,240 | 40,882 | 1,728 |
| **Associate professor** | | | | | | | | |
| 11 or more years | 78,900 | 62,952 | 67,964 | 89,212 | 98,474 | 80,013 | 15,516 | 261 |
| 6–10 years | 80,213 | 64,139 | 70,000 | 88,740 | 100,290 | 82,150 | 16,466 | 230 |
| 3–5 years | 79,743 | 64,076 | 71,776 | 90,397 | 101,201 | 82,314 | 17,944 | 345 |
| Less than 3 | 76,689 | 61,000 | 67,226 | 87,192 | 97,213 | 78,408 | 15,328 | 373 |
| Not specified | 80,255 | 68,013 | 70,245 | 83,000 | 88,039 | 80,065 | 13,984 | 19 |
| All years | 78,771 | 63,011 | 69,477 | 88,512 | 99,760 | 80,573 | 16,395 | 1,228 |
| **Assistant professor** | | | | | | | | |
| 3 or more years | 69,407 | 55,723 | 62,877 | 78,384 | 86,100 | 70,710 | 12,192 | 472 |
| Less than 3 | 67,870 | 53,956 | 61,350 | 75,480 | 82,820 | 68,848 | 11,757 | 459 |
| Not specified | 68,163 | 49,898 | 58,078 | 75,000 | 84,499 | 68,246 | 13,578 | 15 |
| All years | 68,908 | 54,880 | 62,000 | 77,100 | 84,076 | 69,768 | 12,030 | 946 |
| **Lecturer/Instructor** | | | | | | | | |
| 3 or more years | 50,820 | 42,000 | 44,820 | 58,064 | 64,851 | 53,018 | 11,367 | 103 |
| Less than 3 | 47,016 | 41,820 | 44,028 | 53,170 | 58,272 | 49,629 | 9,145 | 61 |
| All years | 50,000 | 41,000 | 44,352 | 55,425 | 64,000 | 51,350 | 10,542 | 178 |

*Note.* Included in this table are only those faculty who are full time, who hold the doctoral degree, and who are in departments of psychology that award the doctoral degree (e.g., psychology departments, educational psychology departments, and schools of professional psychology). All salaries are 9- and 10-month salaries. No statistics are provided where the *N* of faculty is less than 10. From *Faculty Salaries in Graduate Departments of Psychology* (p. 14), by M. Wicherski, A. Hamp, P. Christidis, and K. Stamm, 2014, Washington, DC: American Psychological Association. Copyright 2014 by the American Psychological Association.

to more like an hour and a half. Unlike the working conditions in other large organizations, no one is paying much attention to my comings and goings, as long as I get my work done. I do much of my writing at home, in fact. Academic positions offer great freedom in arranging what is done and when and where the person chooses to do it. In addition, no one tells me what research I should be doing, what books and articles I should be reading or writing, and (within some limits) what courses I have to teach. It is rare in the world of work to be permitted to decide what you want to do and then have someone pay you to do it.

Another advantage of a university atmosphere is continued education. Professors in psychology often know professors in other disciplines and can discuss interesting topics in, say, anthropology or astronomy or history. Universities are abuzz with activities like colloquia, concerts, plays, sporting events, public addresses, and debates. Something interesting is always happening, and the difficulty is usually in being able to go to events and still get work done. Professors usually love to interact and work with students. (If they don't, they are in the wrong field.) The best students are lively, probing, challenging, and fun. They keep the faculty informed and teach the faculty new things just as they are being taught by the faculty. The faculty member ages, but the student body stays at about the same age, so to some degree, students help keep the faculty young.

The detriments of being a professor are, in my opinion, not great. Some faculty members complain about bureaucracy, but every large organization has a bureaucracy. Faculty politics and political bickering sometimes can break out and, in some cases, can achieve legendary proportions. A famous academic law is Sayre's Third Law of Politics: "Academic politics are most bitter, because the stakes are so small" (Otten, 1973, p. 14). The life of a college professor is a wonderful one. I have never for a moment regretted my career choice, and I never want to retire.

## ATTRIBUTES NEEDED FOR SUCCESS IN THE CAREER

Some of the required attributes for success in the academic psychology career are obvious. A certain level of verbal and mathematical intelligence is required. Beyond some required level of intelligence, sheer IQ probably does not account for much in academia (or in any other demanding job). Graduate schools already have selected for intelligence because a person must have good grades in college and reasonably good scores on standardized tests to be admitted to graduate school. And several factors in the 4 to 6 years in a graduate school program further eliminate people along the way, for better or for worse. Many people who enter doctoral programs drop out before obtaining the PhD. Anyone who receives a PhD has the intelligence to be a psychologist in academia or elsewhere.

Besides intelligence, what else matters? As the editor of this volume has maintained (Sternberg, 1988), there are other types of intelligence, too. Practical intelligence (i.e., *street smarts*), social intelligence, and what informally is called *common sense* can all make an important difference, as can the motivation to achieve. The desire to learn, creativity, and communication skills all help, although the stereotype of the brilliant but absent-minded professor did not arise from nothing. Universities do seem to acquire more than their fair share of eccentrics, who excel in their fields but seem barely able to cope with life outside. That helps make universities interesting places, even if the presence of a few unusual people does sometimes strain university administrations that try to manage faculty, who, at the best of times, are an independent and sometimes fractious lot. Faculty are often resistant to change within the university—try changing the required curriculum for students to see this quality come out—even while they profess to like change as a general principle.

If I had to put my finger on two characteristics that predict academic success, the two would be achievement motivation (how much you really want to do this and how hard you are willing to work) and persistence (whether you will keep coming back even if you have suffered setbacks and rejection). Most of the really successful academics have these qualities, in my opinion, although I cannot point to empirical studies to show this.

## RANGE OF OPPORTUNITIES FOR EMPLOYMENT

It is no secret that the academic job market is relatively poor. Although there are about 4,000 junior colleges, colleges, and universities in the United States, the 150 to 200 research universities that produce most of the PhD students still produce them in greater numbers than the academic job market requires. The reasons for this state of affairs are complex. On the supply side, graduate departments have not much reduced the number of graduate students they admit, even though everyone recognizes that the job market in academia is weak. This may be because faculty at research universities enjoy working with graduate students and simply seek students interested in conducting research with them. In addition, many universities (especially large state universities) need graduate students to help teach undergraduates, either in the capacity of teaching assistants or as undergraduate instructors. In addition, schools that do not have graduate programs often want to add them, contributing to the oversupply of new PhDs. So the fact that fewer jobs are available for doctoral-level graduates does not necessarily serve as a disincentive to the admission of new graduate students at most universities.

Why aren't there more opportunities to obtain positions in academia? Again, the causes are complex. Just 35 years ago, predictions were made that there would be an undersupply of candidates for professor positions in the 1990s and into the new century. The federal government, however, banned compulsory retirement at age 70 (as age discrimination) in universities, so some professors are staying on, which prevents openings for younger people just out of graduate school. State governments, which support state universities, colleges, and community colleges, generally have reduced state funding to higher education over the years. The reductions are dramatic in some cases. Many private colleges and universities feel similar financial pressures. Consequently, given that few universities are growing significantly—many are not even replacing faculty who leave—and with fewer professors retiring (or retiring later), the result is that the many students receiving PhDs are chasing too few jobs in academia.

That is the bad news. The good news is that many jobs are still available in higher education. The jobs within academia differ across the specialty areas in psychology and change from year to year. But for those students who establish outstanding records in graduate school, job opportunities are available. In addition, in many fields in psychology, it is possible and even desirable to seek an appointment as a postdoctoral fellow after receiving a PhD to continue conducting research before entering the job market and embarking on a career. Taking a 2- to 3-year postdoctoral fellowship permits a young psychologist to gain additional valuable research experience (usually in a different environment from that in which he or she received the PhD), to build a stronger publication record, and therefore to be in a much more favorable position when he or she enters the job market later (for a discussion of postdoctoral fellowships in academia, see McDermott & Braver, 2004).

The other bit of good news about receiving a PhD in psychology (rather than, say, English or history) is that a wide range of job opportunities exists outside academia. The other chapters in this volume attest to the range of possibilities for a career in psychology outside of an academic setting. Good advice for graduate students in this day and age is to take a wide variety of courses in graduate school and to keep a broad perspective on career opportunities. Many exciting possibilities exist outside university teaching and research.

## A Day in the Life

Contributors to this volume were asked to write about a typical day in their lives. For me, however, no day is really typical. Given the many different activities in which a college professor engages, my activities also differ dramatically from day to day.

I am up at 6:30 a.m. on this Wednesday morning and, with no more than the usual commotion and bother, I leave with my children for their school at 7:35 a.m. I get them deposited and make it to my office by 8:00 a.m.

I have a lecture at 9:00 a.m. for my introductory psychology course, for which I must first prepare. Fortunately, the lecture is on perceptual illusions and the constructive nature of perception. I like to think it is one of my best lectures, but I review my notes, because it has been 2 years since I last gave this version of the lecture, and I go over some 20 slides that I will use. I add two new ones that I have collected. I finish preparing for class in half an hour and decide to see what new messages have come overnight by e-mail. (Telephoning and correspondence by regular mail is becoming obsolete for me and others in academia; most important news is delivered via e-mail.) I read and respond to most of the 13 new messages that have appeared before I leave for class.

The lecture seems to go successfully, and several students ask questions during and after class. On the way back from class, I pick up my mail. I receive considerable mail from a journal that I edit—*Psychonomic Bulletin and Review*, published by the Psychonomic Society—as well as other kinds of mail. I sort the journal mail and discover several reviews of manuscripts and one new manuscript that has been submitted. I go to the journal office and talk about various matters with the assistant for the journal, and then I examine the new submission, which looks quite promising. I assign the manuscript reviewers who will evaluate it for the journal and provide advice that will help me decide on its acceptability. I get back to my office at 10:45 a.m. and finish my e-mail correspondence.

It is now shortly after 11:00 a.m., and I realize that the meeting of my lab group is looming at noon. We are to discuss the draft of a manuscript by Endel Tulving that is being submitted to a journal. I had wanted to read it and thought it would be good for my graduate students to read, too. Now the meeting is less than an hour away, and I have not finished the manuscript. So off I go to a hiding place in the basement (it has no telephone or computer), which I use when I need to read in a quiet environment. (There are too many interruptions in my office.) I finish the manuscript, wolf down some lunch, and go off to my noon meeting. The session is quite lively, with some students suggesting items for further research. We spend some time analyzing statements or passages that seem ambiguous or unclear. One student, in particular, picks up what seems to be a weak point in the logic. I raise some points of my own, which the group discusses. I am jotting down notes, because I promised Dr. Tulving I would respond with comments based on the group's discussion.

After the lab meeting, I have an appointment with a student to discuss her master's thesis. That lasts about 20 minutes, so it is now 1:20 p.m., and I begin to prepare the afternoon lecture for my course on human memory. We are discussing the issues of the malleability of memory and of eyewitness testimony and the possibility of false memories occurring in therapy.

The students are reading *The Myth of Repressed Memory* by Elizabeth Loftus and Katherine Ketcham (1994) at this point in the course, and they seem to be enjoying it. I am discussing evidence for various memory illusions in class. However, I need to prepare some slides to display some recent results, so this chore occupies me until my class begins. After the lecture, two students come by to ask (rather nervously) about the nature of the test to be given the following week. They ask questions about material in one of the textbooks in paralyzing depth, much more than I would ever expect on the test, and we cover the intricate topics they have asked about. I suspect that they have little to worry about if they know the material in such detail, but I keep my suspicions to myself.

The afternoon mail delivery arrives, which includes two journals. I scan the journals' contents and zip through one article that is of particular interest to me. Then it is 4:00 p.m. and time for me to meet with a PhD student about his dissertation. He has some of the first results of a test of nearly 700 subjects in a large-scale project. He lays out the preliminary findings, and the news is exceedingly good: The part of the research that had to work out a certain way for the rest to make an interesting contribution did come out as expected. He is very encouraged, and so am I. He leaves to embark on the additional analyses.

Now it is 4:30 p.m. and I deal with a dozen e-mail messages that arrived during the day. Finally, I turn to a manuscript that I need to evaluate for my journal. The reviews of the manuscript are mixed, so it looks as if a difficult decision will be required. I read until 5:20 p.m. and head for home. That night, after the children are safely asleep, I finish the manuscript and dictate a letter.

This is a reasonably typical weekday, which includes about 10 to 11 hours of work. However, most of my teaching is confined to Mondays, Wednesdays, and Fridays, so on Tuesdays and Thursdays I work more at my own research, writing, and editing. The activities those days would be quite different.

Life certainly has changed. Manuscripts never come through the mail now, only by e-mail or other electronic means. And my e-mail seemed manageable then. Now 100 messages a day is not unusual, and some days, e-mail overpowers me (and most everyone I know) and I can get way behind in responding to it or even reading it.

## Conclusion

The life of a college professor may not be rich and glamorous, but it has its own rewards: being a part of the continual search for knowledge; being surrounded by young, inquisitive minds; being in an academic setting with people interested in every imaginable topic; and having a great degree of personal freedom and autonomy relative to most jobs, among other benefits. Most professors I know would not trade their occupation for any other. Indeed, most do not think of themselves as having a job in the traditional sense. They are doing what they most want to do and getting paid for it, which is a happy bargain.

## References

Bem, D. J. (2004). Writing the empirical journal article. In J. Darley, M. Zanna, & H. L. Roediger, III (Eds.), *The compleat academic: A career guide* (2nd ed., pp. 185–220). Washington, DC: American Psychological Association.

Bernstein, D. A., & Lucas, S. G. (2004). Tips for effective teaching. In J. Darley, M. Zanna, & H. L. Roediger, III (Eds.), *The compleat academic: A career guide* (2nd ed., pp. 79–115). Washington, DC: American Psychological Association.

Darley, J. M., Zanna, M. P., & Roediger, H. L., III (Eds.). (2004). *The compleat academic: A career guide* (2nd ed.). Washington, DC: American Psychological Association.

Elmes, D. G., Kantowitz, B. H., & Roediger, H. L., III (2006). *Research methods in psychology* (8th ed.). Belmont, CA: Wadsworth.

Kantowitz, B. H., Roediger, H. L., III, & Elmes, D. G. (2005). *Experimental psychology: Understanding psychological research* (8th ed.). Belmont, CA: Wadsworth.

Loftus, E. F., & Ketcham, K. (1994). *Myth of repressed memory: False memories and allegations of sexual abuse.* New York, NY: St. Martin's Press.

Lyle, K. B., & Crawford, N. A. (2011). Retrieving essential material at the end of lectures improves performance on statistics exams. *Teaching of Psychology, 38,* 94–97.

McDermott, K. B., & Braver, T. S. (2004). After graduate school: A faculty position or a postdoctoral fellowship? In J. Darley, M. Zanna, & H. L. Roediger, III (Eds.), *The compleat academic: A career guide* (2nd ed., pp. 17–30). Washington, DC: American Psychological Association.

Otten, A. L. (1973, October 20). Politics and people. *Wall Street Journal,* p. 14.

Roediger, H. L., III (2004). Writing textbooks: Why doesn't it count? *American Psychological Society Observer, 17,* 5, 42.

Roediger, H. L., III, & Karpicke, J. D. (2006). Test-enhanced learning: Taking memory tests improves long-term retention. *Psychological Science, 17,* 249–255.

Roediger, H. L., III, Putnam, A. L., & Smith, M. A. (2011). Ten benefits of testing and their applications to educational practice. In J. P. Mestre & B. H. Ross (Eds.), *The psychology of learning and motivation: Advances in research and theory* (pp. 1–36). Oxford, England: Elsevier.

Roediger, H. L., III, & Pyc, M. A. (2012). Applying cognitive psychology to education: Complexities and prospects. *Journal of Applied Research in Memory and Cognition, 1,* 263–265.

Schmidt, S. R. (1983). The effects of recall and recognition test expectancies on the retention of prose. *Memory & Cognition, 11,* 172–180.

Sternberg, R. J. (1988). *The triarchic mind: A new theory of human intelligence.* New York, NY: Viking.

Sternberg, R. J. (2003). *The psychologist's companion: A guide to scientific writing for students and psychologists* (2nd ed.). Cambridge, England: Cambridge University Press.

Sternberg, R. J. (2017). *Psychology 101 1/2: The unspoken rules for success in academia* (2nd ed.). Washington, DC: American Psychological Association.

Wicherski, M., Hamp, A., Christidis, P., & Stamm, K. (2014). *Faculty salaries in graduate departments of psychology.* Washington, DC: American Psychological Association. Retrieved from http://www.apa.org/workforce/publications/13-faculty-salary/report.pdf

*Janet Davidson*

# Psychologists in College Departments of Psychology or Psychological Science

2

W hen standing in long lines, I often play a game of guessing my linc partners' careers and then deciding whether I would trade places with any of them. According to my active imagination, I am waiting alongside actresses, engineers, chief executive officers, doctors, lawyers, electricians, and thieves. This chapter will explain why, for well over 20 years, my game always ends the same way: No other career ever tempts me to give up being a faculty member in a psychology department at a small liberal arts college.

To begin, the term *college* should be defined, and this is a slippery task. Colleges in the United States have a lot in common with universities, and the line between them has grown increasingly blurred. Both types of institution focus on

Janet Davidson is associate professor of psychology and faculty director of advising at Lewis & Clark College, where she won the Teacher of the Year award in 1997. She received her BS from the University of Washington and her PhD from Yale University. Her research interests include giftedness, metacognition, and insightful problem solving.

http://dx.doi.org/10.1037/15960-003
*Career Paths in Psychology: Where Your Degree Can Take You, Third Edition*,
R. J. Sternberg (Editor)

teaching, confer degrees, are public or private, and hire tenure-track and adjunct (i.e., temporary and usually part time) faculty members. Like universities, many 4-year colleges require their tenure-track professors to publish peer-reviewed research and serve on committees to obtain tenure and the job security that comes with it. Distinct differences do exist, however, between the two forms of postsecondary education. Perhaps the most important difference is that colleges tend to be smaller in size than universities and more oriented toward nurturing undergraduates than conducting research. According to a *U.S. News and World Report* survey, 223 national liberal arts colleges had an average of 11.6 students for each faculty member during the fall term of 2012 (Haynie, 2014). Interestingly, some undergraduates purposely choose a college over a university so that they can get to know their professors well. The flip slide means that prospective students and faculty should avoid a college if they want to remain anonymous and skip their classes unnoticed. Furthermore, 4-year (or baccalaureate) colleges typically offer only bachelor's degrees, whereas 2-year ones (e.g., community colleges) grant associate degrees. As a consequence, there are no graduate students to mentor or employ as teaching and research assistants. Some 4-year colleges, including my own, do offer a small number of advanced degrees.

These similarities and differences shape the nature of an academic career in a college's department of psychology or psychological science. This topic will be covered first, followed by various types of information about what to expect from this rewarding vocation.

## The Nature of the Career

Undergraduate education is a college's cardinal mission, which means that standards for teaching are high. Undergraduates, their parents, and administrators expect faculty to be student focused and courses to be captivating. Although lectures do occur, especially in lower level courses, small class sizes promote in-class activities, discussion, and problem-based learning. Excellence in teaching is primarily measured through course evaluations completed by students at the end of each semester. These evaluations, sometimes combined with faculty-peer observation, in large part determine contract renewals, tenure decisions, promotions, and salary increases.

Although class sizes tend to be lower than at large universities, college teaching loads tend to be higher. Full-time faculty at community colleges typically teach five and sometimes six survey courses a semester, although some of these may be multiple sections of the same course. The number of courses for faculty at 4-year colleges ranges from two to four a semester, depending on the college and the department. For example, each tenure-track or tenured professor at Lewis & Clark College offers five courses during an academic year (two one semester and three the other). Fortunately, new tenure-track faculty members receive a one-course reduction their first year to help them prepare their courses and research projects. Each course typically requires 3 hours of class contact a week and each session can be 60, 90, or 180 minutes per week for 15 weeks. (Some colleges have 16-week semesters.) Departments tend to be small, which means that a psychology professor's teaching load at a 4-year college will include lower level survey courses (e.g., introduction to psychology, social psychology) and skill-based courses (e.g., statistics, psychology methodology) in addition to upper level courses in his or her specialty. Psychology is one of the most popular majors nationwide, and it tends to attract a wide-range of undergraduates who want to understand themselves, their dreams, and their families as well as learn how to help others. A sizeable number of nonmajors also want to take psychology courses, which means seats are always in demand.

Scholarship is required at 4-year colleges that have adopted the faculty–scholar model. Research is viewed as informing teaching and vice versa. Training undergraduates to assist in one's empirical work is related to this model and is highly valued. Conducting research with professors fosters students' scientific thinking, connection to the college, and acceptance to graduate schools. It also allows students to apply what they have learned in their psychology courses. As a result, many 4-year colleges provide start-up funds for new tenure-track faculty members. Although these funds are relatively small compared with those at research universities, they generally make it possible for psychology faculty to conduct some type of research incorporating undergraduate assistants. Peer-reviewed publications are necessary for tenure and promotion at these colleges, but the requisite number of publications is relatively small compared with what is expected at research universities.

In addition, colleges cannot function without faculty participation on various committees and task forces; expectations for this type of service are generally greater than at large universities. Depending on the type of committee or task force, members are appointed by the dean of the college, recruited by the committee chair, or nominated and elected by the faculty (Dunn & Zaremba, 1997). College service might sound onerous, but it allows faculty to shape the policies of their institutions and gives them the opportunity to work closely with colleagues from other disciplines.

Being a college psychology professor is a rewarding profession in large part because it involves sharing one's love of learning and passion for the discipline with students and colleagues. Teaching is the main focus of the career, although scholarship and service are also important at some schools. The relevant activities related to each are described in the following section.

# Common Activities of College Professors

The varied tasks that a college professor needs to perform prevent the career from becoming monotonous. For example, if grading or committee work should become temporarily tedious, research pursuits, updating class materials, and meeting with students help compensate.

## TASKS RELATED TO COLLEGE TEACHING

High course loads have consequences. Because of the numerous teaching-related activities that must occur before walking into the classroom for each course, it is often difficult to complete research projects or even grocery shopping during much of the academic year. Without the luxury of graduate student teaching assistants, the majority of a college professor's time is spent single-handedly preparing for classes, writing exams and assignments, grading, and meeting with students. Fortunately, textbook publishers, edited books (e.g., Sternberg, 1997), conferences on the teaching of psychology, the journal *Teaching of Psychology*, and other resources provide valuable information for faculty teaching college-level psychology courses.

### Class Preparation

Several hours are spent getting ready for each hour of a class. Although the amount of time decreases when a course is taught repeatedly, few seasoned college professors walk into a classroom without first updating and reviewing their material. Preparation before and after a term begins is crucial because courses are more successful if the goals are clear, only relevant material is covered, and activities foster hands-on learning and critical thinking.

Course preparation first begins with the selection of interesting and affordable reading material that is pitched at the right level for undergraduates. Appropriate readings can take time to locate because the range of students' abilities and backgrounds is often wide. For example, many undergraduates took psychology courses in high school whereas others did not. Second, each course needs a detailed syllabus that outlines reading assignments; procedures for the assessment of learning; and policies on academic integrity, attendance, classroom behavior, and late work. Syllabi tend to lengthen with teaching experience as it becomes increasingly clear that expectations and requirements should be well specified and documented. Interestingly, the number of topics listed on a syllabus tends to decrease each time a course is taught. It often takes longer than one originally predicts to get through material, especially because both depth and breadth are important. For example, my first Introduction to Psychology course felt like a rushed bus tour through Europe. Every few days we were "back on the bus" headed to a new topic. Now I sacrifice some subjects to present a coherent story about psychology that is relevant to undergraduates' lives. Third, lectures and in-class activities need to be created or updated, which takes a great deal of time. Dunn and Zaremba (1997) recommend having 2-weeks' worth of lectures, exercises, and exams completed in advance for each course. This 2-week rule allows flexibility and reduces stress. Finally, it is important to review one's notes for an hour or two before each class begins. This review often involves refining the material and getting into the mind-set of performing in front of a class.

One of the dangers of course preparation is that it can consume all of an instructor's available time. Rockquemore (2010) refers to this problem as "the teaching trap." New tenure-track professors, in particular, must make a conscious effort to reserve time for research, getting to know colleagues, and sleeping. Overpreparing for courses is inefficient, and it can jeopardize tenure decisions, physical health, and job mobility.

## Writing and Grading Assignments and Exams

When psychology professors congregate, they often remark (or complain) that grading is their least favorite task. Grading takes time and often feels uncomfortably subjective, especially when the criteria are vague. Time and effort put into writing concrete exam questions, specific paper requirements, and clear grading rubrics usually results in less time spent grading and better feedback provided to students. Even well-crafted exams and assignments can take countless hours to evaluate because, unlike at large universities, it typically is expected that undergraduates will receive extensive comments on their work. To make matters more challenging, it is important to hand back work as quickly as possible, preferably within a week, to reduce students' anxiety and provide them with feedback that will help them on future exams and assignments. College faculty members learn to stagger assignment due dates for their various courses; otherwise, the amount of grading becomes overwhelming.

## Office Hours, Open-Door Policy, and Student E-mails

College faculty are expected to hold weekly office hours. The suggested minimum at Lewis & Clark College is 3 hours per week, plus opportunities for students to make appointments for other times. Office hours are generally fairly quiet at the beginning of a semester, with business gradually increasing as the term progresses. Many students voluntarily come to ask question or simply to chat. Others, often those who are performing poorly in a course, need to be encouraged. The transition from high school to college work can be difficult for some students and office hours are a prime time for discussing study skills, motivation, and time management. Tissue is an essential supply because students often want to talk about personal problems that are interfering with their ability to perform well in a course.

In addition to official office hours and appointments, most colleges have an implicit policy that undergraduates can visit a faculty member's office whenever his or her door is open. This increases availability and promotes student–faculty interaction. When undergraduates have extra time, they frequently wander the halls looking for open office doors so they can visit with their professors.

Some students seem to be on e-mail 24 hours a day, and they e-mail questions and comments in lieu of, or in addition to, coming to office hours or dropping by. Replying to these messages is time consuming, which means that many professors respond only at the beginning and end of a workday.

## Advising

Although some colleges hire professional advisors to help undergraduates select courses and careers, others have the faculty conduct pre-major and major advising. Although it doesn't count toward instructors' course loads, advising is viewed as a form of teaching. At least once a semester, it typically occurs during one-on-one sessions involving long-term planning; course selection for the next term; and discussions about the field of psychology, careers, and even relationship problems. Given the small size of departments and the popularity of psychology, it is not uncommon for each psychology professor to have more than 30 advisees each year. Fortunately, advising is a great way to get to know undergraduates, and it is gratifying to help them plan their lives.

## CONDUCTING RESEARCH AT A COLLEGE

As noted earlier, conducting psychological research at a college is often done on a smaller scale than at a research university. Experiments need to be designed without graduate students and expensive equipment in mind, which means they must be relatively simple, compatible with one's course load, and conducive to undergraduate research assistants.

Fortunately, conducting research with undergraduates is rewarding, and effective models demonstrate how best to do it at small colleges. For example, two of my colleagues, Jerusha and Brian Detweiler-Bedell, designed a laddered (or hierarchical) team-based approach (Detweiler-Bedell & Detweiler-Bedell, 2004). This model revolves around three undergraduate researchers per team and each member has a different level of responsibility. A team leader is a senior psychology major who supervises a less advanced psychology major (a team associate) and a student new to psychology (a team assistant). As they gain more experience, team associates and assistants can move up the ladder to become leaders of their own teams. Each team works on its own project and is equated to a highly motivated graduate student, with the added benefit of exposing undergraduates to the collaborative nature of experimental psychology. All teams meet together once a week with their faculty research mentors to discuss progress, share results, and review different aspects of the research process. *Doing Collaborative Research in Psychology: A Team-Based Guide* (Detweiler-Bedell & Detweiler-Bedell, 2013) helps prepare students for their research experience and gain the most from it. The Council on Undergraduate Research also has useful resources.

Also fortunate is that external funding is available for conducting research at 4-year colleges. For example, the National Science Foundation and the National Institutes of Health have special programs for funding research at undergraduate institutions. Internal college funds are often also available for periodic replacement of computers, faculty and student travel to national conferences, summer experiments, and research equipment.

Conducting research with undergraduates involves a variety of activities. First, relatively simple studies need to be designed that fit the college culture and the available pool of participants. (Colleges typically do not have huge introductory psychology courses that require students to be in experiments.) Second, undergraduate research assistants need to be identified and selected. This can be accomplished in various ways. One is to invite students to join one's research team if they have done well in relevant psychology courses. Another is to advertise in the psychology department or campus-wide and interview all applicants. Next, undergraduate researchers need training. This often takes two forms. One is the online training on ethics and other related issues that is mandated by college institutional review boards. The second is specific training and continuing guidance on how to conduct a particular study. Finally, good communication with (and among) undergraduate research assistants needs to occur and this is frequently accomplished through regular lab meetings. At these meetings, information is disseminated, questions are asked and answered, and future studies are proposed.

## COLLEGE SERVICE

In general, college committee work is valued less highly than teaching and research, but it still needs to occur if a faculty member wants to be tenured, promoted to full professor, and viewed as collegial. College service ranges from short-term commitments (e.g., job searches, awards committees) to long-term ones (e.g., the curriculum committees, the institutional human subjects review board). The duties typically involve reviewing materials, attending weekly meetings, making decisions, and writing reports. Committees can help a college run well, and they give faculty members the chance to get to know each other. One must be strategic in accepting requests to serve on these committees, or else there would be no time for teaching, research, and other pursuits. Fortunately, assistant professors usually are protected from large amounts of long-term, time-consuming committee work. Once tenure is received, the expectations for service increase.

## A Typical Day in the Life of a College Professor

Probably every contributor to this book claims there are no typical days in his or her career, and I am no exception. One of the joys of the job is the wide variety of tasks, opportunities, and interactions that occur. However, there are some constant elements.

By choice, I am usually in the office around 7:30 a.m. because the campus is refreshingly quiet. Most of my writing, grading, and course preparation are accomplished before people appear in my building and after they have disappeared. By 9:30 a.m. colleagues and a few students begin to arrive. Liberal arts colleges, my own included, have a strong sense of community, and people stop by to share stories, ask questions, relate news, or simply say hello. On the particular day I am describing, I review course notes for my morning class and then meet with an advisee to discuss graduate schools and how to apply.

I teach Introduction to Psychology from 10:20 to 11:20 a.m. three days a week. There are 40 undergraduates in the course, and I have them use nonpainful behaviorist techniques on each other and record which ones are the most effective. This leads to a lively discussion about why reinforcement tends to be more effective than punishment. Of course, I give lots of praise to good comments and scowl at the mediocre ones.

After class I attend a 1-hour meeting of the tenured and tenure-track members of the psychology department. There are nine of us, and we typically meet twice a month to review upcoming events, course schedules for the next academic year, and requests from the administration. We discuss the need to hire adjunct faculty for the following academic year and set the date for the reception we will have for our graduating majors.

The departmental meeting is followed by a quick lunch on campus with a colleague. While we eat, my companion argues that good teaching is similar to jazz because it involves improvisation, and it requires theatrical skills to keep students interested. It takes me a while to admit that he is right because, being neither musical nor theatrical, I want the clear presentation of material to be sufficient.

My next task is to prepare for my 1:50–2:50 p.m. freshman seminar. This seminar is part of a two-semester interdisciplinary, writing-intensive course that all first-year students take as part of their general education requirements. Each section is discussion based and has no more than 19 students. During this particular class, we talk about Ralph Ellison's *Invisible Man* and how the narrator's identity changes throughout the novel. Questions assigned in advance helped ensure that everyone did the reading and the resulting discussion was a productive one.

I go straight from class to a strategic planning committee meeting. Our mission is to specify what the college needs to have in place to provide a diverse undergraduate population with the skills, knowledge, and experiences necessary for success, leadership, and fulfillment in our 21st-century global society. This task begins to feel monumental and potentially thankless. We are making progress, but it is slow and our strategic plan will need buy-in from students, staff, faculty, and administrators on the undergraduate campus.

At 4:45 p.m., I meet briefly with my team of four undergraduate researchers. Through a subcontract from the Museum of Science in Boston, we are conducting a study on Sunday afternoons in the Science Playground at the Oregon Museum of Science and Industry (OMSI). Interested preschoolers can play our "inhibition games" and OMSI visitors are invited to watch. (Data are recorded only when parents have signed a consent form.) My study is one small part of the Museum of Science's Living Laboratories initiative. The overarching goal is to provide parents and other museum visitors with firsthand knowledge about how psychological research is conducted. At today's lab meeting, my undergraduate research assistants practiced explaining our research to parents. They also asked questions about what to do if a child does not listen to instructions, which resulted in a discussion about when and how to terminate participation.

I work in the office until 6:45 p.m. answering e-mails and writing two letters of recommendation for former students applying for jobs. Then I take grading home with me but don't make much headway on it.

## *Job Options and Prospects*

There are probably never as many jobs in a given field as we would like, and this is certainly the case for positions as a college professor of psychology or psychological science. College jobs are largely dependent on enrollment size and, unfortunately, the number of high school graduates in the United States has declined since 2009–2010 (Prescott & Bransberger, 2012). Within academia, however, more opportunities are available at teaching-oriented institutions than at research-oriented ones. Any psychology student interested in teaching at the postsecondary level should consider working at a 2- or 4-year college.

The good and bad news is that there are different types of positions at teaching-oriented institutions. Many of them, especially at community colleges, are part time and have no job security. To make the equivalent of a full-time salary, some adjuncts work at more than one school. Others take a job outside of academia and then teach a small number of college courses each year. Part-time positions may not be ideal, but they do have advantages. For example, they are not as competitive as full-time positions; they do not require committee work or research; and they add to one's teaching experience. Sometimes these positions turn into full-time ones that may or may not have the option of tenure.

Full-time, non-tenure-track appointments are another option and they take various forms. For example, visiting (or temporary) faculty members are hired when tenure-track or tenured professors are on sabbatical or suddenly leave their institution. In other words, visiting professors typically cover the courses normally taught by someone else. Full-time lecturers and instructors have a similar role except they are more likely to teach only lower level courses and to have renewable contracts. All of these non-tenure-track appointments include health and other benefits, and they do not require research. These appointments allow individuals to acquire more teaching experience and occasionally lead to tenure-track positions.

Tenure-track positions are the most difficult ones to obtain at 2- and 4-year colleges, and the number of positions has decreased as non-tenure-track jobs have increased. An individual usually begins this type of full-time position as an assistant professor of psychology, with the opportunity to become an associate professor (usually when tenure is awarded) and eventually a full professor. Each promotion comes with additional responsibilities and salary.

The bottom line is that jobs are available at 2- and 4-year colleges and not all recipients of advanced psychology degrees pursue them. For individuals devoted to teaching undergraduates, persistence and flexibility in their job searches tend to pay off.

### TABLE 2.1

**Average Salaries for 2- and 4-Year Colleges by Position Title, 2012–2013**

| Position title | Average salary at 2-year colleges granting associate degrees | Average salary at 4-year colleges granting primarily bachelor's degrees |
|---|---|---|
| Lecturer | $45,824 | $52,116 |
| Assistant professor | $52,643 | $58,406 |
| Associate professor | $60,821 | $70,334 |
| Full professor | $74,526 | $91,935 |

*Note.* Only salaries for full-time time faculty are included in this table and all of them are for 9- to 10-month contracts. Public and private institutions are combined. Data from Jaschik (2013).

## Range of Salaries

I have never met colleagues who became college professors because of the money nor do I know any full-time faculty who feel poor. In other words, salaries are usually neither exorbitant nor pathetic, although part-time adjuncts do not always receive a living wage.

In general, full-time faculty salaries tend to be higher at research universities than at colleges, at 4-year colleges than at 2-year ones, at private than at public institutions, and for tenured or tenure-track positions than for positions without the option of tenure. Table 2.1 contains average salary information for different positions at 2- and 4-year colleges. These averages, which are from a 2012–2013 survey conducted by the American Association of University Professors, illustrate the differences in pay between the two types of college and the different full-time jobs within a college (Jaschik, 2013).

Salary surveys should be viewed as only providing ballpark figures. They are conducted on a small minority of faculty working at postsecondary institutions in the United States and they do not always take cost of living by geographic location and other factors into account.

## Advantages and Disadvantages of the College Career

Teaching in a college psychology department has many rewards. Perhaps the greatest is getting to know undergraduates and watching them develop during their college education and beyond. Professors play an important role in this metamorphosis, and one of the best benefits is helping young adults figure out their identities and discover their passions. Students often enter college with a high school mind-set. By their second year, they usually are more creative, independent, and confident in their abilities. At graduation, they are proud of their accomplishments and excited yet nervous about the future. Alumni often stay in touch after their departure from campus, and professors get to live vicariously through the graduate schools, careers, relationships, and travels that their former students pursue. Connections that form in a college setting tend to be numerous, strong, and long lasting.

The second greatest reward is that learning never stops and individual knowledge does not stagnate. No one should become a college professor if he or she does not love to learn. Each semester is different from the previous one, with new psychological literature to explore, new questions to answer, and unexpected challenges to overcome. Undergraduates often help faculty look at material in new ways and prompt them to tackle novel research questions. Working at a small college supports the adage that teaching is the best way to learn.

Autonomy is also an advantage. Although college professors often work 50–70 hours per week, they generally get to determine how they allocate this time. Additionally, when not interacting with undergraduates or colleagues, they also can choose where they work. This flexibility in schedule and location means that a faculty member can work at home during the most productive times for writing and reading, then come to campus for classes, office hours, and meetings. In addition, tenure provides job security and, therefore, the freedom to pursue and communicate any topic of interest as long as this is done in a professional manner. Another type of autonomy stems from 9-month contracts. Faculty members usually have the option of teaching summer courses, conducting research, or completing tasks not accomplished during the academic year.

Finally, numerous opportunities are available to adopt new roles within one's department, college, or discipline. For example, the task of chairing the psychology department often rotates so that every tenured psychology professor serves a 3- or 4-year term. Similarly, many faculty members lead one-semester overseas programs and some move on to become associate deans or deans. Recently, I became the faculty director of advising, which means reduced teaching and increased administrative work. These various opportunities keep the job interesting, help with the development of leadership skills, and provide a deeper knowledge of how one's college functions.

Unfortunately, every career has its disadvantages and being a faculty member in a college's department of psychology is no exception. As noted earlier, college departments tend to be smaller than those at universities. Often, only one or two faculty members represent an entire subdiscipline of psychology, which limits the opportunities for professional discussions and collaborations. As a way to overcome this disadvantage, many college professors develop professional relationships with similar colleagues at nearby institutions. Others pursue interdisciplinary collaborations within their own campuses. Given that there are few unconnected facts and people at a college, it is usually easy to find overlapping interests between members of different departments.

Although community colleges attract an older student population, an unexpected disadvantage of working at a 4-year college is that the majority of undergraduates are always 18 to 21 years old. As professors age, students appear younger each academic year. Eventually, their parents begin to look immature, and it is probably time to retire when their grandparents seem young. The constancy of undergraduates' ages makes one's own mortality increasingly salient. It also means that aging faculty members need to be aware of the changing schemas that undergraduates bring to the classroom. For example, current students weren't alive during the classic cases of flashbulb memories and groupthink. Furthermore, rapidly changing technology often means that undergraduates, rather than older faculty, are the experts on getting classroom equipment to work.

Tenure is an advantage once it is granted but coming up for tenure is stressful even when an assistant professor has done everything right. Compiling a compelling tenure file takes a great deal of time and strategic thought, especially when the tenure committee is composed of colleagues outside one's discipline. Once the file is submitted, a long period of worrying begins because employment is terminated if tenure is not awarded. Typically, the requirements for tenure are not well specified and the decision takes place at several levels, starting with the tenure committee and ending with the college president. Waiting to hear the outcome can be agonizing, and candidates for tenure sometimes apply for other positions so that they have a safety net.

Additionally, having a combination of tenured, tenure-track, and non-tenure-track faculty at a college can create an environment in which some members feel like second-class citizens. Only tenured professors have long-term job security; only tenured and tenure-track faculty can vote at faculty meetings. Furthermore, recent changes in the college culture have caused some untenured faculty to be extremely cautious about the material they present in class (Schlosser, 2015). More specifically, because they fear their jobs might be jeopardized, they no longer cover controversial information (e. g., gender differences, mating) that might disturb some of their undergraduates.

## Preparing To Be a College Psychology Professor

Most colleges require their psychology faculty to have doctorate degrees from accredited graduate schools, although some community colleges hire individuals who have master's degrees. Although it sounds unfair, graduate degrees from top-ranked programs open more doors to employment opportunities than do ones with lower rankings. A PhD or master's degree in psychology, no matter where it is earned, does not automatically prepare an individual to be an adjunct or tenure-track professor at a community or 4-year college. Certain educational, teaching, and research experiences help undergraduate and graduate students know whether they belong in a college's psychology department. They also help individuals obtain and succeed in this type of position. These experiences are discussed in the following sections.

## EDUCATIONAL EXPERIENCES

As an undergraduate, it is beneficial to get good grades, conduct research with one or more faculty members, serve as a teaching assistant for a psychology course if the opportunity is available, and receive a bachelor's degree in psychology or a related field. These experiences help students figure out their career goals and gain admission to graduate school. Attending a community or liberal arts college is not required, but it does provide perspective on small class size and the benefits of faculty–student interactions. During graduate school, taking courses in all areas of psychology helps one acquire the breadth needed to teach a range of topics in the discipline. In addition, taking good notes, being both a teaching and a research assistant, and giving guest lectures as a graduate student provide a foundation on which newly hired faculty members can build their courses. Some graduate programs in psychology provide instruction on how to teach but most do not. Several recent books, such as *On Course: A Week-to-Week Guide to Your First Semester of College Teaching* (Lang, 2010), help prepare individuals to teach at the college level. Other resources, such as *Psychology 101 1/2: The Unspoken Rules for Success in Academia* (Sternberg, 2017), provide useful information on other aspects of the career.

## TEACHING EXPERIENCE

It is advantageous to be the sole instructor of as many undergraduate courses as possible before applying for positions as a college professor of psychology. Community colleges typically require a minimum of 2 to 3 years of full-time teaching or 4 to 6 years part time (Jenkins, 2013).

Many 4-year colleges ask applicants to submit syllabi, course evaluations, a statement of their teaching philosophy, and letters of recommendation addressing their teaching abilities. In addition, on-campus interviews frequently require candidates to give a guest lecture that is evaluated by undergraduates and members of the search committee. Having a battery of lectures and course materials that can be adopted for a new position saves time and reduces stress. Fortunately, teaching experience can be acquired if graduate students are allowed to teach their own courses or if they take temporary teaching positions after receiving their PhDs. The level of experience required, however, depends on the college. While some schools look for a solid record of successful teaching, others focus primarily on published research.

## RESEARCH EXPERIENCE

Evidence of a strong research program is not required for a position at a community college, but it is essential at many 4-year institutions. Doctoral and postdoctoral programs in psychology provide opportunities for research and peer-reviewed publications that help individuals gain these positions. In addition to publications, many 4-year colleges look for a long-term research agenda that can incorporate undergraduate assistants and be conducted in limited laboratory space with relatively small amounts of money. Furthermore, campus interviews often require candidates to give a presentation of their research to students and faculty. Prior experience presenting one's work to a variety of audiences helps during these interviews, as does having empirical studies and hypotheses that intrigue undergraduates.

## *Attributes for Success as a College Professor*

When I began my first position as a psychology department faculty member, a colleague told me that the key to teaching successfully is to like what you teach and to whom you teach. These wise words capture two important attributes. One is a passion for the discipline because enthusiasm is contagious and it makes learning enjoyable for undergraduates. No one wants to listen to instructors who are bored by, or scornful of, the material they present. The other is respect for undergraduates and a strong desire to work with them. Students are more likely to learn if they feel their instructors understand and value them as individuals.

As described earlier, many tasks need to be completed each day of each semester. Except for during a precious sabbatical, one rarely has the luxury of working on one thing for an extended period of time. This means that effective time management and organizational skills are essential. Faculty members who procrastinate or spend time looking for documents tend to struggle more than those who do not.

Obviously, good communication skills are fundamental to college teaching and to the presentation and publication of research. In particular, college professors need to explain concepts in clear terms, listen well to their students, use visual aids appropriately, and model effective speaking and writing. A sense of humor is not essential, but it does put students at ease and keeps them engaged in the material.

Collegiality is probably more important in a small college setting than at a research university because, at some level, everyone needs to work together to accomplish the college's goals. Being viewed as a valued colleague and contributor to the institution's well-being also helps with tenure decisions and promotions (Dunn & Zaremba, 1997). This does not mean, however, that college professors need to be extroverted. Many are team players and excellent classroom performers despite being introverted.

## Conclusion

Let's return to the guessing game that began this chapter. Psychologists in college departments of psychology or psychological science receive rewards not found in most professions. College professors essentially get paid for being professional students. They have the freedom continually to learn about their discipline, their students, and how best to convey information. In addition, they get to talk (almost nonstop) about psychology, be part of a community of inquisitive minds, and play a pivotal role in preparing young adults for the wider world. In short, working at a small college rarely feels like work.

## References

Detweiler-Bedell, B., & Detweiler-Bedell, J. (2004). Using laddered teams to organize efficient undergraduate research. *CUR Quarterly, 24,* 166.

Detweiler-Bedell, J. B., & Detweiler-Bedell, B. (2013). *Doing collaborative research in psychology: A team-based approach.* London, England: Sage.

Dunn, D. S., & Zaremba, S. B. (1997). Thriving at liberal arts colleges: The more compleat academic. *Teaching of Psychology, 24,* 8–14.

Haynie, D. (2014). Liberal arts colleges with low student–faculty ratios. *U.S. News & World Report.* Retrieved from http://www.usnews.com/education/best-colleges/the-short-list-college/articles/2014/04/22/liberal-arts-colleges-with-low-student-faculty-ratios

Jaschik, S. (2013, April 8). On pace with inflation. *Inside Higher Ed.* Retrieved from https://www.insidehighered.com/news/2013/04/08/aaup-survey-finds-average-faculty-salary-increased-rate-inflation-last-year

Jenkins, R. (2013, November 18). How the job search differs at community colleges: The application, the interview, and even the offer are not the same. *The Chronicle of Higher Education.* Retrieved from http://chronicle.com/article/How-the-Job-Search-Differs-at/143089/

Lang, J. M. (2010). *On course: A week-to-week guide to your first semester of college teaching.* Cambridge, MA: Harvard University Press.

Prescott, B. T., & Bransberger, P. (2012). *Knocking at the college door: Projections of high school graduates* (8th ed.). Boulder, CO: Western Interstate Commission for Higher Education.

Rockquemore, K. A. (2010). The teaching trap. *Inside Higher Education.* Retrieved from https://www.insidehighered.com/advice/winning/winning9

Schlosser, E. (June 3, 2015). I'm a liberal professor, and my liberal students terrify me. *Vox.* Retrieved from http://www.vox.com/2015/6/3/8706323/college-professor-afraid

Sternberg, R. J. (Ed.). (1997). *Teaching introductory psychology: Survival tips from the experts.* Washington, DC: American Psychological Association. http://dx.doi.org/10.1037/10228-000

Sternberg, R. J. (2017). *Psychology 101 1/2: The unspoken rules for success in academia* (2nd ed.). Washington, DC: American Psychological Association.

*Kenji Hakuta*

# Psychologists in Schools of Education

3

S chools of education in most colleges and universities mainly provide undergraduate and graduate degrees that lead to professional credentialing for teachers and school administrators. Many also offer advanced degrees (either a master's degree or a doctorate) in education focused on research from various disciplinary and topical perspectives—for example, the learning sciences, the nature of the curriculum, or educational technology to support teaching and learning. Many programs also offer specialized degrees that focus on subgroups of students, such as students with disabilities (special education), gifted and talented students, and bilingual students. Schools of education also may offer clinical or counseling degrees, such as speech therapy or counseling psychology.

Kenji Hakuta, PhD, is the Lee L. Jacks Professor of Education Emeritus at Stanford University. His research focuses on psychological and linguistic perspectives on bilingualism, and he has worked actively in the arena of education policy. His undergraduate degrees and doctorate are in psychology from Harvard University. He has taught at Yale University, the University of California at Santa Cruz, and Stanford University. He was the founding dean for the School of Social Sciences and Humanities at the University of California, Merced.

http://dx.doi.org/10.1037/15960-004
*Career Paths in Psychology: Where Your Degree Can Take You, Third Edition,*
R. J. Sternberg (Editor)

Historically, psychology has been the dominant discipline in education. This dominance is due to the centrality of teaching and learning as the core of educational activity, and the influence of various psychological perspectives on human learning—ranging from behavioral to cognitive to social psychological perspectives. Another contributing factor to the dominance of psychology is the prominent role that American education traditionally has placed on testing and measurement. Thus, psychologists who specialize in the technical issues surrounding the measurement of student intelligence and learning—a specialty known as psychometrics—have played a strong role in establishing psychology as the disciplinary cornerstone of education.

But increasingly, the realization that learning happens within a social and even global context has meant that perspectives from other disciplines—especially sociology, economics, political science, anthropology and linguistics—have come to play a more prominent role. In the 21st century, most schools of education are staffed by faculty and specialists who come from a variety of disciplines who readily acknowledge that a diversity of theoretical and methodological perspectives is an occupational necessity to address the complicated topic. As an interdisciplinary area, education offers an exciting career path within which to pursue your disciplinary interests in psychology, and to reach out across disciplines and employ multiple methodologies.

## Some Common Problems From Psychological and Interdisciplinary Perspectives

As educational professionals, we need a better understanding of a variety of aspects of education. For example, how can we help teachers design more engaging and more effective learning environments? How might this approach differ depending on the nature of the knowledge being taught (such as math versus history)? How do we adapt the learning environment for students who struggle in school? How can we reduce the achievement gap between students in high-poverty and low-poverty schools? How do we help school leaders such as principals and school district administrators become more effective in coaching and leading their students and teachers? How do we communicate what we know about education to key policymakers, such as state lawmakers and governors, the U.S. Congress, and the president? To show the range of disciplinary perspectives that education entails, I'm going to give you a flavor of how some of these questions play out.

# IMPROVING EARLY READING AND LITERACY

Let's say, for example, that you start with the simple problem of wanting to improve early reading and literacy in English. The psychology of reading and literacy development is one of the most developed areas in education. We know quite a bit about how most children learn to read, and about its various components. For example, early on, young children start with knowledge of letters and their correspondence to sound. They develop metacognitive awareness about language and literacy, and how written or printed materials are laid out and how they work. They learn to connect reading with their oral language development whose trajectory began in their homes and communities well before they entered school. By third grade, most children transition from "learning to read," having mastered the mechanics of reading, and move to "reading to learn"—that is, by that grade level, children are expected to move from the decoding and understanding the meaning of texts, to using texts to learn at higher levels. Much of this we know because of a science around the psychology of reading that was built in the 1970s and 1980s using theories and research methods around cognitive psychology.

But the student population in the United States is increasingly diverse. It is estimated that 20% of students enrolled in school nationwide grow up in home environments where a language other than English is spoken (Davis & Bauman, 2011). These children build their literacy not just on their foundation of the English language, but on other languages used in the home, in varying amounts of mixture of English depending on the household structure. And many children grow up in homes where the uses of literacy may be quite different from the expectations of middle-class monolingual English norms. To understand the diverse uses of language and literacy, psychologists have collaborated with researchers whose business it is to understand cultural practices—ethnographers, anthropologists, and sociolinguists—to create new fields of research looking much more broadly at literacy.

Interdisciplinary research on literacy looks at the differing cultural practices, such as differences in adult–child conversations in homes, to construct a better understanding about how home language use and how schools adapt literacy instruction. They also might look at how the home language contributes to the development of English, as well as to the development of literacy in both languages. And they might look at the social status of the languages (in many cases, immigrant languages are stigmatized in many communities) and consider how social marginalization can be addressed in literacy programs. One also might consider how programs can reach out to parents depending on their varied social and cultural backgrounds. A long list of complex factors deserves careful consideration.

## DIGITAL MEDIA AND LEARNING

Another kind of problem addressed in schools of education is how to use technology to increase learning, such as through computer games and simulations. Disciplines are blending around educational technology, both around the design of digital environments and the evaluation of their efficacy to improve student learning.

For example, in design, you might want to create a game to increase student motivation and learning around a curricular unit, such as energy cost reduction that involves trying to reduce energy usage in your school. In crafting the game, you would need to consult with various experts in energy conservation that would involve a multidisciplinary perspective. You would need to think carefully about how to organize requirements of the game, such as whether students should work alone, in pairs, in teams, or in social networks—and therefore examine the literature on learning in different social groupings. You also would need to work with experts in game design and development.

In asking whether the game effectively increases student motivation and learning, you would need to make important evaluation research design decisions. You would need to figure out how to measure the constructs of motivation and learning and to develop a research design. For example, would you want to compare classrooms that use or don't use the technology? If a class does not use the technology (and therefore is in the control condition), should they be given some alternative task or game? Also, should the teacher be the same in both conditions? How would I know if the two classes are equal to begin with? How much of my study should focus on formal evaluations (questionnaires and tests) as compared with observations of students and interviews?

## SCHOOL CULTURE AND CLIMATE

Certain terminology commonly is used in the world of school reform, including what are called *effective schools* and *failing schools*. Effective schools are those that beat the odds as outliers to a usually strong statistical relationship between the demographic composition of the school and its outcomes on measures of academic achievement. Failing schools are those that are persistently in the bottom 10%, including what Secretary of Education Arne Duncan called "dropout factories" (U.S. Department of Education, 2012). Then there are "turnaround schools" that historically did poorly but that have shown strong improvement in student learning outcomes. Obviously, the school reform movement wants more effective and turnaround schools, and fewer failing schools. And, to achieve this reform, researchers have examined the characteristics of these types of schools.

What one usually finds is highly complicated, because schools are complex organizations operating under various federal, state, and local policies and regulations, and they have various leadership structures. Usually, studies find that effective schools have stable leadership, strong and experienced teachers, high expectations of all students, a culture that pays attention to data on student learning outcomes, and strong engagement with the parents and community. They also often are characterized by what sociologists have termed *relational trust* at the level of the school staff, students, and community.

In most cities or regions in the country, education professionals will point to a handful of such schools as success stories, schools teachers and administrators visit for inspiration. But often, when visiting these schools, what is evident is the almost constant state of change in these schools, especially in poor urban districts where the average school superintendent's tenure is just over 3 years. Amid all the change, to produce a stable portrait of leadership, one needs an understanding not just of the psychological characteristics of the leader—the principal or the district curriculum specialist or a lead teacher in a school—but also of the system and its context.

So, the question of what makes an effective leader who facilitates an effective school culture and climate becomes a complex multidisciplinary exercise. It is not just about the psychological traits of the leader but also about how that leader acts within a complex set of circumstances that are fluid and often unpredictable.

## Nature of the Career

Getting into a career in education is both exciting and a bit confusing. It's exciting because so much social good can be accomplished, but confusing because it covers so much range and one cannot be a specialist in so many areas at once. Multiple methods with varying degrees of agreement across disciplines as to the rigor and validity of research methods are a challenge, but the diversity of methods and the constant need for new methods to address emerging data and issues keeps it exciting for the methodologically inclined scholar. All complicated fields require teamwork and collaboration among specialists, and education is no exception. What does set the field aside is the passion that educators bring to their work, which is great because people are highly motivated and work incredibly hard, but it can be problematic because of the high degree of personal investment that these individuals bring to their ideas and perspectives. Of course, psychologists have gotten used to this as part of the discipline—we have long realized that we are not like physics or chemistry, in which the subject of study is not influenced by the process of observation or inquiry.

## KINDS OF ACTIVITIES

The main responsibilities for faculty in schools of education are teaching, research, and various forms of service work for the professional field and university community. The expectations around the distribution of these tasks will vary depending on whether the university mission emphasizes research (and has a doctoral degree program) or teaching. Almost any program, however, will have a particular history of relationships with local schools in the area, and because schools for the most part are locally controlled, most schools of education have acquired a local flavor, and faculty will vary greatly in the extent to which they engage with local schools.

### Teaching

Unlike faculty in psychology departments in colleges and universities, the main teaching responsibility for most faculty in schools of education is for courses taken by students enrolled in the teaching credential program. The structure of teaching credential programs is regulated for the most part by a professional board or commission at the state level, and therefore varies by state. However, they all have in common curriculum and instruction courses that are discipline based and a core set of foundations courses that focus on theories of teaching, learning, and the education system. Additional courses also address the needs of subgroups of students—for example, students with disability and English language learners.

Most schools of education also have a department with varying terms, such as *foundations, leadership*, and *research*, much of which is designed to serve the needs of those seeking administrative credentials (e.g., licensure to become a principal or a district administrator). Faculty with a psychology background often teach courses on leadership development, organizational psychology, innovation, and creativity; basic courses on teaching learning and motivation; courses on socioemotional learning and the role of culture and diversity in schooling; and courses on research methods and on student testing and assessment.

Finally, depending on the school, advanced degrees are offered at both the master's and the doctoral levels. At Stanford, for example, two of the most popular master's programs are in learning, design, and technology and in policy, organization, and leadership studies. Such programs offer multiple opportunities for faculty with a psychological background for teaching and mentoring. At the doctoral level, various training programs are shaped significantly by psychology. The one in which I teach at Stanford—the Social Sciences, Humanities, and

Interdisciplinary Policy Studies program—is a blend of the social sciences, including psychology, as applied to education. Students of mine who have conducted doctoral dissertations recently include those who have asked, How long does it take English language learners to attain proficiency in English and what accounts for their rate of learning? What are the best early childhood education (preschool) learning environments for bilingual children? Does being labeled an "English language learner" have stigmatizing consequences for the student? How do the characteristics of the members and the leaders of teams in online courses influence course completion outcomes? In our program, the methods of psychology, sociology, economics, anthropology, and linguistics are blended to address these complex issues.

Depending on the university, teaching loads can vary considerably. In most research-oriented universities, a typical expectation is to teach four courses per year. In universities with fewer demands on research and supervision of doctoral students, a typical course load may be six courses per year. In all cases, depending on other responsibilities (e.g., if you obtained a large grant that paid for a portion of your time), the chair or dean may grant a lower teaching load.

## Professional Service

Most universities expect faculty to be professionally active and to maintain a public profile. This may include traditional forms of academic service, such as serving on editorial boards for journals or actively participating in your scholarly organization (the American Psychological Association and the American Psychological Society). But education provides numerous opportunities for professional service within the distributed networks of public and private schools at the local, state, and federal or national levels. And most universities will recognize service to the education profession as a consideration for promotion and tenure, even though the university priority remains focused on scholarship. Examples of professional service may include serving on boards and advisory committees, providing data analysis services to school districts or states, and serving on national or state commissions addressing various aspects of education.

Among my own professional service activities, I have served as an expert witness regarding the development of bilingual children to several court cases as well as to the U.S. Congress. Most of these are occasioned around the question of what constitutes an adequate and equitable program for English language learners, in consideration of the length of time it takes students to learn English and how their other educational needs (such as learning math) are addressed in the meantime. Usually, the political and policy alternatives are in conflict with research-based knowledge, so I find these opportunities to "enlighten the public" engaging (if not discouraging, because policy decisions usually are not swayed by research).

I have also served on various committees of the National Academy of Sciences addressing issues of English language learners. These committees usually are formed at the request of the U.S. Department of Education to make recommendations regarding educational programs. The National Academy of Sciences appoints a diverse committee of researchers with different expertise, and the committees go through an elaborate process coming up with their recommendations. This is another form of national service that is highly rewarding, because policymakers seriously consider these recommendations. Committee participation is also another mechanism through which professional networks are reinforced.

Locally, in California, I participate in a number of regional networks of smaller school districts addressing the issue of the implementation of new standards in literacy and math, known as the Common Core State Standards. These are communities of leaders from smaller districts that have few resources to conduct their own autonomous planning, and so they come together to share experience, expertise, and pool their limited resources. I participate by sharing what I know, but also by bringing in experts as well as by helping them find funding to support their continued work.

In all such cases, I am able to bring my knowledge from developmental psychology, psycholinguistics, and education research to contribute to the profession. At the same time, I am able to learn from what issues are considered important by the key decision makers and practitioners in the field, so that my research can be relevant to their needs.

## University Service

A university is a diverse community with multiple constituencies, and most public universities have competing missions, especially for those considered "land grant universities" with a dedicated mission to serve the multiple practical economic interests of the state. Supporting excellence in the K–12 school system is a key interest of any state, and among the main service one can provide the university as a faculty member is to strengthen the ways in which the university views and supports K–12 education. Although this may sound surprising to those who haven't been involved in education, in many universities, the faculty are focused on their own discipline, and do not think much about their own role in supporting K–12 education. Thus, by reminding colleagues of the importance of K–12 education, faculty in education can provide a special brand of service to their university.

In addition, faculty members in schools of education play a role in guiding undergraduate interest in entering the teaching profession. This is an especially interesting time in education, because the field is currently experiencing a cycle of high demand for teachers (fueled by a wave of retirements), moderately high levels of interest among undergraduates in going into teaching, stiff competition from other job sectors because of a stronger economy, and a diversification of pathways into teaching through alternative certification programs, such as Teach for America. Engaging in campus-wide discussions about education is a highly interesting and rewarding form of university service.

## A TYPICAL DAY

A typical day is one that rarely repeats itself, as the life of a professor in a school of education can involve: teaching a large lecture class, conducting a practicum or seminar in small groups, observing student teachers in their classroom placements, leading research seminars, participating in faculty and various university committee meetings, and increasingly doing some of the work virtually. On top of regular work, if you are involved in statewide or national professional activities, plenty of travel can be involved. Also during the day (or in my case, early in the mornings), you find yourself writing for publication in academic and professional venues.

Another reason a typical day may not be typical is that you are on a 9-month appointment, so you usually have either the summer months or one academic quarter *off-duty*, which you can choose to spend concentrating on your research, visiting another institution, or spending more time with your family and friends. So, usually your summer days look quite different from your other months. Thus, in a typical year, you will have several months when you are not teaching or expected to be around for university service, and you can be creative in how you spend it.

## PREPARATIONS

I did not enter education through a typical route, which usually starts with K–12 teaching experience followed by a doctoral degree. Because I started my career as a traditionally trained experimental psychologist, my first job was teaching in the Psychology Department at Yale University (my close senior colleague during that time was the editor of this volume, Robert Sternberg). After an 8-year stint at Yale, my research interests moved over into education sufficiently that when I moved to California, I took a position in education rather than in disciplinary psychology. That said, I always recommend those who want to go into education to begin their careers in K–12 teaching, as the hands-on experience would be invaluable and not something to be gained through books and formal study. It also would lend more professional credibility when working with educational practitioners.

Beyond practical experience, probably the most important preparation would be a combination of strong disciplinary and methodological strengths. As I noted earlier, education is an extremely complex enterprise, and most work that would have a meaningful impact would require a team of collaborators. Being invited to be part of a team requires not just being a nice person but also having some sort of specialized knowledge or skills. In my own case, that was a deep understanding of language and bilingualism and of experimental methodology. Without such expertise, I would not have been as attractive as part of a research collaboration.

## Attributes Needed For Success

Beyond expertise and a collaborative spirit, probably the main attribute for success in education is the ability to tolerate multiple perspectives and to accept incremental progress. We all want to improve education outcomes for all students, but we differ in terms of what we mean by education outcomes and also may differ with respect to how we accomplish those outcomes. For example, we all want children to become successful readers, but some would favor direct teaching, whereas others would favor letting children develop more naturally. Coming to terms with the reality that some approaches work better for some children some of the time—and that there is no silver bullet solution—would enable you to focus your energies on looking for patterns of success, rather than seeking a simple, single solution.

## Pay Range

Faculty members in schools of education earn on par with their academic colleagues in the social sciences within their university. Typically, they will earn less than their peers in higher income professions, such as business, medicine, or engineering. Most data on faculty salaries in public colleges and universities are available online, and inspection of the data will reveal considerable range across institutions. I took an informal survey of recent doctoral students who are in the beginning years of their careers as faculty in schools of education, and in 2015 U.S. dollars, the range is approximately $60,000–$86,000, with the median at around $67,500.

The lower salaries are offset by the benefits of academic freedom and latitude to choose areas of specialization for research, as well as by consulting opportunities that come with increasing specialization in one's line of work. Education faculty have considerable leeway supplementing their income with outside consulting, such as conducting professional development workshops for school districts or supporting data analysis needs of school systems. Because most employment contracts are more than 9 months, this allows up to 3 months of consulting time, and most universities allow faculty to consult some portion of their time even during the regular school year.

## Future Prospects

Education has emerged in recent years as one of the top policy priorities within states as well as nationally. President William Jefferson Clinton coined himself an education president, as did President George W. Bush, and many governors run on their state's economy and education— famous education governors include Dick Riley of South Carolina, Bob Wise of West Virginia, Roy Romer of Colorado, Brian Sandoval of Nevada, and Jim Hunt of North Carolina. Schools of education have an important role to play in this picture, not just as a place where teachers receive their credentials, but also as a knowledge-based voice about effective policy and practice for the education profession.

Still, education as a profession is less valued in the United States than in many other countries. A broad-based discussion around education policy is addressing the status of the occupation and its professionalization, and faculty in schools of education are expected to have a significant role in such discussions.

The newspaper headlines about education include the Common Core Standards, college access, testing, the achievement gap, international competitiveness of our students, teacher tenure policies, bilingual education, and of course, funding. These are all real issues around which educational scholarship and teaching can play a role, conducting research and informing the social policy. There is no shortage of good work to be done, and so this is a great field for those with a strong sense of social mission and a curious mind.

## References

Davis, J. W., & Bauman, K. (2011). School enrollment in the United States: Population characteristics. *Current Population Reports* P20-564. Washington, DC: U.S. Census Bureau.

U.S. Department of Education. (2012, March 19). *Working in the nation's lowest performing schools: A progress report.* Remarks of U.S. Secretary of Education Arne Duncan to the 2nd annual Building a Grad Nation Summit. Retrieved from http://www.ed.gov/news/speeches/"working-nation's-lowest-performing-schools-progress-report"

*Adam D. Galinsky, Malia F. Mason, and Joel Brockner*

# Psychologists in Schools of Business

4

E ach of us (the authors of this chapter) has faced a decision in our careers: accept a professorship in a business school or in a psychology department. When one of us faced this dilemma many years ago, a trusted and admired mentor pushed for the psychology department, derisively saying, "Going to a business school will change you." It did, and, in our cases, for the better.[1]

---

[1] Ironically, this mentor later ended up in a business school!

Adam D. Galinsky is the Vikram S. Pandit Professor of Business and Chair of the Management Division of Columbia Business School, Columbia University. He is the coauthor of the critically acclaimed book *Friend & Foe* (2015). He was trained as a social psychologist.

Malia F. Mason is an associate professor of business in the Management Division of Columbia Business School, Columbia University. She was trained as a social psychologist and cognitive neuroscientist.

Joel Brockner is the Phillip Hettleman Professor of Business and the former chair of the Management Division at Columbia Business School, Columbia University. He is the author of the award-winning book *The Process Matters* (2015). He was trained as a social psychologist.

http://dx.doi.org/10.1037/15960-005
*Career Paths in Psychology: Where Your Degree Can Take You, Third Edition,*
R. J. Sternberg (Editor)

This chapter describes why that move was for the better for each of us as well as why it won't be for everyone. We hope to give you guidance on a decision that many of you will have face as you contemplate doctoral programs: do I get a PhD in a business school or in a psychology department? Or later in your career: do I take a postdoctoral fellowship or professorship in a business school or in a psychology department?

## Relevance

As you consider this dilemma, there is one word that really captures the key, fundamental difference: *relevance*. What are the implications of your research for organizations and the real world? Some business schools want data collected outside the lab, but all want you to articulate why the research matters in a practical sense. This is not to say that faculty in psychology departments conduct impractical research or that research done in a business school is not theoretically rigorous or novel. Rather, we want to highlight that the questions, "Why should anyone care about your findings?" and "How might someone use your findings to inform their everyday behavior, in particular, in their roles as managers, members of work organizations, or in marketing?" loom larger for psychologists who are faculty at business schools.

### RESEARCH CHATTER AND WHO YOUR COLLEAGUES ARE

One of the famous findings in psychology is that peers can matter more than parents for informing teenager behavior (Harris, 1995). The same effect occurs for academics: your colleagues have a role in shaping your research identity, in part, because they expose you to different material. This is true not just for the colleagues in your immediate research area but also for your colleagues who are trained in other disciplines. In a psychology department, your colleagues are likely to be developmental, neuroscience, and cognitive psychologists. In a business school, your colleagues are likely to be economists, accountants, sociologists, and political scientists. You will hear about topics that interest them, be exposed to their methods, and be encouraged to consider their levels of analysis (which may mean analysis at the organizational, industrial, or even societal levels).

So, part of the difference between a psychology department and a business school is the chatter and language you hear in the halls. When we once asked a psychologist why he made the jump from a psychology department to a business school, he responded, "I woke up one morning and enjoyed interacting with and talking to economists more than I did with neuroscientists." So you need to consider which type of colleague inspires you and makes you feel connected.

## NATURE AND SCOPE OF RESEARCH

As we have highlighted, one key difference between research done by psychologists in business schools and psychologists in psychology departments is the emphasis on relevance. You might be wondering, what are typical topics of inquiry for a psychologist in a business school? Before we can address this question, it is important for us to clarify that psychologists who teach in business schools typically work in one of two departments: management or marketing. Although the topics studied by psychologists from these two departments overlap considerably—they are both interested in persuasion, influence, and motivation, for instance—the impetus for the research tends to depend on whether the psychologist is a member of the former or the latter department. That is, psychologists from the two departments likely have different reasons for wanting to know more about a particular topic.

Psychologists in management departments are primarily concerned with people's behavior in organizational settings and as organizational actors. Their research is concerned with such things as identifying barriers to effective teamwork, understanding the forces that shape employees' motivations toward their work, understanding the nature of negotiations, ascertaining the traits and behaviors of effective leaders, elucidating how to motivate people to work toward the organization's goals, and defining how culture shapes organizational behavior. They believe that a more comprehensive understanding of these topics will improve an organization's effectiveness and the well-being of stakeholders of those organizations. Psychologists in management departments tend to publish their research in outlets such as the *Academy of Management Journal, Organizational Behavior and Human Decision Processes,* and the *Journal of Applied Psychology.* It is worth noting that many of them also publish their research in general science (e.g., *Science, Proceedings of the National Academy of Sciences*), general psychology (e.g., *Psychological Science, Journal of Experimental Psychology: General*), social psychology (e.g., *Journal of Personality and Social Psychology*), and cognitive (e.g., *Memory and Cognition*) outlets.

In contrast, psychologists in marketing departments are primarily concerned with people's behavior in the marketplace and as consumers. Their research elucidates how consumers select different alternatives (e.g., brands, products, retailers, ideas); probes the motives behind the use, disposal, and purchase of products; and examines the role of motivation and self-control in consumption. They believe that knowing more about decision making, motivation, influence, self-control, and attitudes can help companies improve their marketing strategies and help consumers make the best purchasing decisions. In addition to publishing in general science, general psychology, social psychology, and cognitive psychology outlets, marketing researchers publish in journals such as *Journal of Consumer Research*, *Journal of Marketing Research*, and *Journal of Consumer Psychology*.

An easy way to parse the complex world of research topics is the following: management scholars focus on organizational actors and behavior in organizations, whereas marketing scholars focus on consumers and behavior that involves purchasing and consumption.

Psychologists in psychology departments also often direct their attention toward a particular set of actors. As detailed in the next section, much of the funding for psychologists in psychology departments comes from grant writing and the funding calls for grant applications that are targeted toward a specific population (e.g., veterans with trauma, children with autism). Therefore, psychologists, depending on the source of their grant, may focus their research questions on topics that are relevant to a specific population (e.g., the elderly, veterans, kids with attention deficit/ hyperactivity disorder) or specific types of behaviors (e.g., health-related behavior). Of course, business school professors may focus on these same populations and behaviors but likely will focus on the implications for organizations or marketing.

This is by no means an exhaustive list of the topics that are of interest to psychologists in business schools. Furthermore, we expect that globalization and technological innovations will shape where psychologists in business school direct their research efforts in the future.

## GETTING RESEARCH DONE

There are three major differences in how psychologists in business schools and psychologists in psychology departments conduct research. These differences pertain to where they do research, where they get participants for their research studies, and how they pay for it.

The first major difference is one that has to do with where the research is conducted. Most psychologists who work in psychology departments have their own dedicated lab space. Typically, when psychologists get hired, they are given start-up money to design and build their own lab space. These labs store the data they collect, house their graduate students, and host lab meetings. Individually run labs are rare for psychologists in business schools, who instead tend to share a centralized laboratory space with other social scientists in the business school that do behavioral research. Typically, such a community-based research laboratory is run by an administrator who coordinates the scheduling of experimental rooms, maintains the equipment, and oversees participant recruiting efforts for all of the social scientists (not just psychologists but also economists) who run behavioral studies in the lab. For instance, Columbia Business School has a research lab that is currently shared by 25 faculty members, their postdoctoral students, graduate students, and research assistants.

The second major difference concerns who participates in research studies. Psychologists in psychology departments often have a pool of undergraduate students who are required to participate in their studies in exchange for course credit. Instead, in business schools, participants are offered monetary remuneration and the participant pool comes from the broader university community. As a result, studies conducted by psychologists in business school are less likely to have samples composed entirely of undergraduates who are enrolled in psychology classes and are more likely to have samples composed of undergraduates majoring in an unrelated discipline, graduate students, and university employees. Of course, given the growing popularity of the Mechanical Turk participant pool, there has been in greater overlap in the research participants in psychology department and in business schools studies.

The third major difference between psychologists in business schools and psychology departments is how they spend their time in conducting research. Psychologists who work in psychology departments generally are expected to find funding for their research by writing grants to external sources, including the government like the National Science Foundation or private sources like the Templeton Foundation. Furthermore, the grant funds go to pay for equipment, software, stipends for graduates students, and salaries for postdocs; in many psychology departments, getting a graduate student depends on having outside funding. Therefore, psychologists in psychology departments spend considerable time writing proposals for funding. And if they are successful, they spend considerable time having to report on how they have used their time (called effort reporting) and on the conclusions of their research to granting agencies.

In contrast, most psychologists in business schools are provided with a modest, annual research budget that they spend on compensation for research participants, experimental software, and attending conferences Funding for doctoral students often comes from a centralized source in the school; furthermore, doctoral students often are admitted to the department through a selection committee rather than being selected by an individual professor. This is not to say that business school psychologists never apply for grants or that they are never awarded them; indeed one of us received a 3-year National Science Foundation grant. But the ability to conduct research on a modest scale is less constrained by success at grant writing in business schools than in psychology departments.

## The Teaching Imperative

Teaching matters in a business school. It matters *a lot*. Simply put, it is difficult to get tenure in a business school if you are not an effective teacher in the classroom.

Whereas psychologists in psychology departments spend a sizable amount of their time identifying funding agencies and writing grant proposals, psychologists in business school spend a considerable amount of time developing teaching materials and meeting with others to talk and strategize about teaching. We take seminars on how to best structure a class, the art and science of PowerPoint, and how to lead a case discussion. We frequently write exercises or cases for use in the classroom.

Although the business school curriculum consists of several courses that psychologists are qualified to teach (including leadership, managing teams, decision making, consumer behavior, advertising, and negotiations), the classroom structure is different from a typical undergraduate lecture. The classes are participative, with students constantly asking or answering questions. Each class session often is structured not only around a topic but also around a case or exercise. For example, in a typical negotiation class, the students will engage in a negotiation exercise at the beginning of class and after the students have reported their outcomes, the professor will debrief the exercise, detailing the learning points, and soliciting the experience of the students during the negotiation. Similarly, an entire leadership session may be structured around a single case in which the students debate different courses of action for a dilemma a leader faces. Given the importance of exercises and cases, psychologists in business schools must learn to do two things. First, they must learn how to teach an exercise or structure a case discussion. Second, they often need to write some of the exercises and cases to be used in the classroom.

Another way in which teaching differs in a business school is that many classes are multisection, multiprofessor classes. For example, at Columbia Business School, we teach 16 sections of our required leadership class, and this class involves between six and eight professors each year. Similarly, we teach more than 20 sections of the negotiations class with more than 10 faculty members involved. What this means is that teaching is a collaborative and collective process. We coordinate on topics and cases or exercises, share materials, and meet frequently. The curriculum is taken seriously at business schools; to ensure coordination and integration, there are often teaching meetings from across all the departments (e.g., finance, accounting, management, marketing, operations).

Once again, *relevance* is the key term for understanding life at business school. This is doubly so in the classroom. Masters in Business Administration (MBA) students will push hard on us during class discussion. Consider the question that one of us faced in the classroom (after this professor was already a chaired full professor who had won teaching awards): "Essentially, all of us in this classroom are practitioners. So what can you teach us, why are we better taught by you than by another fellow practitioner?" The answer that satisfied the student was this, "A practitioner has wonderful and informative experience. But their experience is only one data point and that data point could be an anomaly. What I can offer you as a social scientist is general patterns that exist across many different practitioners. And I can do more than that. I can also tell you *when* something will happen and also *why* it will happen. A practitioner is limited by their experience. A social scientist is not."

Many psychologists have been told that they should not present research in the classroom. This is simply wrong: you need to explain why a research finding matters. How can it help a person make a better career decision, or lead and manage others more effectively? A mantra at Columbia Business School and many others is "blending theory/research with practice." We wholeheartedly agree with the founder of social psychology, Kurt Lewin, who famously proclaimed that, "there is nothing so practical as a good theory" (1951) and we strive to help our business students see the value in theory.

As is probably clear from this discussion, the type of student differs between psychology departments and business schools. Although business schools vary on whether or not they teach undergraduates, almost all business schools offer an MBA. Students enroll in MBA programs for the purpose of reaching higher levels of responsibility in their organizations or learning how to create and grow successful businesses. Most have worked for at least 5 years, making MBA students significantly more experienced than undergraduates. This means they want more relevance and also that they have experiences that may contradict a learning point. So professors have to be ready to be challenged in the classroom (consistent with the previous example about practitioners versus academics).

Business schools have four types of students: undergraduate, MBA, executive MBA (EMBA), executive education. The difference between MBA and EMBA students is the amount of experience—EMBA students tend to be older with more experience. The greater experience that EMBA students have often enriches class discussion on such topics of leadership, negotiations, and ethics. Executive education involves workshops centered on a topic or theme, such as persuasion. For example, current programs taught at Columbia Business School include an Advanced Management Program (a 4-week program), High Impact Leadership (a 5-day program), and Brand Leadership (a 3-day program). These are often open-enrollment programs that offer certificates but no degrees.

## *Preparation and Hiring Trends*

It is not uncommon for marketing or management departments to hire people who have degrees in psychology. In fact, all three of the authors have a PhD in psychology. Many business school departments hire at least some of their faculty from the disciplines (i.e., people who have a PhD in a traditional discipline like economics, sociology, political science).

That being said, the best preparation for a business school professorship probably involves enrolling in a business school PhD program in which you will learn both the art of research and the fundamentals of organizational behavior and consumer behavior. Individuals enrolled in a psychology doctoral program who want to teach in a business school should conduct research that has some relevance for organizational settings or consumer behavior. Taking courses in a business school or from faculty teaching industrial–organizational psychology would be one way to become immersed in problems of relevance to organizations. When business schools do hire a person who has a PhD in psychology, it is generally because the candidate has demonstrated, first and foremost, a capability for impactful, innovative research that has implications for managerial work or informs our understanding of consumer behavior. Moreover, some faculty members who have a PhD in psychology do a 1- or 2-year stint in a postdoctoral program by way of ensuring that their work is more grounded in the realities of organizational life. For example, one of us did a postdoctoral fellowship at a business school that involved not only collaborating with faculty but also teaching an MBA class on negotiations.

Moreover, successful candidates often have demonstrated that they will be good teachers. Job talks in business schools are not just to vet the quality of your research but also to ascertain your prospects as an effective MBA teacher. As a result, job talks often involve frequent interruptions, exactly what a person would face in the MBA classroom. In contrast, most talks in a psychology department involve holding all questions to the end of the talk. The faculty members are looking to how you answer questions and keep command of the room and your ability to handle the room plays a role in hiring decisions.

As higher education is experiencing significant disruption, we hesitate to forecast trends in the hiring of psychology PhDs by business schools. What is clear is that business schools want professors who are conducting theoretically and methodologically strong research that has relevance to organizations and consumers and are also an effective teacher.

## Compensation and Outside Activities

Salaries of psychologists vary tremendously both across and within business schools. According to Association to Advance Collegiate Schools of Business International's Global Survey (AACSB, 2016), the mean 9-month salary for new doctorates that joined management departments between 2015 and 2016 was $113,800. The mean 9-month salary for new doctorates that joined marketing departments at that time was $126,700. It is worth noting, however, that both of these salary figures include candidates with PhDs in fields that generally command higher compensation (e.g., economics) and therefore may be inflated estimates of the average starting salaries of psychologists hired into management or marketing departments. Consistent with the general trend in which professional school faculty are paid more than those in the arts and sciences, the salaries of business school professors typically are higher than those of psychology professors.

Opportunities tend to be greater for nongrant sources of income in business schools than in psychology departments. Psychologists in both psychology departments and business schools serve as legal experts in civil and criminal trails, do paid talks such as keynote addresses, and consult and do workshops for companies around a specific topic (e.g., negotiations, decision making, motivation). Business school professors tend to be more attractive to companies, given the content of their courses and their experience with MBA students and executives. As we mentioned earlier, faculty in business schools can teach not only undergraduates and MBA students but also EMBA students and in executive education programs; often times, these executive education sessions and EMBA classes involve additional compensation, thus providing more opportunities for extra teaching income in a business school.

## Conclusion

Being a psychologist in a business school offers different rewards and challenges than working in a psychology department. A key similarity is theoretically grounded research. Key differences involve a greater focus on teaching and practical relevance. We hope this guided tour of the business school world will help you make the best decision for yourself as you approach doctoral programs, postdocs, or professorships.

## References

Association to Advance Collegiate Schools of Business. (2016). *2015–2016 Global salary survey report: Executive summary.* Tampa, FL: AACSB International.

Harris, J. R. (1995). Where is the child's environment? A group socialization theory of development. *Psychological Review, 102,* 458–489.

Lewin, K. (1951). *Field theory in social science: Selected theoretical papers* (D. Cartwright, Ed.). New York, NY: Harper & Row.

*Aric A. Prather and Elissa S. Epel*

# Psychologists in Medical Schools

5

M edical schools provide a unique setting for those who wish to work at the nexus of psychology and medicine. The interdisciplinary nature of medical schools can lead to surprising collaborations in research and clinical domains. Indeed, our experience is rife with examples where chance and not-so-chance encounters helped push the boundaries of

Aric A. Prather, PhD, is an assistant professor in the Department of Psychiatry and Associate Director of the Center for Health and Community at the University of California, San Francisco (UCSF). He is also a licensed clinical psychologist. Dr. Prather received his PhD in clinical and biological and health psychology from the University of Pittsburgh. He completed a clinical internship at Duke University Medical Center and a postdoctoral fellowship in the Robert Wood Johnson Foundation Health and Society Scholars program jointly housed at UCSF and UC Berkeley.

Elissa S. Epel, PhD, is a professor in the Department of Psychiatry at University of California, San Francisco. Dr. Epel studied psychology and psychobiology at Stanford University (BA), and clinical and health psychology at Yale University (PhD). She completed a clinical internship at the Palo Alto Veterans Healthcare System and a National Institute of Mental Health postdoctoral fellowship at UCSF.

http://dx.doi.org/10.1037/15960-006
*Career Paths in Psychology: Where Your Degree Can Take You, Third Edition*,
R. J. Sternberg (Editor)

understanding about how psychological factors contribute to health and disease. In that way, we are strong supporters of those interested in starting careers in such a dynamic environment. That said, we readily recognize that for all of the potential opportunities afforded a psychologist employed in a medical school, there can also be substantial challenges. In our opinion, the opportunities often win out, but, as will be elaborated on later, the medical school setting often requires certain personality characteristics or mind-sets to enhance one's chance at finding success in a medical school over the long term.

Why would a psychologist choose to work in a medical school and what does that school gain by adding a psychologist to its faculty roster? From the perspective of the medical school, psychologists are well equipped to carry out theory-driven research with important implications for the health and well-being of patients within the medical system. Psychologists readily subscribe to the biopsychosocial model (Engel, 1977) as well as life-course approaches (Kuh & Ben-Shlomo, 1997) that better capture the developmental, psychological, social, and environmental factors that contribute to health. In the end, psychologists are poised to ensure that critical psychosocial contributors to health and wellness are not obscured by the sometimes overly reductionist views held by physicians. Additionally, psychologists with clinical training fill an important role in delivering evidence-based cognitive and behavioral treatments carried out in individual or group settings with patients with and without all sorts of medical complexities.

Medical schools are improved by having psychologists as part of their faculty. The next question is, what is in it for the psychologist? The goal of this chapter is to provide the reader with some insights into the life of a psychologist in a medical school setting, including what can be expected and what, if possible, should be avoided. Although care was taken to discuss different career paths available to psychologists in medical schools (e.g., clinician, researcher), this chapter is weighted toward the experiences of a research psychologist. The decision to focus on research was made based on the fact that many of the complexities characteristic of medical school settings seem to disproportionately affect psychologists engaged primarily in research. Before discussing professional activities, day-to-day experiences, and financial compensation found in medical environments, it is best to describe some of the key characteristics that distinguish medical schools from other employment opportunities for psychologists.

First, the responsibilities that make up one's job description are largely dependent on the types of services provided. As will be discussed in more detail, a day in the life of a clinician within a medical setting, such as serving as a staff psychologist on an interdisciplinary behavioral medicine team or carrying out neurocognitive assessments for patients at risk for Alzheimer's disease, will differ substantially from that of a psychologist whose day-to-day life is centered on conducting research. Naturally, the services provided will dictate with whom a psychologist interacts, which can have implications for job satisfaction. For example, a developmental psychologist working as part of a collaborative clinical team in the department of pediatrics may treasure and thrive in such a fast moving and potentially emotionally charged environment, whereas other personality types who prefer a less hectic research setting may cringe at the prospect of such a position and prefer the more independent and slower moving pace of, for example, conducting neuropsychological assessments.

The second characteristic is the financial structure of medical schools. It is common for psychologists, and to some extent clinicians, to be responsible for the majority, if not all, of their salary. This is what commonly is referred to as having a "soft money" position, meaning that employment depends on continued funding solicited by the psychologist. This funding model contrasts with traditional psychology departments housed in universities, in which faculty often receive a 9-month salary year in and year out, that is, "hard money." For those funded by soft money, sources of funding typically come from extramural grants, such as grants from the National Institutes of Health (NIH) or from clinical service. For instance, a psychologist could generate revenue by seeing patients as part of a medical service, which in turn pays his or her salary. Alternatively, a psychologist may have received several large grants, each of which pays a percentage of the salary. There are many combinations for successfully paying one's salary, but it can be stressful when trying to figure out which combination works best for an individual's interests and skill set and then working to achieve 100% coverage. Relatedly, the financial structure of medical schools has important implications for the tenure process. Although tenure does exist in medical schools, it takes on a different form from what it looks like in traditional academic environments. Tenured research psychologists in medical schools almost always are required to contribute to their salary, although the percentage required may decrease post-tenure and varies a lot by institutions (private universities tend to have larger funds for salary). As such, tenured faculty members are not afforded the same level of job security seen in psychology departments because they must continue to compete for funding to maintain their positions.

Third, unlike psychologists employed in other academic settings, teaching typically is not a high priority role for psychologists in medical schools. That is not to say that teaching opportunities are not available or that teaching from a psychologist would not be welcomed. Psychologists often are called on to teach medical school cohorts about a variety of psychology topics, including heuristics in decision making, stress and illness, and psychosocial interventions, to name a few. Psychologists, however, often have little to no financial incentive to teach.

Last, the number of classes taught does not carry much weight for academic promotion relative to research productivity. As will be elaborated, teaching usually falls under the other hats a psychologist wears from time to time in his or her life as a faculty member in a medical school.

## Professional Activities of Psychologists at Medical Schools

The composition of a medical school faculty differs fairly dramatically from what one would find in a psychology department. First, and perhaps most obvious, the majority of the faculty have medical degrees (MDs). This can pose challenges because medical training differs from that of graduate training in psychology. Indeed, psychologists are often comfortable with ambiguity and nuance, but MDs typically are trained to make calculated decisions based on available evidence. The culture at medical schools also has a hierarchy, and physicians are typically at the top, although that is slowly changing. This does not mean that a psychologist cannot climb the status ladder or that each culture within a medical school is the same, but any psychologist interested in joining a medical school should be aware of this hierarchy.

The professional activities of a psychologist in a medical school broadly fall into two categories: (a) research and (b) clinical service. Embedded in these categories are other varied responsibilities, such as teaching, mentoring or supervision, and administrative or leadership activities.

Research psychologists within a medical school generally carry out research centered on human functioning, either in the context of a medical disorder (e.g., cancer, schizophrenia) or in healthy participants. Because funding agencies that support research typically focus on work in specific health domains (e.g., cardiovascular disease), even when research is carried out in otherwise healthy participants, the work often is framed in relation to some sort of clinical outcome. Research psychologists may serve as either principal investigator (PI) or as a member of a research team. Thus, one's role in the research naturally dictates one's day-to-day activities. Nevertheless, some generalities can be made about the experience of a research psychologist in an academic medical school. In this regard, productivity in the form of grants and peer-reviewed publications (sometimes in that order) remain the currency for promotion for a psychologist in a medical school and a way to establish one's area of expertise. As such, daily activities of a research psychologist typically include culling relevant research literature; writing manuscripts; carrying out data scoring and statistical analyses; planning projects; and meeting with research team members, collaborators, and potential collaborators. Research is a dynamic process that requires persistence and creativity. This is especially true in a medical school, where psychologists are often concurrently involved in multiple projects, in part because of multiple interests and in part because several grants usually are required to cover one's salary. For many psychologists, this is exciting because it provides variety and constant learning about different topics. For others, it can feel overwhelming. It is important to maintain a portfolio of projects that one can manage simultaneously; otherwise one's capacity is spread thin, which hinders productivity.

We would be remiss not to mention the significant amount of time a research psychologist spends writing and revising grants. Grant applications to NIH are accepted three times per year (generally in February, June, October). Other agencies, such as National Science Foundation (NSF), have their own deadlines and cycles. Grant writing takes time and persistence, and those who enjoy grant writing often find the process intellectually stimulating. Because of financial constraints on available grant funding, fewer and fewer grants are funded in any given grant cycle. As such, a successful research psychologist must be resilient to rejection and persistent in resubmitting multiple times.

Clinical service is the other common category of responsibility for a psychologist in a medical school. Whether working in a department of neurology, pediatrics, oncology, psychiatry, internal medicine, or some other department, psychologists providing clinical service typically carry out a set of procedures used for delivering clinical care. These procedures include conducting clinical assessments, intervention (e.g., psychotherapy, psychoeducational groups), writing medical notes and clinical reports, and discussing challenging patients in case conference. Naturally, much of this is limited to the type of clinical population being cared for. For some, clinical service will be carried out in an outpatient setting. In this case, patients will schedule an appointment with a psychologist and be seen at that specific time. In other cases, psychologists may provide service on a more emergent, unpredictable basis, such as treating a patient with acute anxiety in the intensive care unit or carrying out a neurocognitive assessment on a patient who has been hospitalized following a serious car accident.

Many psychologists have a balance of both research and clinical service. Indeed, many medical schools have thriving clinical research programs directed by psychologists. For instance, psychologists across the country direct clinically focused programs in such areas as pain, psycho-oncology, obesity and weight loss (including bariatric surgery), tobacco control, cardiovascular behavioral medicine, insomnia, among others. Many of these programs hire psychologists to conduct research on psychosocial interventions in some form or another. This combination of clinical care and research often fits well for psychologists who have primary interests in clinical research but who wish to maintain their clinical skills.

As noted, psychologists also wear many hats in their positions at medical schools. Although teaching is rarely a substantial part of the job, there are often opportunities to teach formal lectures in medical schools. Indeed, there is a movement across the country among medical schools to increase the amount of psychology, and social and behavioral sciences (SBS) more broadly, into their medical school curriculums (Kaplan, Satterfield, & Kington, 2012). This is further substantiated by the fact that psychological and SBS content are now reflected in the Medical College Admissions Test (MCAT). More medical school curriculums are turning to small-group problem-based learning curriculums that require more faculty to lead small groups of students. It is a great opportunity, and often thrilling or at least highly rewarding, for a psychologist with background in behavioral medicine to teach future doctors about foundational skills in patient care. Thus, medical school faculty members with social science backgrounds are needed to impart this information to the medical classes year after year. Beyond formal lectures, psychologists often provide mentoring to postdoctoral fellows, graduate and medical students, and undergraduates. In our opinion, one of the most rewarding aspects of being a professor is the ability to help shape the next cohort of scientists. Although graduate programs in psychology rarely exist in medical schools, the mentoring responsibilities available to psychologists help fill that void.

## Financial Compensation

The financial compensation afforded a psychologist in a medical school is usually comparable, or sometimes exceeds, that of a faculty with the same level of experience employed in a department of psychology. The most recent salary survey carried out by the American Psychological Association supports this claim (see Finno, Michalski, Hart, Wicherski, & Kohout, 2010, Table 1). Assistant professors employed in the department of psychiatry at a medical school earned a 9- to 10-month median income of $65,455 (mean = $65,927), whereas an assistant professor in a department of psychology over the same period earned $57,000 (mean = $59,196). This disparity continued in associate and full professors. Associate professors employed in psychiatry departments of medical schools earned a median income of $82,636 (mean = $89,967), whereas those in the department of psychology earned $68,000 (mean = $67,616). Full professors in psychiatry departments earned $122,605 (mean = $124,172), whereas those in departments of psychology earned a median income of $100,636 (mean = $109,437). It is notable that although this survey does not provide estimates on the salaries for psychologists in specific other departments in medical schools (e.g., pediatrics, neurology, oncology), psychologists employed in "other than psychiatry departments" earned median incomes similar to those in psychiatry.

As noted earlier, the salary for a psychologist in a medical school is not guaranteed from year to year but rather depends on psychologists' ability to bring in the revenue (through clinical service or research grants) to pay their own salary. It is also common for clinical psychologists to supplement their salary by establishing a private practice, or for nonclinicians, by serving as a consultant. Psychologists outside of medical settings also supplement their income, but because the pressures inherent in raising one's salary in a medical school are higher, such supplementation may be more frequent among psychologists in medical schools.

## Academic and Other Preparation Needed

How does one end up working in a medical school, and what are the skills required for being successful? The answers to these questions depend on what type of position you are seeking. If you are clinically trained, even at the master's level, there are often opportunities to join a clinical service doing psychological assessments and providing counseling in a medical setting. That being said, it is more common to find psychologists in medical schools who have completed a doctorate (PhD or PsyD) and, if interested in clinical work, who are in the process of obtaining a state license to practice.

Preparation for conducting research in a medical school is not much different from conducting research in another setting when it comes to foundational skills, including an ability to critically review existing literature, developing research hypotheses, executing research studies, and reporting the results in peer-reviewed journals. Grant writing may represent a new skill, and although there is no substitution for reading and writing grants yourself, several texts are available to become familiar with the structure and content to be expected (e.g., Gerin & Kapelewski, 2011). As discussed in more detail, obtaining an early career grant is one way to secure a faculty position at a medical school.

Individuals interested in a clinical position at a medical school typically can find employment listings on university websites and other forums where jobs are advertised. It is not particularly common for medical schools to advertise job openings to fill research-psychologist positions. Prospective psychologists more commonly join medical school faculties by (a) being recruited or (b) providing their own funding via a grant mechanism, often starting as a postdoc at that school. For young investigators, the NIH offers a competitive funding mechanism to facilitate such a transition. Specifically, early career psychologists can apply for a Research Career Development Award (K series; NIH, n.d.), which will provide salary support for 4 to 5 years and some additional funding for conducting research (ranging between $25,000 and $50,000 per year). Although this mechanism is not specific to professionals employed in medical schools, the reliance on grant funding by those in medical schools means that the majority of applicants are from soft money environments. All in all, a K award is an excellent mechanism for starting a career in a medical school; however, we would be remiss if we omitted a couple of considerations. One caveat is that the salary a K-series award can provide has a maximum (e.g., as of 2015, the National Institute of Mental Health maximum is $90,000 per year and the National Heart, Lung, and Blood Institute maximum is $75,000 per year). In many areas of the country, these salaries are competitive and well within the starting salary for a psychologist at an institution. In more expensive cities (e.g., New York, Boston, San Francisco), however, a psychologist's salary may exceed the maximum provided by the K award. In this case, the psychologist is left to cover this gap. Ideally, the department or the institution would cover this shortfall, but in instances in which this is not possible, the psychologist often spends a disproportionate amount of time chasing small-grant mechanisms to maintain his or her salary. A second caveat is that once funded by a K award, the psychologist is no longer allowed to receive federal funding from other sources (e.g., being a co-investigator on a NIH grant) until the last years of the award. This is certainly understandable given that training is a primary goal of the K award; however, in a medical school environment in which interdisciplinary collaborations are critical for success, such funding restrictions can hamper productivity. Last, one of the biggest issues is that once the K award ends, psychologists will need to cover their salary through several grants. The ability to secure these grants requires having developed a strong line of research as well as good collaborations.

## *Attributes Needed for Success*

Working within a medical school is ideal for some but not all psychologists. The dynamic and collaborative atmosphere can be invigorating for some and nerve-wracking for others. To be successful in the long term (i.e., more than a couple of years), three clear attributes or characteristics are required. Please note that these attributes are more relevant to research psychologists than to those providing primarily clinical service.

- *The ability to develop a collaborative net.* The nature of the funding environment makes it challenging to carry out independent research in a medical school without the help from good colleagues. As such, it is important, and almost essential, to align yourself with others who are motivated, collaborative, and talented. This is likely to work best if your area of research complements others (i.e., you have a niche). Developing a collaborative net refers to the notion that you and your colleagues submit multiple grants together, each providing some portion of salary support for the other. In the best scenario, this provides a level of financial stability to carry out great science. In the event that one person is unsuccessful in obtaining funding, the interdependence created by the process will help provide some support until the next grant cycle. We have seen this model work well in medical schools.
- *Remain robust yet flexible.* Depending on your graduate school experience, you have been more or less exposed to a fair amount of rejection and yet survived. Unfortunately, rejection only becomes more common once you transition to a medical school. The need to publish scientific papers or obtain grant funding on a regular basis increases one's probability of having unsuccessful experiences. In this respect, success in a medical school requires a short memory, and the persistence to try and try again. Along with having a thick skin (i.e., being robust to criticism), a successful psychologist must be able to see value in varied experiences. The dynamic atmosphere of a medical school, driven in part by the shifting availability of funding for research, may make it necessary to repackage your interests to fit the current funding landscape. For instance, a psychologist who is passionate about the role of depression in patients with pancreatic cancer may need to be open to situating his or her work within a collaborative group studying patients with rheumatoid arthritis. Flexibility in this regard not only helps secure one's position of employment but also helps build productive relationships with new colleagues and further strengthens the collaborative net (i.e., the first attribute).

■ *Know that uncertainty is certain.* If one personality characteristic seems to separate a psychologist who remains employed in a medical school from one who does not over the long term, it is the ability to cope with ambiguity about the future. Put another way, risk-averse individuals need not apply. This comes back to the shifting, unpredictable funding landscape in medical schools. Because grant funding has become increasingly more challenging to obtain, a psychologist is left not knowing whether his or her job will exist when the grant that funds that position ends. Individuals who prefer to plan their lives in 10-year chunks may find it difficult to cope with such uncertainty. This ambiguity, and to some extent, one's limited control over the future, can be a source of substantial stress. Notably, this observation regarding uncertainty applies more strongly to research psychologists than to those who provide clinical service; however, even clinically focused psychologists may experience some difficulties.

## Advantages and Disadvantages of a Career in a Medical School

As we have discussed, medical schools have the potential to provide a thriving and engaging atmosphere for psychologists. Those excited about working with medical populations or carrying out behavioral interventions will find ample opportunity. Likewise, those interested in interdisciplinary collaboration, access to biomedical expertise, limited teaching, and relative independence may be well situated to succeed. A couple more disadvantages should be mentioned when considering a position in a medical school. First, one persistent problem for most psychologists working in a medical school, irrespective of position, is the competition for space. Unfortunately, many working in a medical school have difficulty acquiring laboratory space, which potentially can hinder one's ability to effectively conduct research. A second and related problem is that many psychologists receive little, if any, start-up money upon joining the medical school faculty. Consequently, one must rely on shared resources (e.g., staff, equipment, space), which may or may not provide the ideal environment to begin one's career. This lack of resources is in contrast to joining a department of psychology, where it is standard practice for the university to provide lab space and some funding to an incoming faculty member. This disadvantage also underscores the importance of assessing how a prospective department in a medical school can meet your professional needs.

## *Why I Chose a Career in a Medical School*

### PRATHER

A key landmark that helped shape my path toward a career in a medical school was the research experience I gained after college. I was a research coordinator in a department of psychiatry (coincidently, the very same department I find myself employed in today). Like many students who eventually go on to receive training in clinical-health psychology, I originally had imagined myself as a physician. I found myself fascinated by human biology, aging, and the connection between mind and body. After a year of working as a research coordinator, I realized that I enjoyed conducting, reading about, and analyzing research data too much to put it on hold for 10 years of medical training. Instead, I enrolled in a clinical-health psychology PhD program at the University of Pittsburgh, where I was trained in cardiovascular behavioral medicine and psychoneuroimmunology, two disciplines that depend heavily on interdisciplinary collaborations, including with scientists in the basic sciences.

During my graduate training, I was drawn to clinical experiences in medical settings, including patients undergoing bone marrow transplantation and individuals experiencing chronic pain. In my clinical internship, I continued to work in a medical school by providing therapy to patients undergoing organ transplantation and treating patients with chronic insomnia. It was much more gratifying to provide emergent, short-term therapy for patients undergoing a medical crisis than to meet with someone week after week in outpatient therapy.

Although I treasure my clinical experience and eventually went on to become licensed as a clinical psychologist in California, it was truly the research that brought me to my current job in a medical school. My burning curiosity over the biological mechanisms that link psychological and behavioral factors, such as chronic stress and sleep disturbance, with age-related illness has required close partnerships with immunologists, molecular biologists, biochemists, and neuroscientists, the like of which are hard to come by in traditional psychology departments. I am fortunate to work with like-minded and brilliant health psychologists (my coauthor included). In addition, Elissa Epel and I are fortunate to have a strong campus leader in our department (Nancy Adler, PhD) who has been an incredible advocate for psychologists in our medical school. The enthusiasm for the science is infectious, and despite the continued challenges in regards to funding endemic in science, the collaborative net we have developed as a team provides the needed continuity and stability to propose and test novel scientific hypotheses. A career in a medical school may not be for everyone, but it is an ideal fit for me.

## EPEL

It was also my experiences after college that helped me find my fit for graduate school and my long-term home in a medical school. I had long ago, before entering college, chosen my path toward medical school. I had started studying for the MCAT, and at the same time, I had an exciting job as a research assistant. I was pained to be spending so much time memorizing facts such as chemical structures when I could be reading the research literature and analyzing data. Furthermore, I realized this was just the beginning of a long path toward becoming a clinician with minimal opportunities to learn research methodology. The decision eventually became clear to me that I was more passionate about research than practicing medicine. I never took the MCAT, and instead I took the GRE.

My interest had always been in the intersection between the mind, behavior, and physiology. Health psychology and the more applied behavioral medicine field were cross-cutting areas in psychology that were laying the foundations for the critical role of psychologists in medicine and health. In the early 1990s, there were still few programs in health psychology. I received a PhD in health psychology and completed an internship at a Veterans Administration hospital where psychologists had team roles in many clinics serving the complex needs of aging veterans. The model of having psychologists work in, for example, a primary care clinic side by side with physicians was brand new. Even in the 21st century, the collaboration between psychological and medical clinicians has a novelty and an emergent quality in which everyone learns and patients benefit.

A medical school was the most fitting intellectual home for my interests in disease pathways and interventions. Although I have not continued with clinical work in a traditional model, the training was invaluable and has shaped my intervention research, which applies both theories of behavior change and therapeutic techniques in interventions for groups of people with a common health issue. We study how, for example, stress reduction and self-regulation interventions can help people with weight loss, affect immune function, or help pregnant women have a healthier pregnancy. These interventions have both clinical endpoints as well as address questions about basic mechanism in psychophysiological pathways of health. The new research model is team science, and one of the most gratifying parts of a medical school research career is working with colleagues who share similar values and goals, as I get to do with my coauthor Aric

Prather, and playing a role in furthering our field and the excitement of discovery.

## Conclusion

This chapter laid out the picture of what your career might look like in a medical school, which we view as a high-risk, high-reward endeavor. Research funding likely will remain tight, and one should heed the challenges we lay out in this chapter. If, however, you feel you have both the temperament to deal with uncertainty and the passion for research, we cannot overemphasize the benefits of finding the right fit in a medical school. If you can join or develop a supportive collaborative net, it will allow you to pursue your research interests, develop expertise in several areas, and do meaningful work that will positively affect health and well-being. The daily life of research, with the right balance of support, is tremendously gratifying, with ample independence and creative freedom.

The opportunities for more applied work will grow. The field of medicine is ever changing, especially with the knowledge that the roots of lifelong health lay in part in childhood. The need for care of our aging population is growing, as well as the need to protect the health of the next generation, from gestation onward. Regulations of the Affordable Care Act eventually should have positive implications for the role of psychologists working at the intersection of behavioral medicine and public health, both clinical and research. Support now exists for the prevention of chronic diseases and incentives for health systems to lower acute care costs. In sum, we feel the need is critical and the future is bright for careers in psychology in medical schools, especially for the research-clinician role, in which one can balance flexibly research and clinical work.

## References

Engel, G. L. (1977). The need for a new medical model: A challenge for biomedicine. *Science, 196*, 129–136. http://dx.doi.org/10.1126/science.847460

Finno, A. A., Michalski, D., Hart, B., Wicherski, M., & Kohout, J. L. (2010, May). 2009: Report of the APA salary survey, Table 1. Washington, DC: American Psychological Association. Retrieved from http://www.apa.org/workforce/publications/09-salaries/table-01.pdf

Gerin, W., & Kapelewski, C. H. (2011). *Writing the NIH grant proposal: A step-by-step guide* (2nd ed.). Thousand Oaks, CA: Sage.

Kaplan, R. M., Satterfield, J. M., & Kington, R. S. (2012). Building a better physician—The case for the new MCAT. *New England Journal of Medicine, 366,* 1265–1268. http://dx.doi.org/10.1056/NEJMp1113274

Kuh, D., & Ben-Shlomo, Y. (Eds.). (1997). *A life course approach to chronic disease epidemiology.* Oxford, England: Oxford University Press.

National Institutes of Health. (n.d.). Research career development awards. Retrieved from https://researchtraining.nih.gov/programs/career-development

*Barbara A. Spellman and Jennifer K. Robbennolt*

# Psychologists in Law Schools  6

W hy do people confess to crimes that they did not commit? How do juries, and judges, come to their decisions? For what kinds of injuries should people receive compensation (in dollars) and what should justify how much they get? What makes people more or less likely to cheat on taxes or in business? How do decisions about end-of-life care get made and communicated? How do people understand contractual commitments? What factors influence negotiations? These questions are of interest not only to psychologists but also to lawyers. As psychologists in law schools, we have the opportunity to take knowledge and

Barbara A. Spellman is professor of law (and formerly professor of psychology) at the University of Virginia. She received her PhD (psychology) from the University of California, Los Angeles, her JD from New York University, and her BA (philosophy) from Wesleyan University.

Jennifer K. Robbennolt is Alice Curtis Campbell Professor of Law and professor of psychology at the University of Illinois. She codirects their program in Law, Behavior, and Social Science. She received her PhD (psychology) and JD from the University of Nebraska and her BS (business economics and psychology) from Willamette University.

http://dx.doi.org/10.1037/15960-007
*Career Paths in Psychology: Where Your Degree Can Take You, Third Edition,*
R. J. Sternberg (Editor)

ideas from each of those fields and bring them together in our teaching and research.

## Psychology's Relevance to Law

In the past 20 years or so, the legal profession has increasingly recognized the relevance and importance of psychology for law and legal practice and, perhaps as a result, the number of faculty members with doctorates in psychology who are now professors in law schools has been growing, and we suspect, will continue to grow.

The legal profession has long relied on psychologists for evaluations of individuals—informing legal determinations about whether someone is insane, competent to make decisions or stand trial, or likely to commit more crimes in the future and about whom should receive custody of a child. But several relatively recent (in academic terms) developments have greatly enhanced the visibility and perceived legitimacy of psychological research. Most dramatically, more than 300 people who had been convicted of crimes now have been shown to be innocent by DNA evidence. Spellman has been known to say that DNA evidence is the best thing that ever happened for psychology research in law. Why? Psychology researchers have extensively studied, for example, how eyewitness memory is fallible and how people may mistakenly, but in good faith, pick the wrong person from a line-up. Although these things were repeatedly demonstrated in laboratory settings, the legal system tended to reject the relevance of the findings, noting that the participants in the studies were often college students and that they were neither experiencing real events nor under oath to testify truthfully in a real courtroom. The DNA exonerations revealed that, in many cases, there had been misidentifications in line-ups and fabricated testimony in courtrooms—just as psychology research had predicted. The exonerations also validated concerns psychologists had about how confessions are taken (e.g., that people do confess to crimes they have not committed) and about the analysis and communication of physical forensic evidence (e.g., fingerprints, DNA). Many law enforcement practices have changed as a result of the psychological insights into these failures of justice.

Psychology also has made its way into law schools more indirectly through the field of economics. Starting in the 1960s, economic theory increasingly was used to analyze the substance and sense of laws, cases, and practice. The field of law and economics assumed that people as so-called rational actors would respond to certain incentives by behaving in predictable ways. But by the late 20th century, many economists had recognized that these actors were not so rational—as least not in the ways that had been assumed. The work of psychologists Daniel Kahneman and Amos Tversky, taught in every introductory psychology class, filtered into the economics curriculum and behavioral economics was born. That approach later leaked into law schools as behavioral law and economics.

A third development that has enhanced the perceived relevance of psychology to law schools is related to recent changes in legal practice and the calls for concomitant changes in legal education. Notably, the skills that make good lawyers—skills such as reasoning, creativity, problem solving, communicating, persuasion, planning, negotiating, perspective taking, advising, developing relationships, and more (Schultz & Zedeck, 2009)—are all skills that can be informed by psychology.

Together, these developments have made legal scholars much more accepting of psychological research. It used to seem as if psychologists spearheaded most of the cross-disciplinary initiatives—for example, psychologists dominate the American Psychology-Law Society (American Psychological Association, n.d.) and the pages of the journal *Law & Human Behavior*, and law professors founded the Society for Empirical Legal Studies with its yearly conference as well as the *Journal of Empirical Legal Studies*. Over time it has become increasingly clear to both psychologists and lawyers that virtually any area of psychology has some relevance to law.

## How We Got Here

There are various paths to becoming a psychologist teaching in a law school; we describe the general paths below. But first we tell our own personal stories.

### SPELLMAN

My route was long but it gives me good perspectives on the similarities (and differences) between the two fields from the points of view of both a student and a faculty member. As an undergraduate, I earned the equivalent of a cognitive science major. I attended law school and then worked for a large firm in New York City for several years. I didn't like the practice of law and soon moved to a job as a writer and editor for a legal publishing company. During that time, I took some evening psychology classes, applied to graduate school, and then began my PhD program in cognitive psychology at the age of 30 years old. My advisors kept suggesting that I do law-related psychology research, but I wanted to stay as far away from law as possible (although I was a teaching assistant for a large psychology and law undergraduate lecture class).

I got my first tenure-track position at the University of Texas at Austin psychology department right out of graduate school. After 4 years, I moved to the University of Virginia psychology department, where I advanced from assistant to associate to full professor in 10 years. Over time, my interests shifted from cognitive psychology to social cognition, and my graduate students and I got more interested in legally relevant issues, publishing our research not only in standard psychology outlets (peer-reviewed journals and book chapters) but also in law journals.

During those years, I also taught undergraduate and graduate seminars on psychology and law, and eventually I taught a graduate seminar that was cross-registered in the law school. Teaching a class with 10 psychology students and 10 law students provided much satisfaction as well as many challenges; I often felt as if I were an anthropologist, translating the languages and explaining the actions of two different cultures to each other. (A funny difference is that psychology graduate students would call me by my first name but law students would call me professor; that's the difference between the mentorship model of graduate school in which most of the students want to be you when they graduate and a professional school in which most of the students do not.) Soon after teaching that course, I got a half-time appointment to the law school and soon after that I left the psychology department completely.

## ROBBENNOLT

My path was somewhat different. My undergraduate majors were business economics and psychology. I had considered going to law school but also had considered going to graduate school in psychology or economics. My interest in law and psychology was piqued when I took an undergraduate course in the area, and by the time I applied to graduate school, I was focused on doing work at the intersection of social psychology and law and looking for programs that would allow me to pursue the two degrees simultaneously.

Enrolling in a joint-degree program meant that I began my first year of graduate study as a full-time law student and then started in the psychology department the following year. Being part of an integrated program meant that I was immersed in both disciplines from the beginning and also that the program had a critical mass of both faculty members and other students who were interested in research topics at the intersection of the disciplines. It also meant that I took longer to finish law school, graduating the year after the class with which I started, but I was able to complete both degrees in less time than if I had done them sequentially. It also meant that I spent time moving (mentally and physically) between the law school and the psychology department.

Upon graduating from law school, but before completing my dissertation, I took the bar exam and spent a year clerking for a state Supreme Court justice. I then returned to the psychology department full time to finish my dissertation and receive my doctorate. My next stop was a 2-year postdoctoral position in psychology and public policy.

I began my teaching career at the University of Missouri–Columbia School of Law where I earned tenure and spent a year as the Associate Dean for Faculty Research and Development. After 5 years, I moved to the University of Illinois College of Law where I have been on the faculty ever since.

## Overview of What We Do

Being a psychology professor in a law school is much like being a psychology professor anywhere else (see the previous chapters). Our primary responsibilities are teaching and research; the particulars of how those are done in a law school are described in more detail in the following sections. We may advise a few students on independent writing projects, on their writing for a law review, or on their Doctor of Juridical Science (SJD, a law equivalent of a PhD, typically sought by students who got their initial law degrees in a country other than the United States). We might be asked to write letters of recommendation for our students as they apply for clerkships or fellowships. We evaluate junior law professors—both at our own school and elsewhere—for tenure and promotion. And we serve on law school and university committees. Many of us are engaged in some kind of extra-university intellectual activity that applies our knowledge to a real-world problem. Some law professors will consult on cases or court rules, testify in court or at legislative hearings on the topics of their expertise, write amicus briefs to courts to offer perspective in their areas of specialization, or serve on committees of legal organizations.

### LEGAL EDUCATION

To understand what law professors do, it is important to know what a law school education encompasses. In the United States, a standard law degree (typically called a JD), like a PhD, is obtained after one has earned a bachelor's degree. In most of the rest of the world, law is just another major that one can have when getting a first university degree, equivalent to a bachelor's degree (although sometimes entailing some practical training as well as classroom learning.)

Despite the fact that both law school and graduate school in psychology are postbaccalaureate education, law school is quite different from graduate school PhD programs in psychology. Law school takes 3 years to complete when enrolled in a full-time program—although some people earn their degrees by going to school part time over many more years. Law school is predominantly coursework. First year classes are mostly the same in every law school: contracts, torts, property, civil procedure, criminal law, constitutional law, legal research and writing, and moot court or some other version of appellate advocacy; some schools also have time for electives the first year. After the first year, law students design their own schedules; there are usually no more required courses except for a course in ethics or professional responsibility, although the majority of students take other foundational courses such as evidence, corporations, and federal income tax. There are no majors, but many schools offer concentrations in areas like business law, criminal law, intellectual property, legal history, and tax law.

Most law students do not engage in the extended, self-generated, type of research projects that are typical of psychology and other PhD programs. Law students typically do have a writing requirement that can be fulfilled by writing a long paper for a course. Some students might choose to do an independent writing project or might try to write something to be published in the law school's law review journal. But many students go through law school without ever writing on a self-generated topic that isn't a final paper for a course.

Law schools also have courses in which students learn to do practical legal things, such as write briefs, try cases, negotiate settlements or deals, or draft documents such as contracts or wills. And law schools typically offer a variety of clinics, in which law students, under the close supervision of faculty members or practicing attorneys, work on real cases. Examples of clinics include criminal defense, child advocacy, housing, prisoner's rights, consumer law, environmental law, and immigration law. Currently, much discussion is centered on whether law students are prepared to practice law when they graduate and whether law school should be cut from 3 years to 2 years. Those two ideas seem contradictory: if law students aren't well prepared when they get out, why should law school be cut rather than lengthened? The argument is that although they take many classes, law students don't get enough applied training to be ready for the actual practice of law. The current movement is to offer more practice-focused classes during the second and third year; some law schools now even require practice-focused or clinical-based courses.

## LAW SCHOOL TEACHING

Law professors typically teach two to four classes per year depending on the school, the number of credits for the class, and other factors. First-year law school classes are usually large and meet two to three times per week. These classes typically are graded through a final exam. Second- and third-year students take some large classes with final exams (e.g., evidence, corporations, and tax, as mentioned), but they also are likely to take some seminars which tend to be smaller (10–20 students), meet once per week, more heavily weight class participation, and require multiple short papers or a long final paper. Unlike in many psychology departments, there are no teaching assistants, so faculty members do all of their own grading.

## WHAT A PSYCHOLOGIST MIGHT TEACH

Faculty members in a law school often are expected to teach one of the big first-year courses or a commonly taken upper-level course (as described earlier). Because everyone with a law degree took those courses in law school, it is assumed that everyone, in theory, could teach them. But, of course, people differ in knowledge and preferences, and many psychologists prefer to teach the foundational courses that have significant psychological components such as torts (Robbennolt), criminal law, and evidence (Spellman). As in psychology departments, in addition to large standard courses, faculty members are usually able to teach smaller courses or seminars that dovetail with their own particular expertise and research interests.

Robbennolt regularly teaches the required first-year law school course on torts—covering the law related to whether an injured plaintiff should be able to recover damages from a defendant for having caused her harm. Almost every year, she also has taught some version of a course that she and her co-instructors have come to call empirical methods in law (see Lawless, Robbennolt, & Ulen, 2010). This course introduces law students to basic research design and statistics, topics that until recently were not included in the law school curriculum. She also has taught courses on dispute resolution; psychology for lawyers; a seminar on law, psychology, and economics; and estates and trusts.

Spellman has taught evidence almost every year of her career. Each time she taught it, she saw more relevance to psychology, so she started also teaching an advanced seminar called The Psychological Bases of Evidence Law. (And because of that class, she coauthored a book on exactly that topic.) Recently she developed a popular advanced lecture course called Behavioral Decision Making and Law, which could have been called Memory, Social Cognition, and Judgment and Decision Making Applied to Law and Public Policy. She has also taught Empirical Methods in Law (using Robbennolt's book) and seminars related to her psychology research interests, such as Causation in Law and Psychology of the Deciders: Judges, Jurors, Juries.

We know other psychologists in law schools who teach foundational courses in contracts, civil procedure, property, and constitutional law. Psychologists also often teach courses such as negotiation (as in business schools), dispute resolution, family law, mental health law, scientific evidence, and, like us, variations on courses that combine law with empirical methods in general (e.g., social science and law) or psychology in particular.

## RESEARCH

When Spellman told people that she was leaving a psychology department to become a faculty member in a law school, many people asked, "So are you giving up research?" Such a question shows a lack of understanding of the range of research activities conducted by psychologists in law schools.

It is true that law schools are not typically stocked with laboratories for running research participants. Nor do they have graduate or undergraduate students who are trained to assist with that kind of work. Nonetheless, psychologists in law schools often conduct their own empirical research just as psychologists in psychology departments do. Opportunities exist to hire law student research assistants or even psychology student research assistants and to collaborate with psychologists elsewhere.

Even in psychology, not all research is empirical research. For example, psychologists may write review papers, drawing together related bodies of research, revealing consistencies and contradictions, and evaluating the strengths and weaknesses of existing theoretical explanations. Psychologists may write theory papers, advancing new theories to explain a set of phenomena and push the field forward in new directions. Psychologists in law schools might do any of these tasks and also might write papers analyzing legal cases or legal doctrine, often, but not always, through a psychological lens.

But what we each particularly enjoy, and what people with degrees in both psychology and law should be particularly good at, is what we call "connection" and "translation." Connection means finding new links between the two fields. For example, we have each coauthored books that have explored the connections between theory and research in psychology and particular areas of law—torts (Robbennolt) and evidence (Spellman). Other psychologists have forged connections between aspects of cognitive psychology and questions involving eyewitness memory or between the psychology of affective forecasting and legal issues related to capital punishment, contract law, health law, and more.

Translation means taking what exists in one field and explaining to the other. For example, rather than doing a new experiment to make a point about how analogical reasoning works, a psychologist could just as well describe existing relevant work done by herself or other psychologists of which the legal field is not yet aware and explain the implications of that work for judicial decision making (as Spellman has done). Robbennolt has coauthored a book aimed at legal practitioners that explains a range of psychological theory and research and applies those findings to a collection of tasks—such as interviewing, counseling, negotiating, writing, and being ethical—that lawyers do every day.

We both publish work of all these types in a variety of outlets, including law reviews and peer-reviewed journals, as well as in coauthored books, and our research has spanned a variety of different topics at the intersection of psychology and law. For example, Spellman has conducted research on the use of analogy by judges, differences between law and legal causal reasoning, competency of different bodies for making sentencing decisions, and the importance of evaluating the relation between accuracy and confidence in legal settings. She has also written about the many areas of law that are ripe for social psychology research (Spellman & Schauer, 2013). Robbennolt has explored the role of apologies in legal decision making, similarities and differences in how judges and juries make decisions, lessons of psychology for legal practice, connections between psychological research and tort law, behavioral legal ethics, and other topics at the intersection of psychology and law.

Whether the research is empirical, doctrinal, focused on making connections, primarily translational, or some combination, part of being involved in research means sharing research with others. Law professors routinely travel to present their work at conferences or to give workshops about their research at other universities. (At a workshop, the audience typically has read a draft the presenter's paper, and most of the time is spent in the audience asking questions.) Presenting your own work so that others can engage with it, and hearing and engaging with the work of others, improves research and helps professors generate ideas about new directions to take in their work.

## Becoming a Psychologist in a Law School

About 50 psychologists probably now have tenured or tenure-track appointments in U.S. law schools. Of these 50, most have earned both a JD and a PhD. Other psychologists also have adjunct appointments in law schools but the law school is not their primary home.

Of the few academic psychologists who work in a law school but do not have a JD, some have a degree called a master of studies in law

(MSL). This degree is earned in a 1-year program, offered at only a few law schools, that is designed for experts in other disciplines who want to be exposed to legal education generally and learn how it relates to their field specifically. Some psychologists on law faculties do not have any type of law degree; however, this is becoming less available as a career path.

Faculty members also are doing psychology research in law schools who have a JD but not a psychology PhD. Some of those have master's degrees. Others do not have an advanced degree in psychology but might collaborate with researchers who do.

Most psychology doctoral students probably have considered becoming a professor, and the road from psychology PhD to psychology professor, although not easy, usually is straightforward—get a PhD, probably get a postdoc or visiting professorship or other temporary position, get a tenure-track job. In contrast, most law students do not start out thinking that they would like to become professors, and the road from JD to law professor is not as clear-cut, with a variety of possible paths. How you may become a psychologist in a law school will depend, in part, on how you get your education.

## GETTING THE APPROPRIATE EDUCATION

There are three ways to get both a psychology JD and PhD: earn one degree first, earn the other degree first, or earn both degrees at the same time. Psychologists in law schools have taken each of the three routes.

If you know that you want to get both degrees, the most efficient way to do so is to go to a joint degree program as Robbennolt did. A list of such programs can be found on the American Psychology-Law Society website (American Psychological Association, n.d.) These programs can integrate nicely the two disciplines and can be a great way to become immersed in cross-disciplinary research because of both the structure of the programs and the presence of faculty and students with similar interests. These programs, however, vary in types of financial support available to students, the types of psychology emphasized, and the quality of the experience.

Many of us did not know early on that we wanted to have both degrees, so we got them sequentially. We know some people who got their law degrees and then immediately went into psychology PhD programs. Others (like Spellman) got their law degree and practiced law for a while, and then realized that they were more interested in psychology (either with or without application to the law). And some people have done it the other way, first getting a psychology degree and then a law degree. People who earn their psychology degree first are less likely to take an academic path; often, they get a law degree so that they can be more effective in the worlds of legal policy or practice.

## GETTING AN APPOINTMENT IN A LAW SCHOOL

Law schools tend to give students a lot of help in finding jobs. Many websites of major law schools explain how to prepare for a position as a legal academic. And the WikiHow series lists the nine steps in "How to Become a Law Professor" (n.d.). (No, the Wiki how-to does not give good advice. For much better advice see Denning, McCormick, & Lipshaw, 2010.) Generally, three types of paths can be taken.

One route (the *stellar student* route) is fairly analogous to the route to getting a top research university job in psychology. Go to a very good law school, and while there, get very good grades, be invited onto the editorial board of the law school's top journal (the law review), write a short paper (called a student note) that is published in the journal; and conduct research for and develop relationships with faculty members who will write you strong letters of recommendation and advocate for you. Then, clerk for a judge or judges for 1 or 2 years; spend a couple of years in a fellowship program where you might be teaching legal writing and research and working on publications, and then apply for jobs through a standardized process. Next fill out the standardized form, complete preliminary short interviews at a law conference (known colloquially as the *meat market*), and then possibly receive an invitation to interview at the law school where you present some current research at a workshop for all the faculty and meet individually or in groups with many others.

A second main route to teaching in a law school is to become a lawyer with expertise in a field for which schools need (or want) professors. This process is less standardized. If you follow this path, you already should have some legal publications, so a law school searching for scholars in a particular field might come looking for you. Or, you might contact people at a law school (or have others do so on your behalf). To take this route, many schools want such people to come for a visit— a few weeks or a semester in which you would teach a course, give a workshop, meet a lot of the other faculty members, and be involved in faculty life. This gives the school a good chance to evaluate your teaching and collegiality but also gives you a good chance to evaluate whether the place would be a good fit for you.

As illustrated by our personal stories, people with both law and psychology degrees (or other relevant degrees such as economics, political science, history) can take a variety of routes into the field—both similar to and different from the routes mapped out in this chapter. Robbennolt, for example, got her first job teaching in a law school through the meat market. Spellman moved from a psychology department to the law school at the same university. Others have moved from psychology departments, departments of criminology, or business schools into positions in law schools. As we mentioned, a handful of psychologists have obtained positions in law schools without a JD, but these tend to be exceptions to the rule.

# Pros and Cons for Psychologists Teaching in a Law School

Suppose you are interested in applying psychology to law, and you intrepidly have obtained both degrees. Why might you choose to be a faculty member in a law school rather than a lawyer, a faculty member in a psychology department, or take another job that relies on both of your areas of training?

## LEGAL ACADEMIA VERSUS LAWYERING

Being a lawyer and being an academic involve similar skill sets (although that does depend on what you do as a lawyer). You must be able to analyze complex problems and to communicate logically and clearly in both written and spoken forms. And, whatever you are doing, you must understand your audience. Of course, both professions have several important differences. As a lawyer (again, depending on your job), you often are presented with a client's problem. Your work is bounded by that problem and how to address it with the client. And you must pursue it until you achieve some resolution. As an academic, you choose for yourself which research questions you want to pursue. If it seems to be turning out in a way you do not expect, that's fine, perhaps what you find is more important than what you originally expected to happen. If you lose interest in what you are doing, you can drop the project and move on to something of more interest to you without external consequences. In short, you have more freedom to choose what you want to spend your time thinking about.

Legal practice and academia have other differences. Most notably, in academia, a large part of your time is taken up by teaching. In legal practice, your time might be filled by directly interacting with people to help them with problems in their lives; it also could be filled by drafting contracts for corporations or writing regulations to implement government policy (as usual, it depends on your legal job). Academia runs on a set schedule defined by semesters (or sometime quarters), although, as this and earlier chapters on academic positions should have conveyed, weekends and summer vacations are not exactly free. There is teaching preparation and grading to complete, research to do and present, conferences to attend, evaluation letters to write, and other activities that must be finished during those nonteaching periods. Still, those in academia are more likely to be in control of how to structure their time than those in most legal positions.

Legal academics earn a steady salary; it is not as much as one would earn at a major law firm in a major city, but it may be more than one would earn at a smaller firm or corporation, and it is often more than one would earn working in a public sector or public interest law job. The compensation is steady, unlike being in a small private law practice, in which compensation might depend on how much business was done that year. Like other college and university positions, most law schools offer tenure, so there is generally good job security (although there are still reasons one could get fired). And, most law schools also offer some type of sabbatical leave or course credit banking system so that you may take a semester away from teaching to focus on research. As with other academic positions, law professors typically don't have much choice in where they will live—particularly when starting out, job candidates are unlikely to have a choice from among many job offers. But for various structural reasons (e.g., common foundational courses; no need to move graduate students and labs), moving from law school to law school is done much more frequently and with greater ease than moving between psychology departments.

## LEGAL ACADEMIA VERSUS PSYCHOLOGY ACADEMIA

If you are comparing legal academia to psychology academia—see Chapter 1 on teaching at a university and Chapter 2 on teaching at a college—you will notice that legal academia seems to be a hybrid. Teaching and mentoring activities are more similar to undergraduate institutions—at least in style if not in amount. Undergraduate institutions or law schools tend not to have full-time long-term graduate students, who are trained within specialized labs or areas; who carry on a lot of research under your supervision; and who need special guidance through master's theses, comprehensive exams, dissertations, and so on. Conversely, the faculty research requirements are more comparable to that of university teaching, although the need to try to obtain grant money is given much less emphasis.

Psychologists in law schools tend not to be surrounded by many (or any) other psychologists among their law colleagues, although many tend to affiliate in some way with psychologists on other parts of campus. Instead, psychologists in law schools have the benefits of colleagues who are experts in all different areas of law—a great resource for developing rich and relevant research questions. In addition, in some law schools, a psychologist law faculty member may be surrounded by other interdisciplinary legal scholars—lawyers with training in disciplines such as economics, history, philosophy, political science, sociology, or biology.

Faculty in law schools typically are paid more than those in psychology departments (because, ostensibly, they could choose to leave and get high-paying legal jobs). As mentioned, it's easier to move jobs across law schools; additionally, law schools have a tradition of visiting between institutions—in which case a professor spends a few weeks, a semester, or even a year, teaching at another law school (whether or not they are seeking employment there). Law schools tend to be more formal in style and tone than psychology departments—the buildings are usually better maintained and are likely to include classrooms laid out as courtrooms, the relationship between faculty and students tends to be more formal, faculty are more likely to wear suits or other professional attire, staff and library support is greater, and so on.

## OTHER JOBS FOR WHICH A JOINT DEGREE IS USEFUL

Law schools are not the only place where having both a JD and a PhD (or even master's degree) in psychology is a useful combination. Many people with backgrounds in law and psychology also find satisfying employment outside of academia. For example, many people with degrees in both law and psychology work as litigation consultants—helping attorneys prepare for trials (before either juries or judges), arbitration, mediation sessions, or negotiation by identifying case themes, developing arguments, generating and testing graphics and exhibits, preparing witnesses, conducting analysis of pretrial publicity, and more. Other psychologists with legal backgrounds work in policy development. The federal government now has a *behavioral insights* group to improve government policies and even how the government functions. People with both degrees may work to provide forensic assessments for courts. Plus, others use their psychological training to enhance their own work as attorneys or judges.

## Future of the Field

We are optimistic about the future for psychologists in law schools. We believe that more law schools will be actively seeking more psychologically trained JDs as faculty members. Psychology research has become viewed as respected, relevant, and potentially far-reaching. Additionally, psychology expertise has become viewed as important to the goal of producing well-educated and competent attorneys. These jobs provide both a challenging and rewarding experience.

## References

American Psychological Association. (n.d.). *American Psychology-Law Society, Division 41*. Retrieved from http://www.apadivisions.org/division-41/

Denning, B. P., McCormick, M. L., & Lipshaw, J. M. (2010, July 29). Becoming a law professor: A candidate's guide. *Social Science Research Network*. http://dx.doi.org/10.2139/ssrn.1650713

Lawless, R. M., Robbennolt, J. K., & Ulen, T. S. (2010). *Empirical methods in law*. New York, NY: Aspen Publishers.

Schultz, M. M., & Zedeck, S. (2009, January 30). Final report: Identification, development, and validation of predictors for successful lawyering. *Social Science Research Network*. Retrieved from http://papers.ssrn.com/sol3/papers.cfm?abstract_id=1353554

Spellman, B. A., & Schauer, F. (2013). Social cognition and the law. In D. Carlston (Ed.), *Oxford handbook of social cognition* (pp. 829–850). Oxford, England: Oxford University Press.

WikiHow. (n.d.). *How to become a law professor*. Retrieved from http://www.wikihow.com/Become-a-Law-Professor

*Jennifer S. Lerner*

# Psychologists in Schools of Public Policy 7

What is government itself, but the greatest of all reflections on human nature?
—James Madison, *The Federalist Papers*, Number 51

As James Madison foreshadowed, a career as a psychologist in a school of public policy provides magnificent opportunities to develop fundamental knowledge about human nature. Moreover, it provides opportunities to use such knowledge when informing solutions to challenging public problems, and when teaching a diverse set of well-intentioned students.

Jennifer S. Lerner, PhD, is professor of management, leadership, and decision science at Harvard University in the Harvard Kennedy School of Government. She received her BA from the University of Michigan (Highest Honors in Psychology), and then her master's and doctoral degrees in psychology from the University of California at Berkeley. After completing an NIH postdoctoral fellowship in the Psychology Department at UCLA (emphasizing psychoneuroendocrine systems), she was assistant professor and later the Estella Loomis McCandless Associate Professor in the Department of Social and Decision Sciences at Carnegie Mellon University. In 2007 she became the first psychologist in the history of the Harvard Kennedy School to receive tenure.

I thank Susan Fiske for providing helpful comments on this chapter. I also thank Dacher Keltner, Phil Tetlock, and Shelley Taylor—three brilliant mentors, with whom I have been so fortunate to work.

http://dx.doi.org/10.1037/15960-008
*Career Paths in Psychology: Where Your Degree Can Take You, Third Edition*,
R. J. Sternberg (Editor)

Specifically, I teach four kinds of students: undergraduate[1] and master's students, who idealistically seek to understand psychological science so they can (at least in some small way) make the world a better place; doctoral students who seek to become scholars of public policy; and executive-level students who come for short stints to find new ideas (yours!) for solving pressing public problems. Contrary to my expectations, my favorite students fall in the last category, for two reasons. First, I learn the most from them. Considering myself a student of decision theory, high-stakes decision makers have much to teach me. A second reason I especially love teaching executive-level students is that they often directly translate what they learn in our classes into institutionalized practices. Jumping to the bottom line, I adore this job and daily feel grateful to hold it.

## The Nature of the Career

The job as a psychologist in public policy is not without pressure, however. Despite the supposed comfort of having tenure, I feel more compelled than ever to ensure that our science is accurate, reliable, novel, and meaningful. Global leaders act on what they learn in our classes. In the past 8 years, my executive students have included such participants as three-star army generals, members of royalty, U.S. Navy Seals, mayors, police chiefs, members of parliament, city council members, private sector chief executives officers (CEOs), presidents of nongovernmental organizations (NGOs), intelligence agents, counterterrorism agents, pharmaceutical executives, attorneys, physicians, and more professionals whose work intersects in some way with public purposes.[2] This job is not for the meek. One needs to love the challenge of proving that psychology is useful and not just interesting, even when audiences are skeptical about the value of psychology.

This last point highlights a contrast between teaching in a school of public policy and teaching in a psychology department or even in an interdisciplinary undergraduate department like the Department of Social and Decision Sciences at Carnegie Mellon. Whereas students in my psychology sections at UC Berkeley and students in my Decision

---

[1]My own university does not offer a full undergraduate major or concentration in public policy, but a few schools do (e.g., Princeton's Woodrow Wilson School and Carnegie Mellon's College of Humanities and Social Sciences). I teach advanced undergraduates when they enroll, with special permission, in my master's level courses.

[2]Of course, such experiences reflect my own career, and each career will be somewhat different. Part of the excitement is that one never knows whom one will meet next.

Science classes at Carnegie Mellon all entered my classes with a reasonably positive expectation about learning psychology, the students who enter my classes at the Kennedy School of Government tend to enter with some skepticism about whether someone with a psychology PhD has anything useful to teach them. More often than I would like, students' only concept of psychology revolves around therapy for mental illness. I myself interpret this narrow understanding as a positive challenge and I believe that psychological science can deliver on its promise to improve human health and well-being, ranging from individual to global levels of analysis. I love it when executive-level students in class say variations on "This is cool—why haven't I ever heard of this before?" or "I had no idea that psychology included this stuff." Indeed, at the executive level, most students have not taken a psychology class in the past 15 years, if at all. They are astounded to know that modern academic psychology uses an experimental method for hypothesis testing akin to the randomized-control-trial paradigms with which they are familiar from medication trials. Such aha moments come frequently among students in this environment, triggering transient states of professorial heaven for me. Beyond these transient states, I carry with me a sense of hope that through a classroom of emerging global leaders I might make a contribution, albeit a small one, to the quality and stability of democratic governments around the world. To quote the Kennedy School's outgoing dean, David Ellwood, the Scott M. Black Professor of Political Economy,

> We live in times of great cynicism regarding the ability of our public institutions to perform, but the best antidote to that cynicism is our inspirational students and our astonishing graduates. The best source of hope for the future is these remarkable individuals and the ideas that they carry forward. (personal communication, June 30, 2015)

You may wonder why, if this is such a wonderful career path, you have not heard of it before. The answer may lie in the fact that having tenure-track positions for psychologists in schools of public policy is a relatively new phenomenon.[3] The major prevailing disciplines in both policy research and practice have been economics, political science, sociology, physics, and history. Take the executive branch of government as an example. Notice that U.S. presidents have long consulted their key

---

[3]To the best of my knowledge, Princeton's Woodrow Wilson School ranks first in tenure-track positions for psychologists. They presently have seven jointly appointed tenure track faculty who split time between the psychology department and the Woodrow Wilson School. At other schools, like the Harvard Kennedy School and Berkeley's Goldman School of Public Policy, a small number of tenure-track appointments for psychologists reside fully in the policy school and the faculty holding them sometimes also hold courtesy appointments in the psychology department at their respective institution.

advisors from these disciplines. Presidents routinely draw insights from academic economists who serve as the secretary of the U.S. Treasury, chairs of the Federal Reserve, or as members of the Council of Economic Advisors. They may draw on academic political scientists to serve as secretaries of state or political advisors. They may draw on academic physicists who serve as science advisor to the president and members of the White House Office of Science and Technology, and so on. U.S. presidents have rarely if ever appointed an academic psychologist to an inner-circle position. Presently, the congressional branch of government hardly provides a brighter picture for these roles, and nor does the judicial branch.

But times are changing. Several U.S. universities now actively recruit psychologists to their schools of public policy. Leading the path in terms of numbers appears to be Harvard, Princeton, and UC Berkeley. Although I cannot isolate the impetus for this change without dates, I believe it arises from two interrelated factors. First, the field of economics—the historically dominant field in public policy—has witnessed the growth of a hybrid field called behavioral economics. This new hybrid field combines traditional neoclassical microeconomic theory, which provides prescriptions about how one should make judgments and decisions, with modern scientific psychology, which provides descriptions about how people actually make judgments and decisions. Thus, behavioral economics draws on psychology to provide a more realistic portrait of human behavior, which can make economic models more accurate. It is possible, for example, that the economic crash of 2008 might have been lessened or even prevented if economic models used in financial markets allowed for more behaviorally realistic assumptions to be incorporated.

The second factor responsible for opening the field of public policy to psychologists may simply be a tipping point in recognizing that society's most pressing goals—enhancing physical and mental health, lengthening life, reducing illness and disability, reducing violence, increasing economic growth, and increasing social harmony domestically and internationally—all involve psychology. In this age of exponential technological growth, human beings may become either the key limiting factor or the key catalyst depending on how well we understand and leverage human capacity.

Times may be changing even faster abroad. Opportunities in Europe and in Australia arise from the key role behavioral sciences as a whole (e.g., psychology, economics, sociology, anthropology) play in government. In the United Kingdom, members of a Behavioural Insights Team (also known as the Nudge Unit)—composed of academic psychologists, behavioral economists, and social anthropologists—were the first to hold cabinet-level positions, reporting directly to the prime minister. In this capacity, they conducted numerous randomized controlled trials in social innovation that resulted in such successes as increasing the rate of income tax payments, reducing energy use, and increasing rates of organ donation. A useful summary of this approach and a vision for how psychology might inform policy in the future appears in Cass Sunstein's *Annual Review of Psychology* paper, entitled "The Council of Psychological Advisors" (2016). This review does not represent the full set of possible futures for psychology and public policy, but it is one exciting example of success.

## The Kinds of Activities in Which Professionals in the Career Engage

Psychologists in public policy participate in most of the same activities outlined in the chapters on being a professor in a psychology department or in a business school. That is, these psychologists design courses, teach, create and grade exams, meet with students during office hours, conduct research and supervise students who are conducting research within their research group, maintain a research lab, write letters of reference for students and colleagues, attend faculty meetings and committee meetings at both the school and at the university level, communicate with other scholars who share similar research or teaching interests, attend and present research at professional conferences, write scholarly papers for psychology journals, painstakingly revise scholarly papers, review and evaluate submissions to scholarly journals for potential publication, consult with outside organizations when their expertise is requested, disseminate research findings through major media outlets (television, radio, etc.), and perform pro bono community service. For efficiency, I will not duplicate descriptions of what all these activities involve.

Instead, I will elaborate on some of the additional activities that are relatively unique to conducting research and teaching in a policy school. First, as mentioned, I regularly engage with practitioners—that is, professionals involved in promoting the public good—and the public outside of normal teaching and research settings. For example, I occasionally write an op-ed column for a newspaper on a matter of public interest. I occasionally consult for the United Nations about how to institutionalize better decision environments within their global workforce. I also occasionally consult for or teach in a variety of other public and private sector organizations whose objectives serve the public good. For example, I have consulted for the U.S. Army's Special Forces Airborne

Units (Green Berets), who requested that I provide training on the science of judgment and decision making. I asked for clarification when I first received the call requesting *science* and learned that science was indeed what they wanted. Approximately 90 Green Berets, all of whom can swim the length of an Olympic pool in full combat gear and boots while carrying out, say, a hostage rescue mission sat still for an entire day of classroom-based decision exercises and participatory lectures involving complex graphs, diagrams, and discussion. They asked intelligent questions and offered key insights, which I have learned to expect from interactions with elite-level government and military individuals around the world.

An additional difference between working in a business school and working in a policy school is that policy schools lack funding and therefore require their faculty to write grant proposals to fund research. Our alumni do not typically become investment bankers or CEOs. They become researchers in nonprofit organizations, civil servants, heads of NGOs, elected politicians, foreign diplomats, military officers, and so on. Few of these occupations pay at a level that would allow for million dollar donations to the school. In fact, the Kennedy School receives most of its donations from citizens who never attended the school but simply see us as a source for growing the leaders needed to build smart democratic institutions around the world. The upside is that I can point to individual alumni around the world, such as the head of the United Nations, the president of Liberia, the former president of Mexico, mayors, and members of congress, and know that they all received their respective educations at the Kennedy School. The downside is that I had to spend a large amount of time writing grant proposals to the National Science Foundation, the National Institutes of Health, and to a few select foundations. In a school of business, research funding often is provided without the need to find this outside support.

## A Typical Day in the Career

I first note that it is indeed possible to have a productive, joyful life outside of work if you make strategic choices, outsource tasks, and streamline strategically. Thus, before I arrive at the office, I have had breakfast with my husband, my daughter, and even my dog. On good days, I have gone to the gym. To find time for this, I delegate as much as I can, typically by using federal grant funding to hire inexpensive help from undergraduates. They are resourceful, smart, and eager to learn skills they do not yet possess. They play large roles in my laboratory research and in my teaching.

Having a chronic disease (Systemic Lupus Erythematosus) since I was a child, I also spend a lot of time seeking medical care and figuring out novel ways to work when I experience such conditions as spinal fractures and nerve inflammation. I add this personal information so that readers will know that you do not have to be a super person with unusual levels of energy to pursue this career.

Once at the office, my typical day begins with reading e-mail, catching up with messages from students, collaborators, committees, journals who would like me to review a paper, administrative deadlines, and so forth. On a good day, at least one novel message appears. Recently, for example, one of my former executive-level students wrote to say that he has been promoted from his former position in the National Center for Counterterrorism (the primary organization in the U.S. government for integrating and analyzing all intelligence pertaining to terrorism possessed or acquired by the U.S. government) to a new position in which he directs a program that specializes in interpreting foreign attempts to deceive the U.S. government. His message indicated that he would like to infuse their work with rigorous scholarly and scientific approaches to judgment and decision analysis, and he wondered whether I could help him do so. He asked if I would meet with his deputy in my office, if he dispatched his deputy from Washington, DC. I suggested that we set up a phone call to discuss the matter, wondering why I would not first talk with him by phone. It turned out that we would be discussing content that cannot be discussed via phone. Interesting. I wonder what it is, but I forge on to the next message. A student needs help on her term paper. And so it goes.

I reserve a few hours in the morning for reading, writing, and preparing to teach. Noontime always brings either a research seminar (typically with lunch provided) or a meeting with a colleague about a research or teaching matter. My days are so packed that I have a free lunch hour to myself about once per month. Running to the restroom is a luxury. After lunch, I typically hold back-to-back meetings, including lab meetings (in which we discuss current research projects, meetings with students, or other appointments around campus) and other research meetings. I teach at least two afternoons per week and hold office hours with students. One afternoon per week is devoted to faculty meetings. Being tenured means, among other responsibilities, that I need to become informed about, and vote on, key decisions the school makes. One afternoon per month, I serve on the university-wide Committee for the Protection of Human Subjects. The job of this committee is to ensure that any research involving humans protects human rights and upholds the highest ethical standards. In preparation, I review a set of difficult proposals that have been submitted—ones that the staff cannot handle without faculty insight. I then gather with other faculty around campus to discuss and vote on the proposals.

After dinner at home with my family, I often work in my office at home. This is a good time to write, much like first thing in the morning. Often I will write things that require less systematic thought than do scientific journal articles, such as letters of reference. I do not necessarily recommend the way I do things. I intend for this summary to provide description and not prescription. I continually wish I could find more time to write and often fail to do so.

## Advantages and Disadvantages of the Career

Advantages of a career in public policy far outweigh disadvantages. Some are obvious. It is enormously fun to teach world leaders in executive education who negotiate more effectively, interpret probabilistic evidence more accurately, or enact policies more effectively based on what you have taught them. I frequently receive invitations to teach these leaders not only at Harvard but also at government agencies, at field sites for Special Forces, and at international locations. It is also enormously fun to teach idealistic master's level students whose goal in life is to make the world a better place, not necessarily to earn as much money as possible. It is enormously fun to work with colleagues who share such noble goals. I may even earn a bit more salary than if I were in a psychology department (averages suggest this may be the case).

Other advantages are more subtle. First, I find it enormously rewarding to convert a skeptical student to an eager student. I love, even crave, intellectual challenges. As mentioned, many students come to my class skeptical about learning from a psychologist. This is especially true when a male, senior military official and combat veteran comes in to find that a relatively young Berkeley graduate and female psychologist (i.e., me) is going to teach them about decision making. You can imagine the dynamics of the situation. I need to be on top of my game, making psychology useful, to earn their respect. It is never given automatically.

Another subtle advantage is the diversity of the faculty. Faculty members in a school of public policy come from all walks of life. Some are *professors of practice*, meaning that they earned their credential to teach not by scholarly studies but by practicing public policy. For example, the former U.S. Ambassador to the North Atlantic Treaty Organization (NATO) is a professor of practice on our faculty. So, too, is the current U.S. Ambassador to the United Nations (presently on leave from our faculty). Occasionally, I coteach a session or two with some of these professors, allowing us to unite science and practice. This keeps my science in line with reality, and it helps generate new research ideas.

The faculty members are also diverse in other ways. Whereas most psychology departments lean exclusively to the left side of the political spectrum, policy schools (if they aim to be good ones) must include scholarly thinkers from all perspectives. I find it useful to hear ideas from all perspectives across the political spectrum.

Disadvantages are real, too. In my case, the largest disadvantage has been that finding fellow psychologists in my immediate vicinity who speak the same academic language is difficult. For example, if I mentioned a core concept from psychology like the fundamental attribution error (FAE) in a faculty meeting, only a handful of people out of several hundred would know what I meant. This can create loneliness. The antidote would be to head over to Harvard's psychology department and attend their seminars. I hold a formal affiliation with the department and, theoretically, could show up there whenever I wish, oversee student projects, and so on. But the great social psychologist Kurt Lewin was correct about the power of channel factors—that is, situational factors that appear unimportant on the surface but that actually exert great influence on behavior. Actually spending time in the psychology department turns out to be far more difficult than I expected because of a demanding schedule and the necessity of a 25-minute walk in both directions (sometimes in rain, snow, and ice) to get from my office to the psychology department. To date, I have made far less use of this important connection than I intended—not only because of the difficult channel factors but also because I learned it was necessary to first establish deep roots at the Kennedy School. I hope to establish deeper connections with the psychology department in the future. And I hope that any junior people reading this can take more seriously than I naively did how difficult it is to manage appointments in multiple locations. Ironically, it is sometimes easier to collaborate with psychologists at other schools in the Boston area and around the world (which I often do) because one expects to talk by phone in such cases. In sum, because I love the core of psychology as much as I love to push its outer boundaries, the absence of many fellow psychologists in the same hallway is a real disadvantage but not one that outweighs the advantages.

## Preparation Is Needed for the Career

Because so few of us teach in the field, a clear set of norms and criteria do not exist. To become a tenure-track professor who teaches and conducts research with a great deal of (near-total) intellectual freedom, it is critical to have a PhD and a trajectory of research. Moreover, it is important to have published research that can be applied to solving public problems and to be able to design courses that students of public policy would benefit from taking.

I never set out to work in a school of public policy. I had no idea that such an option existed. Without having a career objective in mind, I did engage, however, in numerous activities in which I learned political science and public policy. Some of my so-called preparation may sound silly, because it was in no way intended as career preparation at the time. Only hindsight reveals ways that my past contributes to what I now do.

As a high school student, I served in the model United Nations, I was vice president of the student government, and I served as a congressional intern to Congressman Barney Frank (D-MA). As a college student, I devoted myself to an honors sequence of psychology courses and to the conduct of an original honors thesis in psychology, but I also took numerous courses in political science and graduated one course short of a double major in political science. I was politically active, participated in a multiweek foreign policy crisis simulation, read a lot of political science and political philosophy, and followed national politics. As a graduate student in psychology, I departed from the standard psychology curriculum and took a course in the Goldman School of Public Policy at UC Berkeley. There I crystallized an understanding of the fact that societal problems do not unfold according to disciplinary boundaries. No societal problem can be solved by psychology alone. If I wanted to tackle some of the biggest problems, I had to learn to understand key aspects of adjacent disciplines like economics. I also participated in a summer institute in political psychology, which included intensive lectures from political scientists (half) and from psychologists (half). Once again, I read literature in political science and public policy while concentrating mainly on psychology.

As a young assistant professor, I worked in an interdisciplinary department inhabited by psychologists, economists, political scientists, and historians. Following the Carnegie Mellon tradition, largely shaped by Nobel Laureate Herbert Simon, the goal was to bring all relevant scholarly disciplines to bear on problems that mattered. The faculty held the highest possible standards for excellence in research, and they paired that with a strong mandate to conduct research that mattered. Thus, my preparation included attending two seminars per week, often by economists or political scientists, and trying to grapple with what psychology could bring to the table. I learned that doing studies simply because they represent the next step in a research program was not good enough to attract the attention of scholars in other fields. I had to conduct research that would matter to multiple disciplines and, better yet, to society as well.

It came as a complete surprise when a faculty member from Harvard called and asked if they could put my name into a search for a tenured position at the Harvard Kennedy School. The chance that such a search would select me seemed close to zero. When I visited Harvard, gave a talk, met the deans and faculty, and toured the campus, I was immediately enthralled. I also met with faculty from psychology, and their faculty voted to offer me a courtesy appointment.

As I understand the tenure process, a committee considers whether a candidate has made fundamental contributions to his or her field as well as whether such contributions would position him or her well to teach and conduct meaningful research in a school of public policy. Now that I am at the Kennedy School, it is clear that the faculty fall at various places along a continuum that ranges from basic to applied. In terms of my research, I fall near the end point on basic, but in terms of teaching, I am much closer to the middle. This may change over time or it may not; either way is okay.

It should be clear at this point that one could be much better prepared than I was. To best strategically position yourself to be a psychology PhD who works in a school of public policy, I recommend the following approach.

As an undergraduate, find a program like one at the University of Michigan where you can attend a summer institute or internship in a school of public policy. The Ford School at Michigan regularly hosts a Public Policy and International Affairs Junior Summer Institute—an intensive program that helps prepare undergraduate students from all over the United States for graduate programs in public policy and international affairs. Students take classes in statistics, economics, and related fields in preparation for graduate school. An ideal option is to find a university that offers an undergraduate major in public policy. As mentioned, such options exist at Princeton and Carnegie Mellon, and other options may exist as well. Independent of any particular program, identify a faculty mentor in a policy school while you are in college or in graduate school. Conduct research or serve as a research assistant for that faculty member. Complete an internship at a state, local, or federal government organization to see what the real-world experience is like. Take courses in microeconomics and in political science or public policy (as well as in psychology, of course) and conduct research in a hybrid field like behavioral economics (psychology and economics) or political psychology (political science and psychology). Consider becoming an intern with an organization like the Behavioral Insights Team in the United Kingdom (described earlier) or with a public policy research organization (e.g., Ideas42, RAND, Mathematica, Brookings, or The Tobin Project). When you design a study to test a psychological mechanism about how the brain works, also think about what (if anything) the results might mean for designing policies that promote human health and well-being. Learn to teach negotiation. All policy schools (and business schools) recruit people with this skill. Above all else, do top-notch work in whatever you do. That is the most important thing.

## Attributes Needed for Success in the Career

First and foremost, a career in public policy requires one to have curiosity about academic work outside of psychology—curiosity about the world of ideas, about economics, about policy, and about politics. If you lack this curiosity, then many seminars will bore you. Academia is replete with opportunities to make trade-offs between depth and breadth. If you choose depth over breadth every time, then this is not the right place for you.

This job also requires being capable of doing research one way, even if most others around you do it in different ways. In other words, you need to be reasonably independent in your abilities, not requiring a cadre of similar others around you. This situation hopefully will change as policy schools begin to recruit more psychologists.

The job requires open-mindedness about methodology and theory. This has been the largest challenge for me. I occasionally have slipped into biased, closed-minded thought when it comes to judging research methodology and theory. I was trained to think that the randomized controlled experiment is the most superior method. I occasionally cast doubt on qualitative methods, most especially on case studies, which seemed to me to encourage unjustifiable post hoc reasoning from a sample size of one. This view has been politically problematic, to say the least. Case studies are the dominant mode of teaching at the Harvard Kennedy School and the Harvard Business School. I have learned that having a healthy skepticism of any method is useful but looking down upon others is not. I have learned that each method provides a different perspective, creating the prismatic whole.

In addition to curiosity and open-mindedness, one needs to think in (what E. O. Wilson calls) *consilient* ways. Consilience is based on the unity-of-knowledge principle, which holds that measuring the same state of nature by several different methods should lead to the same answer. For example, it should not matter whether one measures the height of the Empire State Building with a yardstick, a metric measuring tape, or with a string. In all three cases, the answer should be approximately the same. Thus, studying political behavior using discourse analysis, economic modeling, patterns of neural activation, or Likert ratings scales should all reveal similar truths about political behavior. Wilson argues for "a conviction, far deeper than a mere working proposition, that the world is orderly and can be explained by a small number of natural laws" (1999, pp. 4–5). I ascribe to this view and practice it in my work. My own research methods range from brain imaging to conducting nationwide field surveys, from micro to macro—all aimed at uncovering similar truths about states of human nature.

I noted earlier in this chapter that this line of work is not for the meek. As the proverbial new kid on the block in public policy, psychologists must prove themselves before being welcomed into the pack. I need to prove myself in every class I teach unless it is a doctoral seminar. (Such seminars attract highly specialized students who already know the instructor's credentials and know that they want to take a class from that person.) Thus, doing this work requires a degree of willingness to deal with criticism and challenges. I was used to receiving high teaching evaluations when I taught undergraduates at Carnegie Mellon. When I first came to Harvard Kennedy School, I received mediocre teaching evaluations at best. I have had to work hard on improving my teaching to figure out new strategies for connecting with policy students. Compared with psychology students at UC Berkeley or to decision science students at Carnegie Mellon, the policy students at Harvard are less willing to tolerate learning knowledge purely for knowledge sake. They require me to figure out a meaningful policy or practice implication for most ideas. This is not such a bad thing, especially because they accept conclusions like, "It is too early to know whether this way or that way is better" or "The effect of X depends on the nature of Y" or "No one-size fits all solutions, and here is why."

Finally, one needs to welcome spending considerable time and effort on teaching. Our students are not undergraduates who occasionally sleep through lectures. They are professional students paying large sums of money to Harvard to further their respective capabilities. If you do not like teaching, this would not be a happy place. I used to be only mildly positive about teaching, while I adored research. Having been here for eight years, I still adore research, but I also have come to adore teaching, for the reasons described earlier.

## *Pay Range for the Career*

No aggregate data for faculty holding psychology PhDs in schools of public policy are available. There are too few of us. That said, personal experience tells me that the salaries fall above what psychology departments pay and below what marketing departments in business schools pay. Salaries may be comparable to what an organizational behavior department in a business school would pay, but this is speculation based on a limited sample.

This chapter explicitly provides a description of the faculty role. There are other tracks to consider, however. For example, someone with a PhD in psychology can work in a public policy think tank like RAND, Mathematica, or Brookings. Without access to datasets (again, small numbers), my sense is that those salaries also fall between what one would earn in a psychology department and what one would earn in a policy school.

## Future Prospects for the Career

These are early days for psychologists in schools of public policy. We first-generation folks may mess things up for future generations, or we may lay down wide pathways on which future generations will walk smoothly. There are many bumps in the road. When I arrived at the Harvard Kennedy School, the school did not need me to teach any specific course and that remains the case. I have created from scratch all the courses I teach (which has been fun) but all remain elective courses, not required courses, for the degree.

Looking nationwide at this early point, progress is good. In the past 10 years, some number (less than 10) of psychology PhDs received tenured faculty positions in schools of public policy. We will continue to mentor and hopefully recruit additional psychologists, although the latter is slow going. It appears that psychologists will not soon achieve equal representation with, say, economists or political scientists.

Two key developments in government suggest that progress will continue to improve. One, already described, is the rise of behavioral insight teams around the globe, each powerfully placed in government. They have promoted what they call a "test, learn, adapt" approach to government, all based around the use of randomized controlled trials. For discussion, see Halpern (2014). Their success in the United Kingdom, Australia, and in the Netherlands suggests that a new U.S. team also should meet with success. In 2014, the White House launched the first-ever social and behavioral sciences team (SBST), whose mandate is to make government programs more effective and efficient. SBST includes experts from psychology, economics, political science, and beyond who seek "to harness behavioral science insights to help Federal government programs better serve the nation while saving taxpayer dollars" (Shankar, 2015). This recognition at the highest levels of government that psychologists have a role to play in the policy forum may bode well for faculty composition changes in schools of public policy.

Another key development is somewhat similar, but it goes by a different name. Specifically, it is a growing *Moneyball* approach to government, as described in a new book edited by bipartisan government officials Jim Nussle, former head, Office of Management and Budget under President George W. Bush; and Peter Orszag, former head, Office of Management and Budget under President Barack Obama (Nussle & Orszag, 2014). *Moneyball* is a term coined in Michael Lewis's 2003 book of the same name to characterize how the Oakland A's baseball team increased their prospects of success by taking a data-driven, rather than intuition-driven, approach to hiring players. The approach, as translated to government policy making, argues that government needs to dramatically increase data-driven decision making based on rigorous evaluations of program effectiveness. The overall approach is nicely described by the following quote, excerpted from a chapter by Glenn Hubbard (Hubbard is the former chair of the Council of Economy Advisers under Bush):

> There is no doubt that gathering and evaluating evidence of impact in a complex world is challenging. At the same time, researchers and policy makers across government are already hard at work applying these approaches to build evidence for what works and what doesn't. They're coming to conclusions that are reducing homelessness and improving hospice care. They're simplifying financial-aid forms and boosting college enrollment for disadvantaged students. And they're showing that—with the right resources and a changing landscape that puts evidence-based policy front and center—it's possible to do more than talk about making government work better; we can evaluate the data and marshal the evidence to make it happen. (2014, pp. 21–22)

Presumably, teams of behavioral scientists, including policy school faculty members with psychology PhDs, will conduct such evaluations.

A key development evidenced in academic administration and in federal funding patterns also suggests that progress will continue to improve. Universities and federal funding agencies are increasingly welcoming interdisciplinary work—even while maintaining the highest standards for theory and evidence. The more they do so, the more this career path should open.

# References

Halpern, D. (2014, January). Applying psychology to public policy. *APS Observer*, *27*. Retrieved from http://www.psychologicalscience.org/ index.php/publications/observer/2014/january-14/applying-psychology-to-public-policy.html

Hubbard, G. (2014). The pursuit of evidence. In J. Nussle & P. Orszag (Eds.), *Moneyball for government* (pp. 21–22). Washington, DC: Disruption Books.

Lewis, M. (2003). *Moneyball: The art of winning an unfair game.* New York, NY: W.W. Norton.

Nussle, J., & Orszag, P. (Eds.). (2014). *Moneyball for government.* New York, NY: Disruption Books.

Shankar, M. (2015, February 9). *Using behavioral science insights to make government more effective, simpler, and more people-friendly.* Retrieved from https://www.whitehouse.gov/blog/2015/02/09/behavioral-science-insights-make-government-more-effective-simpler-and-more-user-fri

Sunstein, C. (2016). The council of psychological advisors. *Annual Review of Psychology, 67,* 713–737.

Wilson, E. O. (1999). *Consilience: the unity of knowledge.* New York, NY: Vintage.

# CLINICAL AND COUNSELING PSYCHOLOGY | II

*Christine H. Farber*

# Clinical Psychologists in Independent Practice

8

C linical psychology is the branch of psychology that is concerned with the assessment, diagnosis, and treatment of psychological issues, ranging from minor adjustment challenges (such as a student's struggle to adapt to living in a dormitory away from home) to chronic, severe psychopathology (such as schizophrenia). Psychologists in independent practice, by definition, carry out these activities while working for themselves or within a group practice, independent of larger organizations.

Christine H. Farber is a clinical psychologist in independent practice based in central Connecticut. She received her PhD in clinical psychology from Duquesne University. She is a coauthor of *Treating Traumatic Bereavement: A Practitioner's Guide*, has taught courses as an adjunct professor at University of Hartford's Graduate Institute in Professional Psychology, and has served on the board of directors of the Connecticut Psychological Association. Her clinical practice is informed by her interests in archetypal and phenomenological psychology.

I wish to acknowledge the contributions of Daniel J. Abrahamson, PhD, who cowrote an earlier version of this chapter with me. I also wish to thank Suzanne Hayes for her thoughtful review of and feedback on this chapter.

http://dx.doi.org/10.1037/15960-009
*Career Paths in Psychology: Where Your Degree Can Take You, Third Edition*,
R. J. Sternberg (Editor)

Being a clinical psychologist is akin to cultivating a particular point of view. If I were a fashion designer sitting across from a client, I might take note of the fabric out of which his clothes were made, the shape of his body, and the color palette of his outfit. As a clinical psychologist, I have a different lens and will be attuned to other aspects of the client's presentation and experience. This clinical point of view is informed by knowledge of human development; the biological bases of behavior; ways in which cognition, behavior, and emotion affect one another; how individuals interact with the social environments in which they live; and factors that contribute to resilience. It is informed, also, by theoretical models of personality, motivation, and change, for example, and by questions such as how do people act in certain situations, what factors influence their actions, and when and how are certain behaviors adaptive, or not. A clinical lens takes context into account, as well, which includes past, present, and future influences and group identities that include gender, ethnicity, and race. All of this shapes the ways in which clinical psychologists *see* the world, including how we are attuned to clients.

A clinical point of view is guided by a commitment to evidence-based practice in psychology (EBPP). This means that clinicians maintain an awareness of available research and of our clinical experiences and expertise, carefully thinking through how such knowledge applies to a particular client or group. EBPP requires critical thinking skills, an understanding of the scientific method and statistics (so that we can intelligently read and understand research papers and reports), and an appreciation of the body of knowledge produced by research that pertains to diagnoses, methods of assessment, and effective treatments. The activities performed by clinical psychologists in independent practice are more diversified than ever, and the field continues to evolve. My goal throughout this chapter is to paint a rich, realistic picture of what the field can offer to you as well as what you might bring to it.

## Nature of the Career

Let's consider the fictional case of Louis to illustrate the nature of clinical psychology. Louis, a 37-year-old, heterosexual male, is a construction-machinery operator whose employer put him on leave after noticing that he had been distracted on the job for several days in a row. His employer referred him to me for an evaluation, requesting that I provide a written report addressing whether Louis was fit to return to work. When Louis and I met, he told me that his wife of 11 years had recently filed for divorce. He described himself as "devastated" and reported having difficulty sleeping, eating, and concentrating at work.

He also told me that he was drinking more than usual and "crying at the drop of a hat."

Sitting across from Louis, with my clinical-psychology lens in place, I notice that he looks small despite being of above-average height: His shoulders are rolled forward, his hands clasped in front of him, and his eyes are focused on the floor in a way that makes him look like he is turned inward. When he speaks his voice quivers, and although he is on the verge of tears, he seems eager to articulate his recent experience. As he tells me what happened with his wife, I notice that he uses phrases such as "I failed her."

The further into his story he gets, the more he inches forward, now sitting on the edge of his seat. He makes eye contact with me when he talks about the impending divorce, and I feel as though he is looking for comfort. Grounded in my clinical point of view, I pay attention to all of the clues Louis is providing, and I form hypotheses about his experiences, which he and I can then discuss. As an example, I imagine that if Louis believes he is solely to blame for the divorce, then he likely feels badly about himself, a fact that could leave him vulnerable to depression. I make a mental note of this, as well as a note about the sadness that he seems to embody and what I believe is a willingness on his part to accept help and support.

Later in the interview, I will ask him about symptoms of depression more specifically, as well as about his history of close relationships, whether he has social support, and what his usual coping strategies are and whether they have been effective. I also will administer a few questionnaires that will provide additional information about Louis's symptoms and resources; and he and I will schedule an additional session in which I can present my feedback, discuss the report that I will send to his employer, and develop a plan to get him the support he needs so that he can return to work safely.

## A Variety of Pursuits

Louis's case is an example of a psychological evaluation, which is one of many kinds of activities that an independent practitioner conducts. One of the advantages of private practice is the ability to pick and choose with which activities you most wish to engage.

### PSYCHOTHERAPY

Psychotherapy is perhaps the most recognized of the myriad of activities pursued by psychologists in private practice; and the term psychotherapy itself describes a variety of treatments, interventions, and approaches that address diagnosable disorders and help improve quality of life. Psychotherapy is perhaps the most recognized of the myriad of activities pursued by psychologists in private practice; and the term *psychotherapy* itself describes a variety of treatments, interventions, and approaches that address diagnosable disorders and help improve quality of life. A large variety of treatments exist, and clinicians have expertise recommending and implementing them.

Examples of psychotherapy include an interactive, 6-week, web-based intervention to treat depression; a 12-session course of manualized therapy to treat posttraumatic stress disorder; or a longer term psychotherapy aimed at helping a client to develop coping resources and self-acceptance. Psychotherapy by a clinical psychologist might also include psychopharmacology: in some states, specially trained psychologists have been granted the ability to write prescriptions for psychotropic medications.

Psychotherapy can be conducted with a variety of populations, including children, adolescents, and adults; couples and families; and groups of individuals who share a common concern. Furthermore, psychologists can specialize in the types of problems that we treat. Target issues for treatment are wide-ranging and include interpersonal difficulties, clinical entities such as phobias and mood disorders, and life-changes and the adjustments they require (e.g., a birth or a job change). What is common across approaches to treatment and various subspecialties is that psychologists work in collaboration with clients to address issues that are causing distress or interfering with an enhanced sense of well-being. The therapeutic relationship is the context in which all other techniques and interventions take place, and research consistently demonstrates its significance to effective therapies. As a person who values relationships, I appreciate working in a field in which my relationships with clients are a foundational tool of my work.

## PSYCHOLOGICAL ASSESSMENT AND EVALUATION

Psychological evaluation is a process whereby a psychologist uses a variety of tools—including formalized instruments (such as personality and intelligence tests), interviews, record-review, and observation—to address a specific question posed by the person being evaluated or by a third party. A school may refer a student to a psychologist to ascertain the presence of a learning disability and to suggest modifications that would help the student. A criminal attorney may ask a psychologist to evaluate a defendant in an effort to determine whether psychological issues had some bearing on the alleged crime, thereby introducing mitigating factors into the defense strategy. The case of Louis, described previously, was another example of a client being seen for a psychological evaluation. In each of these cases, the psychologist is asked to answer a specific question or set of questions by performing an assessment of the person(s) being evaluated. She then consults with the appropriate party about findings, opinions, and recommendations, and most often will report her findings in written form.

## PSYCHOLOGICAL CONSULTATION

Many clinical psychologists conduct formal and informal consultations as part of their pursuits, in which they share their knowledge and specific recommendations regarding an issue at hand. A couple might consult with a psychologist to ascertain whether their parenting style contributes to their child's difficulties in school, for example, or a corporation might hire a psychologist to consult about personnel matters in preparation for major changes within the company. Psychologists often consult one another to broaden their perspective or to gain clarity about an issue, and they consult with other health care providers, too. The broad role of psychological consultation underscores the fact that clinical psychologists have knowledge that is valuable to many audiences in a variety of contexts.

## ADJUNCT ACTIVITIES

A psychologist in independent practice can engage in a variety of adjunct activities. I have taught classes; conducted research; written articles, chapters, blogs, and a book about psychological topics of interest; given talks to my community; and engaged in administrative work, including serving on the board of directors of a nonprofit organization and managing grant funds. Other independent practitioners I know serve as expert witnesses in court, supervise graduate trainees, consult to organizations, train psychologists in specific approaches to treatment, and conduct forensic evaluations. The potential for variety within the workweek, the ability to engage with diverse and fulfilling activities, and the freedom to create a unique mix of pursuits are all benefits of independent practice.

## THE BUSINESS OF PRACTICE

Independent practice usually translates into running your own business. Activities within any given workweek will relate to managing the practice of clinical psychology specifically (e.g., maintaining paperwork and communicating with insurance companies) and managing a business more generally (e.g., paying taxes, ordering supplies, and keeping accounting records). This means that clinicians engage in at least several hours per week of paperwork and administrative tasks that we are not paid for, at least not directly, but which support the clinical work we do. Ensuring that you stay on top of such tasks is a significant aspect of running a successful practice.

## PROFESSIONAL ADVOCACY

Some clinicians advocate for themselves, their clients, and the profession. We meet with politicians to fight for legislation that benefits the discipline of and populations served by psychology, write editorials to the local paper about issues upon which psychological study bears relevance, and provide public education through community talks, tweets, or press releases. Being involved with a professional organization such the American Psychological Association allows us to advance the interests of psychology through collective efforts to define the field. Involvement in my state psychological association over many years has been a source of empowerment for me, allowing me to give back to my profession, be a part of the collective force that shapes the discipline, and connect with colleagues. I encourage you to consider joining your state association and the American Psychological Association. Your membership in these organizations will provide you with information about the field in general as well as topics of interest to students in particular. In addition, your membership dues and participation with organizational efforts will support the agenda of promoting and shaping the field of clinical psychology.

# Challenges and Rewards

From practical benefits such as financial compensation to the cultivation of a sense of meaning in one's life, the rewards of pursuing the independent practice of psychology are many. There are challenges, too. The following section discusses some of the more salient advantages and challenges of the career.

## FINANCIAL COMPENSATION

In a survey of its members, the American Psychological Association's Center for Workforce Studies (2010) reports mean salaries of clinicians in individual private practice that range from $54,000, for those working in the field for 5 years or less, to approximately $118,000, for those who have been in the field for 30 years or more. Factors that account for a wide range of reported income include the actual activities pursued and the number of hours of direct, billable services performed in a given week. Spending 1 day a week writing may reduce your income, unless or until you receive compensation or royalties for the work. If you write a popular blog, your time doing so may be rewarded with increased referrals, indirectly affecting compensation. Conducting evaluations for the courts and serving as an expert witness in matters related to civil and criminal litigation can generate fees of $250 per hour or more. Consultants to private corporations sometimes receive fees as high as $5,000 per day. Including such activities within your schedule obviously would enhance your earning potential. Having a specialization that is in high demand, networking with colleagues and agencies in your geographic area, and contracting with insurance companies to serve as one of their network providers can facilitate earning potential by helping you build a full-time practice.

A financial drawback of independent practice is the lack of benefits. Without an employer to offer insurance coverage, paid vacation, or retirement savings, an independent practitioner will need to adopt a business plan that can address these potential financial gaps. Some individuals work in an organizational setting that can offer a stable salary and benefits while establishing a part-time private practice, on the side. Many psychologists I know began their independent practice with part-time work, slowly building up to a full-time practice while working in another setting.

## WORKPLACE AUTONOMY

As mentioned, you can tailor independent practice to best fit your skills, preferences, and needs. The independence afforded by the career also requires you to be self-motivated and self-initiating, which can be an advantage or disadvantage, depending on your personality. You will need to market yourself, hold yourself accountable for the money you make and the services you deliver, and tend to all aspects of the business of practice. Knowing your strengths and weaknesses and seeking assistance in those areas of the business where you most need help can be the difference between having a successful versus an unsuccessful business.

## INTELLECTUAL AND CREATIVE FULFILLMENT

Two of the most appealing aspects of this career for me are intellectual and creative fulfillment. Opportunities to observe, hypothesize, and stretch our knowledge about human existence abound. Activities that call for and foster creativity include the following: formulating a case with the help of a colleague, helping a client to see an old pattern in a new way, and articulating conclusions after several hours of psychological evaluation. If you love to think critically and creatively about human existence, learn new information, contemplate research and theory, integrate extant knowledge with your own experience and observations, or solve problems, this field will not disappoint. It will require, however, a disciplined work ethic and a willingness to grow and expand your perspective.

## A SENSE OF PURPOSE

Clinical psychologists are in the business of understanding human existence and ameliorating suffering. For me, this translates into a sense of purpose that is life sustaining. Witnessing the journeys of individual clients, couples, and families allows me to reflect on questions about human existence as well as gain inspiration from their respective paths, always learning more along the way. Working with human vulnerability and suffering, however, also requires a consistent, serious, and sensitive mindfulness of clients' welfare. A great deal of responsibility is inherent in the practice of psychology. As a career that involves establishing relationships and using those relationships—and therefore, oneself—as a foundational tool of one's work, clinical practice necessitates a commitment to integrity, authenticity, self-awareness, and ethical practice.

## *The Path to Practice*

When undergraduates ask me about pursuing advanced education in psychology, one of the first questions I ask in reply is, "How much do you enjoy school, learning, and studying?" Doctoral-level education requires a substantial commitment of time, energy, and financial resources. Becoming a clinical psychologist is a process that typically takes 6 to 8 years to achieve. It requires that you enroll in a doctoral program,[1] receive your degree, and then become licensed in the state in which you plan to practice.

---

[1]As of this writing, a doctorate is considered the entry-level degree for practice as a clinical psychologist in all but one state. West Virginia is the exception (Association of State and Provincial Psychology Boards, 2015).

## APPLYING TO DOCTORAL PROGRAMS

Applying to doctoral programs is a competitive endeavor. The following list includes a few pieces of information that will help prepare you for the competitive application process:

- If you are interested in a clinical career, then you will want to gain entrance to a clinical program, which is one that prepares you to provide direct clinical services as opposed to a program that focuses mainly on research, for example.
- You have the choice of applying to programs that confer a doctor of philosophy (PhD) or those that grant a doctor of psychology (PsyD). Although the two degrees have similar coursework and training requirements, students enrolled in PhD programs will experience greater emphasis on conducting original research as part of their academic training. Candidates in PsyD programs typically will experience a greater focus on applied aspects of clinical psychology, such as psychotherapy and mental health services administration.
- It will be helpful to familiarize yourself with a program's prerequisites in advance of applying, including coursework requirements. This is especially important for those who have not majored in psychology, as certain psychology courses will be required.

## COMPLETING THE DOCTORATE

Most doctoral programs are structured to be completed in about 5 years, although it is common for people to take 2 or 3 years longer to complete all of the program requirements. Whereas some programs offer tuition reimbursement or stipends to students who engage in research and teaching, not all do; graduate training, therefore, can be expensive. You can prepare for the necessary, long-term training by having a financial and personal plan that will support it. Common requirements for receipt of a doctorate are as followings:

- Two to three years of *coursework* are required. This is measured in credits, and there will be general consistency across programs with regard to many foundational course requirements.
- *Practicum placements* provide your initial, supervised experiences training in the field. A typical placement might entail 2 days per week of clinical work conducting assessments in a rehabilitation clinic, offering psychotherapy groups within a college counseling center, or implementing psychotherapy to patients in a psychiatric hospital. Supervision of your work ideally will provide you with the support you need to develop and hone your skills and cultivate competence in the field.

- A year-long, full-time *internship* (or its part-time equivalent) is a more intensive training experience than is a practicum placement, although it is similar in that it offers organized and supervised training in the field. Students typically pursue an internship after coursework is complete. Because of the competitive nature of internship programs, it is common for students to move to another state for this part of their training. Moreover, not everyone is guaranteed an internship placement on his or her first try (or at all), and this can increase the time it takes to earn the degree.
- *Comprehensive exams*, which cover core areas of the discipline, are given after you complete all coursework. They are intended to test your broad knowledge of the field and can be written, oral, or both.
- The completion of a *dissertation or doctoral project* is typically the final requirement of a doctoral program. A dissertation—which is a substantial written piece of work that represents a new empirically based research contribution to the field of psychology—is required by PhD programs. PsyD programs may require a doctoral project (such as an in-depth case study) instead. A doctoral project emphasizes the application of research and theory rather than the production of new research.

## OBTAINING LICENSURE

To practice clinical psychology, you must become licensed in the state(s) you wish to practice. Each state specifies its own criteria for licensure, such as the following:

- *Eligibility of particular doctoral programs.* A program that is accredited by the American Psychological Association and one of the six regional educational accrediting bodies in the United States will be preferred and in some states, required. Accreditation is a process of quality control, relied on by states to ensure that an education program is comprehensive in its preparation of students for the practice of psychology. When researching potential graduate programs, you should ascertain whether they are accredited, and if not, whether they would meet a particular state's eligibility requirements. The book *Graduate Study in Psychology* (American Psychological Association, 2016) is a good resource for doing so.
- *Additional, required experience in the field.* Some states require additional, supervised experience, over and above the experience acquired in graduate school, before granting a license. The American Psychological Association recommends the equivalent of 2 years of full-time training as a prerequisite for licensure, which includes the doctoral internship and could include practicum hours, as well. Not all states follow this policy, however, and so

it is necessary to familiarize yourself with the requirements of those states in which you wish to practice before accumulating additional, supervised experience.

- *National and state examinations.* All states will require passing a national examination and many require passing a state-specific exam, as well.
- *Mobility among states.* Moving from one state to another is simplified through licensure portability mechanisms such as the Certificate of Professional Qualification in Psychology (CPQ), granted by the Association of State and Provincial Psychology Boards. If a licensed psychologist with a CPQ moves to another state that accepts this certification, he or she will not have to go through the complete credentialing process again. This can be extremely beneficial in those states that have idiosyncratic credentialing requirements.
- *Continuing education.* Psychology is a broad and ever-evolving field. Ethical and competent practice requires ongoing learning—reading research journals, attending workshops and conferences, and collaborating with colleagues are just some of the ways to keep abreast of developments within the field. Most states require that psychologists earn and document continuing education credits to renew their license at appropriate intervals—annually, for example.

# Skills, Attitudes, and Commitments for Success

Intelligence, persistence, and a disciplined work ethic will assist you in your journey through graduate school and beyond. Likewise, certain skills, attitudes, and a commitment to self-awareness will help foster professional success and satisfaction.

## SKILLS

Problem-solving abilities are one of the main staples of a clinical skill set and involve identifying a problem, gathering and analyzing relevant data, considering options, and implementing a solution. A capacity for critical thinking will aid you in effective problem-solving as well as competent, ethical practice more generally. Ideally, you will cultivate the capacity to think critically during your graduate education. This in turn will help you to make sound clinical decisions, think through complex ethical dilemmas, and implement evidence-based practice.

Communication skills, including the ability to write well, are assets for clinicians as well. So, too, are negotiation and diplomacy skills.

Negotiation skills are particularly useful when you are in a position of recognizing and responding to the needs of multiple individuals, such as during couples, family, or group psychotherapy or while conducting assessments and consultations involving third-party payors or multiple individuals or agencies. Negotiating relationships with clients and colleagues also require diplomacy skills.

A successful psychological practice requires attention to financial, managerial, and administrative details; therefore, business aptitude is an asset. For many, administrative work will include working with third-party payors, such as Medicare and private insurance companies, and complying with legal requirements like the Health Insurance Portability and Accountability Act (HIPAA). Your day-to-day tasks will include tending to the paperwork and other arrangements that these systems require. Collaborating with a colleague, hiring a billing manager, and seeking advice from an accountant are ways to supplement your own business skill set if needed. Professional associations are a good resource for practice preparedness, providing resources, tips, and strategies for successful business management.

## ATTITUDES

Many of the activities that characterize clinical practice entail connection with others who are experiencing a great deal of vulnerability. Relating to this vulnerability with compassion, which is further associated with basic listening and empathy skills, is essential for successful practice. An empathic, compassionate psychologist is able to appreciate and respect another's experience while acknowledging that she may never fully understand it. Respect for individual differences and for a client's self-knowledge is another attitude that ought to be cultivated.

Intellectual and existential curiosity helps us to stay interested and engaged with others' lives, our own observations, and the body of knowledge that defines the field. A flexible mind-set and sense of humor are assets, too. One of the gifts of humor is that it allows for shifts in our perspective, helping us to view an issue in a new way.

## COMMITMENTS

Self-awareness is an attribute to which a clinician must aspire, an ongoing commitment which we must make, to practice ethically and competently. Knowing ourselves—through our own psychotherapy, journaling, meditation practice, or ongoing clinical supervision, for example—helps us to acknowledge limits and biases, be aware of our boundaries, take responsibility for the dynamics we introduce into relationships, and find ways to meet our own personal needs so that they do not interfere with our clinical work. If I am aware of my own values regarding marriage and divorce, for example, I will be less likely to impose them on a client and more likely to help her articulate her own values and choices about the same. Self-awareness is also a prerequisite for culturally competent practice. Knowing ourselves is an ongoing process (there is always more to learn and discover!), which allows for increased choice and conscious decision making in our own lives, and is another benefit of this career.

Humility, comfort with vulnerability, and tolerance for that which is unknown go hand in hand with self-awareness. Clinical psychology is an inexact practice that leaves room for interpretation, creativity, and intuitive responses. This can be anxiety provoking as well as exciting, and the individual who can be humble in the midst of not knowing is likely to experience more comfort than one who cannot. Developing strategies that help you to achieve comfort in the face of vulnerability will expand the empathy you have for clients and for yourself.

Finally, attention to self-care and maintenance of balance between the personal and professional realms and within the professional realm are strategies required for long-term success in the field. Self-care is particularly important as a means of preventing or addressing the emotional and psychological challenges of the work. Hearing difficult stories and witnessing the suffering of others can bring about changes to our sense of self, our sense of meaning, and our worldview. Connecting with our inner experiences can ameliorate the challenging effects of this work, and connecting with colleagues who do similar work can help us to feel less alone and to transform distress through sharing, meaning-making, understanding, and humor (Pearlman & Saakvitne, 1995).

## The Future

The evolving landscape of health insurance, the requirements of evidence-based practice, and the prominent role of technology in the 21st-century world are some of the salient influences on the present and future of clinical psychology (Barlow & Carl, 2011). Changes to the delivery of services and the role of independent practitioners will result from these and other influences, although the exact nature of these changes is yet to be determined. And because these changes are yet to be determined, those of us with an interest in the field can shape it through advocacy, involvement with public policy, and consumer education.

The use of electronic communication, practice websites, blogging, and networking via social media are common practices within the field made possible by technological developments of recent decades. Actual interventions, methods of assessment, and psychological instruments are changing within our technological world, as well. Biofeedback, virtual reality tools, and computer applications for self-help are enhancing the quality and delivery of services to target audiences and are helping psychologists reach remote populations and underserved areas. Familiarity with technology may be a prerequisite for living life in general these days; this is no less true for the practice of psychology. Those who can think creatively about the use of technology in the field may find themselves shaping its future.

Another influence within the field is that adherence to evidence-based practice in psychology is becoming a prerequisite for the payment of services by health insurance companies. What this means for the independent practitioner is that the utilization of empirically supported treatments, formal assessment of the effectiveness of our work with clients, and accountability for cost-effective outcomes increasingly are becoming an inherent part of practice.

The evolving health care system, with its emphasis on primary and preventive care, is proving to be a major influence on the field, too. Clinical psychology is becoming more closely aligned with and integrated into the medical profession. As this happens, those in independent practice may find themselves working on multidisciplinary health care teams at least some of the time—consulting with a physician about the long-term psychological impact of chronic illness, screening patients for depression, or working with an individual toward smoking cessation, to give just a few examples. I don't believe that such developments will eclipse independent practice, but I think it's possible that the majority of independent practitioners in the years to come will have a specialty practice that either is supported by health care and health insurance practices or falls outside of the health care system entirely, not relying on insurance reimbursement for payment.

Psychologists can create their own bright future by educating the public about what they have to offer, affecting policy that supports the delivery of and payment for psychological services, and thinking creatively about the breadth of contributions that they can offer the world.

## My Typical Day

I end this chapter with a description of a day in my professional life, although my typical day is not necessarily a typical day.[2] For the most part, conducting psychotherapy has been my primary professional activ-

[2]At the time of this writing I am on an extended sabbatical from my practice to address concerns arising from a chronic, autoimmune disease—a fact that I raise to demonstrate the flexibility that my career path has offered. The typical day I describe represents a day preceding my leave of absence.

ity, and for the most part, I have done this part time. A colleague of mine conducts psychological assessments almost exclusively, dedicating only about 10% of his direct service time to psychotherapy. Another colleague splits her time equally between treatment, forensic-related assessment, and consultation to a nonprofit organization dedicated to the prevention of domestic violence. If you enter the field, you, too, will be able to create a schedule that works for you.

My day starts with a leisurely morning. I wake up with a cup of tea, sitting quietly before I check e-mail correspondence and consult my schedule. I value the fact that I can take my time getting to my office, usually arriving at about noon, ready for the mix of the day's activities. My preference is to tackle administrative work before engaging in direct client services. On this particular day, I begin by working on the annual budget for my state psychological association. Administrative tasks are a source of fulfillment for me. Unlike the psychotherapy I conduct, completing a budget is an item I can check off my list, and this brings a different sort of satisfaction than that which I gain from psychotherapy.

An administrative task that I find less satisfying but which nevertheless requires my attention next is preparation for a scheduled, insurance call. I will be speaking with a care manager at an insurance company to request approval of additional psychotherapy sessions for a client who is making progress in therapy. The client and I are in agreement that further therapy would be useful to her. I have documented her symptoms and progress over time, and demonstrating the effective outcome of our work thus far is an important piece of what I present to the care manager, who ultimately approves eight more sessions for this client.

After completing this call, returning other phone messages, and sorting through my mail, I take a few minutes to prepare for the four psychotherapy sessions I have scheduled this afternoon. I find that my way of being in the world is different when I conduct psychotherapy from when I do administrative work. Whereas administrative work requires a purposeful, goal-directed attitude, engaging in psychotherapy calls forth a quieter, more reflective orientation. Rather than knowing what to do and making that happen, I enter a space of openness in which it is okay to not know, to be surprised, to listen for what has yet to be revealed. Conducting psychotherapy, I am both an expert and not an expert. My knowledge of theory and research is present, my ability to think critically about what a client presents is intact, but so, too, is a more poetic attitude—I enter a space in which associations that are beyond logic or analysis can emerge. The existential space I strive to enter is one of genuineness, authenticity, and presence to the clients with whom I work. How different this is from creating a budget. And how satisfying in its own way.

On this particular day, I will meet with three individual clients—two are childhood trauma survivors working through interpersonal issues and problematic symptoms of anxiety and depression, and one is a newly sober, young adult who is committed to Alcoholics Anonymous and wishes to understand more about his inner experience and the triggers that leave him vulnerable to relapse. These three sessions will be followed by my last session of the day—a couple married for 17 years who feel stuck in the routine of their relationship and would like to prevent potential resentment of one another from building up. To their credit, they can see themselves headed in this direction and want to engage in a therapy that will help prevent resentment and may be even create a spark of excitement and deepen the intimacy between them.

Describing a typical workday reminds me of how much I love the work I have chosen. I am interested in questions such as what makes life meaningful for a given individual and how a person can grow through suffering. I am curious about the depths and complexities of human experience. I care deeply about the individuals with whom I work and am genuinely interested in what matters to them. I am also inspired by their courage and grateful for the invitation and privilege to walk alongside them on their respective journeys through life. To those readers who ultimately may choose to pursue a clinical career in psychology, I trust you will find as much fulfillment as I have on this enriching path.

## References

American Psychological Association. (2016). *Graduate study in psychology, 2016 edition.* Washington, DC: Author.

American Psychological Association, Center for Workforce Studies. (2010). *2009 Report of the APA salary survey.* Washington, DC: Author.

Association of State and Provincial Psychology Boards. (2015). Degree level requirements for licensure by jurisdiction. *Handbook Jurisdictional Summary Reports.* Retrieved from http://www.asppb.org/HandbookPublic/Reports/default.aspx?ReportType=DegreeLevelLiscensure

Barlow, D. H., & Carl, J. R. (2011). The future of clinical psychology: Promises, perspectives, and predictions. In D. H. Barlow (Ed.), *The Oxford handbook of clinical psychology* (pp. 891–911). New York, NY: Oxford University Press. http://dx.doi.org/10.1093/oxfordhb/9780195366884.001.0001

Pearlman, L. A., & Saakvitne, K. W. (1995). *Trauma and the therapist: Countertransference and vicarious traumatization in psychotherapy with incest survivors.* New York, NY: W.W. Norton.

*Jane Annunziata and Marc Nemiroff*

# Psychologists Specializing in Child and Adolescent Clinical Psychology

9

A career in child clinical psychology offers a spectrum of exciting possibilities. A child clinical psychologist is a clinical psychologist who specializes in work with children in a variety of settings, inside and outside the office. A clinical psychologist has specific training and experience in doing psychotherapy and other interventions with people who have a full range of emotional problems. A child clinical psychologist

Jane Annunziata, PsyD, is a clinical psychologist with a private practice specializing in children and families in McLean, VA. She has taught at the University of Bergen (Norway), Mary Washington College, and George Mason University. As a writer, she has contributed parent guidance sections to children's books on such topics as shyness, parental depression, ambivalence, boundaries, and a new baby in the family.

Marc Nemiroff, PhD, is former cochair of the Developmental Psychotherapy program at the Washington School of Psychiatry and maintains a private practice in Potomac, MD. He has written and presented papers on various topics related to the mental health issues of children, clinical work with childhood trauma, and cross-cultural competence.

Together, Dr. Nemiroff and Dr. Annunziata are the authors of several psychological children's books.

http://dx.doi.org/10.1037/15960-010
*Career Paths in Psychology: Where Your Degree Can Take You, Third Edition*,
R. J. Sternberg (Editor)

works therapeutically with children, their parents, and sometimes their whole families to handle the variety of developmental and emotional problems that children may have. Most child clinical psychologists also are trained in psychotherapy with adults. In fact, many of the best adult psychotherapists have specific training in working with children. This is because most adult patients have difficulties stemming from childhood, and child clinical training enhances the ability of the therapist to fully understand the adult patient's childhood experience.

Child clinical psychologists also have specialized training and expertise in psychodiagnostic assessment of children using clinical and developmentally based instruments as well as educational and intellectual tests. Such assessment often is referred to as *psychological testing*. Although clinicians in other disciplines are trained in psychotherapy, only psychologists are trained and authorized to administer psychological tests.

In addition to treatment and assessment, some child clinical psychologists pursue academic careers. Many of those who work in an academic setting engage in research specifically related to child psychology. These psychologists might teach and do research in areas such as child development, behavior problems of childhood, treatment outcomes, and child psychopathology. Child clinical psychologists also engage in professional writing; consultation in, for example, educational or medical settings; and clinical supervision of students and other child clinicians.

The field of child clinical psychology is quite broad and offers important and diverse opportunities that are both intellectually stimulating and personally rewarding. At the core, child clinical psychologists devote themselves to the improvement of the lives of children, adolescents, and their families. One of the great rewards of the field is the variety of ways to help bring about this improvement.

## Professional Activities of Child Clinical Psychologists

Child clinical psychologists engage in a variety of professional activities. They assess children using diagnostic clinical evaluations such as playroom interviews and formal psychological testing instruments. They provide psychotherapy. They also may choose to focus their careers on teaching, conducting research, and providing consultation to a variety of agencies involved directly in the provision of services to children. Many child clinical psychologists choose to engage in several of these activities to provide themselves with a varied and stimulating career and to have an impact on a wide range of people.

Children most often come to a child clinical psychologist with problems such as anxiety, phobias, depression, autism and developmental delays, difficulty with peer relationships, acting-out behaviors at home or school, academic underachievement, parent–child attachment problems, trauma, and the many issues often associated with adoption. Many child clinical psychologists develop an interest in particular populations and specialize in their treatment, or working in specialized settings. For example, many child psychologists may choose to work in medical settings. Some are interested in adoption, children with autistic spectrum disorders, adolescents, very young children, children with attention-deficit disorders, or children with alcoholic parents. Thus, a child clinical psychologist has the opportunity to work with children from birth through adolescence or even early adulthood, in many ways.

## CHILD THERAPIES

There are many ways to intervene clinically with children and adolescents. Play therapy is a common form of individual treatment with younger children, who naturally express themselves through their play. Play is the preferred language of childhood. Play therapy typically is used with children between the ages of 2 and 10 years. Older children can be engaged in a combination of talk therapy with adjunctive play activities, such as crafts, games (e.g., chess), electronic devices, or self-expression through art. The basic assumption of play therapy is that the children's symptoms are really only surface manifestations of underlying conflicts that need to be understood to bring about lasting improvement. Adolescent psychotherapy is almost always talk therapy. At times, the adolescent will share aspects of his or her life by sharing information on his phone, iPad, or laptop, particularly pertaining to social media.

The play therapy approach to treatment also entails active, ongoing child guidance sessions with parents. The goal of such sessions is to help the parents better understand and learn new ways of responding to their child. Sometimes an effective intervention is to work exclusively with the parents, helping them alter their approach to their child to strengthen the parent–child relationship, rather than working with the child directly. Additionally, the child clinical psychologist is in contact with the child's or adolescent's school to facilitate school adjustment and to receive information regarding the child's school functioning. The child clinical psychologist also may intervene with a childcare provider or may consult with a pediatrician on the intersection of the child's psychological and medical problems.

Dyadic therapy is another form of psychotherapy used with children and teenagers. It often is used in the treatment of parent–child attachment and other relational problems. Usually the parent and younger child play or talk together in the presence of the child clinical psychologist, who helps facilitate an improved relationship and greater understanding between the two. The psychologist may provide demonstrations (role-plays), interpret parent–child interactions, and directly teach the parent how to be with the child at the child's developmental level, whether the child is 2 or 17 years old.

In family therapy, members of the family are treated together. Family therapy is based on the belief that an individual's difficulty may be the symptom of a whole family problem. Problems in a family often result from maladaptive patterns of interaction and communication among its members. Family therapy provides family members with an opportunity to learn new and effective ways to communicate and relate to each other. Some child clinical psychologists use *flexible family therapy*, in which various family members are seen in different combinations. For example, if sibling rivalry has become the most obvious problem, the therapist may see just the brothers and sisters for several sessions before reuniting the whole family in their ongoing treatment.

Group therapy can be a powerful form of treatment for children who are uncomfortable in an individual setting, who need feedback directly from peers under the guidance of the therapist, or who need to understand how they affect other children. Sometimes children respond to treatment better in the presence of other children. They learn and receive feedback about their style of interaction with peers, as well as their individual difficulties, and learn new ways to handle their problems from peers and from their therapist. Generally a group consists of six to eight children of approximately the same age, often run by two cotherapists. The children usually are preselected for types of problems, such as those experiencing a parental divorce, children or adolescents with serious peer relationship problems, or those who are developmentally delayed in similar ways. Child clinical psychologists interested in group therapy should receive specialized training in the theory and practice of group psychotherapy with children.

One form of behavior therapy focuses specifically on the child's problematic behaviors. The psychologist intervenes by providing parents or teachers with a systematic plan for modifying those behaviors. This plan may include reinforcement systems and constructive consequences to help children develop more appropriate behaviors. Specific problems a behavior therapist might address include social inhibition, problems with aggression or impulsivity, or poor work habits. Child clinical psychologists who use behavior therapy techniques seek to understand the function of problem behaviors so that they can target those behaviors for modification.

Cognitive behavior therapy (CBT), another form of behavior therapy, focuses on the child's cognitions and on the relationship between the child's faulty thoughts and assumptions that contribute to behavioral or social problems. CBT is often recommended for children with a range of anxiety concerns, depression, and ADHD.

Child clinical psychologists who are behavior therapists often work actively with parents to teach them methods of reinforcing positive behaviors, such as sticker charts or praise, and ways to help their child rethink negative thought patterns and engage in positive self-talk. Parents also are taught appropriate responses to their child's negative behaviors, such as the use of logical consequences, time-outs, and ignoring. Behavior therapists tend to be actively involved with the child's classroom teacher so that the child's problem behaviors at school are addressed. In addition to facilitating better school adjustment, working with the school also ensures consistency between the home and school environments—that is, that teachers and parents are both on the same page in addressing the child's behavior problems.

## TESTING

In addition to providing psychotherapy for children and adolescents, child clinical psychologists also perform psychological testing evaluations. These often are called *psychodiagnostic evaluations* because they are used for the diagnosis of emotional, educational, and cognitive problems. Psychological testing of youth (and adults) is the exclusive domain of psychologists. Psychological testing involves the use of a series of assessment instruments designed to evaluate intellectual and social-emotional functioning. Testing provides information that cannot be obtained through face-to-face interviews. It is, in its way, an X-ray into a child's emotional inner world and cognitive functioning.

The testing instruments include intelligence scales to determine intelligence quotient (IQ), and cognitive strengths and weaknesses, and potential problems in learning, including formal learning disabilities and emotional factors that may be affecting a child's learning. Testing instruments also measure problems with focus and attention as well as diagnose executive functioning disorder and attention-deficit disorder (ADD).

Many projective instruments, such as the Rorschach inkblot technique and projective drawings, are also included in the child clinical psychologist's battery of tests. Projective assessment techniques yield information about the child's unconscious functioning, personality, areas of underlying conflict, and social and emotional strengths and vulnerabilities. Often psychopathology is revealed through this form of testing when it is not accessible through other tests or diagnostic interviews.

## OTHER ACTIVITIES

In addition to engaging in psychotherapy and psychological testing, many child clinical psychologists use their training in other ways. They might teach child-related courses, such as child and adolescent psychopathology and child development, in a college or graduate school setting. They might perform research on topics pertinent to childhood, such as the effects of day care on development, ADD, screens addiction and its implications for brain development, and eating disorders in preteens and teenagers. Child clinical psychologists may work as consultants to agencies that provide services to children other than psychotherapy. Child clinical psychologists may engage in several of these activities simultaneously; they might, for example, practice psychotherapy and provide agency consultation as well as perform university-based research and produce professional writing.

Many child clinical psychologists serve as consultants in a variety of settings. They may work with the staffs of residential child treatment centers, agencies working with at-risk teens, agencies involved with immigrant children, pediatric departments in hospitals, and forensic youth facilities. Child clinical psychologists also serve as consultants to public and private preschools and elementary and secondary schools. They provide child-related presentations to parent groups at schools, churches, and other organizations. These presentations may cover a wide array of topics, including safety from perpetrators, building self-esteem in children, sibling rivalry, sex education, appropriate use of electronics, and the challenges of raising a teenager in the social media age.

Child clinical psychologists also may consult with the media on a variety of topics of concern to children and their parents. These topics may be of general interest to parents or a specific response to a crisis in the community or the world, such as abductions or terrorist attacks. Sometimes an unusual opportunity for consultation may arise. For example, a child clinical psychologist might be asked by a novelist or screenwriter to review the writer's portrayal of a child character, or a psychologist working with an adolescent, for the accuracy of the depiction.

## *Work Settings*

One of the pleasures for a child clinical psychologist is the ability to work in a variety of settings and with a variety of ages, including adults. Many child clinical psychologists do at least some amount of direct clinical service, including psychotherapy and psychological testing. When most people think about child clinical psychology as a career, they picture having a private practice. Although this is certainly the most common setting in which child clinical psychologists work, it is far from the only one. There are also rewarding and fascinating opportunities for clinical and consulting work in preschools, public mental health centers, short- and long-term psychiatric treatment facilities, juvenile detention and other forensic facilities, and various medical settings. They can also focus on specific populations, for example, immigrant children, youngsters who have experienced trauma and abuse, adopted children, and children and teenagers with parents in the military.

A private practitioner may have a solo practice or work independently within a group setting. Solo practitioners enjoy the independence and flexibility that come with having one's own office. Some child clinical psychologists enjoy the diversity of a group practice, where they have the opportunity to work with psychiatrists, social workers, and adult as well as other child clinical psychologists. They enjoy the professional contact with colleagues and the opportunity for sharing and discussing clinical cases.

Public mental health settings are another common venue for child clinical psychologists. In community mental health centers (CMHCs), for example, they engage in the delivery of preventive mental health care, emergency psychological services, and direct treatment to children of all ages and their parents. They supervise students and junior colleagues, perform psychological testing, and consult to community agencies. Many child clinical psychologists enjoy the diversity of the patient population seen in public settings and feel a commitment to serve families who otherwise could not afford mental health services. They also enjoy the fast-paced work environment that most CMHCs provide and the opportunity to be surrounded by a large group of colleagues.

Inpatient treatment facilities (psychiatric hospitals) provide support, safety, and short-term intensive treatment to patients who are severely emotionally disturbed, at high risk of self-harm, or in an acute psychological crisis. One of the reasons to hospitalize a youngster is so that he or she and the family can receive multiple modalities of treatment and psychopharmacological intervention quickly and concurrently to meet the urgency of their situation. Children also are admitted to an inpatient facility for observation and extended diagnostic evaluation in a controlled environment.

Residential treatment centers are another venue for child clinical psychologists. Here, youngsters who cannot be managed because of their behavior and psychopathology are treated in an around-the-clock setting. Child clinical psychologists provide testing and individual and family therapy as well as group treatment.

Day treatment programs primarily are utilized posthospitalization. Youngsters live at home but come to the hospital, most often for the length of a school day, where they receive intensive group therapy offered by child clinical psychologists. The patients receive other forms of treatment, usually including the family, and psychiatric monitoring as well.

Forensic-related work includes child custody evaluations (which involve separate assessments of each parent, each child, and each child together with each parent), ability-to-parent assessments, forensic psychological evaluations of juvenile offenders, and court testimony in criminal and domestic proceedings. Child clinical psychologists may have the opportunity to provide psychotherapy with these populations.

Medical settings offer another venue for practice. A child clinical psychologist may work in a hospital emergency room with families experiencing psychological crisis. Direct intervention and psychological or psychiatric triage ("where should this family go next?") are the two main activities of a hospital emergency room child psychologist.

Child clinical psychologists also work in the pediatrics department of a general medical center or a specialized hospital department, such as pediatric oncology. There they can work directly with children with a range of medical problems, from anxiety about a routine tonsillectomy to the challenges of battling cancer. Play therapy often is used with very young children. The treatment performed in this setting is necessarily short-term, focused therapy centered on the medical issue. Child clinical psychologists also conduct testing for emotional readiness for difficult medical interventions, provide differential diagnoses (i.e., rule out an emotional basis for an apparent physical symptom, or assess level of depression and anxiety while undergoing difficult treatments), consult with medical staff regarding the psychological issues of hospitalized children of differing ages, and do consultative and supportive work with parents. Work with parents may be as simple as helping them talk with their child about an impending surgical intervention or as complex as working with parents whose child is dying.

A child clinical psychologist may work in a pediatrician's office, where he or she functions as a consultant to parents regarding developmental and social-emotional concerns about their children. Within that setting, the child clinical psychologist might see the child directly, in addition to the parents, to determine possible treatment needs and to facilitate appropriate referrals.

Many child clinical psychologists work in academic settings. They seek an academic environment because it enables them to teach, do research, write, and mentor students who are interested in a career in psychology. Many child clinical psychologists particularly value the mentoring role. Of course, child clinical psychologists in academic settings also may have a private practice.

Child clinical psychologists teach at both the undergraduate and the graduate levels. They may teach such topics as child psychotherapy, child development, child psychopathology, psychodiagnostic assessment and testing, and other related courses. In undergraduate courses, they may provide an introduction to child psychopathology and child development and a broad survey of relevant child-related issues.

Undergraduate coursework is not intended to train students to be child clinical psychologists; rather, it provides the building blocks for graduate work in clinical psychology to students who want to become child clinicians. Child clinical psychologists also are employed in graduate school settings, providing supervised training to students who seek to function autonomously as child clinical psychologists.

Academic settings also afford an excellent venue for performing research in areas related to children. Child clinical psychologists who work in academic settings are formally encouraged to engage in research projects relevant to their specific interests. Psychology students are often helpful in assisting their professors in conducting research. This is not only a mutually beneficial arrangement but also a way in which professors can mentor students who are particularly interested in child clinical research. Participation in research provides students with an invaluable opportunity to learn about designing, conducting, and analyzing clinical research. They also learn the essential tools for differentiating well-designed studies from poor ones. A child clinical psychologist needs to be able to recognize good research from poor research.

Child clinical psychologists also engage in research in nonacademic settings. Child-oriented nonprofit organizations, government agencies, and public interest and social policy groups are examples of such settings. Child clinical psychologists might research such issues as the effects of different types of day care on children's social, emotional, and academic development; factors that affect the development of self-esteem in children; effectiveness of different types of treatment; effectiveness of different forms of discipline; effects of various aspects of social, televised, and print media; development of attachment disorders; and effects of parental trauma, substance abuse, depression, and domestic violence on children's psychological and social functioning.

# Academic and Clinical Preparation

Training to become a child clinical psychologist requires at least 3 years of formal graduate-level academic preparation. This is ideally an American Psychological Association–approved graduate program in either child clinical psychology or clinical psychology that offers opportunities for child specialization. Graduate programs include coursework, successful completion of comprehensive examinations, practicum (externship) placements, a full-time full-year clinical internship, and the writing and defense of a doctoral dissertation.

## ACADEMIC PREPARATION

In most states, to call yourself a clinical psychologist, it is necessary to have a PhD or PsyD in psychology, most commonly in clinical psychology. Licensure is necessary before you can practice on your own. Some states require licensure before an individual can refer to herself as a psychologist or a clinical psychologist.

Some clinical psychologists have a doctorate in another area of psychology and then go on for specialized training in the clinical field. In particular, there are child clinical psychologists whose original doctoral degree in psychology was in human development, child development, or personality development. After they received their degree, they realized that they were most interested in working clinically with children, and they pursued formal specialized training in the assessment and treatment of children.

Academic courses cover the entire age range from infancy through late adolescence and usually include core areas, such as child development and theory, child psychopathology, neuropsychology, intellectual and cognitive assessment, personality assessment, and theories and techniques of psychotherapy with children and their parents. Academic training also includes courses about the child's role in the family system. It is important to understand the child's social and emotional development within the context of the family as well as the family dynamics that have an impact on the child.

Child clinical psychologists are trained to utilize the most recent systems of diagnosing pediatric disorders. They currently are the *Diagnostic and Statistical Manual of Mental Disorders* (*DSM–5*; American Psychiatric Association, 2015) and the *International Classification of Diseases-Psychological and Behavioral Conditions* (*ICD–10*; World Health Organization, 2016). They also must be familiar with the requirements of the Health Insurance Portability and Accountability Act (HIPAA), designed to protect patient confidentiality in the age of technology.

The academic culmination of clinical psychology training is the completion of a doctoral dissertation, often in an area of interest to the student. In most programs, this requires a research study, although a comprehensive clinical dissertation is sometimes substituted. The doctoral dissertation is an intensive, lengthy, closely mentored project, and the student must defend his or her work before a number of faculty members.

## CLINICAL PREPARATION

Clinical training includes both the practical experience (practicum placements) undertaken concurrent with the first 3 academic years (or sometimes just the 2nd and 3rd years), and a full-time clinical internship. The internship requires successful completion of formal coursework, practicum placements, and comprehensive academic examinations. Practicum placements provide students with a variety of supervised clinical experiences, usually with children, adolescents, and adults, with an emphasis on youth and their families. Students can be placed in many different settings, including CMHCs, hospitals (both medical and psychiatric), therapeutic nurseries, juvenile detention centers, university counseling centers, and a variety of public and private treatment-focused agencies. Practicum placements are usually about 20 hours per week and may last one to two semesters, sometimes including summers, before the student is rotated to another placement setting. Internship settings are quite similar to practicum settings; the difference is that they require a full-time (at least 40 hours per week) commitment and are always 1 year in length.

Internships are generally a more intense and comprehensive experience in that students work with more difficult patients, a significantly larger caseload, additional seminars, and a greater number of intensive (and sometimes personal) hours of individual supervision. During the internship year, students are usually strongly urged to begin their own treatment. Early internship experiences are closely supervised, but by the end of the internship, the student begins to function more autonomously in preparation for beginning a career.

# *Personal Attributes Needed for Success*

Anyone pursuing a graduate degree in clinical psychology needs to have compassion, empathy, the ability to absorb intense emotions, and skill in relating comfortably to a wide range of people from diverse cultures. Intellectual curiosity and a twofold interest are required: an interest in alleviating the distress caused by psychological problems as well as an interest in the intellectual challenge of figuring people out.

Certain characteristics are particularly necessary in the child clinical psychology field. The first and most obvious is an interest, even a delight, in children and in the multitude of ways they make sense of the world and express themselves. Children know when someone is really interested in them and are more likely to respond in psychotherapy when they sense a genuine connection with the therapist. In addition, child clinical psychologists must have the following characteristics:

- They must be comfortable with their own sense of playfulness without falling into the trap of becoming a playmate. Child clinical psychologists need to be able to be in the moment and involved with the child's concerns but at the same time not get overly caught up in them. This allows them to work with youngsters and parents while maintaining perspective.

- They must have a sense of humor and the ability to adapt it across the age span and across different types of personalities. Similarly, a lack of self-consciousness and a comfort with play and playful thinking are essential.

- They must be quick-witted and flexible, because children think fast and are fluid in their style of relatedness. No two children are alike, and they are always clinically challenging us.

- They must be able to empathize and work with parents and not blame them for their children's problems. In our experience, some clinicians are too prone to see parents as the bad guys, whereas in reality, most parents have their children's best interests at heart and are doing the best they can. Despite this reality, some children do have difficulties and need professional help, and their parents are in need of guidance as well.

- Child clinical psychologists who specialize in play therapy need to have a particular comfort with interactive, symbolic, and fantasy play. They might find themselves being a talking truck, or having a conversation with a misbehaving dog, or acting like a crying baby. This needs to be done without feeling foolish or uncomfortable.

- An insight-oriented play therapist particularly needs to be sensitive to and comfortable with the fact that the play has symbolic meaning. In other words, a tea party is not just a tea party with therapist participation; it is an act of communication from the child to the psychologist. It is just the same when playing war with action figures: It's not just a war between toys; it is about something. It has a meaning beyond what is visible. Thus, the child clinical psychologist must be able to work with play as a metaphor.

- Although all psychologists must be self-aware and have their personal issues well resolved and contained, child clinical psychologists have an additional challenge. Child clinical psychologists must be comfortable with their own childhood histories; their early relationships with their parents; and, if relevant, their own current role as a parent. The unaware child clinical psychologist is at a severe handicap in working successfully with children and parents.

## Financial Compensation

Careers in clinical child psychology are obviously diverse, and so is the financial compensation these professionals receive. On the basis of what we have observed in the field, professionals in child and adolescent psychology tend to earn within the $50,000 to $300,000 range. Variations in compensation depend on whether they are employed by an agency or work in solo private practice, the amount of psychodiagnostic or psycho-neurological evaluations they perform, whether they are primarily practitioners or administrators, and what part of the country in which they practice.

Private practitioners typically earn the highest incomes and can have a quite comfortable lifestyle. The amount they earn depends on the number of hours they work, the geographic location and type of patients seen in their practice, and whether they choose to have junior clinicians working for them.

The salary range in public agencies, community mental health centers, and medical settings tends to be somewhat lower (as for many other careers in those settings). Don't forget, however, that there are many other benefits in public sector employment, including health insurance and paid leave. Clinical and other professional benefits include the following: working with a diverse population of clients; having greater access to colleagues for peer supervision, support, and personal connections; and having a sense of professional community rather than the isolation of private practice. Child clinical psychologists working in other settings, such as academia, research, and consultation, generally fall somewhere in the middle of the salary range. Again, this depends on the particular university, the funding sources of the research, or the type of consultation in which one engages. (And if you should write that million-seller self-help book for parents, one never knows!)

## Choosing To Be a Child Clinical Psychologist: Our Personal Stories

Although our backgrounds are quite different, we had remarkably similar reasons for deciding to become child clinical psychologists. We have both, from early in our lives, been interested in understanding why people do what they do. In high school, this interest deepened, and we realized that it had a name: psychology. We both took high school courses in psychology and found them quite interesting. At this time, during our adolescence, we both did volunteer work with children. Nemiroff worked with intellectually challenged children in a residential facility, and Annunziata worked in a pediatric play program in a medical setting. Our volunteer experiences, along with our abiding interest in what makes people tick and our high school psychology classes, led us to enter college as psychology majors.

For 4 years in college, we took an array of courses in the various fields of psychology. It became clearer to us that children were our primary interest and that we wanted to pursue advanced education and ultimately a career in child clinical psychology. We went to graduate programs where we could specialize in clinical work with children, but we were trained extensively in work with adults as well. Within our programs, we were able to emphasize psychotherapy and psychological testing as opposed to research and teaching. We also both chose to pursue our interest in insight-oriented theoretical and technical approaches to psychotherapy. We were fortunate to have excellent practica and internships that focused on work with children and that provided excellent experience with adults across the age span as well. Thus, although we concentrated on children, the age range of our patients was 2.5 to 85 years old. We were grateful at the time for our training and supervision, and we continue to feel grateful for it on an almost daily basis.

After graduate school, we were both lucky enough to find positions that allowed us to continue our focus on children while also working actively with adult patients. We both began in community mental centers; serendipity, in fact, led us to the same CMHC, which is where we met. Now we both work in separate private practice settings and also teach, supervise, consult, and write.

## A TYPICAL WEEK IN THE LIFE OF A CHILD CLINICAL PSYCHOLOGIST

People often ask us, "What is a typical day like for you as a child clinical psychologist?" A typical week, rather than a day, is a better representation of the variety of our activities. In a typical week we might do the following:

- Spend several days seeing a variety of patients; our patients are diverse in both age and types of problem; within any given day, we might sit on the floor in a playroom with a 3-year-old or enjoy the comfort of our ergonomic office chairs while talking with a 33-year-old; we also might see the parents of the children and teenagers who we treat as well as a couple experiencing marital difficulties and an entire family in formal family therapy. We also treat diverse problems in our patients, ranging from high-functioning patients with mild anxiety and depression to children and adults who have significantly more psychopathology and problematic behaviors.

- Spend time on professional writing (such as the writing of this chapter), although generally we write books for children and parents (i.e., bibliotherapy).
- Spend time preparing and delivering a lecture for students, other professionals, or postgraduates; we might also give a talk to a community parent organization, school, or church or synagogue group on a topic pertaining to children.
- Engage in the supervision of less-experienced clinicians.
- Participate in our own continuing education, including formal presentations and peer supervision groups
- Visit a patient's school for observation or to consult with his teachers.
- Consult with an agency that provides services to children to help staff deal with particularly problematic clients and develop their clinical skills.

As you can see, our week is quite full, meaningful, and wonderfully varied. This is one of the advantages of being a child clinical psychologist. We are never bored.

## PROS AND CONS: ADVANTAGES AND DISADVANTAGES OF THE CAREER

Like any career, child clinical psychology has both positive and negative aspects. We, of course, believe that the advantages far outweigh the disadvantages. Given that the disadvantages are so few, we're going to start with them. Don't be dissuaded.

One of the hardest things about being a clinical psychologist is the burden of listening to and absorbing the pain and suffering of our patients and listening to their difficult histories. It is no different in work with young children, although it is sometimes harder to see a little one suffer, whether it is from extreme anxiety and depression or from the horrors of child abuse. Thus, burnout is an unfortunate hazard of our profession. Burnout can be prevented, however, if one takes proper self-care steps.

Child clinical psychology is different from other clinical work because it involves the added challenge of working with each child's or adolescent's parents. Although most parents are extremely supportive of their children's treatment and are open to the parent guidance that we always provide as part of the child's treatment, at times, work with parents can be the most frustrating aspect of child psychotherapy. It is particularly difficult when parents won't make the necessary changes, either in the family or in themselves, to facilitate the child's emotional growth and behavioral progress. The final disadvantage is that child clinical psychologists often need to spend much time outside of psychotherapy sessions on the phone in case coordination with schools and parents.

The advantages of being a child clinical psychologist, again, far outweigh the disadvantages. This is extremely meaningful life work, and it is most gratifying to help people with their problems and to make a difference in the lives of children and their families. Work with children is uniquely satisfying because you have the opportunity to make a difference early in a child's life and thus to prevent considerable later suffering and hardship.

The work is intellectually stimulating, emotionally engaging, and financially rewarding. Work with children is unique because you can influence the whole system that surrounds a child, including schools, parents, and child-care providers. Thus, you can make a huge impact on a little person's development that helps him well into his adult life. Sometimes a child's therapy alters the entire course of his life.

We've saved the best for last: Work with children is just plain fun. It engages our sense of playfulness and creativity as we sit with a child and participate in his or her emotional growth and psychological development.

## Recommended Readings

Carroll, J., Schaefer, C., McCormick, J., & Ohnogi, A. (Eds.). (2005). *Children talk about play therapy.* Northvale, NJ: Jason Aronson.

Collier, L. (2015). Helping immigrant children heal. *Monitor on Psychology, 46,* 58–62. Washington, DC: American Psychological Association.

Drotar, D. (Ed.). (2000). *Handbook of research methods in pediatric and child psychology.* New York, NY: Kluwer Academic/Plenum. http://dx.doi.org/10.1007/978-1-4615-4165-3

Mikeshell, R. H., & Lusterman, D. D., & McDaniel, S. H. (Eds.). (1995). *Integrating family therapy: Handbook of family psychology and systems theory.* Washington, DC: American Psychological Association.

O'Dessie Oliver, J. (1997). *Play therapy: A comprehensive guide.* Northvale, NJ: Jason Aronson.

Siegel, D. (2013). *Brainstorm: The power and purpose of the teenage brain.* New York, NY: Jeremy P. Tarcher/Penguin.

Sweeney, D. S., & Homeyer, L. E. (Eds.). (1999). *The handbook of group play therapy.* San Francisco, CA: Jossey-Bass.

Walker, C. E., & Roberts, M. C. (Eds.). (2001). *Handbook of clinical child psychology* (3rd ed.). New York, NY: Wiley.

Watson, T. S., & Gresham, F. M. (Eds.). (1998). *Handbook of child behavior therapy.* New York, NY: Plenum Press. http://dx.doi.org/10.1007/978-1-4615-5323-6

## References

American Psychiatric Association. (2015). *Diagnostic and statistical manual of mental disorders* (5th ed.). Arlington, VA: Author.

World Health Organization. (2016). *International classification of diseases–psychological and behavioral conditions (ICD–10).* Geneva, Switzerland: Author.

*Gregory A. Hinrichsen and Michele J. Karel*

# Geropsychologists
*Psychologists Specializing in Aging* | 10

At a family gathering your grandmother asked if
she could speak with you privately. She's concerned
about your grandfather. He's just not his normal self.
Since retiring a year ago, he has lost interest in doing
things, sleeps a lot, seems sad and is irritable, and
dwells on past disappointments. Furthermore, your
grandmother said now she and your grandfather

During almost 40 years in the field of aging, Gregory A. Hinrichsen has
contributed to public policy as an American Psychological Association Con-
gressional Fellow in the U.S. Senate and as National Mental Health Director
for Community Mental Health in the U.S. Department of Veterans Affairs.
Currently, he is assistant clinical professor, Department of Geriatrics and
Palliative Medicine, Icahn School of Medicine at Mount Sinai and Associate
Clinical Professor, Department of Psychiatry and Behavioral Science, Albert
Einstein College of Medicine.

Michele J. Karel is a clinical geropsychologist. She received her PhD in clinical
psychology from the University of Southern California in 1994. She serves
as psychogeriatrics coordinator for Mental Health Services in VA Central
Office. She manages the STAR-VA training program—an interdisciplinary,
behavioral intervention for managing challenging behaviors in CLC residents
with dementia.

http://dx.doi.org/10.1037/15960-011
*Career Paths in Psychology: Where Your Degree Can Take You, Third Edition*,
R. J. Sternberg (Editor)

aren't getting along well with each other. This just doesn't sound like the grandfather you know—the one who was decorated for his military service in Vietnam, founded his own successful business, volunteered in his community, and raised four children. She asks you, "Honey, I know you are majoring in psychology. Is this normal? Can psychologists help someone like your grandfather?"

Although you might feel uncomfortable being cast into the role of the family psychologist, nonetheless, what might you say? What can psychologists do to improve the quality of life for older adults? If you've thought that your career path might be psychology, it's unlikely that you've considered the possibility of specializing in geriatric psychology—or what is called professional geropsychology.

With an undergraduate degree in psychology and hopes to enter a graduate psychology program, Hinrichsen had not considered a career in geropsychology either. Knowing that he needed more social service-related work to enhance his chances of getting into graduate school, in the 1970s, he took a job as a social service outreach worker to older adults in the Boston's Fenway neighborhood. He and the other outreach workers went door to door talking with older adults in their homes. He learned what decades of research studies have documented: Most older adults are remarkably resilient. Some of the older people he met included Tom, whose house he had informally turned into a residence for older gay men; Betty, who was a community activist who helped with an effort to stop landlords from burning down their unprofitable rental buildings; Arlene, who had forged a successful career during an era when women were told that their place was at home and not the workplace; and John, who had been a university professor and had a shelf full of books that he had written.

Hinrichsen also learned what geropsychologists know: A minority of older adults run into problems in later life for which they can benefit by assistance. For example, Joan, who was severely depressed but, after being connected to mental health services, resumed a previously active and meaningful life; and Carla, who had not left her apartment for 5 years because she had been robbed on the street and feared getting robbed again but who was gently coaxed out of her apartment with the help of a mental health worker.

Karel was fairly unusual in discovering an interest in geropsychology early in her career, during college. As a psychology major, she was challenged to choose a topic for her junior and senior year independent research. During that time, her grandmother was suffering from Alzheimer's disease (a condition that was not well understood by the family at the time) and her favorite aunt was busy caring for grandma.

Although Karel enjoyed her college courses in child and adolescent development, she was struck that no coursework was available on issues facing aging families. She decided to focus her independent research projects on issues related to aging and mental health and on family caregiving for older adults. She also started volunteering at a local nursing home where she met many older adults who maintained a sense of humor and appreciation for life despite their health or cognitive limitations as well as some who seemed quite sad or angry about their life situation. She came to realize that even people in wheelchairs who seemed fairly withdrawn had interesting life stories to share if you made the effort to approach and listen to them.

Geropsychologists find their careers meaningful for many reasons. Geropsychology is personally rewarding: Helping older adults overcome late life obstacles and enhance the quality of life for themselves and their families can bring a deep sense of satisfaction. Geropsychology is intellectually rewarding; many factors come to bear in understanding the forces that shape the lives of older people. Geropsychologists assess (and some study) how life experiences, biology, culture, economics, and other factors affect functioning and adaptation in late life. Abundant professional opportunities exist: 10,000 people turn age 65 each day and, by the year 2030, 20% of the U.S. population will be 65 years of age and older. Furthermore, there is a shortage of geropsychology and other geriatric care specialists (Institute of Medicine, 2008, 2012). Geropsychology is personally relevant: While young now, some day—if you are fortunate—you will be old and your experiences as a psychologist likely will enrich your later years. And, if your family members do turn to you for advice on late life issues, you'll be well prepared.

## Professional Activities of Geropsychologists

The vast majority of geropsychologists have graduated from doctoral programs of clinical or counseling psychology. Most geropsychologists provide services to older adults, their families, or the teams that provide care for older adults in health care or residential settings. In addition to providing services to clients, the range of activities in which geropsychologists may engage reflects those for which psychologists are often prepared: research, teaching, consultation, and advocacy. Being a psychologist or geropsychologist affords the opportunity to shape your career in directions that are most meaningful to you.

## SETTINGS OF CARE

Geropsychologists who provide direct services to older adults and their families usually work in independent practice (also called *private practice*) or within organizations. Organizational practice includes work in hospitals, clinics, universities, and other settings that provide health and mental health related services to older people. It is worth noting that the Veterans Health Administration of the U.S. Department of Veterans Affairs (VA) provides health care to military service veterans and is a major employer of psychologists, including many who work in geriatric care programs.

A geropsychologist in independent practice often will have an office where older people are seen for psychological evaluation and treatment or may independently provide services in another setting, such as residential care. Common examples of residential care facilities include in the older adult's home, assisted living (independent residential living with some help), and long-term care (often referred to as *nursing homes*, where older adults who have serious and often chronic health or cognitive health problems live and receive care).

For geropsychologists who work in organizations, a wide range of possible settings exists. Some work in mental health programs, such as outpatient clinics, partial mental health hospital programs (for those who need more care than can be offered on an outpatient basis), or inpatient mental health care settings. Some geropsychologists work in health care settings such as primary health care, rehabilitation programs for people with medical problems (e.g., stroke), medical inpatient services, and long-term care residences. Of note, a growing area of practice for psychologists, including geropsychologists, is *integrated care*, wherein psychologists are important members of the health care team in these traditionally medical care settings. Research increasingly shows that physical and mental health are closely interrelated; treating mental health problems often leads to improvements in physical health and functioning, so including behavioral or mental health professionals in health care settings can be a great benefit (American Psychological Association, 2008).

## ACTIVITIES IN WHICH GEROPSYCHOLOGISTS ENGAGE

What geropsychologists do often includes the following activities:

> *Clinical assessment.* Geropsychologists make an assessment of the concerns raised by older adults or the people who care about them. The geropsychologist will talk with the older adult to get a history and characterize the nature of concerns, learn about past and current life, understand cultural factors that are rel-

evant to the person, obtain information about current medical problems and medications, and determine whether the individual has a mental disorder. Psychological instruments may be administered that help to evaluate psychological issues, including depression, anxiety, substance misuse such as alcohol, personality, cognitive functioning, and everyday decision making and functional abilities. Optimally, assessment (and later treatment) efforts are coordinated with other health service professionals, often the primary care medical doctor or sometimes a team of professionals. The assessment generally will lead to a plan for providing services to the older person to overcome problems, achieve well-being, and maximize potential (American Psychological Association, 2014).

*Psychological treatments.* Geropsychologists provide psychological treatments to older adults. Psychological treatments are typically in the form of psychotherapy. Psychotherapies may be in individual, couple, family, and group format. Geropsychologists sometimes do an analysis of environmental factors that contribute to an older adult's emotional distress and behavioral difficulties and then implement a plan to change those environmental factors. Research has found that many of the psychotherapies that were developed for younger adults are effective for older adults (Scogin & Shah, 2012).

*Consultation.* Geropsychologists are sometimes consultants. Medical care providers might consult with the geropsychologist about how to understand and manage psychologically relevant issues in their patients (e.g., not following through with medical recommendations, changes in mental abilities). A residential care facility might ask a geropsychologist about how to best respond to a resident who is having difficulties adjusting to living in the facility. A community agency that serves older adults might ask the geropsychologist to develop a program to screen for depression in its clients, to explain how to best deliver mental health services for those who are depressed, and then to evaluate whether the program worked.

*Supervision and training.* Geropsychologists often play an important role in training others to develop skills for providing clinical care for older adults and their families (Knight, Karel, Hinrichsen, Qualls, & Duffy, 2009). Geropsychologists teach and supervise the clinical work of psychologists-in-training, including in graduate school programs as well as doctoral internships, postdoctoral fellowships, and even for midcareer professional psychologists who are looking to develop skills to serve older adults. Likewise, geropsychologists often provide training in interprofessional care settings, helping trainees and professionals in medicine, nursing, social work, and other fields to learn about mental health and aging.

*Blended and other roles.* Many geropsychologists blend a variety of roles. For example, a university-based geropsychologist might do research, teaching, and consultation and also provide some psychological services to older adults. Some geropsychologists who primarily provide services to older adults integrate the collection of research data into their work and subsequently publish the findings and present them at professional meetings. Some geropsychologists advocate for older adults by engaging in efforts to educate governmental officials and legislators about the needs of older adults and propose policies and programs that will better serve those needs (Hinrichsen, 2010). Some geropsychologists direct local or national programs related to the mental health needs of older people.

There are many opportunities for leadership in the field of geropsychology because it is a relatively young field. Geropsychology students and early career geropsychologists are making important contributions to the field and have access to mentoring from a particularly generative and generous community of geropsychologists. As an example, Karel spent the first 16 years of her career working as a geropsychology clinician and supervisor at a VA Medical Center. With excellent mentoring and collaboration with more senior geropsychologists, she had the opportunity to publish in the field and cochair a major national geropsychology training conference (Knight et al., 2009). She later took a position with the national VA Central Office to help coordinate the integration of psychologists into two national geriatric care programs: Home Based Primary Care (where the care team provides primary care in the homes of veterans who are too sick to get to the medical center) and Community Living Centers (nursing home care settings). Opportunities for leadership and to make a difference abound in this field, for those who are motivated to do so.

## OLDER ADULT CONCERNS THAT ARE OFTEN A FOCUS OF TREATMENT

Older adults often seek treatment from a psychologist because they are dealing with emotional distress. Sometimes a family member or staff person has urged the older person to see the psychologist. Common examples of emotional distress include depression, anxiety, subjective stress, or unhappiness. Distress may be associated with problems with day-to-day functioning, sleeping, fatigue, changes in appetite, and other issues. Some older adults seek psychological assistance because they feel their mental abilities are changing. For example, an older person believes his or her memory is not as good as when he or she was younger.

Certain life problems are often the focus of psychotherapy with older adults. Life transitions are common in late life. Some examples include retirement, moving to a new residence, the onset or exacerbation of medical problems, and care for a spouse or partner with medical or cognitive problems. Conflict with others is a frequent focus of psychotherapy. Examples include conflict with a spouse or partner, adult child, sibling, friend, or residential staff. Some older adults experience the death of an important person, such as a spouse or partner, sibling, adult child, or friend, and have difficulties coming to terms with the loss. Social isolation can be a focus of psychotherapy. Some older adults have longstanding problems making or keeping connections with other people. For others, life circumstances have changed and, for the first time in their lives, they find it challenging to establish new relationships. As noted earlier, an assessment will precede psychotherapy. Taking into account the older adult's values, abilities, and goals, the psychologist will propose a plan of treatment. For example, the geropsychologist might conduct a course of cognitive behavioral therapy (CBT) to reduce depression and anxiety symptoms and improve the older person's capacity to deal with the onset of medical problems.

## A Typical Day for a Geropsychologist

A typical day for a geropsychologist would be one that is varied. For most, the work is satisfying and interesting. For many geropsychologists, job satisfaction comes from the fact that the clients with whom they work are quite different from each other and come to later adulthood with the accumulation of a lifetime of experience. For example, Hinrichsen provides clinical services in a large outpatient geriatric medical clinic that is part of an urban medical center. The physicians in the medical clinic are all geriatricians—medical doctors who specialize in older adults—or are in training to become geriatricians. The average age of patients in the clinic is 85 years. For this author, a typical day would look something like this.

Morning: Provide consultation to two staff members who he is teaching how to conduct an evidence-based psychotherapy for depression (interpersonal psychotherapy, IPT; Hinrichsen & Clougherty, 2006) that has been found effective with older adults. Listen to portions of audiotaped sessions and give feedback to the staff members on their psychotherapeutic work with older adults.

Complete administrative tasks, including returning patient calls and e-mails. Work on an ongoing study of the usefulness of cognitive behavioral therapy for insomnia (CBT-I), an evidence-based treatment for sleep problems in older adults. Also, speak with a medical doctor of a patient who he will see for an evaluation in the afternoon.

Afternoon: Patient 1. See an older adult in psychotherapy who has a 10-year history of chronic insomnia who is being treated with CBT-I. The patient has shown considerable improvement. The therapist reviews a sleep diary from the prior week and then discusses with the patient a plan to finish up psychotherapy.

Patient 2. Conduct an assessment of a woman who is highly anxious because she believes she has Alzheimer's disease. The psychologist had spoken earlier in the day with the patient's primary care doctor who has doubts that her patient has Alzheimer's disease and thinks the patient needs education about changes in cognitive abilities over the life span and instruction in anxiety management techniques.

Patient 3. Continue psychotherapy with a woman struggling with depression and anxiety who is being treated with chemotherapy for metastatic cancer. In this session, the therapist works with the patient to better handle conflict with her sister over the choices the patient has made about her medical care and her need for help.

Patient 4. Continue IPT with a woman who is depressed because of problems in adjusting to living with her daughter and her family. Because of failing eyesight, recently she moved in with her daughter. She is distressed that her daughter and her children do not include her in the family in a way that she had hoped. She is having frequent arguments with her daughter and scolds her grandchildren who she believes avoid her.

At the end of the day, take part in a conference call with a geropsychology organization of which he is a member of the board. The call's purpose is to continue work on a project to create geropsychology educational opportunities for psychologists interested in providing services to older people but who have no formal training in aging.

## Potential Advantages and Disadvantages of Being a Geropsychologist

As noted earlier, there are many advantages to being a geropsychologist: taking part in a variety of roles, experiencing satisfaction in helping improve the quality of life of many older adults, serving a population of older adults that will grow significantly in number in the coming years and for which there are not enough providers, being part of a field that is relatively new, and learning lessons through your work that may prepare you for a productive and satisfying life when you are older.

There are some potential disadvantages. Some psychologists find it uncomfortable working with older adults because they have concerns about their own aging or the aging of close relatives. Some psychologists may not find working with persons with cognitive impairment such as Alzheimer's disease interesting or challenging because there is no cure for the condition but rather it is managed in collaboration with family members and other professionals. The problems of some older adults are highly complex and require attention to medical, social, environmental, cognitive, and psychological factors. Some psychologists may find this complexity frustrating. It's not clear how systems of care will evolve to meet the needs of what will soon be a large population of older people, nor is it clear how reimbursement for mental health services might change in the future. Medicare—the federal program of health insurance for people 65 years of age and older as well as younger people with disabilities—pays for most mental health services for older people. Some believe that Medicare does not adequately reimburse geropsychologists for their services especially because some efforts on behalf of the older patient—such as coordination of care—are not paid for directly.

## PREPARATION NEEDED TO BECOME A GEROPSYCHOLOGIST

If you are now an undergraduate in college, it would be helpful to take a course that includes topics related to aging. For example, some universities and colleges have courses on psychological development throughout adulthood (courses usually referred to as adult development and aging). Other courses might have a more sociological focus that review societal forces that shape adulthood and older adulthood (often called social gerontology). Some professors integrate aging issues into survey courses on psychopathology; psychological development; and even demographics, economics, and biology.

It can be especially interesting and satisfying to have experience meeting and talking with older adults. Some colleges and universities offer service programs to older adults who may want assistance (e.g., friendly visitor programs, escorts to medical appointments, help with household chores). Opportunities for intergenerational contact might exist in which you meet older people to learn about their lives and for them to learn about you. Spending some time talking with older relatives may yield a deeper appreciation of their lives and how you share many commonalities. Academic courses and contact with older people likely will give you a sense of whether you may have a career interest in geropsychology. If so, after college, you might consider taking a job in an agency that serves older adults or work in a research study of older people.

Some individuals who are interested in pursuing a doctorate in clinical or counseling psychology want a program that offers opportunities to build knowledge and skills about aging. A few programs in the United States have a focus on preparing psychologists to become geropsychology specialists. Others have faculty with expertise in aging that will offer opportunities to take courses in aging and receive training experiences with older adults. (See Recommended Resources at the end of this chapter.)

Students who attend graduate psychology programs with geropsychology faculty, aging courses, and training experiences with older adults often are well prepared to take the next step in the path of becoming a geropsychologist, which is a psychology doctoral internship. An internship is a year of supervised experience providing psychological services after completion of graduate coursework. An internship with opportunities to provide assessment and treatment services to older adults will incrementally build geropsychology acumen for those who have had courses and training experiences with older people. For others, the internship will afford an opportunity to gain initial professional experience with older adults, which at this point, may lead to a career in geropsychology.

Those who want to become geropsychology specialists often do one more year of training after obtaining a doctorate in psychology. This is called postdoctoral fellowship. Postdoctoral fellowships in professional geropsychology exist. Other postdoctoral fellowships in clinical or counseling psychology offer a major focus on aging-related issues. In either case, trainees build competencies in geropsychology assessment, treatment, and consultation. For some psychologists, interest in geropsychology comes later in their careers, and then they obtain the needed knowledge and skills through continuing education courses, supervised experiences, and related work to become competent geropsychology specialists. A framework for building competencies in geropsychology is called the Pikes Peak Model for Training in Professional Geropsychology (Knight et al., 2009). Other documents discuss pathways to becoming a professional geropsychologist based on the Pikes Peak Model (Hinrichsen, Zeiss, Karel, & Molinari, 2010; Karel, Knight, Duffy, Hinrichsen, & Zeiss, 2010).

## Qualities That Make for a Successful Geropsychologist

We believe that professional success is ultimately a subjective judgment. The reasons that people enter any field, including psychology, reflect their hopes and values as well as practical considerations like how much income they want or need and to what degree a career facilitates a balance between work and other interests. Among the geropsychologists that we know who say their careers are meaningful and successful, the following qualities appear to be important: comfort with older adults and families, an appreciation of and curiosity about life history, capacity to understand issues from multiple perspectives, skillfulness in working with other professionals, ongoing curiosity about developments in the field of aging, and commitment to making the world a better place. We believe these qualities facilitate high-quality professional services to older clients and a personally meaningful and sustaining career.

## What Geropsychologists Get Paid

Like all psychologists, geropsychologist earnings vary widely according to work settings, years in practice, and region of the country. Information about psychologist salaries is available through the American Psychological Association's Center for Workforce Studies website (http://www.apa.org/workforce/index.aspx). Unfortunately, there are no data regarding salaries of geropsychologists compared with psychologists in other specialty areas. Geropsychologists who work in the VA Healthcare System are General Schedule (GS) federal employees, usually starting at the GS-12 grade level and moving to the GS-13 grade level; psychologists who take on significant leadership roles may be promoted to the GS-14 grade level. These salaries vary widely across the country because of locality pay variations (see U.S. Office of Personnel Management, 2015). As noted, geropsychologists who work in the private sector generally depend on Medicare reimbursement for clinical care services since Medicare is the primary insurer for older adults. Medicare reimbursement rates may be lower than rates that psychologists can receive via other insurance reimbursement or via private pay.

## Future Prospects for a Career in Geropsychology

A career in geropsychology likely will have abundant professional possibilities. A fact mentioned earlier is that the number of Americans who will be 65 years of age and older is growing—and growing rapidly. Currently, 13% of the U.S. population is 65 years and older. By the year 2030, the percentage will be 20% (Federal Interagency Forum on Aging-Related Statistics, 2012). A population of older adults this large in the United States is historically unprecedented. A major factor driving this growth is the fact that after World War II, large numbers of children were born between 1946 and 1964—the so-called baby boom generation of which there are 76 million members. Other factors bearing on a growing percentage of the population that is older include many more people, relative to earlier generations, actually living to age 65 years, and older people living somewhat longer than they did in earlier eras.

Currently, about 20% of older adults have a mental disorder, which is about the same proportion as younger adults (Karel, Gatz, & Smyer, 2012). Although older adults have lower rates of conditions such as depression and anxiety than younger adults, they have higher rates of dementia (a progressive loss of mental abilities). On the basis of current estimates, it appears that the baby boom generation likely will have higher rates of mental disorders than the current generation of older adults. Furthermore, baby boomers likely will access mental health services in greater numbers than the current generation of older people, in part, because baby boomers generally have more favorable attitudes toward mental health services than earlier generations.

The workforce of specialists to serve the health and mental health needs of older adults is highly inadequate (Institute of Medicine, 2008, 2012). Efforts to recruit and train health and mental health professionals with expertise in geriatrics have not met with a great deal of success. In the future (as now) it is likely that generalist health and mental health care providers will be serving the health care needs of most older adults. Sometimes those providers lack adequate knowledge and skills to deal with problems that get increasingly complex with advanced age. Future geropsychologists will have busy and successful professional lives that make a substantive contribution to meeting the mental health needs of older Americans.

The U.S. health care system is in evolution. One trend is in the delivery of more holistic, integrated, and coordinated health care. These approaches hold promise for better quality and less expensive care. The fields of geriatrics and geropsychology have been in the forefront of advocating for integrated, coordinated, and holistic care to older adults (American Psychological Association, 2008), which health care policymakers have learned is good for all ages. Another trend is for the integration of mental health care into physical health care settings—an effort for which individuals in the aging field also have made major contributions (Unützer et al., 2002).

Beyond currently existing roles, it is likely in the coming decades that opportunities will grow for psychologists to provide care in primary care settings, improve the quality of life for people with dementia and their families, consult with legal professionals on the capacity of some older adults to competently make decisions, and help older people at the end of life (Karel, Gatz, & Smyer, 2012). Furthermore, geropsychologists likely will be sought after by nongeriatric specialists to provide consultation on how to address mental health concerns of older people and enrich and enhance their quality of life.

## Conclusion

If you are considering becoming a psychologist, it is likely that you have not considered geropsychology as a possible specialization. The field is relatively new and, like many others, you may not be aware that older adults can greatly benefit from the efforts of psychologists. Geropsychology affords an opportunity for a rich, interesting, and meaningful professional career that contributes to the quality of life for older Americans and their families. Unprecedented in American history, 20% of the population will be 65 years and older by 2030, and the need for psychological services will be considerable. The workforce of specialists with geriatric expertise is quite small, and the need and future professional opportunities for geropsychologists likely will be huge.

## Recommended Resources

American Psychological Association, Division 20, Adult Development and Aging: http://www.apadivisions.org/division-20/
American Psychological Association, Office on Aging: http://www.apa.org/pi/aging/
Council of Professional Geropsychology Training Programs (CoPGTP): http://copgtp.org/
GeroCentral: http://gerocentral.org/
Psychologists in Long Term Care: http://www.pltcweb.org
Society of Clinical Geropsychology: http://www.geropsychology.org/

## References

American Psychological Association. (2008). *Blueprint for change: Achieving integrated healthcare for an aging population.* Washington, DC: Author. Retrieved from http://www.apa.org/pi/aging/programs/integrated/integrated-healthcare-report.pdf

American Psychological Association. (2014). Guidelines for psychological practice with older adults. *American Psychologist, 69,* 34–65. http://dx.doi.org/10.1037/a0035063

Federal Interagency Forum on Aging-Related Statistics. (2012). *Older Americans 2012: Key indicators of well-being.* Washington, DC: U.S. Government Printing Office.

Hinrichsen, G. A. (2010). Public policy and the provision of psychological services to older adults. *Professional Psychology: Research and Practice, 41*, 97–103. http://dx.doi.org/10.1037/a0018643

Hinrichsen, G. A., & Clougherty, K. F. (2006). *Interpersonal psychotherapy for depressed older adults*. Washington, DC: American Psychological Association. http://dx.doi.org/10.1037/11429-000

Hinrichsen, G. A., Zeiss, A. M., Karel, M. J., & Molinari, V. A. (2010). Competency-based geropsychology training in doctoral internships and postdoctoral fellowships. *Training and Education in Professional Psychology, 4*, 91–98. http://dx.doi.org/10.1037/a0018149

Institute of Medicine. (2008). *Retooling for an aging America: Building the health care workforce*. Washington, DC: National Academies Press. Retrieved from http://www.iom.edu/Reports/2008/Retooling-for-an-Aging-America-Building-the-Health-Care-Workforce.aspx

Institute of Medicine. (2012). *The mental health and substance use workforce for older adults: In whose hands?* Washington, DC: National Academies Press. Retrieved from http://www.iom.edu/Activities/MentalHealth/GeriatricMentalHealth.aspx

Karel, M. J., Gatz, M., & Smyer, M. A. (2012). Aging and mental health in the decade ahead: What psychologists need to know. *American Psychologist, 67*, 184–198. http://dx.doi.org/10.1037/a0025393

Karel, M. J., Knight, B. G., Duffy, M., Hinrichsen, G. A., & Zeiss, A. M. (2010). Attitude, knowledge, and skill competencies for practice in professional geropsychology: Implications for training and building a geropsychology workforce. *Training and Education in Professional Psychology, 4*, 75–84. http://dx.doi.org/10.1037/a0018372

Knight, B. G., Karel, M. J., Hinrichsen, G. A., Qualls, S. H., & Duffy, M. (2009). Pikes Peak model for training in professional geropsychology. *American Psychologist, 64*, 205–214. http://dx.doi.org/10.1037/a0015059

Scogin, F., & Shah, A. (Eds.). (2012). *Making evidence-based psychological treatments work with older adults*. Washington, DC: American Psychological Association. http://dx.doi.org/10.1037/13753-000

Unützer, J., Katon, W., Callahan, C. M., Williams, J. W., Jr., Hunkeler, E., Harpole, L., . . . Langston, C., for the IMPACT Investigators, Improving Mood-Promoting Access to Collaborative Treatment. (2002). Collaborative care management of late-life depression in the primary care setting: A randomized controlled trial. *JAMA, 288*, 2836–2845. http://dx.doi.org/10.1001/jama.288.22.2836

U.S. Office of Personnel Management. (2015). *Pay & leave*. Retrieved from https://www.opm.gov/policy-data-oversight/pay-leave/salaries-wages/2015/general-schedule/

*Paul L. Craig*

# Clinical Neuropsychologists | 11

*Clinical Neuropsychology: Brain–Behavior Relationships*

"I love neuropsychology!" When I heard Erin Bigler proclaim his passion for clinical neuropsychology while being honored with the Distinguished Neuropsychologist Award at the 1999 annual meeting of the National Academy of Neuropsychology

Paul L. Craig, PhD, ABPP-CN, is a clinical professor at the University of Washington School of Medicine, Department of Psychiatry and Behavioral Sciences. He received a BS in biopsychology at Nebraska Wesleyan University in 1974 and a PhD in clinical psychology at the University of Wyoming in 1980. Dr. Craig completed postdoctoral fellowships at the University of Washington School of Medicine and the University of Oklahoma Health Sciences Center. He delivers neuropsychological services through his private practice in Anchorage, Alaska.

http://dx.doi.org/10.1037/15960-012
*Career Paths in Psychology: Where Your Degree Can Take You, Third Edition*, R. J. Sternberg (Editor)

(NAN; Ruff, 2003), I realized he was speaking for the entire profession. It is rare for a leader in any scientific or health care field to make such a spontaneous and genuine public declaration of love for his or her profession. But as Dr. Bigler spoke from his heart, silence spread throughout the audience. I noted several affirming nods acknowledging that he was speaking for all of us in the field. Neuropsychologists love neuropsychology.

Bigler's declaration was followed by an erudite lecture concerning the pathophysiology of traumatic brain injury, neuroimaging, and neuropsychological functioning (Bigler, 2001). This invited lecture was not without controversy and stimulated further discussion and scholarly debate in peer-reviewed journals (Bigler, 2003; Lees-Haley, Green, Rohling, Fox, & Allen, 2003; Ruff, 2003). The healthy debate regarding the neuropathological and neuropsychological consequences of mild and moderate traumatic brain injuries persists into the 21st century. During recent years, the media has focused the public's attention on traumatic brain injury more than ever by covering the head-injury–related litigation among National Football League players (e.g., Gladwell, 2009) as well as reports about thousands of combat veterans returning from the Middle East with reports of blast injuries from improvised explosive devices.

This chapter provides an overview of clinical neuropsychology as a potential career. The amount of change I have witnessed in the field of neuropsychology during the past 40 years has been staggering. I suspect the rate of change in the profession will increase exponentially as a result of advances in assessment technology, neurosciences, and neurocognitive research as well as developments in connate fields such as neuroimaging. If you chose to pursue a career in neuropsychology, you will need to be a lifelong learner given the inevitable changes on the road ahead.

Reading this chapter will introduce you to the profession as it now exists. I can only begin to speculate what the profession may look like after a few more decades have elapsed when you may be approaching retirement. In that context, if you pursue training as a clinical neuropsychologist, you will have the opportunity to mold the future for the profession through your research, clinical practice, involvement with professional societies and associations, and advocacy regarding public policy pertaining to research and practice in the field of clinical neuropsychology.

The American Psychological Association (APA) includes more than 50 divisions focused on interest areas and specialties within psychology. The Society for Clinical Neuropsychology (SCN) is one of those APA Divisions. Neil Pliskin, the 2015 president of the SCN, has focused the Society on preparing clinical neuropsychologists for the profession's future under the Patient Protection and Affordable Care Act of 2010 (PPACA). In a letter to the membership of the SCN, Pliskin states,

> SCN has been examining the role that neuropsychologists play in interdisciplinary patient centered care settings. The idea of patient care settings is that patients are more likely to receive the behavioral health services they need if all specialists are either co-located or fully integrated (embedded) into one medical home. (2015)

This integration would ensure that behavioral health and cognitive wellness screenings required under PPACA are provided. Pliskin continues, "there are incentives for performing these behavioral health (including cognitive) screenings and potential penalties when they are not addressed" (2015). Later in this chapter, I will discuss some preliminary findings from a recent survey completed by the SCN regarding neuropsychology's current involvement within these integrated health care teams.

Many changes are afoot—some of which will dramatically change the landscape of clinical neuropsychology as a profession during the next few years. Although these changes can be unnerving to neuropsychologists who are entrenched in the independent practice model of service delivery, the inevitable changes within the U.S. health care system will create new opportunities for those who are willing and able to help create efficient and effective integrated models of service delivery that will address physical, behavioral, and cognitive health.

## Neuropsychology as a Profession

What exactly is neuropsychology? I frequently am called on to explain the field of neuropsychology to the public. For example, when I serve as an expert witness in the courtroom, one of my first tasks is to educate jurors about the profession. I begin by saying, "Neuropsychology is the scientific study of brain–behavior relationships." Then I explain, "Clinical neuropsychology is the application of this scientifically derived knowledge for purposes of evaluating and treating individuals with known or suspected brain disorders." I emphasize that clinical neuropsychologists may provide assessment or treatment services to children, adolescents, and adults—depending on their specific competencies and interests.

Neuropsychological evaluation techniques typically involve observing and measuring the behavior of an individual with a known or suspected brain disorder that may be developmental or acquired. In almost all circumstances, the neuropsychologist completes an assessment by administering standardized neuropsychological tests, recording the patient's responses, and comparing his or her test performances with normative performances expected among demographically similar individuals. To determine whether neuropsychological test results are normal or abnormal, the neuropsychologist must analyze not only the patient's level of ability but also the patient's pattern of strengths and weaknesses among the various skills assessed. Moreover, it is important for the neuropsychologist to analyze the problem-solving process used by each patient when responding to various tasks to better understand why he or she may be evidencing difficulty on that task (Kaplan, 1990). A competent neuropsychologist must combine objective data and clinical judgment to ensure that an individual is not being incorrectly diagnosed or categorized strictly based on a test score. Individuals may perform poorly on one or more neuropsychological tests for many reasons, including motivational deficits, cultural and linguistic factors, emotional disorders, sensory impairment (e.g., poor visual acuity), or uncooperativeness. Brain dysfunction is only one of many putative explanations for poor performance on neuropsychological tests.

The practicing neuropsychologist must be thoroughly familiar with human neuroanatomy. In this context, neuroanatomy from a structural perspective is an important subject in which the neuropsychologist should be fluent. Functional neuroanatomy is equally important—in other words, understanding the connections and functional relationships among the various neuroanatomical structures subserving various aspects of cognition, emotion, and behavior. A neuropsychologist also needs to be knowledgeable about the neuropathology associated with various developmental and acquired brain disorders.

Neuropsychological assessment does not involve direct investigation of brain structures and neural pathways. Rather, a neuropsychologist uses behavioral assessment techniques to infer how well the patient's brain is functioning in relation to memory, problem solving, language and communication, visuospatial and constructional skills, and related mental abilities. The neuropsychologist usually can address the patient's neuropsychological prognosis by examining the patient's history and the neuropathological condition thought to be causing the patient's current neuropsychological deficits.

In addition to neuropsychological evaluation services, many neuropsychologists are involved in treatment. For example, some neuropsychologists provide cognitive rehabilitation, psychotherapy, and related psychoeducational services to patients experiencing neurocognitive deficits following a traumatic brain injury or some other acquired insult to the central nervous system (e.g., Prigatano, 1999; Prigatano, Gilsky, & Klonoff, 1996; Sohlberg & Mateer, 2001). Vigorous debate has surrounded the efficacy of various approaches used to rehabilitate brain-impaired patients (e.g., Salazar et al., 2000). However, various reviews of outcome research generally have supported the clinical utility of specific cognitive rehabilitation techniques (Charters, Gillett, & Simpson, 2015; Cope, 1995; NAN, 2002; National Institutes of Health Consensus Development Panel on Rehabilitation of Persons With Traumatic Brain Injury, 1999; Park & Ingles, 2001). Certainly, innovative approaches to neuropsychological rehabilitation should continue to be developed and researched so that the treatment needs of individuals who have survived a significant insult to the brain can be optimally met. Another valuable use of neuropsychological assessment involves identifying and quantifying the cognitive benefits associated with specific forms of psychotherapeutic treatment for emotional disorders (e.g., Groves et al., 2015).

## Work Settings and Activities

Clinical neuropsychologists work in a broad array of settings, including medical-surgical hospitals, psychiatric facilities, rehabilitation programs, multidisciplinary primary-care health clinics, and others. Some neuropsychologists have academic positions at universities within psychology departments or within a medical school department (e.g., neurology or rehabilitation medicine), where they may be involved in training and supervising students, interns, residents, and postdoctoral fellows in clinical neuropsychology. Each year, I teach first-year medical students at the University of Washington School of Medicine about clinical neuropsychology. As a result, these medical students learn when and how to call on a clinical neuropsychologist to assess or treat patients with known or suspected brain disorders.

As a result of the tireless efforts of Jerry Sweet and his colleagues during the past 25 years (Sweet, Meyer, Nelson, & Moberg, 2011; Sweet & Moberg, 1990; Sweet, Moberg, & Suchy, 2000a, 2000b; Sweet, Moberg, & Westergaard, 1996; Sweet, Peck, Abramowitz, & Etzweiler, 2002, 2003) much has been learned about the range of professional activities associated with the practice of clinical neuropsychology, including the economics of practice. An updated survey completed by Sweet and colleagues recently was published in *The Clinical Neuropsychologist* (Sweet, Benson, Nelson, & Moberg, 2015).

Before Sweet's repeated efforts to characterize neuropsychological practice patterns, Putnam and DeLuca (1990) published data they had gathered regarding the practice of clinical neuropsychology by way of a survey completed 25 years ago. If you are seriously interested in a career in neuropsychology, read the historical surveys as well as the more recent surveys cited earlier. These surveys may provide you with some important insights regarding historical and current trends that may be of value as you attempt to predict what a career in clinical neuropsychology might look like over the next few decades.

In addition to Sweet's efforts, in 2014, the SCN established a task force investigating integrated models of care involving neuropsychologists. As chair of this SCN task force, Cynthia Kubu (personal communication, June 13, 2015) shared some preliminary data with me.

The most recent surveys completed by Sweet and colleagues (Sweet et al., 2011; Sweet et al., 2015) were cosponsored by the APA's SCN and the NAN. Kubu's (personal communication, June 13, 2015) survey was exclusively sponsored by the SCN.

Sweet's 2015 survey included data from 1,777 respondents as contrasted with 1,685 respondents in 2010. In 2000, about 37.6% of Sweet's respondents were women. By 2010, 52.8% of the respondents were women. Female representation in the field continues to grow with 55.7% of the respondents being female in the 2015 survey, soon to be published by Sweet and colleagues.

Private practice was a predominate employment setting for neuropsychologists in the survey completed during 2000. At that time, more than two thirds of the respondents reported some involvement in private practice, and 38.7% reported that they were exclusively working in a private practice setting. Ten years later, in 2010, two thirds of the respondents reported some involvement in private practice but only 27.5% reported exclusively working in a private practice setting. Preliminary data from the 2015 survey suggest that only 22.4% of clinical neuropsychologists are working exclusively in private practice settings. Clearly, the trend is moving away from independent private practice and toward employment in institutional settings, where 52.8% of the 2015 respondents report their exclusive employment.

It is very important to note that "decreased reimbursement" was noted by 65.2% of Sweet's 2015 survey respondents when asked about the "influence of recent healthcare system changes on clinical practice." The claim of decreased reimbursement is not directly supported, however, by the mean level of income reported by all respondents. Specifically, in 2010, the mean annual income for all neuropsychologists responding to the survey was $132,400. Preliminary data from the 2015 survey report a mean annual income of $143,400. It is also noteworthy that the 2010 data support the notion that clinical neuropsychologists who are board certified by the American Board of Clinical Neuropsychology (ABCN) earn significantly higher annual incomes than their non-board-certified peers ($158,400 versus $118,600). Despite differences in income, both board-certified and non-board-certified neuropsychologists report fairly high job satisfaction, which harkens back to Dr. Bigler's proclamation, "I love neuropsychology!"

Consistent with the trends reported by Sweet in the series of surveys cited previously, preliminary data from SCN's task force survey led by Kubu suggests that 64% of the 405 SCN respondents indicated that they were working within an integrated care team. The majority of the SCN task force respondents (72%) were members of teams within neurology or neurosurgery clinics (e.g., epilepsy, movement disorder), followed by rehabilitation (25%), other medical specialty clinics (15%), primary care (15%), psychiatry or psychology clinics (14%), university and counseling centers (2%), and other settings (9%). You will note that these percentages total more than 100 insofar as 40% of the respondents reported working on more than one integrated care team. According to Kubu, "Neuropsychologists in integrated care teams provide a variety of services including assessment, diagnostic and treatment recommendations, behavioral interventions, clinical research, therapy (psychotherapy and cognitive rehabilitation), and program evaluation." She continues, "It is anticipated that even more neuropsychologists will be working as members of integrated care teams with ongoing changes associated with healthcare reform" (personal communication, June 13, 2015).

On the basis of all of the available data, the trends suggest that the future of clinical practice in neuropsychology will increasingly involve working within integrated multidisciplinary teams of health care providers.

On a personal level, I have provided neuropsychological services in a variety of settings throughout my career. In the past, I have been employed as a consultant to a comprehensive outpatient rehabilitation facility as well as to two acute inpatient rehabilitation programs located within medical-surgical hospitals. With a partner in the early 1990s, I cofounded a multidisciplinary outpatient mental health clinic through which I delivered neuropsychological services.

Since 1997, I have been in solo private practice almost exclusively providing neuropsychological assessment service on an outpatient basis. During each stage of my career, a typical day in my professional life has varied significantly depending on my involvements and commitments. When I was providing services as a consultant to the outpatient rehabilitation program, I participated in group counseling sessions with patients with brain injuries and consulted with the multidisciplinary rehabilitation team to ensure that services were appropriately integrated and individualized on the basis of each patient's neuropsychological strengths and weaknesses. I provided similar services as a consultant to an acute inpatient rehabilitation program. In the inpatient setting, I spent a significant amount of time meeting with family members to help them understand the neuropsychological consequences of an acute insult to the brain incurred by their loved one (e.g., traumatic brain injury or cerebrovascular accident).

In my current outpatient practice, I am actively involved day-to-day in the assessment of individuals with known or suspected brain disorders.

I spend an hour or more interviewing each patient to obtain a thorough health and psychosocial history. If a family member is available, I prefer to have him or her participate in the clinical interview to augment the history provided by the patient. Likewise, I review any records that have been made available to me through the referral source. Depending on the current level of patient functioning and the clinical questions to be answered, test administration can be brief (e.g., administration of a dementia screen instrument in the case of a patient with advanced dementia) or can last up to a day and a half when a comprehensive neuropsychological and psychological evaluation is required to answer complex referral questions. Consistent with the practice pattern of about half of the clinical neuropsychologists responding to Sweet's 2010 survey, I employ a testing technician in my practice. About half of the neuropsychologists practicing in 2010 administered their own tests and about half used a testing technician. Professional standards regarding use of non–doctoral-level personnel when conducting a neuropsychological evaluation have been promulgated by the American Academy of Clinical Neuropsychology (Brandt & Van Gorp, 1999).

A typical day at this point in my career might involve one or more clinical interviews, an hour or more of record review, a few hours of dictating and proofreading reports, and meeting with patients and family members to provide feedback and recommendations derived from the neuropsychological test results. I also encourage the patients to discuss the findings and recommendations with the referral source (e.g., primary care provider or vocational rehabilitation counselor).

Occasionally, I am asked to travel to a remote Alaska bush village to provide neuropsychological services (Craig, 2005). Although I could easily decline this remote work, I gladly accept these referrals with the same spirit of adventure that brought me to Alaska in 1980.

On some days, I find myself sequestered in my office—or in a lawyer's conference room—for a few hours with a court reporter and two or more attorneys, responding to their questions during a deposition. Likewise, I sometimes am asked to serve as a witness in the courtroom regarding civil or criminal cases. If I have seen a patient in the context of a clinical referral from a physician and, later, a neuropsychological issue arises that pertains to a legal matter before the court, I am typically called to testify as a fact witness. If my professional involvement in the case was premised on being retained by legal counsel or by the judge to serve as an expert relative to a civil or criminal case, my role in the courtroom as an expert witness is significantly different. In either case (i.e., fact witness or expert witness), I must remain unbiased and base my testimony on objective data interpreted in the context of neuropsychological research published in peer-reviewed journals rather than expressing a personal opinion or a subjective impression. Attorneys function as advocates. Neuropsychologists must avoid advocacy and should remain objective and scientific when providing testimony during a deposition or in a courtroom setting.

When I was actively involved in providing neuropsychological services to hospitalized patients in a medical-surgical hospital, my day frequently concluded with a couple of hours at the hospital evaluating patients with impaired mental functions at the request of neurologists, neurosurgeons, internists, and related health care providers. Since 1997, my outpatient practices followed a fairly predictable weekly schedule, with each new patient scheduled for the next available evaluation appointment. However, when working in an inpatient setting, the flow of work is not unlike drinking water from a water fountain connected to an antiquated plumbing system. One minute, you're gazing at the fountain with nothing but an occasional gurgle emerging from the spigot; a moment later, as you hold your mouth close to the fountain, water is gushing toward your face, and you wonder if you can drink fast enough to avoid aspiration. Making yourself available in an inpatient setting can be quite rewarding professionally but also can be taxing because of the unpredictable demands on your time.

In addition to the activities I've described, many university-affiliated neuropsychologist are actively involved in research as well as teaching and supervising graduate students, interns, postdoctoral fellows, and related trainees. Some private practice neuropsychologists also maintain active research programs in association with their clinical practice. A few neuropsychologists have contracts with pharmaceutical companies to participate in clinical trials to objectively determine whether and how proposed drugs influence cognition. Professional neuropsychologists are applying specialty knowledge regarding brain-behavior relationships in a broad array of settings.

## Academic Preparation

Sweet et al. (2002) reported that 64.9% of the respondents to the survey completed during 2000 stated that they had completed doctoral programs in clinical psychology. In the 2010 survey, 74.0% of the respondents reported clinical psychology as their field of doctoral study. Consistent with most of my peers, I completed my doctoral training at an APA-accredited clinical psychology program at the University of Wyoming in 1980. Although my undergraduate major at Nebraska Wesleyan University was biopsychology, I did not become aware of clinical neuropsychology as an area of professional specialization until my second year of graduate school. During September 1977, a doctoral program classmate, Dean Delis, returned from a summer practicum completed at the Boston Veterans Administration hospital. Dean enthusiastically shared stories about the clinical neuropsychologists he had met and worked with in Boston. My intellectual curiosity was piqued, and I began reading everything I could find on neuropsychology in the University of Wyoming library.

During the last year of my doctoral studies, I completed an internship in health care psychology at the University of Minnesota health sciences center where I had the privilege of being supervised in clinical neuropsychology by Manfred Meier. Thereafter, I completed a postdoctoral fellowship specializing in rural community mental health, an area of professional interest throughout my training and career, through the University of Washington School of Medicine. During this fellowship, I primarily lived and worked in Ketchikan, Alaska. In retrospect, this adventuresome lark in Alaska defined the rest of my career. Thirty-five years later, I am still living and working in Alaska.

After a 3-year stint as the program director and psychologist of the community mental health center in Homer, Alaska, I decided that I wanted to specialize in clinical neuropsychology. I applied for a fellowship in clinical neuropsychology at the University of Oklahoma Health Sciences center and was delighted when I received notification of acceptance. After completing this fellowship, I returned to Alaska. Since 1981, I've maintained a clinical faculty appointment at the University of Washington, School of Medicine, through the multistate regional health care training consortium known as WWAMI (an acronym for Washington, Wyoming, Alaska, Montana, and Idaho).

APA Division 40, Clinical Neuropsychology (1989)—now the SCN—defines the training that is required to be a clinical neuropsychologist as follows: doctoral-level training, including successful completion of didactic and experiential training in neuropsychology and neuroscience at a regionally accredited university; 2 or more years of supervised training applying neuropsychological services in a clinical setting; licensure to provide psychological services in the state in which services are being delivered; and review by one's peers as a test of these competencies. This definition states, "Attainment of the ABCN/ABPP Diplomate in Clinical Neuropsychology is the clearest evidence of competence as a clinical neuropsychologist, assuring that all of these criteria have been met" (APA Division 40, Clinical Neuropsychology, 1989, p. 22). The ABCN is one of several boards affiliated with the American Board of Professional Psychology (ABPP). As of July 2015, more than 1,100 neuropsychologists have achieved board certification by the ABCN/ABPP. In 2001, the NAN also issued a definition of a clinical neuropsychologist (Barth et al., 2003).

In 1992, I passed the ABCN examination and became board certified in clinical neuropsychology through ABPP—a credential I value quite highly. If you are serious about becoming a clinical neuropsychologist,

I strongly encourage you to pursue the necessary training and supervised experience to eventually obtain board certification. As is the case with board certification in medicine, bright and talented professionals sometimes fail the ABCN examination. When I was examined, the pass rate was about 70%. Obviously, failing the ABCN examination can feel like a significant blow to a newly trained neuropsychologist, who probably has never failed a test before in his or her life. However, well-trained and qualified applicants who initially fail the ABCN examination can use the feedback from the exam to continue to develop expertise within neuropsychology. Frequently, these promising new professionals are able to pass the examination when they persist and are reexamined. Ivnik, Haaland, and Bieliauskas (2000) published a useful article regarding the steps involved in obtaining board certification through the ABCN/ABPP. This article may be of interest if you decide that a professional career neuropsychology is consistent with your interests.

Similarly, if you want to learn more about how to become a neuropsychologist, you should read the proceedings from the Houston Conference on Specialty Education and Training in Clinical Neuropsychology (Hannay, 1998). You also may benefit from visiting the database of training programs that can be found on the APA SCN website. This database provides a current list of doctoral programs, internships, and postdoctoral fellowships in clinical neuropsychology (SCN, 2015).

During the past several years, finding an appropriate internship has proved to be a bottleneck for doctoral students in psychology in general, and neuropsychology in particular. Mittenberg, Petersen, Cooper, Strauman, and Essig (2000) surveyed clinical neuropsychology internship programs and found that, "Selection criteria reflect a vertically integrated model of education and training in accordance with the Houston conference model" (2000, p. 1). In other words, to enhance your chances of being accepted into an appropriate internship program focused on clinical neuropsychology, it would be in your interest to apply to a doctoral training program that adheres to the Houston Conference model. Moreover, you may benefit from reading a recently published overview regarding postdoctoral training in neuropsychology (Bodin, Roper, O'Toole, & Haines, 2015) to understand the spectrum of training experiences required if you choose to pursue a career in clinical neuropsychology.

## Financial Compensation

Independent practice in clinical neuropsychology has provided me with a healthy income, allowing me to lead a comfortable middle-class lifestyle. I have worked hard and have been sufficiently rewarded financially throughout my professional career to be able to raise a family on a single income, enjoy an occasional fly-in fishing trip to various lakes and rivers in Alaska, and savor some family trips to international destinations, creating memories that will last a lifetime. I have not created the personal wealth enjoyed by my age-mates who majored in business and pursued entrepreneurial goals since they were in their 20s. My quality of life, however, has been outstanding as a result of the intellectual and financial rewards associated with my professional activities in neuropsychology.

As reported previously, Sweet's surveys completed in 2010 and 2015 suggest that the earning power of the average clinical neuropsychologist has remained relatively stable throughout the United States during the past 5 years after considering changes in the consumer price index. At the same time, you should take note that a majority of the 2015 survey respondents indicated that "decreased reimbursement" was a specific concern. In light of this concern, it is not surprising that fewer and fewer clinical neuropsychologists are exclusively working in private practice settings. Premised on the service delivery systems and payment models authorized by the PPACA, it is highly probable that this trend will continue and that the clinical neuropsychologist of the future will be employed in an integrated multidisciplinary health care system. Hopefully, the value that clinical neuropsychologists bring to the health care team will continue to be recognized by way of reasonable financial compensation within integrated healthcare delivery systems.

For a much more detailed review of the range of salaries enjoyed by clinical neuropsychologists, you are encouraged to read Sweet's 2015 survey results that are currently being summarized for publication in *The Clinical Neuropsychologist* during 2015 or 2016. The previous surveys also should be reviewed to better understand the long-term trends in financial compensation within the field of clinical neuropsychology.

Viewed from a business perspective, selling your professional time by the hour is not a business model that leads to the financial wealth that some enterprising entrepreneurs have achieved. But a career in neuropsychology certainly can be financially, intellectually, and professionally rewarding.

## Attributes of the Successful Neuropsychologist

Many personal characteristics collectively contribute to a successful career in clinical neuropsychology. Certainly, learning to be a clinical neuropsychologist is intellectually demanding. By way of example, the neuropsychological trainee must learn the nuances of neuroanatomy. In the case of dementia of the Alzheimer's type, it is helpful for the neuropsychologist to know about the substantia innominata, which is the brain tissue located in the basal forebrain below the anterior perforated substance and anterior to the globus pallidus and ansa lenticularis. In particular, the substantia innominata is inclusive of the nucleus basalis of Meynert, which is thought to provide a significant percentage of cortical cholinergic innervation and has been the focus of intense research in the field of dementia.

The neuroanatomical information contained in the previous paragraph is not intended to intimidate prospective neuropsychology students. Many students studying medicine, neuropsychology, neuroscience, and related fields learn structural and functional neuroanatomy. Learning neuroanatomy requires a lot of rote memory as well as three-dimensional spatial reasoning skills to conceptualize how various brain structures fit together and interconnect. One neuroanatomical structure may be known by two or more names, all of which are considered correct labels. Likewise, two or more adjacent or functionally connected brain structures may collectively be described by yet another name. In addition to mastery of the fundamentals of neuroanatomy, training in neuropsychology requires a student to learn about neuropathology, neuroimaging (including functional magnetic resonance imaging), neurophysiology, and related fields within the neurosciences.

Neuropsychologists must have extensive training in clinical psychology to practice competently. When observing and measuring behavior, it is important to be knowledgeable about and attentive to the cornucopia of variables that can influence performance—for example, motivation, prior learning, emotional disorders, personality and character structure, and cultural factors, to name but a few. The brain is not a binary computer crunching algorithms; it is an incredibly complex organ subserving sensory functions, perception, cognition, emotions, and associated behavioral responses of the individual.

Multicultural competence is becoming increasingly important in psychology generally and clinical neuropsychology specifically (APA, 2003). Participating in neuropsychological evaluation is a culturally defined endeavor. Interpreting neuropsychological test results and providing patients with feedback and recommendations requires the neuropsychologist to be familiar with the cultural context of both the tests and the patient. Although I was not formally providing neuropsychological services while on vacation in Thailand several years ago, an experience I had while trekking with my daughters in the mountains near Chiang Mai opened my eyes to the importance of cultural factors with respect to interpretation of neuropsychological phenomenon. Through a series of unexpected circumstances, I found myself in a small mountain village communicating through a translator with a Thai gentleman who obviously had experienced a right hemisphere cerebrovascular accident about

1 month earlier. About a year earlier, he reportedly had another much milder right hemisphere stroke, from which he had enjoyed an excellent recovery. Unfortunately, he was not recovering as well following the more recent cerebrovascular event. After struggling to help him understand through the translator what probably had occurred to his brain (e.g., "The right half of your brain controls the left side of your body"), I stopped talking and began listening to the interpreter more carefully. I discovered that this man's explanation for each cerebrovascular accident was that one or more chickens had stolen half of his spirit. Following the first stroke a year earlier, he sacrificed a chicken in front of his hut, after which his symptoms began to improve rapidly. He had sacrificed several chickens during the month following his more recent stroke, but to no avail. As I pondered his interpretive model for his neurological condition, I wryly wondered how many of our current scientific models for understanding neuropathological conditions and techniques for remediating neuropsychological impairment will be viewed in the future as equally primitive, if not absurd. In any case, adhering to the APA's multicultural guidelines cited earlier cannot be overemphasized in our increasingly multicultural world.

Each year, I have the pleasure of introducing the WWAMI medical students in Alaska to clinical neuropsychology. I typically begin the lecture with a caveat: "If anybody ever tells you they know how the brain really works, hold them immediately suspect!" While studying neuropsychological research, a student inevitably learns how far our knowledge has advanced with regard to understanding the structure and function of the human brain. But the more you learn, the more you begin to realize how much remains unknown regarding the conundrum of the brain.

In short, a successful clinical neuropsychologist must be bright in relation to verbal and spatial thinking and broadly knowledgeable about neurosciences and psychology, enjoy working with people, have good critical thinking skills, enjoy report writing, and be meticulous when dealing with all of the details associated with completing a neuropsychological evaluation. A full-day neuropsychological evaluation contains a huge amount of data the must be correctly scored and interpreted. The professional neuropsychologist must attend to all of the details associated with completing a neuropsychological assessment as precisely as possible. However, a competent neuropsychologist also needs to be able to rise above these details to think more abstractly about the context from which these data emerge for purposes of arriving at a reliable and valid diagnostic and prognostic conclusion. Finally, a student who wants to become a clinical neuropsychologist must be both patient and tenacious. The number of years of training necessary to become a board-certified clinical neuropsychologist can be daunting. But senior professionals in the field usually remember those years of training as some of the most intellectually rewarding years of their lives.

## *Opportunities for Employment*

When preparing the survey of clinical neuropsychologist completed during 2010 (Sweet et al., 2011), Sweet's research team identified more than 7,000 professionals who were identified by way of combining the lists of members of the American Academy of Clinical Neuropsychology, the SCN, and the NAN. As stated previously, only about 1,100 of these individuals are board-certified neuropsychologists. Neuropsychologists who belonged to more than one of the organizations were included only once in this blended mailing list of 7,000 professionals. Ten years earlier, the number of professionals identified within the field of clinical neuropsychology was more than 4,000 (Sweet et al., 2002). The APA SCN—previously named the Division of Clinical Neuropsychology— was created in 1979 with 441 founding members (Goodglass, 1979). As of 2015, the SCN's membership roster has grown to 3,531 psychologists, making it the largest of the 55 divisions housed within the APA.

Many other examples could be provided to support the notion that the profession of neuropsychology has grown exponentially during the past 35 years. Despite this growth, the academic arena and health care marketplace appear to have absorbed the ever-increasing pool of clinical neuropsychologists who have emerge from postdoctoral fellowships. During each of the past 35 years in which I have practiced, I have attended one or more professional meetings with my neuropsychological colleagues (e.g., SCN, NAN, International Neuropsychological Society). Although I recall several colleagues describing anxiety caused by the vicissitudes of private practice and others lamenting the interprofessional political battles that sometimes occur within institutions, I cannot recall ever hearing a board-certified neuropsychologist complain that he or she could not find work. On the basis of ongoing personal communication with various colleagues and early career neuropsychologists, my impression is that newly trained professionals are finding employment in their field of specialization.

Some neuropsychologists are primarily involved with grant-funded research projects, which frequently are housed at university-affiliated teaching hospitals. Others are employed institutionally and spend most of their time providing neuropsychological services to patients within that institution. Some enjoy a combination of grant-supported research comingled with clinical service delivery. Private practice neuro-psychologists work with a variety of populations depending on their area of expertise, specialization, and referral sources. Pediatric neuro-psychologists receive specialized training that allows them to evaluate brain disorders among children and adolescents in the context of the template of normal development. The ABCN recently began subspecialty credentialing in pediatric clinical neuropsychology. Other practitioners primarily work with adults, and some specialize in the assessment of older individuals. Some neuropsychologists exclusively evaluate and treat physician-referred patients. Others mostly evaluate and treat individuals who are referred by mental health professionals. These patients may have a primary psychiatric diagnosis with no other neurological problems identified. Some neuropsychological colleagues have built private practices focused on serving as forensic consultants and expert witnesses (Heilbronner, 2005). Each of these niches is unique, but they all have a common denominator—a clinical neuropsychologist who is trained and credentialed to practice in this field of professional specialization.

## Conclusion

For those who want to learn more about the scientific underpinnings of neuropsychology, the *Fundamentals of Human Neuropsychology* (Kolb & Whishaw, 2008) is an outstanding text. Likewise, if you want to learn more about assessment, *Neuropsychological Assessment* (Lezak, Howieson, Bigler, & Tranel, 2012) is considered by many to be the definitive book in the field. The APA SCN has a student organization, the Association of Neuropsychology Students in Training (ANST). You may want to join ANST. Roaming the Internet, you can quickly learn more about the various professional organizations relevant to training and practicing clinical neuropsychology (e.g., the SCN, NAN, International Neuropsychological Society, Association for Internship Training in Clinical Neuropsychology, in the Association of Postdoctoral Programs in Clinical Neuropsychology). The ABCN has some useful links on its website (http://www.theabcn.org) and may be a good starting point for the inquisitive reader.

If you are an energetic student who wants to pursue a professional career in clinical neuropsychology, follow your passion. As anybody who has lived for more than a handful of decades knows, life never precisely follows the plan a young person envisions. If you are focused on the goal of becoming a clinical neuropsychologist and tenaciously work toward that goal, it is possible that you may one day address a group of your colleagues and find yourself proclaiming, "I love neuropsychology!"

# References

American Psychological Association. (2003). Guidelines on multicultural education, training, research, practice, and organizational change for psychologists. *American Psychologist, 58,* 377–402.

American Psychological Association Division 40, Clinical Neuropsychology. (1989). Definition of a clinical neuropsychologist. *Clinical Neuropsychologist, 3,* 22. http://dx.doi.org/10.1080/13854048908404071

Barth, J. T., Pliskin, N., Axelrod, B., Faust, D., Fisher, J., Harley, J. P., . . . the NAN Policy and Planning Committee. (2003). Introduction to the NAN 2001 definition of a clinical neuropsychologist: NAN Policy and Planning Committee. *Archives of Clinical Neuropsychology, 18,* 551–555.

Bigler, E. D. (2001). The lesion(s) in traumatic brain injury: Implications for clinical neuropsychology. *Archives of Clinical Neuropsychology, 16,* 95–131. http://dx.doi.org/10.1016/S0887-6177(00)00095-0

Bigler, E. D. (2003). Neurobiology and neuropathology underlie the neuropsychological deficits associated with traumatic brain injury. *Archives of Clinical Neuropsychology, 18,* 595–621. http://dx.doi.org/10.1016/S0887-6177(02)00156-7

Bodin, D., Roper, B. L., O'Toole, K., & Haines, M. E. (2015). Postdoctoral training in neuropsychology: A review of the history, trends, and current issues. *Training and Education in Professional Psychology, 9,* 99–104. http://dx.doi.org/10.1037/tep0000057

Brandt, J., & Van Gorp, W. (1999). American Academy of Clinical Neuropsychology policy on the use of non–doctoral-level personnel in conducting clinical neuropsychological evaluations. *Journal of Clinical and Experimental Neuropsychology, 21,* 1. http://dx.doi.org/10.1076/jcen.21.1.1.941

Charters, E., Gillett, L., & Simpson, G. K. (2015). Efficacy of electronic portable assistive devices for people with acquired brain injury: A systematic review. *Neuropsychological Rehabilitation, 25,* 82–121. http://dx.doi.org/10.1080/09602011.2014.942672

Cope, D. N. (1995). The effectiveness of traumatic brain injury rehabilitation: A review. *Brain Injury, 9,* 649–670. http://dx.doi.org/10.3109/02699059509008224

Craig, P. L. (2005). On the far edge of the last frontier: The Alaska experience. In R. L. Heilbronner (Ed.), *Forensic neuropsychology casebook* (pp. 167–184). New York, NY: Guilford Press.

Gladwell, M. (2009, October 19). Offensive play: How different are dog fighting and football? *The New Yorker.* Retrieved from http://www.newyorker.com/magazine/2009/10/19/offensive-play

Goodglass, H. (1979). *Letter to the APA division of clinical neuropsychology.* American Psychological Association Division 40 (Clinical Neuropsychology) Records. Washington, DC.

Groves, S. J., Porter, R. J., Jordan, J., Knight, R., Carter, J. D., McIntosh, V. V. W., . . . Joyce, P. R. (2015). Changes in neuropsychological function after treatment with metacognitive therapy or cognitive behavior therapy for depression. *Depression and Anxiety, 32,* 437–444. http://dx.doi.org/10.1002/da.22341

Hannay, H. J. (1998). Proceedings: The Houston Conference on specialty education and training in clinical neuropsychology. *Archives of Clinical Neuropsychology, 13,* 157–158.

Heilbronner, R. L. (2005). *Forensic neuropsychology casebook.* New York, NY: Guilford Press.

Ivnik, R. J., Haaland, K. Y., & Bieliauskas, L. A. (2000). American Board of Clinical Neuropsychology special presentation: The American Board of Clinical Neuropsychology (ABCN), 2000 update. *Clinical Neuropsychologist, 14,* 261–268. http://dx.doi.org/10.1076/1385-4046(200008)14:3;1-P;FT261

Kaplan, E. (1990). The process approach to neuropsychological assessment of psychiatric patients. *Journal of Neuropsychiatry and Clinical Neurosciences, 2,* 72–87. http://dx.doi.org/10.1176/jnp.2.1.72

Kolb, B., & Whishaw, I. Q. (2008). *Fundamentals of human neuropsychology* (6th ed.). New York, NY: Worth Publishers.

Lees-Haley, P. R., Green, P., Rohling, M. L., Fox, D. D., & Allen, L. M., III (2003). The lesion(s) in traumatic brain injury: Implications for clinical neuropsychology. *Archives of Clinical Neuropsychology, 18,* 585–594. http://dx.doi.org/10.1016/S0887-6177(02)00155-5

Lezak, M. D., Howieson, D. B., Bigler, E. D., & Tranel, D. (2012). *Neuropsychological assessment* (5th ed.). New York, NY: Oxford University Press.

Mittenberg, W. S., Petersen, R. S., Cooper, J. T., Strauman, S. M., & Essig, S. M. (2000). Selection criteria for clinical neuropsychology internships. *Clinical Neuropsychologist, 14,* 1–6. http://dx.doi.org/10.1076/1385-4046(200002)14:1;1-8;FT001

National Academy of Neuropsychology. (2002). *Cognitive rehabilitation: Official statement of the National Academy of Neuropsychology.* Retrieved from http://www.nanonline.org/NAN/Files/PAIC/PDFs/NANPositionCogRehab.pdf

National Institutes of Health Consensus Development Panel on Rehabilitation of Persons With Traumatic Brain Injury. (1999). Rehabilitation of persons with traumatic brain injury. *JAMA, 282,* 974–983. http://dx.doi.org/10.1001/jama.282.10.974

Park, N. W., & Ingles, J. L. (2001). Effectiveness of attention rehabilitation after an acquired brain injury: A meta-analysis. *Neuropsychology, 15,* 199–210. http://dx.doi.org/10.1037/0894-4105.15.2.199

Pliskin, N. (2015, June 1). *President's corner: Dear SCN/Division 40 member.* Retrieved from https://www.scn40.org/scn-neuroblog/presidents-corner

Prigatano, G. P. (1999). *Principles of neuropsychological rehabilitation.* New York, NY: Oxford University Press.

Prigatano, G. P., Gilsky, E. L., & Klonoff, P. S. (1996). Cognitive rehabilitation after traumatic brain injury. In P. W. Corrigan & S. C. Yudofsky (Eds.), *Cognitive rehabilitation for neuropsychiatric disorders* (pp. 223–242). Washington, DC: American Psychiatric Association.

Putnam, S. H., & DeLuca, J. W. (1990). The TCN professional practice survey: Part I. General practices of neuropsychologists in primary employment and private practice settings. *Clinical Neuropsychologist, 4*, 199–243. http://dx.doi.org/10.1080/13854049008401906

Ruff, R. M. (2003). A friendly critique of neuropsychology: Facing the challenges of our future. *Archives of Clinical Neuropsychology, 18*, 847–864. http://dx.doi.org/10.1016/j.acn.2003.07.002

Salazar, A. M., Warden, D. L., Schwab, K., Spector, J., Braverman, S., Walter, J., . . . Ellenbogen, R. G., for the Defense and Veterans Head Injury Program (DVHIP) Study Group. (2000). Cognitive rehabilitation for traumatic brain injury: A randomized trial. *JAMA, 283*, 3075–3081. http://dx.doi.org/10.1001/jama.283.23.3075

Society for Clinical Neuropsychology. (2015). *Neuropsychology training programs* [Database]. Retrieved from http://www.training.scn40.org

Sohlberg, M. M., & Mateer, C. A. (2001). *Cognitive rehabilitation: An integrative neuropsychological approach.* New York, NY: Guilford Press.

Swcct, J. J., Benson, L. M., Nelson, N. W., & Moberg, P. J. (2015). The American Academy of Clinical Neuropsychology, National Academy of Neuropsychology, and Society for Clinical Neuropsychology (APA Division 40) 2015 TCN professional practice and "salary survey": Professional practices, beliefs, and incomes of U.S. neuropsychologists. *Clinical Neuropsychologist, 29*, 1069–1162. http://dx.doi.org/10.1080/13854046.2016.1140228

Sweet, J. J., Meyer, D. G., Nelson, N. W., & Moberg, P. J. (2011). The TCN/AACN 2010 "salary survey": Professional practices, beliefs, and incomes of U.S. neuropsychologists. *Clinical Neuropsychologist, 25*, 12–61. http://dx.doi.org/10.1080/13854046.2010.544165

Sweet, J. J., & Moberg, P. J. (1990). A survey of practices and beliefs among ABPP and non-ABPP clinical neuropsychologists. *Clinical Neuropsychologist, 4*, 101–120. http://dx.doi.org/10.1080/13854049008401504

Sweet, J. J., Moberg, P. J., & Suchy, Y. (2000a). Ten-year follow-up survey of clinical neuropsychologists: Part I. Practices and beliefs. *Clinical Neuropsychologist, 14*, 18–37. http://dx.doi.org/10.1076/1385-4046(200002)14:1;1-8;FT018

Sweet, J. J., Moberg, P. J., & Suchy, Y. (2000b). Ten-year follow-up survey of clinical neuropsychologists: Part II. Private practice and economics. *Clinical Neuropsychologist, 14*, 479–495. http://dx.doi.org/10.1076/clin.14.4.479.7201

Sweet, J. J., Moberg, P. J., & Westergaard, C. (1996). Five-year follow-up survey of practices and beliefs of clinical neuropsychologists.

*Clinical Neuropsychologist, 10,* 202–221. http://dx.doi.org/10.1080/ 13854049608406681

Sweet, J. J., Peck, E. A., III, Abramowitz, C., & Etzweiler, S. (2002). National Academy of Neuropsychology/Division 40 of the American Psychological Association practice survey of clinical neuropsychology in the United States, Part I: Practitioner and practice characteristics, professional activities, and time requirements. *Clinical Neuropsychologist, 16,* 109–127. http://dx.doi.org/10.1076/clin.16.2.109.13237

Sweet, J. J., Peck, E. A., III, Abramowitz, C., & Etzweiler, S. (2003). National Academy of Neuropsychology/Division 40 of the American Psychological Association practice survey of clinical neuropsychology in the United States: Part II. Reimbursement experiences, practice economics, billing practices, and incomes. *Archives of Clinical Neuropsychology, 18,* 557–582.

*Melba J. T. Vasquez and Puncky Paul Heppner*

# Counseling Psychologists 12

Counseling psychology is a strong and vibrant specialty in psychology. Our historic roots go back to the early 1900s in the settlement houses of Boston, when the pioneering social justice advocate Frank Parsons worked to help immigrants find work in their new environment. Since that time, our specialty has broadened and deepened. In the 21st century,

Dr. Melba J. T. Vasquez, PhD, ABPP, is in full-time independent practice in Austin, TX. She is former president of the American Psychological Association (APA) and has served in various other leadership roles in psychology, including as president of the Society of Counseling Psychology. She has coauthored three books and more than 80 book chapters and journal articles, is a fellow of 11 divisions of the APA, and holds the Diplomate of the American Board of Professional Psychology.

Puncky Paul Heppner, PhD, is a Distinguished Curators Emeritus Professor at the University of Missouri-Columbia. He has been actively involved in research and has published more than 200 refereed journal articles and book chapters. Dr. Heppner also has served in a wide array of professional leadership positions in counseling psychology, including as president of the Society of Counseling Psychology and editor of *The Counseling Psychologist*.

http://dx.doi.org/10.1037/15960-013
*Career Paths in Psychology: Where Your Degree Can Take You, Third Edition,*
R. J. Sternberg (Editor)

counseling psychology is an applied specialty that prepares exceptional scientists and practitioner-oriented psychologists who provide a wide array of remedial, preventative, and developmental psychological services. Counseling psychologists work in diverse settings including university counseling centers, academic training programs, Veterans Affairs (VA), the military, independent practice, and community agencies. Moreover, counseling psychology has a long history that focuses on a person's strengths (rather than deficits) and optimal functioning across a developmental, lifespan perspective.

Counseling psychology has been consistently recognized for its emphasis on social justice and for the inclusion of the environmental context and culture to more fully understand human behavior. We are a specialty that emphasizes the integration of science and practice in all professional activities (the scientist–practitioner model), with an outstanding history of rigorous research on a host of topics, such as psychotherapy process and outcomes, multicultural and cross-cultural issues, prevention, and vocational development.

We have an exceptionally strong professional organization, the Society of Counseling Psychology (SCP) within the American Psychological Association, which not only provides strong leadership for the profession of counseling psychology but also has become a leading division within the larger association. The SCP actively prepares the next generation of counseling psychology through systematic mentoring and leadership training with students and young professionals (many of whom later assume major leadership roles in our field and beyond).

This chapter first defines counseling psychology and then describes the varied career opportunities in counseling psychology. We discuss both the academic and applied professional practice of counseling psychology (e.g., university counseling centers, independent practice, business and industry, medical settings, community mental health centers and clinics, and schools). We also provide information about applying for graduate schools in counseling psychology as well as an overview of graduate training in counseling psychology.

## What Is Counseling Psychology?

Counseling psychology has long been acknowledged as one of the original four specialty areas within professional psychology (clinical, counseling, school, and industrial–organizational psychology). We will first define counseling psychology by discussing central values and distinguishing features of the work of counseling psychologists; in doing so, we borrow heavily from the description formally approved in 2013 by the governing body of psychological specialties within the United States, the Committee for the Recognition of Specialties in Professional Psychology (CRSPP; APA, 2016a).

## HELPING PEOPLE RESOLVE NORMAL DEVELOPMENTAL LIFE CHALLENGES

Counseling psychology addresses a variety of concerns, focusing on typical developmental life stresses as well as more severe issues with which people may struggle as individuals and as part of families, groups, and organizations. In essence, counseling psychologists help people improve their sense of well-being, alleviate feelings of distress, and resolve crises. They also provide assessment, diagnosis, and treatment of more severe psychological symptoms. Common problems addressed by counseling psychologists include (but not limited to) the following: (a) personal and social adjustment; (b) stress management and coping with negative life events; (c) mental disorders; (d) the development of one's identity; (e) persistent difficulties relating to other people; (f) dealing with and adjusting to physical disabilities, disease, or injury; (g) organizational problems; (h) relationship difficulties, including marital and family difficulties; (i) school and career or work adjustment concerns; (j) making decisions about career and work, including school–work–retirement transitions; and (k) learning to overcome skill deficits.

The training of counseling psychologists is such that they typically have specialized knowledge across all stages of development, and in particular: (a) emphasize healthy aspects and people's strengths; (b) environmental and situational influences (e.g., how cultural, gender, sexual orientation, other identity factors and lifestyle issues shape people's experiences and concerns); (c) issues of diversity and social justice, including advocacy; and (d) the role of career and work in people's lives.

## EMPHASIS ON STRENGTHS OF NORMAL PEOPLE

Counseling psychology has long focused on the needs of relatively normally functioning people across the life span. Counseling psychology is distinguished by its focus on the nonpathological—on normality and day-to-day problems of living, with an emphasis on strengths and adaptive strategies and resilience (see Gelso, Nutt Williams, & Fretz, 2014; Heppner, Casas, Carter, & Stone, 2000). Such a focus is reflective of what is now referred to as positive psychology (see Lopez & Snyder, 2011; Snyder & Lopez, 2002), which emphasizes strengths rather than deficits in people.

## THE INTEGRATION OF SCIENCE AND PRACTICE

The integration of science and practice has a long and important history in counseling psychology (see Heppner et al., 2000; Heppner, Wampold, Owen, Thompson, & Wang, 2015). The knowledge of our profession must be empirically based and verifiable, rather than subjective and untestable. This does not mean that we cannot learn a great deal about human behavior from the more subjective ways of knowing; however, it is of utmost importance that such ideas be empirically tested. Thus, a great deal of quantitative and qualitative research appears in our professional journals. Counseling psychologists also acknowledge the importance of methodological diversity, and the need to examine and expand our assumptions regarding human nature as we continue to learn about the capabilities and sensibilities of human beings as well as how people learn and change over time.

## A PREVENTATIVE AND DEVELOPMENTAL FOCUS

Related to the emphasis on people's strengths, counseling psychology is also unique in its historical focus on preventative and developmental interventions (see Hage et al., 2007). Preventative interventions are those that help people recognize and deal with issues before they become problematic. For example, a preventative intervention may involve consulting with members of a community to prevent gang involvement and providing seminars in the schools for parents and teachers to discuss and prevent bullying. Counseling psychologists, in collaboration with others such as school psychologists, are currently active in promoting prevention science as "a public health model to guide the design, delivery, and sequence of research and intervention strategies" (Herman et al., 2010, p. 654). For example, collaborative research by counseling and school psychologists has found that children can be identified in the first grade who will likely experience academic failure, delinquency, conduct disorders, and school dropouts in high school (e.g., Darney, Reinke, Herman, Stormont, & Ialongo, 2013).

Developmental interventions are those that are educational in nature and are designed to help people understand the issues, factors, and skills involved in normal human development (e.g., communication skills training, or a death and dying seminar). Because the majority of counseling psychology programs are housed in Colleges of Education, the historic emphasis of this specialty has been on developmental issues, skill training, and cultural diversity and on affecting the lives of large numbers of people (Kagan et al., 1988). This unique developmental and educative perspective positions the profession of counseling psychology to more easily expand work in new areas, such as in sports psychology as well as in business and industrial settings.

## DIVERSITY AND CONTEXTUAL PERSPECTIVES

A major theme in counseling psychology for almost four decades now has been an awareness of the need to view people and their behavior within a sociocultural context influenced by such variables as culture, race and ethnicity, gender, sexual orientation, and age (e.g., Heppner et al., 2000; Sue & Sue, 2013). For example, counseling psychology focuses particularly on how the various strands of identity, such as culture, gender, and lifestyle issues, shape people's experiences and concerns. Because counseling psychologists view environmental and social factors as important in human development (in addition to individual or familial factors), they tend to be leaders in the psychological profession in attending to research, training, curriculum development, and interventions involving human diversity (e.g., Gelso et al., 2014; Vasquez, 2003).

Congruent with its emphasis on human diversity, counseling psychology programs tend to accept a higher percentage of racial and ethnic minority students (25%) than other specialty areas in psychology (e.g., see Norcross, 2000; Norcross, Sayette, Mayne, Karg, & Turkson, 1998). Because of counseling psychology's respect for diverse perspectives, the faculty of counseling psychology programs have been in the forefront of not only increasing the preparation of more ethnic minority psychologists but also promoting the multicultural and cross-cultural competencies of all counseling psychologists. Thus, since the 1980s, significant strides have been made in integrating diversity issues into the counseling psychology curriculum, and counseling psychology has been recognized repeatedly for many years as leading the discipline of professional psychology (e.g., see Heppner et al., 2000; Kagan et al., 1988). Not surprisingly, many counseling psychology training programs also emphasize multicultural psychology as a research area—for example, Norcross et al. (1998) reported that 69% of the counseling psychology programs did so.

## A BROAD ARRAY OF HELPING SKILLS

Given the emphasis on normal people's strengths, preventative and developmental, diversity and contextualization, the skills used by counseling psychologists are quite broad, and include skills relevant to both research and clinical practice settings, such as (a) individual, marriage and couple, and family and group counseling and psychotherapy; (b) both prevention and developmental interventions, such as emphasizing school performance as well as crisis interventions and disaster and trauma management; (c) assessment techniques for the diagnosis of a wide array of stressful challenges and psychological disorders; (d) preventative and developmental programs and workshops that educate and inform the public about mental health and about school, family, relationship, and workplace issues before they start or reduced before they get worse;

(e) consultation with organizations; (f) program evaluation; (g) quantitative and qualitative research methodological skills; (h) scale and test construction and validation; (i) mentorship of the next generation of counseling psychologists; and (j) clinical supervision.

In sum, counseling psychology is a strong and vibrant specialty within the larger profession of psychology. We strongly encourage interested readers to visit the SCP website (http://www.div17.org) to learn much more about counseling psychology in the 21st century.

## Career Paths

In 1988, the Georgia Conference Work Group Task Force on Professional Practice concluded that counseling psychologists have demonstrated that they have been able to effectively work in a wide array of settings, including academia, university counseling centers, independent practice, business and industry, medical settings (e.g., VA settings), community mental health centers and clinics, and schools (Kagan et al., 1988). We will discuss several career paths of counseling psychologists to depict the multiple and varied careers in counseling psychology. We will describe these paths separately, although in reality counseling psychologists often are engaged actively in activities related to more than one path at any particular time or in different paths at different times during the course of their career.

## ACADEMIC CAREERS

An academic counseling psychologist often serves as a professor within psychology or education departments. Academic positions usually contain activities within three broad areas that we will describe briefly: teaching, research, and service. Counseling psychologists teach undergraduate classes in 2- or 4-year undergraduate institutions as well as graduate-level classes in colleges and universities. They may teach, conduct research, engage in a wide range of professional service, serve as administrators in academic settings, or even work part time in applied settings such as university counseling centers or independent practice.

### Teaching

People who tend to do well in academic environments are people who enjoy educating students, not only within classrooms but also in a broad array of educational activities outside of the classroom (e.g., learning to publish in professional journals), and even mentoring individual students one on one across one or more years. Counseling psychologists may teach a wide array of undergraduate courses, such as introductory psychology, personality, and research methods; they also may teach in master's level or doctoral-level counseling courses to provide higher level knowledge and skills related to both the research and practice of counseling At this level, they may teach a wide array of courses, such as counseling methods, interviewing, diagnosis and assessment, multicultural psychology, and group counseling.

Moreover, because psychology has long focused on the psychology of human learning and development, counseling psychologists often are focused on ways to improve teaching and learning across all levels of education through research, evaluation, and the creation of textbooks and workshops. Faculty in master's and doctoral programs are actively involved in training students to conduct scientific research and thus are engaged in promoting students' independent research by supervising their master's theses or doctoral dissertations. In addition, faculty members typically are engaged in a number of other university-related committees.

## Research

Faculty in undergraduate, master's, and PhD programs often are involved in research, but in general this is more often the case in the doctoral programs. People who do well in such activities tend to like investigative activities; they enjoy reading, thinking, and discovering or creating new knowledge on particular topics that interest them. Those counseling psychologists typically are involved in a programmatic line of research on a particular topic of interest. For example, a faculty member might investigate a particular topic for many years, or even throughout their career. Examples of some research topics include, but certainly are not limited to the following: resilience and racial discrimination, reduction of drug and alcohol abuse, school-to-work transition, reduction of discrimination against marginalized groups, prevention of depression and anxiety, career development of women, coping and well-being across different cultures. Much of our psychological research is aimed at not only increasing our understanding of particular psychological topics but also, and most important, promoting effective psychological interventions to help those individuals in need as well as to prevent problems from occurring (e.g., promoting greater levels of social justice within communities).

## Professional Service and Administration

Typically, most academic faculty are involved in an array of professional service activities, either related to their department, college, or the larger university. For example, all faculty serve on departmental and university committees as part of their professional service to their institution (e.g., departmental student admissions committees, university awards committee). Some counseling psychologists enjoy such leadership activities in academia, and serve in larger administrative roles, from departmental-level positions, such as chair of a psychology department, to higher level administrative appointments, such as president of a university. Because of the emphasis on work and career as well as development or prevention in the field of counseling psychology, counseling psychologists typically have the knowledge, skills, and attitudes to serve effectively in administrative roles and promote successful and healthy organizational climates.

## UNIVERSITY COUNSELING CENTERS

University counseling centers are usually part of student services at public and private colleges and universities, and they offer a wide range of services. Counseling center psychologists provide remedial and developmental services related to assessment, individual and group psychotherapy, program development, and crisis intervention services. Psychotherapy services at most university counseling centers have instituted time limits, because of the high demand for services and funding limitations, which can range from a couple of sessions to between 6 and 10 sessions.

Counseling psychologists also provide additional preventive and developmental services and serve as consultants and program specialists. Prevention programs include psychoeducational programs, such as date-rape workshops, alcohol and drug abuse prevention seminars, and suicide-prevention programs, all of which may be offered to students, faculty, and staff.

Because most university counseling centers also serve as training sites for practicum and intern students from various doctoral programs, counseling psychologists also serve as supervisors and trainers. They engage in research and sometimes hold appointments in academic departments, such as psychology or educational psychology. In addition, counseling psychologists serve in administrative roles, such as training director, director of the counseling center, or vice president of student affairs.

## INDEPENDENT PRACTICE

Since the 1980s, external forces and changes in the health care market have resulted in a significant increase in the job market for the practice of psychology, including for counseling psychologists, particularly in independent practice (Heppner et al., 2000). Services include individual, couple, family, and group psychotherapy. Some psychotherapists offer services to adults only or to older adults; others serve only adolescents and children. Many offer psychological testing and also may provide consultation, workshops, and seminars. Forensic services, including testifying as an expert witness and providing psychological evaluations for use in the court system (either criminal or civil courts), are other services that counseling psychologists provide. The counseling psychologist may be self-employed or may join other professionals in group practices or partnerships.

Business is an important aspect of independent practice in which most graduate students have not been traditionally trained, but more graduate programs are providing some information in this area, including business management skills, marketing and advertising skills, and guidelines for obtaining relevant consultant services (e.g., accountants, attorneys). Other counseling psychologists acquire this crucial information through training after graduation, including continuing education workshops and classes, consultation, or reading (Pope & Vasquez, 2005).

## New Directions in Independent Practice

The changing face of independent psychology practice is largely driven by the changing needs of society. Understanding the landscape of reimbursement policies is important.

The passage of the Patient Protection and Affordable Care Act (ACA) provides a number of benefits, including increased access to mental health, but variations in health insurance and reimbursement rates create challenges. A primary benefit of the ACA is that more Americans have increased access to adequate mental health care, one of 10 areas that insurance must cover. An advantage of the ACA is that patients cannot be denied coverage if there is a preexisting condition. So, theoretically, all can have access to care regardless for which condition they previously received treatment (Vasquez & Kelly, 2016). This historic health care reform has resulted in enactment and implementation of rules that fully integrate psychological services into primary care, prevention, and benefits packages (APA Practice Organization, 2010).

Information technology advances have begun to exert an influence on the health care industry. The result is an integrated, primary health-oriented, market-driven, employer-focused, information technology–assisted health care delivery system.

Psychologists have expanded their practices into sports psychology, forensic psychology, executive coaching, and gerontology. Growing societal awareness and attention to the effects of lifestyle and behavior on health and illness is creating important roles for psychologists in prevention, health promotion, and disease management. Counseling psychologists have the skills, training, and perspective to provide services—including psychotherapy, consultation, and training—to solve behavioral problems with individuals, groups, organizations, systems, or even the population at large. Learning how to apply those abilities and knowledge in new settings is a lifelong strategy for success.

Training other providers is also an activity in which counseling psychologists with unique skills may specialize. For example, one colleague provides training for employee assistance program counselors who provide telephone services for employees of a major international corporation. One recent training program involved skill development in dealing with anger management issues for couples who called in for telephone services.

## Prescription Privileges

One of the newest roles for counseling and clinical psychologists in independent practice is that of obtaining prescriptive authority. Former APA president Pat DeLeon saw prescriptive authority for psychologists as part of promoting the health care system's ability to be more responsive to consumer needs (Heiby, DeLeon, & Anderson, 2004). The APA has approved this goal and developed a model of training for prescription privileges and as of 2015 three states have such privileges.

Counseling and clinical psychologists with prescriptive authority are in a unique position to improve the quality of medication utilization for clients. They may modify previously ordered dosage levels, substitute more appropriate medications, and ensure that the "all-important psychosocial aspects of therapy are incorporated into the treatment regime. They often take patients off inappropriate medications. In essence, they effectively utilize their psychological expertise" (Heiby et al., 2004, p. 337).

## OTHER HUMAN SERVICE AGENCIES

Community health agencies or clinics employ counseling psychologists as providers and administrators. Some are federally, state-, or county-funded community mental health clinics; others are privately funded agencies (usually, but not always, nonprofit settings), such as a women's agency focusing on rape, domestic violence, or related issues. Community agencies often offer psychotherapy services; some provide preventive and developmental services, although probably to a lesser extent. Assessment services and forensic work also may be involved.

## HOSPITAL SETTINGS AND MEDICAL CENTERS

Typically, hospitals and medical schools hire counseling psychologists to provide skills and knowledge that supplement the services provided by other professionals in these settings and to design and teach courses in patient counseling and patient education (APA Practice Organization, 2014; Kagan et al., 1988). In such settings, the counseling psychologist may provide direct counseling services to either the patient or the patient's family. Counseling interventions may include such interventions as stress management for heart patients and support groups for families of terminally ill patients. Counseling psychologists in medical settings also may serve as consultants to treatment teams regarding the psychological well-being of patients and may provide recommendations for psychiatric or psychological treatment. They also may fill the role of psychoeducator to teach medical students and residents how to increase interpersonal sensitivity and to recognize patients who should be referred for psychiatric or psychological services.

Since the end of World War II, the VA has hired counseling psychologists, and the VA continues to be a major employer of these professionals. According to Kagan et al. (1988), duties typically involve career development for former military personnel; intervention with problems, such as posttraumatic stress disorder and other effects of war trauma; and treatment of disorders that the general population exhibits, including alcohol and drug abuse, depression, and anxiety.

## SCHOOLS

The roots of counseling psychology are in educational settings (Gelso et al., 2014). A primary function of counseling psychologists in the school is to create and maintain a psychologically healthy climate within a school system. Thus, counseling psychologists often serve as a consultant to administrators, teachers, parents, students, and the community (e.g., provide preventive services such as parent effectiveness classes or suicide prevention for the community). Development of a counseling curriculum might involve designing courses for students grades K–12 that focus on healthy development (e.g., peer relationships, conflict-management skills, bully prevention).

A counseling psychologist may engage in crisis intervention in schools that have experienced a loss of a student or teacher, a shooting in the school, and any other traumatic situation. They facilitate groups for children and adolescents experiencing divorce, for those with single parents, and for depressed students and may supervise other school counselors and social workers. Some states require additional credentials or certification for work in the schools.

## BUSINESS AND INDUSTRY

The skills and perspectives of counseling psychologists have been valued by business and industry for decades. A corporation or organization might hire counseling psychologists on a full-time, part-time, or contract basis to provide services in three areas: counseling and psychotherapy, corporate consultation, and direct management (Kagan et al., 1988).

### Counseling and Psychotherapy

Employee assistance programs (EAPs) provide employment opportunities for counseling psychologists. EAPs help with early identification and treatment of employee problems and provide in-house counseling and psychotherapy services, often short term. Counseling psychologists assess issues related to absenteeism, loss of productivity, substance abuse, and marriage and family problems and provide career development services.

### Corporate Consultation

Companies that hire psychologists as consultants include high-technology, financial, and health companies and mega-conglomerates, as well as large nonprofit organizations. Consultants in business and industry offer assistance, usually to top management, on such matters as executive education, executive coaching, team building and effectiveness, supervisor–staff relationships, management assessment and development, diversity management, conflict resolution, and enhancement of communication within and across departments (Gelso et al., 2014; S. L. Shullman, personal communication, August 15, 2005).

### Direct Management

Psychology consultants also provide performance consulting or executive coaching. Hays and Brown (2004), for example, have described how performance consultants provide consulting in three domains: the performing arts (e.g., composers, dancers, actors, talk show personalities), business (e.g., attorneys, bankers, advertising executives, insurance salespeople, corporate executives), and high-risk professions (e.g., neurosurgeons, emergency room physicians and nurses, combat medics).

# Academic Preparation of Counseling Psychologists

This section discusses the admissions process into graduate school and provides some resources so students can quickly begin to identify relevant schools and types of training programs that seem most suitable to them.

## THE APPLICATION PROCESS

The application process in counseling psychology takes a great deal of time and dedicated effort.

### *Resources*

A number of resources discuss the process of applying to graduate school in psychology that can be helpful to students applying to both master's and doctoral programs in counseling psychology: (a) *Applying to Graduate School in Psychology: Advice From Successful Students and Prominent Psychologists* (Kracen & Wallace, 2008); (b) *Getting In: A Step-by-Step Plan for Gaining Admission to Graduate School in Psychology, Second Edition* (APA, 2007); (c) *Insider's Guide to Graduate Programs in Clinical and Counseling Psychology* (Norcross & Sayette, 2014); and (d) *The Complete Guide to Graduate School Admissions: Psychology, Counseling, and Related Professions* (Keith-Spiegel & Wiederman, 2000). These books contain a wide array of useful information, from preparing yourself during the undergraduate years to become academically competitive to selecting the right counseling psychology program (for you), completing the application process, and accepting admission.

### *Important Deadlines*

The deadline for applying to graduate work in counseling psychology varies across different counseling psychology programs, but many of the application deadlines are in early December. Thus, ideally, undergraduate students will begin the process of applying to graduate schools in counseling psychology 2 years in advance of graduation. We recommend beginning the process during junior year for two reasons: (a) it takes a great deal of time and effort to collect relevant information about counseling psychology training programs, and (b) students will have more time to acquire relevant training experiences to become more competitive applicants. It is advantageous not only for applicants to have good interpersonal skills but also to have worked with a wide array of people. These kinds of experiences provide a strong base for becoming a psychologist whose career requires high levels of interpersonal skills. Likewise, having a wide range of research experiences as an undergraduate student also provides a strong foundation to develop critical or scientific thinking skills.

### *Collecting Information and Comparing Programs*

A list of the doctoral programs in counseling psychology currently accredited by the APA is provided both in *Graduate Study in Psychology*

(APA, 2016b) and online (SCP, APA Division 17, 2014). Accreditation by the APA is considered a hallmark of quality and serves as a guide for quality control; most state-licensing boards require that candidates for licensure have attended APA-accredited graduate programs and APA-accredited internship sites to be eligible for the licensure examination. Some employers (e.g., the VA) require that one has completed an APA-accredited program and internship to be eligible for employment.

As of 2015, there are 67 accredited doctoral programs in counseling psychology; in addition, a handful of other programs are jointly accredited as counseling and clinical psychology; counseling and school psychology; or counseling, clinical, and school psychology. The APA book (2016b) and website (SCP, APA Division 17, 2014) also describe the kinds of degrees that are offered by each program, admission requirements, and an array of other information, such as the number of applications received or accepted and available financial support. Every APA-approved program is required to have current information on the front page of their website clearly titled "Student Admissions, Outcomes and Other Data" indicating the following: (a) time to completion for all students entering the program, (b) program costs, (c) internship placements, (d) student attrition from the program, and (e) licensure percentage. This information is invaluable because it allows prospective students to easily compare and contrast programs on at least these important evaluative criteria.

We strongly encourage students to closely examine the respective websites of these programs to learn more about the similarities and differences among the programs and to identify which programs seem to be the most appealing. Some programs may emphasize practice more than research or vice versa. Some programs may emphasize multicultural or diversity issues more than other programs. Although the program websites contain a vast amount of information, the information often is insufficient for most applicants to adequately assess that particular program. It is essential not to stop at this initial phase of collecting information from websites, but rather to collect additional information (e.g., talk to students currently in those programs, or one's current psychology teachers). Students might even conduct an on-site visit after they have gone through a lengthy process of collecting information about different programs. It is extremely important to be well prepared for interviews, having specific questions about the program as well as questions especially for those faculty members whose research interests and other professional activities match the student's interests.

In addition, students should tailor their applications to each particular institution and should explain why they are interested in that particular program, noting for example, which faculty members they might want to work with. We strongly encourage students to apply to fewer programs and to tailor their applications to specific programs, rather than to submit a mass-mailing of applications to many programs, with little attention given to each site.

In essence, we suggest that applicants take an active approach to learn about and compare counseling psychology programs that are especially appealing to them. We also encourage students to examine the websites of specific faculty in each of the graduate programs that they are interested in attending to more fully understand the kinds of interests held by those faculty, the type of research they are publishing, and the courses they teach. In addition, as students examine the various training programs, they likely will find a great deal of similarities across programs as well as some important differences. Some programs will emphasize much more involvement in research-related courses, whereas others will emphasize more applied or practice experiences. Some programs will heavily emphasize diversity issues—some will have a broad array of courses related to multicultural topics, whereas others may have but one multicultural counseling course. As students collect additional information, they typically narrow their list to 5–20 programs. We recommend that students apply to around 10–12 programs. Also note that fees are associated with applying to many graduate programs.

## Common Admission Criteria

A wide array of admission criteria generally is considered across counseling psychology master's and doctoral programs in counseling psychology. In general, applicants should do their best to describe their strengths and relevant skills for both the scientific and applied or practice work of counseling psychologists. With that in mind, we will briefly list several admission criteria that commonly are used in training programs: (a) grade point average, (b) GRE scores, (c) quality of the student's undergraduate training and institution, (d) quantity and depth of previous research experiences, (e) quantity and depth of previous experiences in serving in various helping roles, (f) investigative interests, (g) social or interpersonal skills, (h) interest in and skills associated with diversity issues (e.g., multicultural awareness, knowledge, skills), (i) statistical skills, (j) compassion for others or social justice, (k) leadership experience or skills, and (l) the fit between the student's interests or skills and each program's training focus. Thus, applicants should do their best to address these qualifications as they respond to the required application materials in each of their applications for doctoral study.

Prospective students should be familiar with the two general routes to gain admission into doctoral programs in counseling psychology. The first route is to gain acceptance into a doctoral program in counseling psychology after completing an undergraduate degree. The second route is to first gain acceptance into a master's program, and typically after 2 years of study (and a master's degree), the student then applies for admission into a doctoral program in counseling psychology. Most important, students should understand the different criteria for admission into master's versus doctoral programs in counseling psychology.

Describing which of these two general routes to choose is more than a little complicated. For example, some doctoral programs prefer doctoral applicants to already have a master's degree, and so perhaps 80 or 90% of their entering doctoral students in any given year will be limited to those who already have a master's degree. Not only is a master's degree required, but also usually previous counseling experience. Conversely, the opposite can be the case with other doctoral programs, which prefers to admit undergraduate students who recently have completed their bachelor's degree. These programs often emphasize undergraduate research experience. Other graduate programs may prefer students who have a wide array of people-related experiences, either in previous work environments, during their undergraduate years, or after obtaining a master's degree.

Although most students who enter graduate school in counseling psychology have undergraduate degrees in psychology, others have related undergraduate or master's degrees. Students with nonpsychology undergraduate degrees may need to take extra courses to gain the basic foundations of psychology. Some students have found that obtaining a master's degree provides significant research experiences and counseling practica, which increases their chances of being accepted into a doctoral program. In general, doctoral programs housed in psychology departments tend to admit more students directly upon completion of their bachelor's degree, and programs housed in colleges of education tend to be more likely to accept those students with the master's degree, although there are exceptions to this general practice.

## GRADUATE TRAINING IN COUNSELING PSYCHOLOGY

The entire graduate school process usually takes 5–6 or more years from the beginning of graduate studies to the awarding of the doctorate. The actual coursework for most doctoral programs in counseling psychology typically consumes 3 or 4 years of coursework and applied supervised practice experience.

### Coursework

The coursework typically includes courses related to the following: (a) core areas of psychology (e.g., personality or individual differences, social psychology, human development, experimental psychology); (b) research skills (e.g., statistics, research design, quantitative and qualitative methodologies, professional writing); (c) communication skills, including developing therapeutic alliances and helping people change; (d) individual and group counseling, consultation, and program development; (e) career theory and development; (f) multicultural and cross-cultural competencies; (g) measurement and scale construction; and (h) leadership development.

## Comps, Internship, and Dissertation

After the majority of this coursework is completed, students typically have three more major educational tasks. One often is referred to as the comprehensive examination (or more colloquially, comps). Comps may take many forms across the different counseling psychology programs. One possibility is an all-day, sit-down comprehensive examination of what students have learned in their major topics of study; another possibility is preparation of a comprehensive portfolio (including artifacts, such as major papers they have written during graduate school); still another possibility is documentation of most of the important learning outcomes during their doctoral study. The second major educational task is the dissertation, which is original research that the student conducts to illustrate their ability to conduct scientific research on a topic of their interest. Most programs prefer that students have proposed their dissertation, if not completed their dissertation, before fulfilling the year-long internship experience, which is the final major educational task. Students are required to complete a 1-year internship. The APA also accredits qualified internship sites. A list of these accredited internships is available online (APA, 2016c). These internship sites range from university counseling centers to VA hospitals and behavioral medicine centers. The internship usually includes a full year of supervised practice, for which students typically receive a stipend. The Association of Psychology Postdoctoral and Internship Centers (APPIC, 2016) provides an online directory and facilitates the matching of students to internship programs. Most students travel to a setting in another city or state for their internship.

## State Licensure

The required internship experience culminates with the student's entry into the workforce (assuming the dissertation is completed), and he or she obtains licensure usually after 1 or 2 years of supervised experience. Most counseling psychologists who acquire state licensure must apply and provide verification of their academic and supervised training experiences and must take a state licensing examination in the state they will work to become a licensed counseling psychologist. The examination for licensure is called the Examination for Professional Practice in Psychology (EPPP). Further information can be found on the Association of State and Provincial Psychology Boards website (http://www.asppb.net). Most states also require an ethics or jurisprudence exam relevant to state mental health laws, and some states also require an oral exam. When students complete these requirements, they become licensed psychologists in the state in which they have taken the exam. Psychologists maintain their license by paying an annual fee and taking a prescribed number of continuing education credits to remain current in the field and thus be able to deliver the highest quality care.

## Financial Costs

Financial support throughout the process varies. The majority of doctoral programs in counseling psychology require that students attend full time. Many of the APA-accredited programs provide research or teaching assistantships, and some fellowships or grants are available through the university or from other sources. During the internship, a stipend often is provided but not always; stipends vary greatly depending on the type of setting, with VA's and other government agencies generally having higher salaries. The stipends also vary depending on the part of the country or size of the city where the internship is located. Thus, the training to become a counseling psychologist involves both time and significant financial costs, and it is important to understand these costs when making a decision to start the process of becoming a counseling psychologist.

## ACCREDITED MASTER'S PROGRAMS

Until recently the only accreditation of programs at the master's level occurred for trainees in counselor education programs as opposed to counseling psychology programs. However, the Masters in Psychology and Counseling Accreditation Council (MPCAC) is now available in 13 programs across the United States, with many more programs at some stage of accreditation review. The information about this accreditation process and a list of approved master's programs is available online (MPCAC, 2013). States also allow licensure as counselors at the master's level. The American Counseling Association has compiled survey results of each state and their (a) title credential, (b) educational requirements for licensure, (c) experiential requirements (i.e., how many supervised hours), and (d) required examination. This information also can be found online (American Counseling Association, 2010).

## Financial Compensation

The report of the 2009 Doctorate Employment Survey indicated that the median salary in 2009 for licensed counseling psychologists in direct human services was $81,000 (APA Research Office, 2009). Salaries vary by setting and years of experience. At 6 to 9 years of experience, counseling psychologists in university counseling centers reported a median salary of $53,000, whereas their colleagues in independent practice claimed median salaries of $79,000. According to the APA Research Office report "Faculty Salaries in Graduate Departments of Psychology" (2013–2014), the median salary for educational, counseling, and school psychology assistant professors was $63,334; the median salary for associate professors was $70,233; and the median salaries for full professors was $100,242.

## Conclusion

We believe that counseling psychology is a strong, viable specialty that continues to help people understand normal human behavior as well as complex problems and challenges that are a part of life and living. The field prepares exceptional scientists, professors, and practitioner-oriented psychologists who provide a wide variety of services to diverse populations in a number of settings. The authors of this chapter have thoroughly enjoyed their respective careers, and we hope that this helpful information will aid those considering a career in this vibrant specialty.

## References

American Counseling Association. (2010). *Licensure requirements for professional counselors 2010.* Retrieved from http://www.counseling.org/docs/licensure/72903_excerpt_for_web.pdf

American Psychological Association. (2007). *Getting in: A step-by-step plan for gaining admission to graduate school in psychology* (2nd ed.). Washington, DC: American Psychological Association.

American Psychological Association. (2016a). *Counseling psychology.* Retrieved from http://www.apa.org/ed/graduate/specialize/counseling.aspx

American Psychological Association. (2016b). *Graduate study in psychology.* Washington, DC: American Psychological Association.

American Psychological Association. (2016c). *Search for accredited programs.* Retrieved from http://apps.apa.org/accredsearch/?ga=1.235148737.173120886.1450277224

American Psychological Association Practice Organization. (2010). *Health care reform.* Retrieved from http://www.apapracticecentral.org/advocacy/reform/index.aspx

American Psychological Association Practice Organization. (2014, Fall). Alternative practice models for psychologists: An overview. *Good Practice Magazine.* Retrieved from http://www.apapracticecentral.org

American Psychological Association Research Office. (2009). *Report of the APA salary survey. Table 6: Direct human services positions (licensed only): Counseling psychology doctoral-level, 11–12 month salaries for selected settings: 2003.* Washington, DC: Author. Retrieved from http://www.apa.org/workforce/publications/09-salaries/index.aspx?tab=4

American Psychological Association Research Office. (2013–2014). *Faculty salaries in graduate departments of psychology. Table 8: Salaries for full-time faculty in the U.S. doctoral departments by type of department, rank, and years in rank.* Washington, DC: Author. Retrieved from http://www.apa.org/workforce/publications/13-faculty-salary/table-8.pdf

Association of Psychology Postdoctoral and Internship Centers. (2016). *APPIC directory.* Retrieved from https://appic.org/directory/

Darney, D., Reinke, W. M., Herman, K. C., Stormont, M., & Ialongo, N. S. (2013). Children with co-occurring academic and behavior problems in first grade: Distal outcomes in twelfth grade. *Journal of School Psychology, 51,* 117–128. http://dx.doi.org/10.1016/j.jsp.2012.09.005

Gelso, C. J., Nutt Williams, E., & Fretz, B. R. (2014). *Counseling psychology* (3rd ed.). Washington, DC: American Psychological Association.

Hage, S. M., Romano, J. L., Conyne, R. K., Kenny, M., Matthews, C., Schwartz, J. P., & Waldo, M. (2007). Best practice guidelines on prevention practice, research, training, and social advocacy for psychologists. *The Counseling Psychologist, 35*(4), 493–566. http://dx.doi.org/10.1177/0011000006291411

Hays, K. F., & Brown, C. H., Jr. (2004). *You're on! Consulting for peak performance.* Washington, DC: American Psychological Association. http://dx.doi.org/10.1037/10675-000

Heiby, E. M., DeLeon, P. H., & Anderson, T. (2004). A debate on prescription privileges for psychologists. *Professional Psychology: Research and Practice, 35,* 336–344. http://dx.doi.org/10.1037/0735-7028.35.4.336

Heppner, P. P., Casas, J. M., Carter, J., & Stone, G. L. (2000). The maturation of counseling psychology: Multifaceted perspectives, 1978–1998.

In S. D. Brown & R. W. Lent (Eds.), *Handbook of counseling psychology* (3rd ed., pp. 3–49). New York, NY: Wiley.

Heppner, P. P., Wampold, B. E., Owen, J., Thompson, M. N., & Wang, K. T. (2015). *Research design in counseling* (4th ed.). San Francisco, CA: Cengage Learning.

Herman, K. C., Reinke, W. M., Stormont, M., Puri, R., & Agarwal, G. (2010). Using prevention science to promote children's mental health: The founding of the Missouri Prevention Center. *The Counseling Psychologist, 38*, 652–690. http://dx.doi.org/10.1177/0011000009354125

Kagan, N., Armsworth, M. W., Altmaier, E. M., Dowd, E. T., Hansen, J., Mills, D. H., . . . Vasquez, M. J. T. (1988). Professional practice of counseling psychology in various settings. *The Counseling Psychologist, 16*, 347–365. http://dx.doi.org/10.1177/0011000088163004

Keith-Spiegel, P., & Wiederman, M. W. (2000). *The complete guide to graduate school admission: Psychology, counseling, and related professions.* Hillsdale, NJ: Erlbaum.

Kracen, A. C., & Wallace, I. J. (2008). *Applying to graduate school in psychology: Advice from successful students and prominent psychologists.* Washington, DC: American Psychological Association.

Lopez, S. J., & Snyder, C. R. (2011). *Oxford handbook of positive psychology* (2nd ed.). New York, NY: Oxford University Press.

Masters in Psychology and Counseling Accreditation Council. (2013). *Accredited programs.* Retrieved from http://www.mpcacaccreditation.org/masters-in-psychology-mpac/accredited-programs/

Norcross, J. C. (2000). Clinical versus counseling psychology: What's the diff? *Eye on Psi Chi, 5*, 20–23.

Norcross, J. C., & Sayette, M. A. (2014). *Insider's guide to graduate programs in clinical and counseling psychology.* New York, NY: Guilford Press.

Norcross, J. C., Sayette, M. A., Mayne, T. J., Karg, R. S., & Turkson, M. A. (1998). Selecting a doctoral program in professional psychology: Some comparisons among PhD counseling, PhD clinical, and PsyD clinical psychology programs. *Professional Psychology: Research and Practice, 29*, 609–614. http://dx.doi.org/10.1037/0735-7028.29.6.609

Pope, K. S., & Vasquez, M. J. T. (2005). *How to survive and thrive as a therapist: Information, ideas, and resources for psychologists in practice.* Washington, DC: American Psychological Association. http://dx.doi.org/10.1037/11088-000

Snyder, C. R., & Lopez, S. J. (2002). *Handbook of positive psychology.* New York, NY: Oxford University Press.

Society of Counseling Psychology, American Psychological Association Division 17. (2014). *List of APA-accredited counseling psychology PhD and PsyD programs.* Retrieved from http://www.div17.org/about-cp/list-of-apa-accredited-counseling-psychology-phd-and-psyd-programs/

Sue, D. W., & Sue, D. (2013). *Counseling the culturally diverse: Theory and practice*. Hoboken, NJ: Wiley.

Vasquez, M. J. T. (2003). Extending the ladder of opportunity: Breaking through the colored glass ceiling (2002 presidential address). *The Counseling Psychologist, 31,* 115–128. http://dx.doi.org/10.1177/0011000002239568

Vasquez, M. J. T., & Kelly, J. F. (2016). Independent practices. In J. C. Norcross, G. R. VandenBos, & D. K. Freedheim (Eds.), *APA handbook of clinical psychology: Vol. 1. Roots and branches* (pp. 435–447). Washington, DC: American Psychological Association.

*Joseph E. Comaty*

# Psychologists Specializing in Psychopharmacology

13

The field of study called psychopharmacology is quite broad and diverse. Pharmacology involves the development and study of all types of drugs, such as drugs used to treat disorders of the heart and vascular system, drugs used to treat disorders of the respiratory system, or drugs used to treat disorders of the endocrine system. Psychopharmacology is

Joseph E. Comaty received his MS in experimental psychology from Villanova University; his PhD in psychology with a specialization in clinical neuropsychology from the Rosalind Franklin University of Medicine and Science, in Illinois; and his postdoctoral master's degree in clinical psychopharmacology from Alliant University/CSPP of California. He is a licensed psychologist under the Louisiana State Board of Examiners of Psychologists (LSBEP) and a licensed medical psychologist (i.e., prescribing psychologist) under the Louisiana State Board of Medical Examiners. He is an adjunct assistant professor in psychology at Louisiana State University (LSU) in Baton Rouge and serves as emeritus faculty of the Southern Louisiana Internship Consortium in psychology at LSU. He is the author of more than 60 articles, book chapters, and presentations. He is a coauthor of the psychopharmacology textbook, *Julien's Primer of Drug Action* (2014).

http://dx.doi.org/10.1037/15960-014
*Career Paths in Psychology: Where Your Degree Can Take You, Third Edition*,
R. J. Sternberg (Editor)

a subset of the field of pharmacology. Psychopharmacology specifically involves the development and study of those drugs that have an effect on the brain and behavior.

Although some people may think that being a psychologist who can prescribe medications is the only option available to someone interested in this field, I hope to show in this chapter that there are a variety of career options for individuals interested in the area of psychopharmacology. I will present information that will be helpful to someone who is contemplating entering the field and what level of training is needed to work at various jobs within the area of psychopharmacology. Some form of advanced degree beyond the baccalaureate level usually is needed to gain employment in the field.

Those individuals who go on to obtain a master's degree will find that several options are open to them. For example, they can work within college, university, or medical school departments of psychology, physiology, or pharmacology as research assistants or research associates. They also can work as research assistants or associates in the research and development laboratories of a pharmaceutical company. Or, they can work for a pharmaceutical company in their marketing department as a pharmaceutical representative. These individuals are trained to provide information about the company's products to clinicians who will be using those products to treat their patients.

Another area of employment for those who obtain the master's degree is within government agencies. For example, such jobs may include being a researcher, analyst, or project coordinator for federal agencies, such as the National Institute of Mental Health (NIMH), National Institute of Drug Abuse (NIDA), or the Centers for Disease Control and Prevention (CDC). There are also employment opportunities within public state government agencies, such as departments of mental health, substance abuse, or public health.

Individuals with a master's degree also may find employment in clinical private practice settings where they would work for and under the supervision of a licensed psychologist, perhaps administering and scoring standardized psychological tests.

Individuals who wish to advance to the doctoral degree would be able to find employment in the same areas as noted for the master's degree, but the range of opportunities would be greater. For example, they would be able to be lecturers or professors in academic and medical school departments. They would be able to be independent researchers in pharmaceutical companies. And, with the proper training, they could become eligible to be licensed as a practicing psychologist. The following sections of this chapter will describe these opportunities in more detail.

# The Nature of the Career

When you discuss the issue of psychologists and psychopharmacology, people might assume you are talking about psychologists who have earned the authority to prescribe medications. That is not the only option, however, for those students in psychology who are thinking of specializing in the area of psychopharmacology. As an example, I will describe my career path to show the different employment settings for individuals with training in psychopharmacology.

As an undergraduate, I knew that having only a bachelor's degree with a psychology major would not permit me much of a career opportunity. So, I went to graduate school. It was as a graduate student in experimental psychology that I first was exposed to psychopharmacology through one of my graduate courses. After graduating with a master's degree in experimental psychology, I was employed as a research assistant in a public state mental health and substance abuse agency. I first worked in the laboratory of an experimental psychologist studying the effects of drugs on the behavior of animals. Then, I worked in the laboratory of a pharmacologist where I learning biochemical techniques to assess the effects of drugs. These experiences shaped my interest in psychopharmacology.

My employer became the chair of the pharmacology department of a Midwestern medical school and I was his laboratory associate. Within the medical school, I had the opportunity to work with pharmacologists, research physicians, biochemists, and other research psychologists.

To pursue my career goals, I needed to seek a doctoral degree. I chose to enter a clinical program with a specialty in neuropsychology. I completed the traditional clinical training, including academic courses, clinical practica, and an internship. In reviewing the choices for my practica and internship, I sought placements that were in facilities that conducted clinical research. My internship placement was with a public state research institute conducting clinical trials of drugs for pharmaceutical companies and clinical research on the medications used to treat severe mental illness. This training melded my background in experimental research in pharmacology with the clinical application of somatic treatments for mental illness.

After completing my PhD in psychology, I was fortunate to be living in one of the two states that had passed legislation to allow specially trained psychologists to prescribe medication. I completed the additional training needed to become a prescribing psychologist, which includes completing a postdoctoral academic program that grants a master's degree in clinical psychopharmacology. I will describe in detail the additional requirements to become a prescribing psychologist in the section "Preparation Needed for the Career."

It has now been 10 years since both prescribing psychologists in New Mexico and medical psychologists in Louisiana have had the authority to prescribe. They have improved access to behavioral health care for many of the citizens of their states who otherwise would have had difficulty finding a qualified professional to meet their needs. As of this writing, hundreds of thousands of prescriptions have been written between the two states by these professionals without a single complaint about their practice being received by their respective regulatory boards. Illinois recently passed legislation to allow specially trained psychologists to prescribe medication, and as of this writing, they are currently in the rule writing process to implement the law.

The pioneers of the prescribing psychologist movement were the 10 military psychologists who participated in the Psychopharmacology Demonstration Project (PDP) under the auspices of the Department of Defense (DoD) in the 1990s. They effectively demonstrated that psychologists could be trained to safety administer psychotropic medications.

Prescribing and medical psychologists practice in a wide variety of settings that include private practice, private hospitals, on consultation liaison services in general hospitals, state public mental health centers and agencies, centers for the treatment of developmental disabilities, within the Indian Health Service, within the Public Health Service, and within several branches of the military. The career includes combining traditional psychotherapeutic services with pharmacotherapeutic services in these settings.

## Activities in Which Professionals in the Career Engage

The areas of practice for someone who has training and expertise in the area of psychopharmacology are quite broad. Follow the outline at the start of this chapter, we can see the kinds of tasks carried out by individuals at the master's level and then at the doctoral level of training.

### MASTER'S DEGREE LEVEL WITH BASIC SCIENCE OR CLINICAL TRAINING

In academic settings, individuals might teach undergraduate courses in community colleges, but to go further in the academic area, one would need to get a doctoral degree. Individuals at this level of training can be laboratory assistants in academic departments of psychology, pharmacology, basic sciences, or other science-related departments; in medical school departments of pharmacology and physiology; or in commercial and industrial settings, such as pharmaceutical companies.

In pharmaceutical companies, individuals with this level of training can be employed as protocol monitors. These individuals are in charge of ensuring that clinical research studies are conducted according to the company protocols and that the data are submitted and entered into the company's database for analysis. Pharmaceutical companies also hire individuals with a master's degree as sales representatives. These individuals contact health care service providers and support their use of company products through education and by providing samples.

At this level of training, you could be hired by government agencies, such as NIMH, CDC, and NIDA among others, as a laboratory assistant or technician. Some of the studies conducted at this level involve animal testing that is part of Phase I studies required by the U.S. Food and Drug Administration before a drug can be used in human studies.

With a master's degree in psychology and courses in clinical or counseling psychology, individuals can be hired by licensed psychologists in private practice or group practice settings as psychometricians. A psychometrician can administer and score psychological tests for the licensed psychologist to review and use as part of the process of assessment before treatment.

## DOCTORAL DEGREE LEVEL WITH BASIC SCIENCE OR CLINICAL TRAINING

In academic settings, individuals at this level can be faculty members of psychology departments and teach courses at both the undergraduate and graduate level. These courses might have titles such as drugs and behavior, physiological psychology, neuropharmacology, psychopharmacology, and clinical psychopharmacology. In addition to teaching responsibilities, these faculty members are responsible for carrying out research in their area of interest and mentoring undergraduate and graduate students in the field.

Individuals at this level could be faculty members of medical schools. They likely would teach academic courses in clinical psychopharmacology or conduct research in their area of interest. Within national and state government agencies, doctorally trained psychologists function as heads of laboratories or directors of divisions. In these positions, they head special projects that promote the advancement of technology for the treatment of mental health and substance abuse disorders. They may serve on national committees that advise the federal government on a wide variety of matters that pertain to evidence-based treatment of mental illness and substance abuse. They also may serve on committees within these agencies that review grant applications submitted by academic researchers to help fund their projects.

Psychologists who wish to become licensed as health care providers have additional employment opportunities. Such psychologists can be part of clinical teams in inpatient psychiatric and general hospital settings. They provide education to their patients about the importance of medications to treat their illness, about the possible side effects of medications, and about the need to take medications as prescribed. They provide guidance to physicians about what types of psychotropic medications might be helpful to treat patients who have behavioral health disorders in conjunction with the treatment for their medical conditions and about how to avoid possible drug interactions that would interfere with the individual's treatment.

Licensed psychologists also can be in private practice. They would open an office and provide treatment to individuals with a variety of behavioral health needs. In this setting, psychologists can make recommendations to an individual's primary care physician (PCP) about what medications might be helpful in treating the behavioral health issue. If a psychiatrist or nurse practitioner is prescribing the medications, the psychologist could report any side effects the individual may be experiencing and collaborate with the prescriber on a plan to resolve the issue.

Psychologists in states that have passed laws allowing them to prescribe medication can work in multiple settings that include inpatient general hospitals, outpatient mental health clinics, forensic settings, and private practice settings. Such prescribing or medical psychologists treat behavioral health conditions in the same way that psychiatrists treat patients. Prescribing and medical psychologists consult with the patient's PCP to ensure integrated and coordinated care and to avoid interfering with the medical treatment being provided by the PCP for the patient's general health care.

## A Typical Day in the Career

Those individuals with a master's degree who work in an academic setting (college, university, or medical school) usually will be working for a doctoral-level academician, scientist, or clinician who would be in charge of a research laboratory within an academic department. As their laboratory assistant, you would be assigned tasks that are part of a particular research project. Your duties might include conducting planned experiments that involve working with scientific equipment, chemicals, biological samples, whole animals, or even human subjects. You would monitor the experiments, record the data, and then review the data with your supervisor. If you have a background in statistics, you could assist in data analysis and write parts of the report for publication. You would participate in laboratory meetings and journal clubs in which the latest research being published in the area is reviewed. And, you may get to go to scientific meetings at which your laboratory's research is being presented.

In an industry or government agency setting, you could work as a laboratory assistant, much the same as in the academic setting. You also may be employed as a protocol monitor who would be tasked with ensuring that researchers who are contracted to perform studies, carry out the experiments precisely as designed by the agency or company. This would involve tracking progress on the project and collecting data on subject's responses or results of other pharmacological tests. That data would be entered into the agency or company database for analysis. You may be asked to generate progress reports on the status of the project for your supervisor. You also could be employed by a pharmaceutical company as a pharmaceutical sales representative. This job involves being on the road most of the time, meeting with various individual clinicians or those who work in group practices, clinics, and hospitals. You would provide them with information and literature about the company's products and answer any questions they have about the product. You also would provide them with samples of the company's product for their patients.

Finally, if you work for a licensed psychologist in their office or group practice as a psychometrician, you would interact with a variety of individuals who are being seen by the licensed psychologist for assessment and treatment. For example, you may get to work with children, adolescents, adults, and older adults. Depending on your supervisor's practice and area of expertise, you may get to work with individuals who have conditions such as autism, intellectual disabilities, learning disabilities, substance abuse problems, mental health problems, and cognitive problems from trauma or medical disease, as well as with older adults with dementia.

Individuals who complete the doctoral degree and work in an academic setting (college, university, medical school) could be a faculty member in a department of psychology, pharmacology, or physiology, for example. Duties would include designing and conducting research projects, writing grant applications to support your research, teaching, and consulting. You would write your research results and publish them in recognized professional journals. You would teach undergraduate and graduate courses or medical school courses on topics within your area of expertise. Teaching at this level involves preparing the material, choosing the textbooks and other reading assignments, actually teaching the classes, constructing examinations, scoring the examinations, and submitting grades. You would have office hours to assist students who have questions about the class and the exams. A faculty member also sits on thesis or dissertation committees (in college or university settings) as well as departmental or school-wide committees. Faculty duties also include supervision and mentoring of graduate students for advanced degrees (in college or university settings). If you have a laboratory that employs assistants, you would provide them with their job duties, teach them research techniques, monitor the research, meet with them, and analyze the data for eventual publication. Being an expert in a certain area allows you to provide expert advice to organizations, companies, and other individuals. You also may travel to conferences, meetings, and other public sessions to learn about new developments in your field and also present the results of your own experiments. Sometimes, faculty experts are asked to testify in court.

Duties for those in an industry or a government setting are similar to those in an academic setting. For example, you may be in charge of a division, section, or laboratory focused on research for a particular drug or health condition. Within a government agency, you could be asked to review scientific grants that other investigators would submit to the agency in search of funding for their research. Or you could be asked to do complex analyses on data collected by national health surveys conducted by these agencies.

Within an industry setting, you could be employed as a scientific liaison officer. These individuals spend a lot of time traveling regionally. Their job is to make connections with key opinion leaders in a particular field. They then exchange information with these thought leaders and invite them to speak to other groups of physicians about their experience using the company's products.

As a licensed psychologist, you would set up a private practice or join a group of psychologists in a group practice to provide services to the public. Other settings in which you may work include psychiatric units in general or public hospitals and community mental health centers or outpatient clinics. In these settings, your typical day might include seeing several patients either in your office or on a hospital unit for assessment and treatment or to perform psychological testing.

If you are a prescribing or medical psychologist, in addition to psychotherapy, you can also write prescriptions for medications that will help with treating the person's behavioral health disorder. At each subsequent visit, you would assess the person's progress in therapy and also check for any side effects they may have from the medications. You would call the person's PCP and consult with them about your proposed medication treatment plan and whether this would interfere with or cause a problem for any medical treatments being provided by the PCP. Prescribing psychologists also order laboratory tests and review the results of those tests to check on the health of their patients.

In a private practice setting, a psychologist makes notes in the patient's chart to document what is being done, scores and interprets the results of psychological tests, and writes a report to present results and provide a diagnosis. A psychologist in private practice submits bills for services either to patients directly or to their insurance companies and sometimes calls the insurance companies to inquire about payment. Psychologists also testify in court on behalf of their patient or on other clinical matters related to the care of the patient.

## Advantages and Disadvantages of the Career

Those in the scientific, research, and academic fields have the opportunity to engage in exciting research and add to an important and expanding field. You may also make an exciting contribution to the technology for the treatment of behavioral health disorders. The possibility of interacting with colleagues nationally and internationally who have similar interests and of collaborating with them on research projects is rewarding. In academia, the reward is the opportunity to share knowledge with students and inspire them to consider a career in the field of psychopharmacology. As a mentor and supervisor to graduate students, the reward involves shaping the skills of future researchers and clinicians in the field.

Advantages of working for a pharmaceutical company as a pharmaceutical representative or liaison officer include a variable schedule and a good salary with benefits and profit-sharing plans in the company. Advancement is also available either within or between companies. Additional advantages include travel, a personal vehicle, expense account, personal electronic devices (i.e., tablets, phones, etc.) to support you in doing your job, and the ability to work from home.

Advantages of working in the clinical field include having the opportunity to provide psychological assessment, psychological treatment, and also medications if needed (for those who are prescribing or medical psychologists) to your patients.

The disadvantage of being in an academic, research, and scientific field is that these jobs may not be as prevalent as they once were. The competition for grants to support your research is increasing, and the money to support such grants is decreasing. Additionally, there is the drive to publish and provide academic service to qualify for tenure on an academic faculty. Failing to get tenure would mean losing your job and having to find another position.

The disadvantage of working in the research division of a pharmaceutical company includes the lack of ability to work on your own projects or in areas of your interest. Most of the time you will be working on company projects. You also need company permission to collaborate with anyone outside the company or to talk about what you are working on and to publish your work. Some people may find this somewhat constricting. Sometimes the company shuts down your laboratory or research project without warning based on a business decision by the company officers. Because the company owns your work, the company would take possession, and it can store it or destroy it as they decide. You may even lose your job because the company decides to go in another direction with its research or drug development targets. This lack of predictability may not be to your liking.

The disadvantages of working in a clinical field, particularly in private practice, is the need to constantly ensure that you have enough business to make a living and support the infrastructure of your practice (office rent, equipment, utilities, staff, benefits, insurance). Also, because you do not make any money when you are not seeing patients, you have to plan to cover your costs when you are sick or go on vacation or otherwise not able to be in the office. Plus, you have to provide your own benefits and retirement planning.

As a prescribing psychologist, you have all of the same issues as any other solo practitioner, plus you have the risk of liability related to any untoward events from medications you prescribe for the treatment of behavioral health disorders. You also have to worry about individuals who may be seeking to have you prescribe controlled substances for them when they are not needed. As a prescriber, you have a license from the Drug Enforcement Agency (DEA) and part of their task is to monitor prescribers to ensure that controlled substances are not being diverted to nonapproved uses.

Getting paid for your services in private practice is getting more difficult. As more managed care organizations (MCOs) and insurance companies are involved in the delivery of and payment for behavioral health services, many private providers are complaining that the services they bill for are being denied or they have to wait long periods of time before being reimbursed. That usually means taking time out of your schedule to call the insurer to appeal their decision and hope to get some payment for services. It is this part of the business that has caused many solo practitioners to drop from all insurance panels and to simply charge cash.

And given the movement toward reducing costs in health care, much of what psychologists used to do in private practice is now being done by social workers and professional counselors. This has caused some psychologists in the field to seek alternative opportunities by contracting with facilities and agencies to provide specific specialized services. For example, some psychologists contract with nursing facilities to provide psychological evaluations of residents and collaborate with nursing facility physicians on treatment options for residents with behavioral health issues. Others join group practices that share overhead expenses and are able to negotiate contracts more easily with hospitals, outpatient clinics, and MCOs.

## Preparation Needed for the Career

To prepare for a career in basic research as a laboratory technician or research assistant, you would take courses at the undergraduate level that would give you training in the basic psychological techniques related to research. Usually, this means being a psychology major with science courses such as physiological psychology, perception and sensation, cognitive psychology, psychopharmacology, statistics, and experimental design. This coursework is followed by graduate training at the master's degree level. Usually this means obtaining a master of science (MS) degree from a university program with courses in experimental psychology, physiological psychology, and biopsychology. These are usually 2-year programs and may require a thesis, which includes conducting a research project and then writing a report. After graduation, you could apply for jobs in academic or medical school laboratories, industry, or government agencies.

If you wanted to work as an associate or assistant within a clinical field, then you would follow the same undergraduate path as a psychology major, but the courses would include more clinically relevant areas such as social psychology, psychopathology, abnormal psychology, and psychopharmacology. This would be followed by graduate training in clinical or counseling psychology culminating in a master of arts (MA) degree. Courses would include abnormal psychology or psychopathology, diagnosis, tests and measurement, and psychopharmacology. These are also 2-year programs and may require a thesis for graduation. After graduation, you could find a career working as a psychometrist in the office or group practice of a licensed psychologist. You also could work as a clinical research assistant for an academic psychologist who specializes in research with humans in the area of psychopharmacology. This may involve administering various psychological and psychiatric rating scales of symptoms related to psychological disorders before, during, and after treatments. And this degree would also prepare you for a job in industry as a pharmaceutical sales representative.

The preparation for faculty positions in a college, university, or medical school includes completing a doctoral degree (either a PhD or PsyD [doctor of psychology]). This level of training would prepare you for a position in industry or government agency doing clinical research. The doctoral degree also prepares you to be employed as a scientific liaison officer with a pharmaceutical company.

Doctoral training usually takes 4 to 5 years of study beyond the bachelor's degree. It also can include a thesis (for the midpoint master's degree in some programs) and a dissertation (for the PhD) or major project or literature review (for the PsyD). The dissertation is an independent research project that you develop and complete under the direction of your major academic supervisor.

To be a provider of health care services to the public, you need a PhD or PsyD in a specialty area such as clinical, counseling, school, or neuropsychology. This graduate training requires academic coursework and several clinical practica. Practica are rotations in various areas of clinical practice or clinical settings that provide experience working with patients and clients in different settings under the supervision of a licensed psychologist. Some programs also require the completion of a 1-year internship that is a focused clinical placement in a program that specializes in providing direct care services in a specific area. Internships can be in psychiatric hospitals, university or college counseling centers, or community clinics or mental health centers. After graduation, you would be supervised for another year in a clinical setting by a licensed psychologist to be eligible to apply for a state license to practice psychology independently. Requirements for licensure vary by state but usually involves passing a national examination (the Examination for Professional Practice in Psychology), completing a criminal background check, submitting all of the documentation of your doctoral training and internship, passing a state jurisprudence examination, and perhaps sitting for an oral examination by the state regulatory board of psychology.

Finally, to become a prescribing psychologist (the term used in New Mexico and Illinois) or medical psychologist (the term used in Louisiana), you would need to follow the path described previously for becoming a licensed psychologist. That path includes the doctoral degree—from an American Psychological Association (APA)–accredited program—with practica training, internship (APA accredited), and postdoctoral supervision. The next step is to apply for licensure to practice psychology in New Mexico, Louisiana, or Illinois.

Once you are a licensed psychologist, then you can register to enter one of the programs designated by the APA to provide the training necessary to earn a postdoctoral master's degree in clinical psychopharmacology (MSCP). At present, three such programs are designated by the APA: Southwestern Institute for the Advancement of Psychotherapy/ New Mexico State University, Fairleigh Dickinson University, and the California School of Professional Psychology/Alliant International University. These programs offer courses such as biochemistry, pathology, anatomy, pharmacology, psychopharmacology, laboratory tests and their interpretation, and physical examination. Essentially, these are the same types of basic science courses taken by medical students. In addition to the didactic training, many of the courses require some form of clinical experience. This usually means shadowing or working with licensed prescribers to treat individuals with behavioral health disorders. After graduating with an MSCP, you would need to take another national examination especially designed for psychologists pursuing prescription privileges. This exam is called the Psychopharmacology Examination for Psychologists. If you pass the exam, then you can apply to one of the states that currently allow licensed psychologists with specialized training to prescribe. In New Mexico, you would apply to the state regulatory board of psychology and you would be granted a certificate of prescriptive authority. In Louisiana, you would apply to the state regulatory board of medicine and you would be granted a license to prescribe. In addition to your state certificate or license to prescribe, you also would need a state-controlled substances license from the state pharmacy board and the federal DEA license, which allows you to prescribe what are called *scheduled* drugs or controlled substances.

As noted previously, as of early 2016, Illinois was the third state to pass a law to allow specially trained psychologists to prescribe. The requirements in Illinois to qualify for prescription privileges are different than they are in New Mexico and Louisiana and may require more didactic training and a longer period of clinical supervised experience before applying to the Illinois board of psychology for a certificate of prescriptive authority.

## *Attributes Needed for Career Success*

Regardless of what area you intend to pursue, the attributes for success include interest in education on a variety of topics related to your field of study. Good study habits are essential. Being able to do well in formalized testing will be needed because you often will be tested in this area. You must have an interest in learning about science, both basic science and clinical science. You will need to remain focused on your goals, because if you intend to pursue a career path that requires the doctoral degree, then you will need to dedicate a substantial amount of time and money to achieve that goal. Remaining focused will move you along your career path in a timely manner. Having an aptitude for learning and understanding the basic biological sciences will be helpful. If you are thinking about moving forward in the clinical field and pursue a research career or a career as a licensed professional, you need to have people skills, including empathy, understanding, and a desire to help others as well as the ability to keep a healthy emotional distance from others.

Good organizational skills are essential. Having a good analytical mind is always helpful when working in scientific areas. It is critical to understand how to conduct a competent experiment and to think critically when reading the literature. It also is important to be able to work well with others as part of a team. If you plan to go into industry either as a sales representative or liaison officer, then good speaking skills, command of the literature, and good social skills are a must.

## Pay Range for the Career

For jobs as a research or clinical assistant (i.e., master's degree positions), the pay would start at about $40,000 per year and go up to about $80,000 per year. Academic positions and private positions would fall in the lower part of this range, whereas medical school and industry positions would fall in the upper part of this range.

At the doctoral level, salaries for academic faculty start at about $50,000 per year as an assistant professor and go up to about $140,000 or more at the full professor level. The starting and top salary levels will vary depending on the level of college or university. Top-tier universities usually pay more than smaller private colleges. Medical schools pay higher salaries across the board compared with universities and colleges.

Salaries for pharmaceutical representatives could range from $50,000 to $120,000 per year with a potential for bonuses based on sales performance, plus commissions, and profit sharing. For doctoral-level scientific liaison officers with pharmaceutical companies, salaries may range from about $90,000 to $180,000 per year with bonuses and profit sharing adding to the base salary.

For prescribing or medical psychologists, it is difficult to predict the salaries. Private practice salaries depend on volume of clients seen per day, contracts, and reimbursement rates from MCOs. An estimate would range from about $60,000 per year when starting out to about $200,000 per year when established.

## Future Prospects for the Career

In general, the projection for future demand in the health care industry is high. Thus, it is expected that careers in any of the health care areas discussed in this chapter would continue to be in demand. This is especially true given that the baby boomer population is now beginning to enter the senior citizen age range and will require more health care.

For prescribing and medical psychologists, the future remains bright. The need for behavioral health specialists who also can provide medication treatment will only increase. The trend is for a decrease in physicians across all specialties because the average age of physicians is now about 55 years old, and ongoing retirements from practice are expected. This trend is more acute in the psychiatry subspecialty because fewer medical graduates are entering this specialty.

In addition, with the full implementation of the Patient Protection and Affordable Care Act, parity, and the integration of behavioral health care into primary health care, the need for highly trained behavioral health care professionals who can work with other medical professionals as an integrated team will only increase. Therefore, the future continues to look bright for those who choose a career in psychology with a specialty in psychopharmacology.

*Joseph F. Rath, Hilary Bertisch, and Timothy R. Elliott*

# Psychologists Specializing in Rehabilitation Psychology

14

R ehabilitation psychology is a dynamic and wide-ranging field that offers a wealth of opportunities to psychologists who enter the specialty. According to a recent statement by the Division of Rehabilitation Psychology (Division 22) within the American Psychological Association (APA),

Joseph F. Rath, PhD, is associate director for psychology research and director of the Psychology Postdoctoral Fellowship in Advanced Rehabilitation Research Training (ARRT) at the Rusk Institute of Rehabilitation Medicine, New York University (NYU) School of Medicine. He currently serves as Secretary of APA's Division 22 (Rehabilitation Psychology).

Hilary Bertisch, PhD, ABPP-CN, is a senior psychologist at the Rusk Institute of Rehabilitation Medicine and a clinical assistant professor at NYU School of Medicine. Her clinical, research, and supervisory work has focused on assessment and rehabilitation for individuals with a variety of medical and psychological conditions impacting cognitive and emotional functioning.

Timothy R. Elliott, PhD, ABPP, is a professor in the Department of Educational Psychology in the College of Education and Human Development at Texas A&M University. He is executive director of the Telehealth Counseling Clinic, a nonprofit training and service clinic at Texas A&M University that provides long-distance psychological services to low-income residents throughout the Brazos Valley of Texas.

http://dx.doi.org/10.1037/15960-015
*Career Paths in Psychology: Where Your Degree Can Take You, Third Edition,*
R. J. Sternberg (Editor)

> Rehabilitation psychology is a specialty area within psychology that focuses on the study and application of psychological knowledge and skills on behalf of individuals with disabilities and chronic health conditions in order to maximize health and welfare, independence and choice, functional abilities, and social role participation across the lifespan. (Scherer et al., 2010, p. 1444)

These goals are achieved through a variety of professional activities, which vary depending on the type of setting in which the psychologist works and the population they treat.

## Nature of a Career in Rehabilitation Psychology

Psychologists specializing in rehabilitation psychology help people with disabilities address limitations in psychological, familial, social, and vocational aspects of their lives because of physical, cognitive, or emotional aspects of their conditions. They provide services to individuals with a wide range of disorders typically encountered in medical rehabilitation settings, including catastrophic illness (e.g., cancer), traumatic injuries (e.g., spinal cord injury [SCI]), and chronic disabling conditions (deafness and hearing loss, impaired vision). It is not uncommon for rehabilitation psychologists to cover a particular area or unit of an outpatient or inpatient setting serving a specific diagnostic group or to specialize in working with one particular patient population (e.g., individuals with traumatic brain injury [TBI], chronic pain, amputations) or age-group (e.g., older adults, children; Cox, Cox, & Caplan, 2013; Elliott & Rath, 2011; Scherer et al., 2010).

Conditions addressed by rehabilitation psychologists range from neurologic (e.g., SCI, TBI, stroke, Guillain-Barré syndrome) to orthopedic (e.g., joint replacements, fractures,) to general medical (e.g., multiple sclerosis, HIV/AIDS, vestibular disorders) to psychiatric (e.g., major depression, schizophrenia) to developmental (e.g., intellectual and developmental disabilities, cerebral palsy) to any combination of these (e.g., polytrauma secondary to motor vehicle accidents). Conditions may be acute (e.g., stroke, concussion) or chronic (e.g., rheumatoid arthritis, fibromyalgia, diabetes), static, or progressive (Cox et al., 2013; Elliott & Rath, 2011; Scherer et al., 2010). In addition, substance use disorders are prevalent in medical rehabilitation settings (e.g., dependence on pain medication, alcohol abuse) and may contribute to the onset of disability, development of preventable secondary complications following disability (e.g., skin ulcers, infections), and poor outcome (Heinemann, 1993).

Psychologists specializing in rehabilitation psychology practice in a wide variety of inpatient and outpatient settings that serve individuals living with chronic illnesses and disabilities. Common settings include public and private acute care and postacute care hospitals, other post-acute inpatient settings (i.e., intermediate care facilities and skilled nursing facilities), comprehensive outpatient rehabilitation facilities, specialty clinics (e.g., cardiac rehabilitation), and private practice, and also include schools, universities, nonprofit organizations, and state and federal agencies (Scherer et al., 2010). In hospitals and other institutional practice settings, rehabilitation psychologists typically work within interdisciplinary teams. Depending on the particular setting and the individual's needs, these teams generally include some combination of the following disciplines: physiatrists (physicians specializing in rehabilitation medicine), nurses, physical therapists (PT), occupational therapists (OT), speech and language pathologists (SLP), social workers, audiologists, vocational counselors, and recreational therapists, as well as consulting physicians, such as neurologists, orthopedists, psychiatrists, internists, and others (Strasser, Uomoto, & Smits, 2008).

Over the past 20 years, there has been a trend for rehabilitation resources to be reallocated from traditional acute and postacute inpatient settings to outpatient and home-based programs (Elliott & Andrews, 2016). In response to these shifts, new initiatives such as telehealth approaches are being developed to augment ongoing treatment after discharge from acute and postacute treatment facilities and return to the community. These innovations accompany the long-standing educational or vocational rehabilitation programs (often provided by state agencies) for individuals who may qualify for assistance. These programs were developed to augment the rehabilitation process and in many cases may subsidize rehabilitation therapies.

## Professional Activities of Psychologists Specializing in Rehabilitation Psychology

Regardless of the specific practice setting, the wide array of circumstances confronting individuals with disabilities and chronic health conditions demands a broad skill set and flexibility in the rehabilitation psychologist's approach. For example, on any given day in many general rehabilitation settings, a psychologist may consult with nursing staff regarding behavioral management of a patient with TBI, provide supportive psychotherapy to a polytrauma patient grieving the loss of a loved one, and offer counseling to the spouse of a patient with SCI with questions about sexual functioning (Elliott & Rath, 2011).

Psychologists specializing in rehabilitation psychology routinely provide services informed by other academic and practice areas of psychology, including, but not limited to, social, clinical, and counseling psychology; rehabilitation counseling; behavioral neuroscience; and neuropsychology (Elliott & Rath, 2011). In planning clinical services, rehabilitation psychologists are sensitive to issues of social stigmatization resulting from disability, confidentiality, and consumer protection (e.g., laws related to the Americans With Disabilities Act), as well as multicultural and diversity issues (e.g., race or ethnicity, gender, age, sexual orientation). In addition, they take into account limitations that may be imposed by such factors as socioeconomic status, geographic location, and architectural barriers; they are knowledgeable about, and recommend as necessary, relevant environmental modifications and assistive technologies, devices, products, and services (Cox et al., 2013; Elliott & Rath, 2011; Hibbard & Cox, 2010; Stiers et al., 2015).

Services typically provided by rehabilitation psychologists can be divided into three broad categories (Elliott & Gramling, 1990): assessment (e.g., psychological, neuropsychological, and psychosocial), consultation (e.g., with interdisciplinary teams, family members, or outside parties and regulatory systems), and intervention (e.g., counseling and psychotherapy, psychoeducation, behavioral management, family interventions, sexual counseling, and cognitive rehabilitation).

## ASSESSMENT

Psychologists specializing in rehabilitation psychology are involved in the formal psychometric assessment of intelligence, cognition, personality, mood, social functioning, or outcome. In addition, they use a variety of standardized and nonstandardized methods, including structured and unstructured interviews, rating scales, and questionnaires to assess aspects of adjustment, such as extent and nature of disability, sexual functioning, pain level, and substance use (Cox et al., 2013; Elliott & Rath, 2011; Hibbard & Cox, 2010; Stiers et al., 2015). Regardless of the setting or specific disability, assessment often involves adaptations of traditional tests for patients with mobility and sensory limitations (e.g., Caplan & Shechter, 2008). Rehabilitation psychologists thus are acutely aware of, and skilled in, issues such as test selection, administration and interpretation issues, and threats to test validity that may exist in a given case (Cox et al., 2013; Hibbard & Cox, 2010; Stiers et al., 2015). They use a flexible approach to balance proper test administration with effective accommodations for specific disabilities. A primary concern is making evaluation data relevant to the individual's functional life skills, including, but not limited to, vocational or educational capacities (Elliott & Rath, 2011).

Inpatient rehabilitation settings typically require rapid assessment of cognitive and emotional functioning, preexisting and reactive psychological adjustment concerns, and motivation for treatment. In situations in which the individual is experiencing extreme distress, the rehabilitation psychologist may be called on to differentiate between situational and characterological sources of psychological symptoms. Especially in acute inpatient settings, but in other settings as well, rehabilitation psychologists also use both formal and informal methods to assess family, partner, and caregiver adjustment (Cox et al., 2013; Elliott & Rath, 2011; Hibbard & Cox, 2010).

When developing treatment plans for individuals with cognitive deficits because of TBI, stroke, or other conditions that affect neurological functioning, rehabilitation psychologists typically employ a process approach to assess patients' strengths and limitations. A comprehensive neuropsychological evaluation typically is completed to identify specific cognitive deficits, intact abilities, and measurable goals to guide treatment planning. Once again, a primary concern is making the assessment data relevant to the patient's functional life skills (Wilson, 1997).

## CONSULTATION

Psychologists specializing in rehabilitation psychology routinely provide consultations regarding patient behavior, especially in inpatient settings. Consultations address such diverse issues as adherence to treatment regimens, motivational issues, behavioral disturbances, vocational potential, and family concerns. Rehabilitation psychologists provide guidance to the treatment team regarding the patient's specific learning style, needed accommodations, motivational needs, cognitive abilities, and emotional reactions. Such collaboration can help the interdisciplinary team establish realistic treatment goals. Psychologists may consult individually with specific staff members or develop large-scale psychoeducational interventions for staff (Cox et al., 2013; Elliott & Rath, 2011; Hibbard & Cox, 2010; Stiers et al., 2015).

In many practice settings, rehabilitation psychologists formally communicate with team members during weekly meetings, but they are available for informal consultation between meetings. In addition to working directly with interdisciplinary teams, rehabilitation psychologists play a key role in providing consultations to authorized outside parties, such as family members, attorneys, courts, schools, employers, government and social service agencies, and insurance companies (Cox et al., 2013; Elliott & Rath, 2011; Hibbard & Cox, 2010; Stiers et al., 2015).

## INTERVENTION

For psychologists specializing in rehabilitation psychology, interventions focus on the provision of therapeutic strategies designed to help individuals, their families, and primary support systems cope with, and adapt to, the effects of disability. Rehabilitation psychologists address the implications of disability in the context of the individual's life circumstances, both currently and developmentally, as the person's needs change over time (e.g., Elliott, Kurylo, & Rivera, 2002). They are skilled in a variety of psychotherapeutic strategies and treatment options appropriate to various stages of adaptation to physical injury or disabling illness. Intervention techniques and modalities include, but are not limited to, individual and group psychotherapy, behavioral intervention and management, cognitive rehabilitation, couples' counseling and family therapy, psychoeducation, sexual counseling, pain management, biofeedback, and clinical hypnosis (Cox et al., 2013; Elliott & Rath, 2011; Hibbard & Cox, 2010; Stiers et al., 2015).

In inpatient settings, the rehabilitation psychologist's psychotherapeutic interventions often are focused on facilitating psychological adjustment to new physical disability, traumatic injury, or catastrophic illness. Depending on theoretical orientation, the psychologist may incorporate psychodynamic formulations or learning theory as well as specific cognitive-behavioral interventions (Chan, Berven, & Thomas, 2004). Regardless of theoretical orientation, psychologists specializing in rehabilitation psychology stress the development of flexible coping and problem-solving approaches (Elliott & Rath, 2011; Rath & Elliott, 2012).

Throughout the course of treatment, rehabilitation psychologists tailor treatment options and psychotherapeutic strategies to the individual's stages of adaptation to illness or injury. For example, to further a patient's overall rehabilitation goals, the psychologist initially might focus on maintaining day-to-day motivation but then later address issues of long-term adjustment to disability and future educational and vocational goals. Sexual counseling may include educational and counseling strategies to encourage communication, increase sexual satisfaction, and reduce the impact of disability (Cameron et al., 2011). When providing sexual counseling services, rehabilitation psychologists are mindful not to limit their interventions to married couples or presume heterosexuality. Similarly, they are sensitive to the sexual concerns of individuals who are not in relationships and may be struggling with issues related to stigma and disability (Cox et al., 2013; Elliott & Rath, 2011; Hibbard & Cox, 2010; Stiers et al., 2015).

To address maladaptive behaviors, rehabilitation psychologists employ a variety of behavioral management techniques, such as positive reinforcement, shaping, timeouts, and modeling (Stoll, 2004). Behavioral intervention techniques may be especially useful in reducing impulsivity and improving self-control in patients with TBI and in addressing aggressive or disruptive behavior in general. When implementing behavioral management plans, rehabilitation psychologists typically work closely with interdisciplinary team members, including nursing, PT, OT, and SLP (Cox et al., 2013; Hibbard & Cox, 2010; Stiers et al., 2015).

When working with individuals with TBI, stroke, and other conditions that affect brain functioning, rehabilitation psychologists typically employ cognitive rehabilitation, which encompasses a range of systematic interventions designed to improve everyday functional abilities and increase levels of independence (Cicerone et al., 2011). The restoration approach to cognitive rehabilitation is based on the premise that repetitive exercise can restore compromised cognitive abilities. Techniques include visual and auditory exercises; numerical tasks; computer-assisted exercises; and feedback on performance, practice, and reinforcement. In contrast, the compensation approach reinforces the individual's cognitive strengths, while teaching strategies to circumvent impaired cognitive abilities, with the goal of increasing independent functioning (Dams-O'Connor & Gordon, 2013). Compensatory strategies include the use of cues, notes, written instructions, calendars and datebooks, and electronic devices such as beepers and pagers. The individual is taught to minimize distractions, break down complex tasks into steps, and self-monitor and self-regulate behavior (NIH Consensus Development Panel on Rehabilitation of Persons With TBI, 1999).

Because disability and chronic illness affect not only the individual with the disability but also the individual's primary caregivers and support systems, rehabilitation psychology practice includes provision of psychoeducational and psychotherapy services to family members and primary caregivers (Kosciulek, 2004). Psychologists specializing in rehabilitation psychology are proficient in engaging couples and families and formulating and executing systemic interventions (Cox et al., 2013; Hibbard & Cox, 2010; Stiers et al., 2015). Typical interventions include stress management or problem-solving training, with emerging evidence from randomized clinical trials that these interventions may be provided effectively in the home via long-distance technologies (Berry, Elliott, Grant, Edwards, & Fine, 2012; Bombardier et al., 2013; Elliott, Brossart, Berry, & Fine, 2008).

Psychologists specializing in rehabilitation psychology offer psychoeducational services to provide family caregivers with specific information about the particular chronic illness or disability, along with skills for coping with their family member's disabling condition (Cox et al., 2013; Elliott & Rath, 2011; Hibbard & Cox, 2010; Stiers et al., 2015).

Similarly, psychoeducational training programs may be provided for interdisciplinary team members to improve practical skills and coping. Psychoeducational groups also can be used to connect individuals coping with the same type of chronic illness or disability (Rath, Bertisch, & Elliott, 2014). Learning that occurs through the group process of sharing similar concerns and developing strategies for overcoming them may be more effective than direct didactic transmission of information (Hale & Cowls, 2009).

Finally, psychologists specializing in rehabilitation psychology may incorporate any number of specialized intervention methods tailored to individual patient needs (Cox et al., 2013; Elliott & Rath, 2011; Hibbard & Cox, 2010; Stiers et al., 2015). For example, when working with patients with chronic pain, rehabilitation psychologists may utilize clinical hypnosis or biofeedback, in addition to more routine pain and anxiety management treatment strategies (e.g., progressive muscle relaxation, visualization, diaphragmatic breathing). In some settings, biofeedback therapy may be provided for individuals with such diverse conditions as migraine, diabetes, fibromyalgia, and Guillain-Barré syndrome (e.g., Huyser, Buckelew, Hewett, & Johnson, 1997) as well as with orthopedic and neurological conditions such as TBI, stroke, SCI, and cerebral palsy (Ince, Leon, & Christidis, 1987).

# A Typical Day for Psychologists Specializing in Rehabilitation Psychology

Overall, across practice settings and clinical populations, psychologists specializing in rehabilitation psychology use a broad skill set and a flexible approach while working with patients, families, and interdisciplinary teams to facilitate maximal functioning and adjustment (Elliott & Rath, 2011). These psychologists perform a wide range of professional activities, depending on the type of setting in which the psychologist works and the populations treated. For example, for a rehabilitation psychologist working on a specialized outpatient brain injury rehabilitation service, a typical day might begin with conducting a comprehensive neuropsychological evaluation with a patient who sustained a TBI or stroke. This evaluation typically includes a number of standardized tests and unstandardized methods that help the psychologist better understand the patients' ability to concentrate, remember things, and solve problems and determine how these skills may have been affected by the injury, which will inform treatment planning. During the same day, the psychologist might conduct two or three treatment sessions in which patients are helped to address cognitive difficulties through individual or group cognitive rehabilitation, or any psychological adjustment issues related to the injury through individual or group psychotherapy. In addition, the psychologist may spend an hour supervising an intern or postdoctoral fellow. Finally, an hour or so typically is spent writing reports, documenting treatment, and billing. The rehabilitation psychologist also may have informal meetings with therapists from other disciplines, such as SLP, OT, or PT, to discuss a particular patients' progress and treatment plan.

In contrast, a typical day for a psychologist working on a general inpatient rehabilitation unit might begin with multidisciplinary team consultation meetings to discuss how patients are progressing, and any barriers to their treatment or progress. Sometimes, psychologists make rounds with medical doctors, nurses, and residents to check on patients and identify any concerns that need to be addressed. They typically conduct individual and family sessions to address these concerns and any other psychological adjustment issues related to rehabilitation; they also may lead patient and family education or support groups or even staff intervention and support groups. They might work with administrators to coordinate hospital staff education and support to prevent burnout. If the hospital is a teaching setting, they may conduct supervision with students, and they may seek supervision or consultation themselves to discuss challenging cases (L. Nash, personal communication, June 3, 2015).

## Advantages and Disadvantages of a Career in Rehabilitation Psychology

For many psychologists, a primary advantage of specializing in rehabilitation psychology is the reward associated with being an integral component of a team of professionals that helps people cope with serious injuries or illnesses. Working with an interdisciplinary can be intellectually and professionally stimulating. In addition, many choices are available, because as described previously, rehabilitation psychologists work in a wide range of settings such as hospitals, rehabilitation centers, and specialty clinics for patients with physical, neurological, or psychiatric disabilities across the life span. Potential professional activities for rehabilitation psychologists are extensive, including assessment, support, educational programming, consultation, research, and the promotion of public policies and legislation to facilitate independence for individuals with disabilities (Scherer et al., 2010).

One potential disadvantage of pursuing a career in rehabilitation psychology is the length and expense of the education and training necessary to enter the profession, discussed in the following section. In addition, these professionals may experience a sense of isolation from psychologists in other disciplines because rehabilitation psychology addresses medical and physical-health concerns that are less common in mainstream psychological research and practice. Finally, although the medical rehabilitation enterprise idealizes teamwork for all involved, in many situations, the physician is the head of the team with the latitude to dismiss or ignore psychological expertise. Being active and involved in professional psychological associations can offset some of these potential disadvantages.

## Preparation Needed for a Career in Rehabilitation Psychology

As with all disciplines of professional psychology, psychologists specializing in rehabilitation psychology are required to complete a doctoral degree, which includes rigorous predoctoral training (Scherer et al., 2010). Most rehabilitation psychologists are graduates of APA-accredited clinical psychology doctoral programs, with a smaller percentage earning doctorates from APA-accredited counseling psychology programs, and an even smaller percentage earning degrees from doctoral programs in other psychological specialties. These doctoral training programs take a minimum of 5 years to complete.

To provide clinical services, rehabilitation psychologists also are required to successfully complete the licensure process in the state where they work and provide evidence of ongoing continuing education (Sherwin, 2012). Many states require a postdoctoral fellowship to qualify for licensure, and rehabilitation psychologists typically complete specialized postdoctoral training in health care settings working with individuals who have physical or cognitive disabilities (Stiers et al., 2012; Warschausky, Kaufman, & Stiers, 2008).

To further deepen their knowledge of the field of rehabilitation psychology and to attain formal credentialing and recognition, many psychologists specializing in rehabilitation psychology also elect to attain specialty board certification through the American Board of Professional Psychology (Cox et al., 2013). To become board certified, rehabilitation psychologists are required to demonstrate competencies in the domains of interpersonal relationships, multifaceted patient assessment, team consultation, patient protection and advocacy, a variety of interventions, scientific evidence basis for activities, supervision, teaching, and ethical standards and to show expertise in these areas. Rehabilitation psychologists also demonstrate proficiency in multicultural issues and are equipped to understand and serve patients from diverse backgrounds (Cox et al., 2013; Hibbard & Cox, 2010; Stiers et al., 2015).

## NECESSARY ATTRIBUTES FOR SUCCESS IN A REHABILITATION PSYCHOLOGY CAREER

In addition to clinical training and skills, the ability to instill confidence and trust and provide reassurance is an important attribute for all psychologists (Ackerman & Hilsenroth, 2003; Holdsworth, Bowen, Brown, & Howat, 2014; Jung, Wiesjahn, Rief, & Lincoln, 2015). These attributes are essential to the success of psychologists specializing in rehabilitation psychology, especially given the often-vulnerable nature of the patient population. Individuals who receive services from rehabilitation psychologists may not have pursued psychological services were they not living with chronic illness or disability, and some may still be learning how their condition affects day-to-day life. Building and maintaining an alliance therefore may be a particularly complex process that requires compassion and good self-awareness on the part of the psychologist, especially in the initial stages of adjustment. The rehabilitation psychologist's skill in empathetically instilling confidence and providing reassurance while maintaining the boundaries of a short-term treatment plan is particularly applicable in acute care settings.

The parallel between the nature of the professional relationship in rehabilitation psychology and other specialties is well recognized. Attributes including high ethical standards, compassion, awareness of self and others, good relationships with others, multicultural sensitivity, conscientiousness, good stress management skills, and ability to establish boundaries have been described as essential in rehabilitation environments (Cox et al., 2013; Hanson & Kerkhoff, 2011). Perhaps more so than for psychologists practicing in other specialties, the traditional role of the rehabilitation psychologist on interdisciplinary teams requires a particularly strong interpersonal skill set, which is essential for effective communication and teamwork.

As new practice guidelines continue to emerge and evidence for specific rehabilitation treatments grows (Bayley et al., 2014), techniques become increasingly scientific and outcomes based (Stiers et al., 2015). Nonetheless, psychologists specializing in rehabilitation psychology must be able to balance the systematic nature of evidence-based interventions with the innovation required for direct application of the interventions to patients' individual lives. Therefore, such attributes as attentiveness, exploration, activity in session, affirmation, and accuracy are required, but with sufficient creativity and openness to adapt the intervention for individual patients, while still maintaining the fidelity of the treatment.

## Pay Range for Rehabilitation Psychologists

The Veterans Health Administration is the largest single provider of rehabilitation services in the United States, and it is the largest single employer of psychologists. Their pay schedules for psychologists are publicly available from the Office of Personnel Management, and these probably provide the best up-to-date and reliable information about salaries for early career and midcareer psychologists. Salaries vary by region and specific location, and they are subject to federal budgets (which may or may not include cost-of-living increases). Beginning salaries for a recent doctoral graduate are higher if the applicant has completed a postdoctoral fellowship. Psychologists are hired as clinical psychologists. On the basis of posted information, the lowest current salary for a licensed rehabilitation psychologist who completed a postdoctoral fellowship and was hired into their first position would be $83,468, and the highest possible starting salary would be $98,815 (for the same position in the San Francisco Bay Area).

## Future Prospects for a Career in Rehabilitation Psychology

Rehabilitation psychologists usually are attuned to public, educational, and health care policies because these policies directly affect the lives of individuals with disabling health conditions and have direct implications on professional practice. Recent data indicate almost one in five adults in the United States report some form of disability (Courtney-Long et al., 2015). The overall increase in the number of people living with disabilities may be attributed to the disabling features and sequelae of chronic disease (e.g., diabetes, hypertension) and health issues that accompany the aging of the nation's population. Veterans who incurred some form of injury (e.g., TBI, limb loss, chronic pain, burns) during the armed conflicts in Iraq and Afghanistan also contribute to the increase of disability rates, and many of these injuries (and secondary complications) can persist throughout the life span.

These trends financially strain individual and public resources. In the federal fiscal year of 2010, more than 43% of total Medicaid payments were made to people with disabilities (Houtenville, 2013). Programs and services that facilitate quality of life, reduce disability, and prevent further complications are needed to curtail costs. The Veterans Health Administration has steadily and dramatically increased the number of psychologists to serve veterans with disabling conditions. Programs that help place veterans with disabilities into competitive employment are being developed and evaluated by rehabilitation psychologists (Ottomanelli et al., 2012). Others are involved in developing innovative telerehabilitation services in the home (Brennan et al., 2011).

Rehabilitation psychologists also are examining innovative uses of emerging technologies to facilitate adjustment and participation among persons with disabilities. For example, virtual reality technologies are being used to help patients with severe burns manage their pain during intensive procedures (with self-hypnotic and imagery techniques; Patterson, Jensen, Wiechman, & Sharar, 2010) and to assist gait training and driving simulations. There also are opportunities to assist patients with limb loss in adjusting to and learning the use of robotics and other advanced prostheses.

New roles for rehabilitation psychologists are emerging in Level 1 trauma centers because many individuals with little or no health insurance are admitted with severe and disabling injuries, and they are discharged without inpatient medical rehabilitation care (Warren, Stucky, & Sherman, 2013). Level 1 trauma centers are mandated to have active educational, research, injury prevention, and public outreach programs. Rehabilitation psychologists use their professional skills to help the trauma team provide a continuum of care, support, and strategic services.

Consequently, future prospects for careers in rehabilitation psychology are bright. Opportunities for psychologists specializing in rehabilitation psychology likely will proliferate in medical and community settings as their work is critical in alleviating the concerns that individuals with disabilities face by improving access to care; enhancing the quality of available services; and optimizing quality of life and full participation in social, vocational, and personal roles.

# References

Ackerman, S. J., & Hilsenroth, M. J. (2003). A review of therapist characteristics and techniques positively impacting the therapeutic alliance. *Clinical Psychology Review, 23*, 1–33. http://dx.doi.org/10.1016/S0272-7358(02)00146-0

Bayley, M. T., Tate, R., Douglas, J. M., Turkstra, L. S., Ponsford, J., Stergiou-Kita, M., . . . the INCOG Expert Panel. (2014). INCOG guidelines for cognitive rehabilitation following traumatic brain injury: Methods and overview. *Journal of Head Trauma Rehabilitation, 29*, 290–306. http://dx.doi.org/10.1097/HTR.0000000000000070

Berry, J. W., Elliott, T. R., Grant, J. S., Edwards, G., & Fine, P. R. (2012). Does problem-solving training for family caregivers benefit their care recipients with severe disabilities? A latent growth model of the Project CLUES randomized clinical trial. *Rehabilitation Psychology, 57*, 98–112.

Bombardier, C. H., Ehde, D. M., Gibbons, L. E., Wadhwani, R., Sullivan, M. D., Rosenberg, D. E., & Kraft, G. H. (2013). Telephone-based physical activity counseling for major depression in people with multiple sclerosis. *Journal of Consulting and Clinical Psychology, 81*, 89–99. http://dx.doi.org/10.1037/a0031242

Brennan, D. M., Lum, P., Uswatte, G., Taub, E., Gilmore, B. M., & Barman, J. (2011). A telerehabilitation platform for home-based automated therapy of arm function. *Conference Proceedings of the IEEE Engineering in Medicine and Biology Society*, 1819–1822.

Cameron, R. P., Mona, L. R., Syme, M. L., Cordes, C. C., Fraley, S. S., Chen, S. S., . . . Lemos, L. (2011). Sexuality among wounded veterans of Operation Enduring Freedom (OEF), Operation Iraqi Freedom (OIF), and Operation New Dawn (OND): Implications for rehabilitation psychologists. *Rehabilitation Psychology, 56*, 289–301. http://dx.doi.org/10.1037/a0025513

Caplan, B., & Shechter, J. (2008). Test accommodations for the geriatric patient. *NeuroRehabilitation, 23*, 395–402.

Chan, F., Berven, N. L., & Thomas, K. R. (Eds.). (2004). *Counseling theories and techniques for rehabilitation health professionals*. New York, NY: Springer.

Cicerone, K. D., Langenbahn, D. M., Braden, C., Malec, J. F., Kalmar, K., Fraas, M., . . . Ashman, T. (2011). Evidence-based cognitive rehabilitation: Updated review of the literature from 2003 through 2008. *Archives of Physical Medicine and Rehabilitation, 92*, 519–530. http://dx.doi.org/10.1016/j.apmr.2010.11.015

Courtney-Long, E. A., Carroll, D. D., Zhang, Q. C., Stevens, A. C., Griffin-Blake, S., Armour, B. S., & Campbell, V. A. (2015). Prevalence of disability and disability types among adults—United States, 2013. *Morbidity and Mortality Weekly Report, 64*, 777–783. http://dx.doi.org/10.15585/mmwr.MM6429a2

Cox, D. R., Cox, R. H., & Caplan, B. (2013). *Specialty competencies in rehabilitation psychology*. New York, NY: Oxford University Press.

Dams-O'Connor, K., & Gordon, W. A. (2013). Integrating interventions after traumatic brain injury: A synergistic approach to neuro-rehabilitation. *Brain Impairment, 14*, 51–62. http://dx.doi.org/10.1017/BrImp.2013.9

Elliott, T. R., & Andrews, E. E. (2016). Physical rehabilitation facilities. In J. C. Norcross, G. R. VandenBos, & D. K. Freeheim (Eds.), *APA handbook of clinical psychology: Vol. 1. Roots and branches* (pp. 509–524). Washington, DC: American Psychological Association.

Elliott, T. R., Brossart, D., Berry, J. W., & Fine, P. R. (2008). Problem-solving training via videoconferencing for family caregivers of persons with spinal cord injuries: A randomized controlled trial. *Behaviour Research and Therapy, 46,* 1220–1229. http://dx.doi.org/10.1016/j.brat.2008.08.004

Elliott, T. R., & Gramling, S. E. (1990). Psychologists and rehabilitation: New roles and old training models. *American Psychologist, 45,* 762–765. http://dx.doi.org/10.1037/0003-066X.45.6.762

Elliott, T. R., Kurylo, M., & Rivera, P. (2002). Positive growth following an acquired physical disability. In C. R. Snyder & S. Lopez (Eds.), *Handbook of positive psychology* (pp. 687–699). New York, NY: Oxford University Press.

Elliott, T. R., & Rath, J. F. (2011). Rehabilitation psychology. In E. M. Altmaier & J.-I. C. Hansen (Eds.), *Oxford handbook of counseling psychology* (pp. 679–702). New York, NY: Oxford University Press.

Hale, S., & Cowls, J. (2009). Psychoeducational groups. In I. Soderback (Ed.), *International handbook of occupational therapy interventions* (pp. 255–260). New York, NY: Springer Science. http://dx.doi.org/10.1007/978-0-387-75424-6_24

Hanson, S. L., & Kerkhoff, T. R. (2011). The APA Ethical Principles as a foundational competency: Application to rehabilitation psychology. *Rehabilitation Psychology, 56,* 219–230. http://dx.doi.org/10.1037/a0024206

Heinemann, A. W. (Ed.). (1993). *Substance abuse and physical disability.* Binghamton, NY: Haworth Press.

Hibbard, M. R., & Cox, D. R. (2010). Competencies of a rehabilitation psychologist. In R. Frank, M. Rosenthal, & B. Caplan (Eds.), *Handbook of rehabilitation psychology* (2nd ed., pp. 467–475). Washington, DC: American Psychological Association.

Holdsworth, E., Bowen, E., Brown, S., & Howat, D. (2014). Client engagement in psychotherapeutic treatment and associations with client characteristics, therapist characteristics, and treatment factors. *Clinical Psychology Review, 34,* 428–450. http://dx.doi.org/10.1016/j.cpr.2014.06.004

Houtenville, A. J. (2013). *2013 annual compendium of disability statistics.* Durham: University of New Hampshire, Institute on Disability.

Huyser, B., Buckelew, S. P., Hewett, J. E., & Johnson, J. (1997). Factors affecting adherence to rehabilitation interventions for individuals with fibromyalgia. *Rehabilitation Psychology, 42,* 75–91. http://dx.doi.org/10.1037/0090-5550.42.2.75

Ince, P. L., Leon, M. S., & Christidis, D. (1987). EMG biofeedback with the upper extremity: A critical review of the experimental foundations of clinical treatment with the disabled. *Rehabilitation Psychology, 32,* 77–91.

Jung, E., Wiesjahn, M., Rief, W., & Lincoln, T. M. (2015). Perceived therapist genuineness predicts therapeutic alliance in cognitive behavioural therapy for psychosis. *British Journal of Clinical Psychology, 54,* 34–48. http://dx.doi.org/10.1111/bjc.12059

Kosciulek, J. F. (2004). Family counseling. In F. Chan, N. L. Berven, & K. R. Thomas (Eds.), *Counseling theories and techniques for rehabilitation health professionals* (pp. 264–281). New York, NY: Springer.

NIH Consensus Development Panel on Rehabilitation of Persons With Traumatic Brain Injury. (1999). Consensus conference. Rehabilitation of persons with traumatic brain injury. *JAMA, 282,* 974–983. http://dx.doi.org/10.1001/jama.282.10.974

Ottomanelli, L., Goetz, L. L., Suris, A., McGeough, C., Sinnott, P. L., Toscano, R., . . . Thomas, F. P. (2012). Effectiveness of supported employment for veterans with spinal cord injuries: Results from a randomized multisite study. *Archives of Physical Medicine and Rehabilitation, 93,* 740–747. http://dx.doi.org/10.1016/j.apmr.2012.01.002

Patterson, D. R., Jensen, M. P., Wiechman, S. A., & Sharar, S. R. (2010). Virtual reality hypnosis for pain associated with recovery from physical trauma. *International Journal of Clinical and Experimental Hypnosis, 58,* 288–300. http://dx.doi.org/10.1080/00207141003760595

Rath, J. F., Bertisch, H., & Elliott, T. R. (2014). Groups in behavioral health and medical settings. In J. L. DeLucia-Waack, C. R. Kalodner, & M. T. Riva (Eds.), *Handbook of group counseling and psychotherapy* (2nd ed., pp. 340–350). Thousand Oaks, CA: Sage.

Rath, J. F., & Elliott, T. R. (2012). Psychological models in rehabilitation psychology. In P. Kennedy (Ed.), *Oxford handbook of rehabilitation psychology* (pp. 32–46). New York, NY: Oxford University Press.

Scherer, M., Blair, K., Bost, R., Hanson, S., Hough, S., Kurylo, M., . . . Banks, M. (2010). Rehabilitation psychology. In I. B. Weiner & W. E. Craighead (Eds.), *The Corsini encyclopedia of psychology and behavioral science* (4th ed., pp. 1444–1447). Hoboken, NJ: Wiley.

Sherwin, E. (2012). A field in flux: The history of rehabilitation psychology. In P. Kennedy (Ed.), *The Oxford handbook of rehabilitation psychology* (pp. 10–31). New York, NY: Oxford University Press. http://dx.doi.org/10.1093/oxfordhb/9780199733989.013.0002

Stiers, W., Barisa, M., Stucky, K., Pawlowski, C., Van Tubbergen, M., Turner, A. P., . . . Caplan, B. (2015). Guidelines for competency development and measurement in rehabilitation psychology postdoctoral training. *Rehabilitation Psychology, 60,* 111–122. http://dx.doi.org/10.1037/a0038353

Stiers, W., Hanson, S., Turner, A. P., Stucky, K., Barisa, M., Brownsberger, M., . . . the Council of Rehabilitation Psychology Postdoctoral Training

Programs. (2012). Guidelines for postdoctoral training in rehabilitation psychology. *Rehabilitation Psychology*, *57*, 267–279. http://dx.doi.org/10.1037/a0030774

Stoll, J. L. (2004). Behavior therapy. In F. Chan, N. L. Berven, & K. R. Thomas (Eds.), *Counseling theories and techniques for rehabilitation health professionals* (pp. 136–176). New York, NY: Springer.

Strasser, D. C., Uomoto, J. M., & Smits, S. J. (2008). The interdisciplinary team and polytrauma rehabilitation: Prescription for partnership. *Archives of Physical Medicine and Rehabilitation*, *89*, 179–181. http://dx.doi.org/10.1016/j.apmr.2007.06.774

Warren, A. M., Stucky, K., & Sherman, J. J. (2013). Rehabilitation psychology's role in the Level I trauma center. *Journal of Trauma and Acute Care Surgery*, *74*, 1357–1362.

Warschausky, S., Kaufman, J., & Stiers, W. (2008). Training requirements and scope of practice in rehabilitation psychology and neuropsychology. *Journal of Pediatric Rehabilitation Medicine*, *1*, 61–65.

Wilson, B. A. (1997). Cognitive rehabilitation: How it is and how it might be. *Journal of the International Neuropsychological Society*, *3*, 487–496.

# SPECIALIZED SETTINGS

*Rebecca M. Puhl and Marlene B. Schwartz*

# Psychologists Working in Independently Funded Research Centers and Institutes

15

This chapter focuses on careers of psychologists who work in independently funded research centers. Although research centers can vary considerably in terms of their size, scope of research, funding sources, and whether or not they are linked to academic institutions, we address some of the common characteristics, benefits, and challenges of working in this type of setting. Our insights about these issues come from

Rebecca M. Puhl, PhD, is deputy director of the Rudd Center for Food Policy and Obesity and professor in the Department of Human Development and Family Studies at the University of Connecticut. She received her BA from Queen's University in Ontario, Canada, and her PhD in clinical psychology from Yale University. Her research addresses bullying, bias, and discrimination experienced by children and adults who have obesity.

Marlene B. Schwartz, PhD, is director of the Rudd Center for Food Policy and Obesity and professor in the Department of Human Development and Family Studies at the University of Connecticut. She received her BA from Haverford College and her PhD in clinical psychology from Yale University. Her research and community service address how home environments, school landscapes, neighborhoods, and the media shape the eating attitudes and behaviors of children.

http://dx.doi.org/10.1037/15960-016
*Career Paths in Psychology: Where Your Degree Can Take You, Third Edition*,
R. J. Sternberg (Editor)

our professional experiences working as researchers and in leadership roles at an independently funded research center called the Rudd Center for Food Policy and Obesity. We have worked at the Rudd Center since its establishment at Yale University in 2005 and through the center's recent move to the University of Connecticut in 2015. What makes our center different than most is its dual focus on both research and policy. Our center's mission is to use research to help reverse the environmental and societal contributors of childhood obesity and weight bias, which can be best achieved by influencing public policy. The inclusion of public policy in our center's mission is not typical of most research centers, and it provides us with unique opportunities in our research and in working with individuals and organizations outside of academic and scientific settings. We highlight some of these distinctive features of our center, in addition to the characteristics that are more common across independently funded centers.

## The Structure of an Independently Funded Center

### OPERATING WITHIN OR OUTSIDE OF ACADEMIC INSTITUTIONS

Independently funded research centers can exist within a university setting or be completely unaffiliated with an academic institution. Each of these scenarios comes with advantages and challenges.

Being an independently funded research center within a research university setting can have scientific and financial benefits for both the center and the university. In this case, scientists in the center often have faculty appointments as professors in departments at the university with similar responsibilities as other faculty members in the institution. This scenario has considerable advantages as it anchors researchers as faculty members to the university, increases access to university resources otherwise not readily available to independent centers, allows multiple opportunities for collaboration with other researchers across the university, and provides more financial stability that otherwise must be obtained through grant funding. However, it also can slow down the pace of research given that center scientists have faculty responsibilities within the university, such as course preparation, teaching, grading, meeting with students, attending faculty and committee meetings, and completing other professional service activities. In addition, a center that is within an academic institution is expected to contribute to the research and scholarship of the university community more broadly and is accountable to the university's established evaluations and standards that apply to other university-based centers.

Centers that are truly independent and unaffiliated with academic institutions have more freedom to operate under their own authority, choose the areas of research they wish to pursue, and determine the types of funding sources they wish to seek. This scenario provides an environment that allows researchers to potentially be more productive because scientists are not serving multiple roles as faculty members and devoting time to teaching or other faculty responsibilities. Overhead infrastructure costs for independent centers or institutes can be substantial, however, and they often lack access to the breadth of fund-raising opportunities to which universities or hospitals dedicate significant resources.

Regardless of whether independently funded centers are within or unaffiliated with an academic institution, they face an ongoing challenge of securing sufficient funding to continue producing research and maintaining center operations. Centers that depend on federal grants, such as the National Institutes of Health (NIH), are particularly vulnerable to financial struggles in light of fierce competition for a reduced amount of available NIH funds. Centers increasingly may be forced to look for alternative funding sources, such as industry funding or financial donors whose interests guide the research areas that define the center's work. Centers that cannot find sufficient funding sources, regardless of whether this comes from external granting agencies, industry, or private donors, may be vulnerable to financial strains that make it difficult to remain independent or necessitate closing their doors altogether.

## THE INTERNAL ORGANIZATION OF A CENTER

The structural organization within independently funded research centers can vary, but typically, a center director oversees the research activities conducted by a staff of PhD-level scientists, research assistants, and other research personnel who are working on the center's identified research mission. At the Rudd Center, our director (Dr. Marlene Schwartz) fills a number of additional key roles, including meeting with potential funding agencies or donors, representing the center at national meetings and events, initiating collaborations with other organizations, and establishing connections with researchers within and outside of the university.

Our center also has a team of multidisciplinary faculty who have been trained in fields of psychology, economics, law, public health, and policy. Each of our faculty members leads a team of research staff, and each team works both collaboratively and independently on distinct research and policy initiatives that together meet our center's primary mission. This structure works well for multifaceted research topics (like the topic of obesity, the focus of our center's work), as it brings together scientists from different disciplines that can work collaboratively for a long period of time to facilitate progress on our mission. Each of our faculty also have academic appointments at different departments within the university, which means they work as both center scientists and faculty members.

Because our center is situated within a university, we also have students who work with us, either as summer interns, as research assistants during the academic year, or on projects supervised by faculty that can serve as independent studies to fulfill course requirements or graduate-level theses or dissertation studies. Having students work with us is an important aspect of our center's structure, not only because student involvement is valuable to the completion of our center's research but also because it provides opportunities to train, stimulate, and deputize young researchers to pursue and further these research topics in their own research careers.

Finally, as a center that prioritizes the translation of science for public policy and public consumption, our structure requires expertise in communications and policy. Our center has a communications team that translates and disseminates our research evidence for broad audiences, works with media outlets and reporters who seek our expertise, maintains an active presence for our center in social media, and manages all aspects of our center's website, newsletter, and other forms of external communication. In contrast, our policy experts educate federal, state, and local policymakers about our center's research, and work with state and local advocacy groups to develop the tools and resources necessary to support policy improvements. The addition of communications and policy expertise is not common in independent research centers, but we believe these areas of expertise are key to promote and optimize the impact of our research.

## Key Features of Working at an Independently Funded Center

When a center initially is launched or established, it is critical to have a clearly defined research mission.

### IDENTIFYING THE PRIMARY MISSION OF THE CENTER'S RESEARCH

For many academic psychology labs, the scientific method defines the research trajectory—each study builds systematically on the previous study by changing one variable at a time to refine the theory being tested. This method makes sense when the mission of the lab is to further knowledge about a specific phenomenon or aspect of human behavior. In the case of the Rudd Center, however, our mission is to use research to reverse the environmental and societal contributors to childhood obesity and weight bias. We are interested in the factors that cause childhood obesity and weight bias, but only as a starting point— our work is driven by a desire to change those factors, and our belief is that large societal changes are best achieved through influencing public policy.

Our structure reflects the domains in which we would like to see policy change, and we are willing to end some lines of research and begin new ones as opportunities arise. For example, over the years, we have research programs that focus on strengthening policies in specific settings that influence children's diets (e.g., schools, child care centers), strengthening the federal food programs (e.g., Women, Infants and Children; Supplemental Nutrition Assistance Program), and pressuring the food industry to change its practices (e.g., restaurant menu calorie labeling, child-directed food marketing, product reformulation). As new policies are created, such as the federal requirement for all restaurant chains to post calories on their menus and menu boards, we are comfortable ending that line of research and using our resources to focus on new areas.

## CONDUCTING WORK RELEVANT TO THE DONOR'S INTENT

Funding from individual donors is a consistent source of support for some research centers. In these cases, it is important to ensure that a clear connection exists between the donor's vision and the center's mission and that the funder's priorities match those of the organization.

Our center was established by a donation from an individual donor, and our mission and primary initiatives were developed in collaboration with our donor's vision. This required establishing a clear and specific understanding of the aims and mission of our funded work, the target populations we hope to reach, and the potential impact and long-term benefits that our work aims to achieve. For our center, funding from our donor was particularly fundamental in providing opportunities for us to conduct research in novel and innovative areas that typically are not funded by government or other publicly funded sources and to pursue policy-focused work that is rarely funded through traditional grant mechanisms. Thus, this funding helped to establish the unique strengths of our center as both a research and policy organization pursuing novel work to inform public policy and public health.

Although our center receives research funding from other external granting agencies and foundations, our founding donor's vision remains a central part of our center's identity, ongoing research, and long-term goals. We are in regular communication with our donor to report progress of relevant research initiatives and accomplishments and to discuss new projects and future directions of our work. In the years since our center was established, our donor has attended important meetings and conferences hosted by our center on areas of our work that are of shared interest, and these events have provided unique opportunities to obtain input and guidance on future priorities for our center alongside feedback from other experts in our field.

Over time, as our research has evolved and moved in new directions, it has been important to maintain good communication with our donor and to reevaluate how our work continues to align with the overall mission of our center. We have been fortunate to have a donor whose vision continues to match the goals of our organization, who has afforded us considerable freedom to prioritize what research is needed most, and who has trusted our expertise to carry forward our center's mission.

## SEEKING GRANT FUNDING FROM EXTERNAL FUNDING AGENCIES

Although the Rudd Center was founded with a gift from an individual donor, we have always sought funding from a variety of other sources to diversify our support and engage with different stakeholders. The majority of additional funding for our work has come from private foundations (such as the Robert Wood Johnson Foundation [RWJF], Dell Foundation, Horizon Foundation, Claneil Foundation) and government agencies (NIH and the U.S. Department of Agriculture).

Each source of funding has different requirements, and we have had to learn how to match projects with funding sources. NIH funds traditional research studies, for which scientific rigor is paramount. Foundations often are less interested in funding scientific research and are more interested in funding demonstration projects or creating practical resources for use by practitioners in the field. For example, we created a psychometrically sound assessment tool to code school wellness policies using research funding from RWJF's Healthy Eating Research Program. After it was published in the peer-reviewed literature, RWJF used a different funding mechanism to help us create an online version of the measure that could be used by researchers and school administrators throughout the country. Similarly, Dr. Puhl has used funding from the Rudd Foundation to create resources such as evidence-based films to educate health professionals and teachers about weight bias, an online course for continuing medical education about weight stigma, and a media gallery of respectful images of children and adults with obesity for journalists to use when publishing media reports about obesity. We feel that these nonresearch resources augment the societal impact of the Rudd Center beyond the influence of scholarly articles we publish in academic journals.

## ESTABLISHING PARTNERSHIPS WITH NATIONAL ORGANIZATIONS

One of the benefits of participating in a foundation's overall funding program is that it provides the opportunity to meet other researchers and members of national nongovernmental organizations who are interested in the same issues. For many academics, their primary colleagues outside of their own university are researchers in other universities who do similar work; you meet up at scientific meetings and may collaborate on multisite studies.

At the Rudd Center, in addition to these scientific collaborations, we prioritize meeting people from national organizations who have the capacity to engage in activities that are beyond our scope, yet important to the movement overall. One such relationship is with the Center for Science and the Public Interest (CSPI), which is an advocacy organization that works on changing federal and state nutrition policies. When we publish a study that is relevant to their work, they can help get our research into the hands of advocates all over the country. Furthermore, because CSPI is able to engage in lobbying, they can speak with legislators when bills have been introduced and can share our research with policymakers if it is relevant.

Another important relationship for our center is with the Partnership for a Healthier America (PHA), which is an independent organization that brokers commitments between the First Lady's *Let's Move* initiative and for-profit companies to improve policies relevant to childhood obesity. For example, several large commercial childcare companies in the United States have joined PHA and promised to stop serving sugary drinks, increase fruits and vegetables, limit screen time, and promote breastfeeding. Our center's role is to be the independent evaluator of these commitments, but through that process, we have come to know PHA and have had the opportunity to provide feedback on its initiatives.

A third example is an important relationship that our center has with the Centers for Disease Control and Prevention (CDC). The CDC oversees federal health policy and funds individual states to engage in health promotion initiatives through grants to their Departments of Public Health. We have had the opportunity to work with the CDC to provide expert opinions on their planned activities and feedback on national surveillance measures, such as assessment of school health policies and practices.

## PRESENTING RESEARCH TO DIVERSE AUDIENCES

Disseminating our research to diverse groups is a key component of efforts to motivate broad-level changes with science. At our center, an important aspect of our approach to research involves presenting our scientific findings to diverse audiences who can use our research evidence to inform actionable goals in public health or public policy.

Like other academics, our faculty members regularly present their research findings at national scientific conferences and meetings where the audience members are typically other researchers in the fields of obesity, nutrition, or public health. Presenting our research at conferences is important to maintain scholarly credibility of our center's work and to stimulate ideas for new science. We also prioritize opportunities to present our research to nonscientific groups, such as government agencies, advocacy organizations, school boards, community groups, and policymakers. These types of groups are especially relevant given our center's mission to use research to inform public health and public policy. The topic that we study at our center is obesity, which remains a national public health priority across multiple disciplines, including medicine, public health, nutrition, economics, education, government, and legislation. In light of the ongoing attention to obesity across these areas and broad consensus about the need to find effective prevention strategies for obesity, our center's faculty and staff regularly present our research to diverse audiences who can use scientific evidence to push forward positive public health policy changes.

As examples, our faculty members have presented their research to national medical panels such as the CDC and Institute of Medicine, the National Parents and Teachers Association, national organizations like the American Heart Association and National Cancer Institute, state departments of health, community health organizations, local and state food policy councils, public health coalitions, and nonprofit organizations focusing on obesity. Our outreach also extends to groups directly involved in policy making. We regularly create and distribute reports, policy briefs, and amicus briefs based on our research findings to policymakers, and our faculty routinely are called upon to provide expert testimony at state and national legislative hearings. In addition, our policy experts and faculty interact with key policymakers, including state house representatives, senators, and attorneys generals, about policy strategies to promote healthy changes in the food environment that can be informed by our research.

## COMMUNICATING RESEARCH FINDINGS THROUGH THE MEDIA

It is difficult for science to have a broad impact if no one knows about it. This is especially true when science aims to improve public health and individual health behaviors. In academia, researchers often think about the end goal of their work as publishing their findings in a peer-reviewed journal. But the process shouldn't end there. At the Rudd Center, we believe that research findings need to be disseminated more broadly to maximize the likelihood that scientific knowledge can reach people who can use it in ways that are most likely to have a meaningful impact. Conducting and publishing research is key, but translating this work so that the public can understand it and use it in actionable ways is equally important.

Researchers don't routinely ask themselves how they should communicate their research findings to the groups that can use their evidence. An important question that often is missing from the research process is, "How can I translate my research findings in ways that are meaningful for others to take action with?" This question needs to be a regular part of research, not just for the work of individual scientists but also for independently funded research centers. One of the most efficient and far-reaching strategies to disseminate science is through the mass media. We live in a culture that consumes large amounts of media every day, whether it occurs through television, radio, websites, social media, or cell phones. Media has a strong influence on shaping public attitudes about social and health-related topics, and thus it provides an important tool for scientists to use to communicate their research to broad audiences.

At our center, we spend a lot of time translating our research findings in multiple media formats. Our ability to have a consistent media presence means that our faculty members regularly spend time talking about their research or sharing their expertise with news reporters; writing op-eds for newspapers; writing articles for popular news websites, blogs, or magazines; and doing media interviews on radio or television. As a result of these efforts, our center has become a trusted and regularly called-on source for science and policy recommendations in national and international press.

Having a social media presence is also important, as it allows our center to contribute to the national discourse on important topics. Our communications team makes this happen by maintaining our center's website, disseminating monthly online newsletters about our center's work, arranging webinars for our faculty to host, and managing our Facebook and Twitter pages to promote our research and garner discussion. With more than 10,000 Twitter followers, social media has become an important way for our center to engage key groups on topics that are important to our center's mission and work.

Being able to communicate research findings through multiple media formats is an important way for independently funded research centers to remain key contributors to the national discourse on relevant issues. Media reach can serve as one indicator of a research center's impact and reputation, which are important in the eyes of potential funders. Being able to explain, to the public, the significance of one's research and how it is useful is a key catalyst for people, in turn, to use that science to motivate action.

## A Closer Look at Working at the Rudd Center

### A TYPICAL WORKDAY

One positive aspect of working in a place like the Rudd Center is that every day is different. Sometimes the day is spent meeting with fellow faculty and students, discussing research studies, running statistical analyses, and planning our next project. Other days are spent writing—most commonly research manuscripts or grant applications. Our faculty routinely spend time talking with news reporters and policymakers about our center's work. Other days, our faculty may be traveling to meetings, where they interact with other researchers or with policymakers, advocates, or health professionals. Finally, because our colleagues and collaborators are all over the country, we often spend time on conference calls and webinars, which have the advantage of saving the costs of travel but typically are not as fulfilling as in-person meetings.

### UNIQUE ASPECTS OF THIS CAREER

This career offers unique aspects that aren't typical of traditional research settings. For example, the center's core faculty members routinely have opportunities to represent our center at national meetings with other organizations. Because childhood obesity is such a complex problem, one conclusion that has emerged in the discourse about how to solve it is that many segments of society must be engaged, including the food industry. As a result, we have had the opportunity to attend meetings with representatives of major food and beverage companies and national trade associations for the food, beverage, and restaurant industries. Our faculty have met state attorneys general, public health attorneys, and legislators and who also are interested in pressuring companies to change their practices through litigation or legislation. By listening to all of these players, we have come to appreciate the challenges in changing the behavior of an entire industry and the pros and cons of government versus self-regulation as well as the potential role of litigation. There are many paths one can take to improve the food environment in our country. By listening to people who have vested interests in the outcomes of a lawsuit or new piece of regulation, we have been able to identify some of the unanswered questions where the two sides disagree (e.g., Does food marketing actually make people eat more? When is a child old enough to resist the influence of food marketing?). These insights have guided our research.

## ADVANTAGES AND DISADVANTAGES OF WORKING AT A PLACE LIKE THE RUDD CENTER

The advantage of working at an independently funded research center or institute like the Rudd Center is that new ideas are encouraged and innovation is rewarded. The disadvantage, however, is that we straddle the different worlds of research and policy simultaneously, which sometimes can be confusing. We are stronger advocates than any other scientific research center, but remain more focused on science than any other advocacy center. We must tolerate tension from wanting to advocate for an action to improve public health that does not yet have enough scientific evidence, and resisting the pull to support a politically feasible policy that may be too weak to make a significant difference.

## PREPARATION NEEDED FOR A CAREER AT A PLACE LIKE THE RUDD CENTER

Being trained in a research-focused clinical psychology program is excellent preparation for a career working at an independently funded research center or institute. Strong scientific skills are a must, but knowledge of group dynamics and personality traits, as well as understanding the science of persuasion and behavior change, all have been useful. Given the policy focus of our center, obtaining work experience with policymakers also would be quite useful, such as working for a federal legislator on Capitol Hill to observe the policy process up close.

## ATTRIBUTES NEEDED FOR SUCCESS IN THIS TYPE OF CAREER

To be successful in a place like the Rudd Center, you need to have curiosity, an optimistic outlook, and an interest in working with people from diverse organizations who may have different research or policy priorities than your own. It can be a challenge to spend your career working toward an ambitious public health mission while interacting with others in the field who are being paid to protect the interests of for-profit companies. It also can be challenging to spend time with government employees who are not allowed to make partisan comments or politicians who are worried about reelection. But if you are someone who likes to figure out how to get diverse individuals (and organizations) who have different viewpoints and ambitions to work together toward a common goal, this type of work can be immensely rewarding.

## Conclusion

No two research centers are exactly alike, and they vary according to size, scope of research, and funding sources and whether they are linked to academic institutions or operating independently. Research centers that are linked to academic institutions have advantages of anchoring researchers as faculty members to the university, increasing access to university resources, and providing opportunities for collaboration across the university. Independent research centers typically have more freedom to operate under their own authority, choose the areas of research they wish to pursue, and the types of funding sources they wish to seek. In both cases, however, centers may face challenges of securing sufficient funding to continue producing research and maintaining center operations. Despite this challenge, working at a research center can offer unique opportunities for multidisciplinary research collaboration, interacting with national organizations, presenting research to diverse groups, and being in an environment that encourages innovative research ideas.

*Natalie M. Anumba and Ira K. Packer*

# Forensic Psychologists | 16

A s John Smith awaited his trial in jail, his attorney visited him to discuss a recent motion she had filed. During their conversation, she noticed that he had not been showering or eating. He appeared distracted, talked to himself, could not remember what she had just said, and started talking excessively about things that had nothing to do with his case. She knew that he had a history of mental illness, and grew

Natalie M. Anumba, PhD, assistant professor of psychiatry at the University of Massachusetts Medical School, is a forensic psychologist at Worcester Recovery Center and Hospital. She received her BA from the George Washington University, received her PhD in clinical psychology from Drexel University, and completed her postdoctoral residency in forensic psychology at the University of Massachusetts Medical School.

Ira K. Packer, PhD, is clinical professor of psychiatry at the University of Massachusetts Medical School. He directs the University of Massachusetts Medical School's Postdoctoral Residency Program in Forensic Psychology, the Forensic Evaluation Service at Worcester Recovery Center and Hospital, and the Massachusetts Center of Excellence for Specialty Courts. He has served as president of both the American Board and the American Academy of Forensic Psychology.

http://dx.doi.org/10.1037/15960-017
*Career Paths in Psychology: Where Your Degree Can Take You, Third Edition,*
R. J. Sternberg (Editor)

concerned about his ability to pay attention to his case and tell her how he wanted to proceed.

When Jane Johnson was arrested and brought to court, the allegations against her were so bizarre that there were questions about whether Ms. Johnson may have been mentally ill at the time. Her mother told the attorney that Ms. Johnson had been diagnosed with schizophrenia several years ago, had been hospitalized several times, and had stopped taking her psychotropic medications months ago. The defense lawyer thought it was possible that mental illness actually might have been responsible for Ms. Johnson's alleged behavior.

Both of these cases illustrate how mental health issues can work their way into legal proceedings. Before deciding how to proceed, the attorneys in these instances may solicit additional information and recommendations from professionals with knowledge of and expertise in mental illness. In seeking input from mental health professionals, the attorneys likely will derive particular benefit from consulting with professionals who not only have a great deal of knowledge of mental illness, but also are familiar with legal concepts—that is, forensic mental health professionals. In this chapter, we will focus specifically on the broad and varied contributions of forensic psychologists.

## The Nature of the Career

In essence, forensic psychology is the application of psychology to aspects of the law. The *Specialty Guidelines for Forensic Psychology* provides a comprehensive definition of the term *forensic psychology*:

> For the purposes of these guidelines, *forensic psychology* refers to professional practice by any psychologist working within any sub-discipline of psychology (e.g., clinical, developmental, social, cognitive) when applying the scientific, technical, or specialized knowledge of psychology to the law to assist in addressing legal, contractual, and administrative matters. Application of the *Guidelines* does not depend on the practitioner's typical areas of practice or expertise, but rather on the service provided in the case at hand. These *Guidelines* apply in all matters in which psychologists provide expertise to judicial, administrative, and educational systems including, but not limited to, examining or treating persons in anticipation of or subsequent to legal, contractual, administrative, proceedings; offering expert opinion about psychological issues in the form of amicus briefs or testimony to judicial, legislative or administrative bodies; acting in an adjudicative capacity; serving as a trial consultant or otherwise offering expertise to attorneys, the courts, or others; conducting research in connection with, or in the anticipation of, litigation;

or involvement in educational activities of a forensic nature. (American Psychological Association [APA], 2013, p. 7)

This definition is broad because psychologists can practice in a number of specialty areas or subdisciplines, and can serve many different functions, all of which can be of potential use in the legal setting. This chapter will briefly discuss the broad field of psychology and law, identify some applications of psychology to the law, and focus on the role of the clinical forensic psychologist.

Many trace the beginning of psychology's involvement in the U.S. legal system to the early 1900s. Hugo Münsterberg generally is credited with founding the field via his 1908 book *On the Witness Stand*. In it, he argues that psychologists should be involved in the legal system, in areas such as memories of witnesses, crime detection, untrue confessions, hypnosis and crime, and crime prevention. However, he was not able to provide an adequate scientific basis for many of his arguments, his work was mocked by legal scholars (Wigmore, 1909), and the matter of psychological contributions to law was largely ignored (Costanzo & Krauss, 2015; Heilbrun, Grisso, & Goldstein, 2009).

Over the following decades, psychology continued to grow as a scientific field. Psychologists designed, conducted, and published empirical studies in a variety of areas, and in some instances, the research was of relevance to legal proceedings. For instance, the U.S. Supreme Court's 1954 decision, *Brown v. Board of Education* (holding that school segregation was illegal) drew in part from contemporaneous research on the psychological effects of segregation on children (*Brown v. Board of Education*, 1954). Additionally, the American Association of Correctional Psychologists was founded in 1954, marking the beginning of forensic psychology as a formally organized field (Heilbrun et al., 2009).

Psychologists slowly began to get involved in court proceedings by testifying as expert witnesses. Because psychologists do not possess a medical degree, and because psychology is a broad field, their qualifications were sometimes questioned. In 1962, the D.C. Circuit Court of Appeals (*Jenkins v. United States*) ruled that psychologists could provide expert opinions in court regarding mental illness at the time a defendant committed a crime. The court also held that training, skills, experience, and knowledge should serve as the basis of expert qualification, rather than the presence of any particular degree, and this finding eventually was incorporated into the Federal Rules of Evidence (Heilbrun & LaDuke, 2015).

Beginning in the 1970s, psychologists' involvement with the courts became much more formalized. Professional organizations representing forensic psychology were established, including the American Psychology-Law Society (AP-LS). Scholarly journals (such as *Law and Human Behavior*; *Psychology, Public Policy, and Law*; and *Behavioral Sciences and the Law*) that disseminated peer-reviewed research on topics related to psychology and the legal system were developed. The University of Nebraska established a joint-degree graduate program in law and psychology (DeMatteo, Marczyk, Krauss, & Burl, 2009). In addition, the American Board of Forensic Psychology was created to credential psychologists who specialize in advanced-level forensic practice (Heilbrun et al., 2009; Packer & Borum, 2013). Importantly, scholars identified weaknesses and inadequacies prevalent in psychologists' work for the courts, which served to prompt self-examination and the development of standards of quality (Heilbrun et al., 2009). During the 1970s and 1980s, forensic assessment instruments, or structured and standardized tools used to measure psycholegal concepts, were developed. Additionally, in the 1980s, textbooks in forensic psychology began to be published (Heilbrun et al., 2009).

The field of forensic psychology has grown steadily since then. The professional society representing psychologists in the United States, the APA, submits *amicus* briefs summarizing psychological research or adopting a position to assist the courts in deciding certain cases, such as those concerning same-sex marriage, defendants with intellectual disabilities within the criminal justice system, and false confessions. Every year, a number of professional and academic conferences focus on issues relevant to psychology and law. Classes in forensic psychology have become more available at the undergraduate level, and increasing numbers of graduate programs focus on training forensic psychologists (DeMatteo et al., 2009).

In 2001, the APA recognized forensic psychology as an official specialty in psychology. In addition, APA adopted *Specialty Guidelines for Forensic Psychology* (2013), developed by AP-LS and the American Academy of Forensic Psychology, for psychologists engaging in forensic work. Psychology as applied to legal matters also makes appearances in popular media (such as the television shows *Law & Order*, *Lie to Me*, and *Criminal Minds*) or high-profile cases (such as the case of Eddie Ray Routh, who was convicted of the 2013 killing of U.S. Navy SEAL and sniper Christopher Kyle; or that of Andrea Yates, who was found not guilty by reason of insanity of killing her five children in 2001).

Psychologists serve a number of functions within the broad field of psychology and law. For instance, psychologists conduct research, which has been and is applied to legally relevant issues, such as eyewitness testimony (Wells et al., 1998). This work can be used in trials or hearings by way of expert testimony at hearings or submission of *amicus* briefs. They can present to or testify in hearings held by legislative bodies and help write and disseminate policy statements and position papers by professional societies (Costanzo & Krauss, 2015; Cutler & Zapf, 2015). Psychologists who contribute in this way tend to come from a number of disciplines within psychology, such as cognitive, social, developmental, clinical psychology, or neuropsychology. For the purposes of this chapter, we will focus on clinical psychology as applied to legal questions. For overviews of the notable contributions of other psychological disciplines to the law, please see Costanzo and Krauss (2015) or Packer and Grisso (2011).

## Clinical Forensic Psychology

Clinical psychology, as applied to legal matters, looks at the relation between psychological disorders, symptoms, and legally relevant behaviors and capacities. Sometimes clinical psychologists are involved in mental health treatment in forensic contexts, such as in correctional facilities or providing outpatient psychotherapy to consumers who have been ordered into treatment by the court. Clinical forensic psychologists also assist nonclinician consumers (judges, jurors, attorneys, or law enforcement agencies) by providing information to the consumer that they otherwise may not be familiar with, for the purpose of assisting them in making some kind of decision. This can occur in both criminal and civil contexts (Cutler & Zapf, 2015).

One such form of assistance offered by clinical psychologists occurs by conducting forensic evaluations, or psychological evaluations relevant to litigation. Typical psycholegal questions addressed by forensic evaluations for criminal cases can include a defendant's competence to stand trial, competence to waive one's rights while being interrogated by the police, criminal responsibility or insanity at the time of an alleged offense, risk of dangerousness or reoffending, or competence to be executed. In civil cases, psychologists may be asked to address issues surrounding child custody, personal injury, employment discrimination, competence to refuse medical or psychiatric treatment, competence to make a will, and competence to manage one's personal affairs and finances.

Conducting forensic evaluations is a different type of work from what is more typically considered clinical work in psychology (i.e., therapy and treatment-oriented evaluations). As a result, it is important that psychologists (and consumers) are clear on the distinction between the functions, as well as the nature and demands of the forensic role. Major differences between forensic work and more general clinical work include the following (for more information, see Greenberg & Shuman, 1997; Heilbrun et al., 2009; Melton, Petrila, Poythress, & Slobogin, 2007):

- *The psychologist's role and the client.* When a psychologist does therapy, the patient undergoing therapy is considered the client, or the person whom the psychologist serves. The psychologist strives to work toward the direct benefit of the patient and is responsible to that patient. Conversely, when conducting a forensic evaluation, the attorney, judge, or agency that requests the evaluation is the client—not the person being evaluated. That means that if a judge orders an evaluation with a report, the psychologist is obligated to provide one, regardless of the potential benefits (or detriments) to the person being evaluated.

- *The stance*. Therapy often involves a supportive, empathic approach with the intention of helping the person, and the understanding that the professional service is expected to benefit them. Forensic evaluation, on the other hand, requires being open and respectful, but in general, it involves a more detached, neutral, or impartial approach. The intention is to convey the results accurately, and there is no expectation that the service will necessarily help the person.

- *Voluntariness*. Most people who undergo mental health treatment do so after seeking a clinician and voluntarily presenting to appointments. In contrast, forensic evaluations are done with individuals involved in litigation, at the request of an attorney, court, or agency. Sometimes (but not always) the individual has no legal right to refuse to participate in a forensic evaluation or could face negative consequences from not participating.

- *Trust in the patient's responses*. When doing therapy, it may not be common or even necessary to question the patient's truthfulness or motivations. When conducting forensic assessments, however, the psychologist must be aware of the motivation to consciously distort information, mislead the evaluator, or minimize socially undesirable behaviors and must take this into account. Therefore, it is important that in conducting a forensic evaluation, a psychologist will rely not only on the patient's perspective and reports but also will gather additional information from other sources (such as treatment records, family members, and witnesses).

## Typical Activities of the Forensic Psychologist

Many of the functions performed by forensic psychologists are similar to those of other types of psychologists, particularly clinical psychologists. That is, psychologists will interview patients and collateral sources of information, administer and interpret tests, consult with other clinicians, review treatment records, diagnose mental illnesses, and (in some instances) identify relevant treatment needs based on a clinical conceptualization of the patient's referring problem. These tasks are completed not for the purpose of furthering a patient's treatment, but for the purpose of providing information to the court. Thus, a forensic psychologist may spend more time gathering certain information (i.e., arrest history, violence history, substance use history) than a treating psychologist and may spend less time gathering certain information that is not directly relevant to the patient's legal situation. Forensic psychologists also tend to place greater emphasis on gathering information from collateral sources, such as family members, friends, arresting police officers, alleged victims or witnesses, or others who would be able to provide information about the patient's history and clinical functioning. A forensic psychologist's case conceptualization will be more focused on the specific legal question, rather than a broad summation of the person's clinical functioning.

Like many other psychologists, forensic psychologists will spend time writing reports. Unlike some other psychologists, however, these reports are not intended to be read by other health professionals, the patient, or the patient's family members. Forensic reports are to be read by legal professionals (such as judges and lawyers), and thus they have to be written in a way that renders them understandable and useful to this audience. Legal considerations, like a prohibition against the inclusion of certain types of information in particular reports, also will affect the structure and content of the report. Again, the reports will be focused on a specific psycholegal question, rather than on a general history and clinical functioning.

In addition, forensic psychologists engage in professional activities that are unique to the demands of their positions. One such activity includes consulting with attorneys, as most patients evaluated by forensic psychologists will have legal representation. For psychologists who are privately retained, the attorney is often the means by which they acquire cases. In these instances, the attorney will contact the psychologist, explain the details, and ask whether the psychologist is willing and able to take the case. In other instances, an evaluation is ordered by a judge and could be funded by the state as a public service. In either circumstance, the psychologist will be in contact with attorneys on a regular basis either to gather background information, explain clinical findings and opinions, or prepare for courtroom proceedings.

Forensic psychologists may expect to testify in court as expert witnesses during the course of their careers. Doing this requires familiarity with the specific case, mental health concepts, psychological principles and methods, relevant legal cases and statutes, and courtroom culture. Courtroom testimony is a unique skill that is best obtained through training, observation of other clinicians in court, and practice, and this skill will be refined by experience.

Forensic psychologists may have some freedom in how they structure their time on a day-to-day basis. For instance, you may decide to spend the mornings writing reports and the afternoons interviewing patients and collateral sources of information. Or perhaps you decide to dedicate one day to interviews, and the next to writing. Regardless of what is done with each day, the forensic psychologist generally has to meet overarching deadlines, which are likely to be relatively inflexible. As a forensic psychologist, you can expect to spend at least some portion of your time obtaining clinical information from the patient, records, or other collateral sources. A substantial amount of time will be spent preparing reports for consumption by legal professionals. Forensic psychologists may spend time traveling, either for the purpose of conducting interviews in various locations or to testify in courts.

## Advantages and Disadvantages of Being a Forensic Psychologist

Being a forensic psychologist carries unique advantages. Forensic psychologists may be able to exert some form of control over their day-to-day schedule, work flexible hours, or write reports from home without having to travel to an office. Additionally, engaging in forensic work on a full-time basis (either as a public employee or via private retention) eliminates the psychologist's dependence on managed health care for reimbursement for service. Forensic work often brings interesting cases and exposure to a variety of symptoms and mental illnesses. Forensic psychologists can make an impact beyond the face-to-face contact with a patient by educating nonclinicians about mental illnesses, diagnoses, and treatment. This education also may serve to provide assistance to judges in making legal decisions.

Being a forensic psychologist, however, also comes with drawbacks. Forensic psychologists can face significant time pressure, with limited flexibility in deadlines; this means that work can pile up and may require working extended hours. In some cases, forensic psychologists have to review overwhelming amounts of information in the form of several hours of patient interviews, multiple interviews with collateral sources, and hundreds of pages of records. Because reports are considered legal documents and are used in legal proceedings, psychologists' work can be subject to high levels of scrutiny from judges, attorneys, or even the media. This is particularly so when the psychologist testifies in court. Also, because the psychologist's work product will be reviewed by nonclinicians, the potential exists for others to misunderstand or misrepresent the psychologist's statements and opinions.

# Preparation Needed

Work in the field of psychology and law requires extensive education. A bachelor's degree (in psychology or a related field) is just the beginning. This degree lays the foundation in learning about human behavior, cognition, and emotions; engaging in critical thinking and analysis; and becoming familiar with research. Job opportunities in the field are rather limited for those with a bachelor's degree, although it certainly is possible to become probation officer in a courthouse or mental health worker in a hospital setting.

A master's degree in psychology generally takes 2 years of studying a particular, more narrowed area of interest than at the undergraduate level. People typically enter a master's program either to gain extra training and credentials to enter a doctoral program or to acquire skills for advancement in a particular career. A master's degree requires classes in human behavior, mental illnesses, research design, and statistics. Some master's programs require an internship for the purpose of gaining direct experience. Some programs require completion of a thesis, or an independent research project that students design and conduct, and then present to a committee to prove that they have acquired the research and scientific knowledge. After schooling, individuals with a master's degree can do therapy, assist in research, or assist in the administration of testing under the supervision of a doctoral-level psychologist. However, to practice as a forensic psychologist, a doctoral degree is required.

A doctorate in psychology requires extended, in-depth study that includes both breadth of training in the general field of psychology as well as focus in a more specific areas (such as clinical psychology, counseling psychology, or school psychology). Graduate training programs award a PhD (doctor of philosophy in psychology) or a PsyD (doctor of psychology) degree. The PhD tends to feature a significant research component and involves an original and intensive research project that is the doctoral dissertation. The PsyD tends to focus on intensive preparation in clinical work, but it also may require a research or clinical project. The doctorate usually takes 5 to 6 years to complete (including an internship year), although those who enter doctoral training with a master's degree may finish somewhat sooner. Doctorates in psychology also require clinical practicum or externship placements, in which trainees learn to do the hands-on work of a psychologist while under close supervision of a licensed psychologist for at least 2 years. The final year of the doctoral degree is a predoctoral internship—a calendar year of full-time supervised experience. The internship is required for practitioners (as contrasted with researchers and academics) and is likely to involve moving, given that the competitive internship application and placement process occurs on a nationwide basis.

Increasing numbers of graduate degree programs after some form of exposure to forensic training, and some offer an emphasis in an area such as forensic psychology. Forensic training during graduate education may involve training in forensic mental health assessment, forensically oriented research, law classes, or practicum placements with forensic or correctional populations. There are also dual-degree programs, in which graduates earn a joint doctoral degree and a professional law degree (DeMatteo et al., 2009; Packer & Borum, 2013). Those who are interested in the availability of graduate-level training in forensic psychology should view the Students section of the AP-LS (2016) website for the most up-to-date listings of programs. For more information about variations in training and coursework in graduate programs, please see Packer and Borum (2013) and DeMatteo et al. (2009).

In addition to the doctoral degree, many jurisdictions require state-level licensure for an individual to be allowed to identify oneself as a psychologist and engage in independent practice. This usually will require taking the nationwide exam, and states vary in terms of additional requirements (e.g., a separate test specific to the state, supervised experience obtained after the completion of the degree). For more information about licensure and individual state requirements, the Association of State and Provincial Psychology Boards (2016) is a valuable source of information.

It is also beneficial to receive postdoctoral-level training in forensic psychology after completing one's degree. A formal postdoctoral training position typically involves 1 year of additional training, includes close supervision, tends to focus on a relatively limited area of practice (such as criminal forensic assessment), and provides more in-depth training than can be provided in other levels of training. A postdoctoral fellowship allows the psychologist to develop high-level skills in this specialty area and will count toward the supervised experience required for licensure in some states. For these reasons, completing formalized postdoctoral training may also make a psychologist more competitive for employment. Formal postdoctoral training programs are relatively rare, however, compared with the number of opportunities for graduate training (Packer & Borum, 2013). Some forensic psychologists instead receive supervised training on the job. Psychologists also may become involved in forensic training by way of various continuing education (CE) seminars and workshops. Forensic CE programs are beneficial because many states mandate that psychologists demonstrate they are current in the field to renew their licensures, and the CE credits may fulfill these requirements. Some states also require that psychologists obtain an additional credential demonstrating competence in forensic evaluation before they are allowed to engage in forensic work, particularly if the work is in the public service sector.

Once a forensic psychologist establishes a career and gains experience, he or she may choose to obtain board certification. Board certification through the American Board of Forensic Psychology (a specialty board of the American Board of Professional Psychology) denotes an advanced level of competence in forensic practice. The board certification process involves an application, review of the applicant's credentials and experience, a written examination, review of written sample reports submitted by the applicant, and an oral examination based on the samples. More information is available on the American Board of Forensic Psychology (2016) website.

## Personal Attributes Desirable in Forensic Psychologists

Psychologists in general benefit from the ability to analyze information, establish rapport with others, and observe subtle behaviors. Forensic psychologists may benefit from personality traits, such as conscientiousness and attention to detail, which may facilitate combing through mountains of clinical data and completing thorough evaluations. Also important is a firm sense of boundaries and awareness of professional ethics—again, forensic evaluation is different from therapy, and psychologists must recognize these differences to engage in quality practice. Toward this end, forensic psychologists must possess self-awareness and the ability to identify situations in which they may have trouble maintaining impartiality. Forensic psychologists must be able to communicate clearly and effectively, both verbally and in writing. Forensic psychologists also must be able to understand and appreciate the more concrete, structured, and logic-driven structure of legal thinking as well as be able to reconcile this with the aspects of mental health that may be relatively nuanced and mushy. A tough skin is also helpful, for two reasons. First, forensic work, particularly in criminal matters, by its nature involves exposure to some of the worst aspects of human behavior and experiences. Second, some cases may require being subject to bruising cross-examination that is rife with insinuations (or outright statements) that one is incompetent, negligent, or malevolent. Finally, in forensic psychology, and arguably any other field, a sense of humor and a willingness to learn are beneficial qualities.

## Pay and Future Prospects

No data focus on forensic psychologists specifically, but a 2009 study by APA found a median income of $87,000 for clinical psychologists (Finno et al., 2010). Once again, this information collapses many types of psychologists practicing in many settings across the United States, so it may not fully represent the subfield. Income also can be influenced by factors such as experience, work setting, and geographic location. The income for forensic psychologists is likely higher than the median, as hourly rates for private forensic practice exceed the typical rate for clinical services.

Forensic psychology is a growing field with numerous applications to law. Future directions and applications of the field may include the following:

- Aspects of immigration law, particularly evaluations of individuals seeking asylum (how traumatized is traumatized enough to merit asylum?).
- Racial and cultural considerations in legal competencies and capacities. This topic is particularly pressing given the increasing diversity of the American population.
- Social media, specifically the analysis of an examinee's online presence and behavior. Such information may reveal aspects of the patient's clinical functioning or may be particularly necessary in cases that focus on online behavior (e.g., cyberstalking, sexting, and others).

The field of forensic psychology is relatively new and has developed significantly over the past four decades. It is a fully recognized specialty by APA and the American Board of Professional Psychology, and as of the publication of this chapter, there are more than 300 board-certified specialists in forensic psychology. Given the large demand for forensic services, it is likely that there will be an increased need for well-trained forensic psychologists.

## References

American Board of Forensic Psychology. (2016). Retrieved from http://abfp.com/

American Psychological Association. (2013). Specialty guidelines for forensic psychology. *American Psychologist, 68*, 7–19. http://dx.doi.org/10.1037/a0029889

American Psychology-Law Society. (2016). *Students*. Retrieved from http://www.apadivisions.org/division-41/education/students/index.aspx

Association of State and Provincial Psychology Boards. (2016). Retrieved from http://www.asppb.net/

Brown v. Board of Education, 347 US 483 (1954).

Costanzo, M., & Krauss, D. (2015). *Forensic and legal psychology: Psychological science applied to law* (2nd ed.). New York, NY: Worth.

Cutler, B. L., & Zapf, P. A. (Eds.). (2015). *APA handbook of forensic psychology* (Vol. 1). Washington, DC: American Psychological Association.

DeMatteo, D., Marczyk, G., Krauss, D. A., & Burl, J. (2009). Educational and training models in forensic psychology. *Training and Education in Professional Psychology, 3*, 184–191. http://dx.doi.org/10.1037/a0014582

Finno, A. A., Michalski, D., Hart, B., Wicherski, M., & Kohout, J. L. (2010). *2009: Report of the APA salary survey*. Retrieved from http://www.apa.org/workforce/publications/09-salaries/index.aspx#section5

Greenberg, S., & Shuman, D. W. (1997). Irreconcilable conflict between therapeutic and forensic roles. *Professional Psychology: Research and Practice, 28*, 50–57. http://dx.doi.org/10.1037/0735-7028.28.1.50

Heilbrun, K., Grisso, T., & Goldstein, A. M. (2009). *Foundations of forensic mental health assessment*. New York, NY: Oxford University.

Heilbrun, K., & LaDuke, C. D. (2015). Foundational aspects of forensic mental health assessment. In B. L. Cutler & P. A. Zapf (Eds.), *APA handbook of forensic psychology* (Vol. 1, pp. 3–18). Washington, DC: American Psychological Association. http://dx.doi.org/10.1037/14461-001

Jenkins v. United States, 307 F. 2d 637 (1962).

Melton, G. B., Petrila, J., Poythress, N. G., & Slobogin, C. (2007). *Psychological evaluations for the courts* (3rd ed.). New York, NY: Guilford Press.

Münsterberg, H. (1908). *On the witness stand: Essays on psychology and crime*. New York, NY: Doubleday.

Packer, I. K., & Borum, R. (2013). Forensic training and practice. In R. K. Otto (Ed.), *Handbook of psychology: Vol. 11. Forensic psychology* (2nd ed., pp. 21–32). Hoboken, NJ: Wiley.

Packer, I. K., & Grisso, T. (2011). *Specialty competencies in forensic psychology*. New York, NY: Oxford University Press. http://dx.doi.org/10.1093/med:psych/9780195390834.001.0001

Wells, G. L., Small, M., Penrod, S., Malpass, R. S., Fulero, S. M., & Brimacombe, C. A. E. (1998). Eyewitness identification procedures: Recommendations for lineups and photospreads. *Law and Human Behavior, 22*, 603–647. http://dx.doi.org/10.1023/A:1025750605807

Wigmore, J. H. (1909). Professor Münsterberg and the psychology of testimony being a report of the case of Cokestone v. Münsterberg. 3 Illinois LR 399.

*John P. Sullivan, David B. Coppel, Sam Maniar,*
*and Antoinette M. Minniti*

# Sport Psychologists | 17

## *Working With Sports Teams and Individuals*

The current chapter is a collective effort, much like the dynamic world of sport, for which the authors will share their combined professional experiences related to the practice, scholarly work, and education of sport psychology. The objective of this chapter is to provide insight to you, the

---

John P. Sullivan, PsyD, has worked with the same team in the National Football League for the past 15 years. He has also worked with the National Basketball Association, Major League Soccer, and Olympic national teams, among others. He maintains positions at Providence College and the University of Rhode Island and serves as an instructor/supervisor for the Brown University Medical School Sports Medicine Fellowship.

David B. Coppel, PhD, FACSM, CC-AASP, is a professor in the Department of Neurological Surgery and the director of Neuropsychological Services and Research at the University of Washington Sports Concussion Program. Dr. Coppel is the consulting neuropsychologist and clinical/sport psychologist for the Seattle Seahawks.

http://dx.doi.org/10.1037/15960-018
*Career Paths in Psychology: Where Your Degree Can Take You, Third Edition*, R. J. Sternberg (Editor)
Copyright © 2017 by the American Psychological Association. All rights reserved.

reader, who may have an interest in joining the growing group of sport psychologists who have a shared passion for improving and optimizing performance. The chapter is organized into two overarching sections—we focus primarily on practical or applied work, and we briefly discuss research and educator pathways. Within those two sections, we discuss the following: (a) the nature of the career, (b) the types of activities in which sport psychology professionals engage, (c) a typical day in the career, (d) preparation that is needed for this career, (e) attributes that typically exemplify successful sport psychologists, (f) salary ranges for different careers in this area, and (g) the anticipated horizon and future prospects for sport psychology professionals.

Working with sport teams and individuals as a sport psychologist offers continual opportunities to be both proactive and responsive to ever-changing environments. The nature of sport psychology as a career often mirrors that dynamic. This is particularly the case if you are interested in practice (also known as consultancy or applied work), as you need to be aware of the importance of flexibility and adaptability. Sport psychology also provides avenues for those attracted to an academic environment—such as you would find in higher education or through scholarly work and research—and the nature of the career for an individual who opts for this pathway provides its own set of opportunities and experiences. Quite often, sport psychology professionals engage in some combination of the three areas (practice, scholarly work, and education), and this provides various strings to their bow, which allows for the following: research-informed practice (learning about current techniques, and then implementing them with athletes and coaches), practice-informed research (identifying athletes' patterns or responses to techniques, which can lead to conducting deliberate research about the phenomena), and research- or practice-based education (transferring knowledge from either or both of the other two domains to share stories with students, which allows them to gain a deeper understanding of phenomena).

As you can see, it is difficult to describe the nature of the career of sport psychology without making reference to the context of the environment, because the approach that you would take to engage with the field would depend on what you are most interested in doing within the field. The following sections provide an overview of what

Sam Maniar, PhD, serves as the sport psychologist for the Cleveland Browns. Dr. Maniar has also worked with amateur, Olympic, and professional athletes from virtually all sports, focusing on both counseling and performance enhancement interventions.

Antoinette M. Minniti, PhD, CPsychol, is the associate executive director for the Office of CE Sponsor Approval at the American Psychological Association.

to expect and some key factors regarding sport psychology in terms of practical or applied work. The importance of both research and scholarly work and also educational settings is briefly addressed in the context of their complementary and critical supporting role, as these two activities are necessary components of applied work of sport psychologists.

## PRACTICAL OR APPLIED WORK

Practitioners primarily provide direct services to athletes and teams to improve well-being and performance. An integral part of the work of practitioners includes assessment. This section outlines the requirements and rationale for conducting certain types of assessment— including clinical (mental health specific), health promotional, talent identification, and sport psychological evaluations. To begin, sport psychology can be viewed with skeptical eyes by some traditionalists, so assessment can be an essential aspect of demonstrating the impact of interventions. It also can be used to assess and identify areas of concern as well as to identify and diagnose mental health concerns. The specific assessments one may be interested in will depend on the role being served.

### Requirements to Administer and Interpret Tests

Overall, assessment tools and tests require different qualifications of practitioners. The best way to learn what is required for a particular test is to consult the specific test manual for the assessment being used. At the very least, prior supervised experience is a prerequisite for using any type of assessment. Many tools that are psychological in nature also require the training earned through a doctoral degree in psychology (PhD, PsyD, or EdD) or licensure as a psychologist.

### Clinical Evaluations

Mental health assessments can be used to help understand the presenting problems of a client. Commonly used mental health assessments used in sport are the Minnesota Multiphasic Personality Inventory— 2 Restructured Form (MMPI–2–RF; Ben-Porath & Tellegen, 2011) and Sixteen Personality Factor Questionnaire (16PF; Cattell & Mead, 2008), although some organizations may also use the Millon Clinical Multiaxial Inventory—III (MCMI–III; Millon, Millon, Davis, & Grossman, 2006) or Personality Assessment Inventory (PAI; Morey, 1991). Each of these has its own strengths and limitations, but the reason for using a mental health assessment should be clear upfront. In other words, it shouldn't be used as a probing tool without some prior hypothesis. Moreover, these tools should be used only by professionals who are qualified to do so.

Some mental health assessments may be used to measure progress and improvement. These measures are usually quicker to complete and are specific to a presenting problem. Some examples of these types of tools are the Beck Depression Inventory–II (BDI-II; Beck, Steer, & Brown, 1996) and Beck Anxiety Inventory (BAI; Beck & Steer, 1993).

## Health Promotion

Various assessments can be used to promote healthy behaviors, such as exercise. For example, spending time understanding where a client falls relative to the transtheoretical model (TTM; Prochaska, Norcross, & DiClemente, 1994) can help direct the appropriate intervention. The TTM is an integrative, biopsychosocial model to conceptualize the process of intentional behavior change. Stages of change lie at the heart of the model. Studies of change have found that people move through a series of stages when modifying behavior and certain principles and processes of change work best at each stage to reduce resistance, facilitate progress, and prevent relapse. Likewise, identifying barriers to exercise in advance can help a professional work with his or her clients to develop strategies to work through or around them.

## Talent Identification and Selection

A wide range of personnel and intelligence assessments have been brought from the field of industrial–organizational psychology to utilize these measures to identify and select high-performing athletes. There is much debate as to the merit and validity of these practices; however, it is a widely conducted practice. These can range from personality-based to behavior-based measures as well as from crystallized intelligence to fluid intelligence to emotional intelligence. Before using any type of assessment for selection or identification, practitioners generally are required to consult with the rules and regulations of their specific sport and governing body to be clear about benefits and implications of its implementation in that particular context.

## Sport Psychology Assessments

Before working with a team or individual athlete for performance enhancement (e.g., mental skills training), typically some form of assessment should be used. That is, assessments can serve as a type of *needs analysis* as well as a baseline measure to evaluate athletes' progress. For this reason, the same assessments used at the beginning of an intervention program should be used to monitor progress and to evaluate the impact of the interventions at the conclusion of the program.

A sport psychologist may want to incorporate a battery of assessments to evaluate factors such as anxiety, confidence, composure, attention or concentration, motivation, group dynamics, and rest or recovery. Although the breadth and range of instruments that are available to practitioners are far too extensive to list here, some useful resources can be found in the works of Duda (2000) and Tenenbaum, Eklund, and Kamata (2012).

Alongside the importance of assessment, a key component to understanding the work of sport psychology practitioners is recognizing that each psychologist has his or her own approach to working with athletes and clients. Furthermore, the individual approaches of psychologists are based on theoretical frameworks that have been studied and evaluated in their own right. The following section outlines a widely studied and utilized approach—psychotherapy—and identifies what is central to its implementation in terms of applied sport psychology work.

## Psychotherapy and Sport Psychology

When most people think of psychology, the therapeutic process that involves the application of psychotherapy is typically what comes to mind. In the field of sport psychology, working in a psychotherapeutic context means focusing on individual athletes' well-being and overall health. Equally, practitioners must be able to understand complex sporting cultures in which athletes are based. In many ways, psychotherapy has evolved to meet the varied and unique demands of the athletic population.

First, critical to the success of this (or any) therapeutic process is a solid ethical foundation, which—particularly in dynamic, multidimensional, and interactive sporting environments—often can prove difficult (e.g., to meet the needs of both athletes and coaches). To be effective, working in a sport setting requires being aware of and addressing the frequent and distinctive ethical challenges that have the potential to affect consistent quality practice. Ethical challenges can stem from issues dealing with the athlete, coach, athletic department personnel, and professional league rules as well as compliance with governance rules and regulations or the legal issues surrounding the particular setting.

Another important set of factors that is key in the psychotherapeutic context when working with athletes involves attention to logistical components—for example, athletes have to manage stress and adaption for training, travel (particularly in cases of time zone changes), disruption in schedules, unpredictable work flow, irregular work–rest cycles, reduced social connections (depending on the sport and required commitments), health risks and dangers (e.g., orthopedic and concussive injuries), and retirement from sport. In addition, it is necessary to address the demands relevant to various sporting levels—for example, when working with student-athletes, sport psychologists need to understand that this population typically has greater demands and risks compared with their peers, but not necessarily any greater internal resources (such as effective coping skills) to meet these demands. In contrast, in elite-level sport, applied sport psychologists commonly assist athletes with challenging factors, such as dealing with their sport as a job, and the need to cope with internal (e.g., competing for a place on the team) and external (e.g., adapting to being away from loved ones) demands that are unique to elite sport.

## Psychotherapy in Sport Versus Nonsport Environments

Psychotherapy in a sporting context is not much different to its application in nonsporting domains; however, it has necessarily evolved such that scientific evidence is based on sport-specific research and application, and findings have focused on ways to stabilize both health and performance maintenance and optimization. The psychotherapy process in sporting and nonsporting environments is similar because the fundamental demands of sport and life are similar in relation to mental health. This is true in three significant ways: (a) mental health issues do not discriminate, so physically gifted sportswomen or men are equally as susceptible as nonathletes to managing challenges related to mental health; (b) when athletes are dealing with physical or mental health issues, the effects are not restricted to a particular aspect of their life (e.g., just to their personal or family life, or only in their sport); and (c) stigma is an issue that is equally dealt with by athletes and nonathletes—although this issue sometimes can be magnified by the sporting culture because of the tendency for sport cultures to shun or ignore mental health needs because "athletes are supposed to be tough."

Individual and group-format psychotherapy both focus on assessing athletes' mental health and various aspects of performance. It is important to remember that mental health and an athlete's ability to perform are inextricably linked. An athlete may be focused entirely on his or her performance, but other influencing factors outside of the sport environment may contribute to poor performance. Once these factors are evaluated and understood by a sport psychology clinician, it means that this information also can be used for good to provide constructive solutions. The typical goals of individual and group psychotherapy are to provide support and to promote health, skill development, self-awareness, behavior change, interpersonal connectedness, and emotional or personality development. Key elements of psychotherapy when working with athletes include empathy, affect and cognition, activation and deactivation (being stressed and relaxed during therapeutic sessions), increased tolerance (e.g., to improve resiliency), and instillation of hope.

As alluded to earlier, psychotherapy can be conducted with individual athletes or in sport teams. For either setting, psychotherapy work consists of assessment, treatment planning, treatment execution, and follow-up. Assessment in a performance context is optimal when it involves collaboration with others in a sports medicine or sport science team. This process may include, but is not limited to, the following: a clinical interview, use of self-report measures that include standardized questions (see previous section in this chapter), computer-based assessments, measures taken on the body or biometric data, as well as use of smartphone applications, and use of psychophysiological (mind–body) evaluation methods (e.g., biofeedback and neurofeedback).

## Biofeedback and Neurofeedback

With regard to the use of psychophysiology technology, both biofeedback and neurofeedback have shown great efficacy as an approach for working in a sport environment. Biofeedback and neurofeedback have been integrated to clinical settings for nearly 50 years. Biofeedback achieves its results by observing and then gaining control over psychophysiological connections toward learned self-regulation. This technique helps the user and clinician to measure skill adaption by looking at changes in physiology, behavior, and even lifestyle to promote well-being and health. In biofeedback therapy, individuals are trained on electronic monitors to exert control over bodily processes, such as heart rate, respiration, blood pressure, muscular tension, body temperature, and brain activity. By observing and monitoring shifts in bodily functions, athletes learn to adapt and modify their mental and emotional responses to alleviate symptoms and to help regulate emotional and cognitive responses to specific situations.

Neurofeedback is also a way to quantify and train brain activity. During a neurofeedback session, sensors detect brainwaves to see the brain in action. A neurofeedback computer system compares brain activity with targets and goals to attain specific brainwave frequencies.

Sounds and images tell the user when goals have been reached and when they are activating or suppressing target wavelengths on the brain. Users learn how to quiet brainwaves associated with low performance as well as how to increase brainwaves associated with optimal brain function.

Assessment that involves using either technique generally requires medical-grade technology as well as specialty training to implement and appropriately interpret data. Also, similar to the way that psychotherapy has evolved to meet the unique needs of sport, many of the devices and applications in the biofeedback and neurofeedback arenas have protocols that are focused on athletes' specific needs (e.g., to manage emotions, energy, and improve focus), and the demands of sport (e.g., to improve stress responses and recovery for training and competition). Additionally, research has provided sport psychologists with guidance and protocols regarding proper implementation and incorporation of these forms of technology.

## BEYOND APPLIED WORK: RESEARCH AND EDUCATOR PATHWAYS

It is clear from the previous sections of this chapter that the work of an applied sport psychologist can be widely varied. Certainly, sport psychologists require a breadth of skills and training to be effective and ethically responsible when working with athletes. That being said, for applied sport psychologists, it is also important that they are continuously up to date with current research. This point brings us to the important aspects of research or scholarly work and education settings with regard to the development of the sport psychology field. The next section will briefly discuss scholarly work in sport psychology and the educator pathway—both of which are hugely important components of the field and, for some, may be their preferred options for engaging with the field.

### Research and Scholarly Work in Sport Psychology

As sport has evolved, so too have sport psychologists' methods of researching and understanding key factors that contribute to athlete performance and well-being. For example, related to training, competition, coaching, and cultural factors within sport environments, research in the field has evolved to provide information about ways to promote leadership, team cohesion, motivation, and confidence, to name a few. Additionally, many sport psychologists work in multi-disciplinary environments (e.g., with other disciplines such as sports nutrition, physiology, biomechanics) and thus need to know the evidence base regarding best practice for optimally working with other sport support professionals.

## The Educator Pathway and Sport Psychology

Another type of activity and important contribution to sport psychology involves the educator pathway. This area of the profession is arguably the focal point at which practice, research, and lessons derived from across the sport psychology profession all converge. In other words, as we referred to earlier, both the practical and scholarly work that sport psychology professionals contribute to the field should make their way to the classroom setting. A primary objective in sport psychology education is that you, the students, benefit from the range of experiences within the field that represent real-life scenarios and research that has been conducted rigorously.

As the profession of sport psychology grows and evolves, we continue to build a foundation of knowledge and insight as to how to best work with teams and individuals. That work typically includes supporting coaches in their role as well as working with and needing to understand enough about other sport science disciplines (such as those referred to earlier) to be able to optimize yourself as a resource and, in turn, optimize athlete performance. This brings us to a typical day in the career of an applied sport psychologist. This chapter will focus on the practical realm—that is, an applied sport psychologist's professional day.

# The Typical Day of an Applied Sport Psychologist

One of the best (or worst, depending on your perspective) aspects of being a sport psychologist is that there is no such thing as a typical day. The various components of the job will vary not only by day but also by the setting in which you work. Nevertheless, the main components of a sport psychologist's practice likely will be divided between seeing clients, consulting with a team or presenting psychological skills to the team, observing training and practice, and consulting with coaches and medical staff.

## SEEING CLIENTS

A sport psychologist undoubtedly will meet with athlete-clients. Meetings typically are done on a one-on-one basis. When working with athletes, the psychologist will need to be flexible in terms of hours (early and late) as well as missed appointments. Although college athletes may prefer to set scheduled times, it is common for professional athletes to prefer to pop in when they have a moment. Sport psychologists must be agile in navigating the multiple roles they may be serving in the organization. For that reason, in many ways, being a sport psychologist is similar to being a rural psychologist because both professionals often need to wear a variety of hats. Finally, because of the stigma athletes have in seeking out mental health services (for a review, see Hughes & Leavey, 2012; Maniar, Curry, Sommers-Flanagan, & Walsh, 2001; Simon & Docherty, 2014), athletes may view one-on-one sessions with hesitation and skepticism. For these reasons, it may be safer for an athlete to present for performance improvement as opposed to mental health-related concerns. Thus, it is important for the psychologist to conduct a comprehensive intake assessment to determine all of the potential factors contributing to the presenting problems.

## CONSULTING WITH THE TEAM

In some, but not all, cases it is common to have regular meetings with a team. In these meetings, the sport psychologist typically covers a different mental skills training topic (e.g., imagery, goal setting, concentration, relaxation). These sessions serve as an overview of a topic that may whet the appetite of athletes who may want to further develop these skills in individual sessions. It is best to keep these sessions brief and interactive to hold the athletes' attention. This is another great opportunity to break down barriers and stigma, as research with college athletes indicated that those who had team meetings with a sport psychologist were three times more likely to seek out individual sport psychology services (Maniar, Carter, & Smith, 2003).

## OBSERVING TRAINING

Observing training (or practice) is important for two reasons. First, showing an interest in the sport and making yourself available in a nonthreatening environment can help reduce the barriers and stigmas toward seeking help. Second, it can serve as a good data point for identifying needs as well as assessing the effectiveness of interventions. When doing so, it is best to take mental notes and record any observations after practice. Having a notebook out at practice likely will cause anxiety and increase the fear inherent in seeking help.

## CONSULTING WITH COACHES AND MEDICAL STAFF

Part of a sport psychologist's schedule will no doubt involve consulting with coaches. In fact, the sport psychologist may serve as more of a behind-the-scenes practitioner who advises the coach on how to approach performance issues. In other cases, and with appropriate releases of information, the psychologist may want to advise the coach on how to best approach or work with an athlete (Baker, Côté, & Hawes, 2000; Becker, 2009; Gillet, Vallerand, Amoura, & Baldes, 2010; Meeusen et al., 2013). Ideally, the psychologist will be part of an integrative medical team (Neal et al., 2013; Pinkerton, Hinz, & Barrow, 1989; Schwab Reese, Pittsinger, & Yang, 2012). In these cases, time will be spent consulting other medical providers (e.g., trainers, physicians) on symptoms to look for, psychological concerns in the rehabilitation process, and how to effectively make referrals for counseling.

## *Preparation for a Career in Sport Psychology*

When considering a career in sport psychology prospective students should take this to heart—to be a competent sport psychologist one first needs to be a capable and skilled clinical or counseling psychologist. Thus, the journey for any student starts with finding an American Psychological Association (APA)–accredited clinical or counseling doctoral program (e.g., PhD, PsyD, EdD) and then looking for the following aspects contained within its curriculum:

- *Coursework* available in sport psychology fulfilling the APA proficiency criteria
- The opportunity for *supervision* and practicum hours in applied sport psychology
- *Research* opportunities in areas of sport psychology and a history of publication
- Postgraduate *supervision* and consultation during postdoctoral training

The main three elements of relevant coursework, supervision, and research allow aspiring sport psychologists to assemble the proper academic journey so they may achieve competency for both application and research facets of psychology within sport. The APA recognized sport psychology as a proficiency in 2003, which has provided a source of formal recognition of this practice of psychology (see APA Division 47, 2016).

Although the field is becoming increasingly globalized, and sport psychology professionals are obtaining work in various countries, the field is not yet a mobile field whereby credentials from one country directly translate across to another. So, for example, if you choose to be educated overseas in Australia or the United Kingdom, and obtain the equivalent to licensure there (i.e., chartered psychologist or CPsychol), the qualification is not recognized as a practicing credential in the United States (and vice versa); thus, additional education or credentialing would be required to practice in the United States (or overseas).

Taken as a whole, the information about the field of sport psychology, and the three main areas of applied work, research or scholarly work, and education provide some insight as to the attributes that would be associated with success in any or all of the career paths outlined. That being said, there is no definitive road map to becoming a sport psychologist, but several ideal criteria will help provide credibility and may increase the likelihood of success in this field. First, the term *psychologist* is regulated by state law (APA, 2010), and only those who are licensed psychologists with expertise in sport psychology may refer to themselves as a *sport psychologist*. Second, the psychologist should have a sound understanding about the interplay and interaction between an athlete's physiology and his or her mind. Third, prior experience playing or coaching a competitive sport is helpful in building credibility as well as providing relevant experience on which draw. Fourth, a sound understanding of navigating multiple relationships in an ethical manner is essential. Fifth, excellent interpersonal skills (e.g., communication and presentation skills as well as being able to relate to people from various backgrounds) combined with having a thick skin, as you will be met with skepticism and distrust, is imperative.

Now that you know more about the field of sport psychology, you now might by asking, "How much money would I make in this profession?" Given the varied nature of the possible activities we have described for which sport psychology professionals might engage, it is not surprising that the salary range is equally as varied. The APA featured an article in their student magazine, *gradPSYCH*, that included estimations from individuals in the field (Voelker, 2012). To best illustrate the salary range, Table 17.1 provides information about typical salaries associated with the most common types of jobs in sport psychology. The level of education typically associated with each of the

## TABLE 17.1

**Estimated Salary Ranges for Sport Psychology Professions**

| Job title or role | Anticipated salary range |
| --- | --- |
| University professor[a] | $35,000–$100,000 |
| University athletic department sport psychologist[b] | $60,000–$100,000+ |
| Self-employed sport psychology consultant | $30,000–$100,000+ |
| Military (e.g., Department of Defense) | $90,000–$125,000 (GS13–GS15) |

[a]Data from Sports Psychology Professor (n.d.). [b]Data from Voelker (2012).

positions indicated in the table is at the doctoral and postdoctoral level, which demonstrates the overall investment on balance with projected earning power.

The sport psychology profession is relatively new compared with other more established professions in psychology (e.g., clinical, counseling, school psychology); however, the horizon looks promising as the field navigates its way through a continuously evolving landscape. For example, sport psychologists increasingly are recognizing that their qualifications are in demand in disciplines outside of sport psychology (e.g., business, military, music). Another area of growth within sport psychology and psychotherapy includes the use of real-time data via smartphone platform advancements in neurobiological contexts. Smartphones are now ubiquitous and can be harnessed to offer sport psychologists with a wealth of real-time data regarding athlete-client behavior, self-reported symptoms, and even physiology. There are also ongoing developments in the field related to professional training, and these developments are essential for the growth of the field. For instance, Hays (2012) described the future direction of sport psychology with respect to education, including the need to ensure comprehensive graduate-level training for future practitioners, and the need for professional programs to clearly define competency standards, which ultimately must be met by professionals, and that include the necessary benchmarks for practice and ethics.

One challenge for the field may be the same as its strength—that is, its professionals and the nature of their work are such that there is far-reaching scope for where and how sport psychologists could implement their skill sets. So perhaps a difficulty for the profession to be considered is the extent to which the field defines itself so that it remains sufficiently inclusive, without extending itself too broadly. In looking ahead, and viewing the overall picture, the landscape is a positive one that is promising and exciting in equal measure.

## Recommended Readings

Baillie, P. H., & Danish, S. J. (1992). Understanding the career transition of athletes. *The Sport Psychologist, 6*, 77–98.

Brenner, J. S., & the American Academy of Pediatrics Council on Sports Medicine and Fitness. (2007). Overuse injuries, overtraining, and burnout in child and adolescent athletes. *Pediatrics, 119*, 1242–1245. http://dx.doi.org/10.1542/peds.2007-0887

Bricker, J., & Hanson, A. (2013). The impact of early commitment on games played: Evidence from college football recruiting. *Southern Economic Journal, 79*, 971–983. http://dx.doi.org/10.4284/0038-4038-2010.119

Buysse, D. J. (2014). Sleep health: Can we define it? Does it matter? *Sleep, 37*, 9–17.

Caine, D., Maffulli, N., & Caine, C. (2008). Epidemiology of injury in child and adolescent sports: Injury rates, risk factors, and prevention. *Clinics in Sports Medicine, 27*, 19–50, vii. http://dx.doi.org/10.1016/j.csm.2007.10.008

Capranica, L., & Millard-Stafford, M. L. (2011). Youth sport specialization: How to manage competition and training? *International Journal of Sports Physiology and Performance, 6*, 572–579.

Good, A. J., Brewer, B. W., Petitpas, A. J., Van Raalte, J. L., & Mahar, M. T. (1993). Identity foreclosure, athletic identity, and college sport participation. *Academic Athletic Journal, Spring*, 1–10.

Harmison, R. J. (2011). Peak performance in sport: Identifying ideal performance states and developing athletes' psychological skills. *Sport, Exercise, and Performance Psychology, 1*, 3–18.

Luke, A., Lazaro, R. M., Bergeron, M. F., Keyser, L., Benjamin, H., Brenner, J., . . . Smith, A. (2011). Sports-related injuries in youth athletes: Is overscheduling a risk factor? *Clinical Journal of Sport Medicine, 21*, 307–314. http://dx.doi.org/10.1097/JSM.0b013e3182218f71

National Collegiate Athletic Association. (2014). *Mind, body and sport: Understanding and supporting student athlete mental wellness*. Retrieved from http://www.ncaapublications.com/productdownloads/MindBodySport.pdf

## Recommended Resources

Association for Applied Sport Psychology: http://www.appliedsportpsych.org/

American Psychological Association, Division 47, Society for Sport, Exercise, and Performance Psychology: http://www.apadivisions.org/division-47/index.aspx

*Sports psychology careers* from Careers in Psychology: http://careersinpsychology.org/becoming-a-sports-psychologist/

# References

American Psychological Association. (2010). *Model act for state licensure of psychologists.* Retrieved from https://www.apa.org/about/policy/model-act-2010.pdf

American Psychological Association Division 47. (2016). *APA sport psychology proficiency.* Retrieved from http://www.apadivisions.org/division-47/about/sport-proficiency/index.aspx

Baker, J., Côté, J., & Hawes, R. (2000). The relationship between coaching behaviours and sport anxiety in athletes. *Journal of Science and Medicine in Sport/Sports Medicine Australia, 3,* 110–119.

Beck, A. T., & Steer, R. A. (1993). *Beck Anxiety Inventory Manual.* San Antonio, TX: Psychological Corporation.

Beck, A. T., Steer, R. A., & Brown, G. K. (1996). *Manual for the Beck Depression Inventory–II.* San Antonio, TX: Psychological Corporation.

Becker, A. J. (2009). It's not what they do, it's how they do it: Athlete experiences of great coaching. *International Journal of Sports Science and Coaching, 4,* 93–119. http://dx.doi.org/10.1260/1747-9541.4.1.93

Ben-Porath, Y. S., & Tellegen, A. (2011). *MMPI–2–RF (Minnesota Multiphasic Personality Inventory—2 Restructured Form): Manual for administration, scoring, and interpretation.* Minneapolis: University of Minnesota Press.

Cattell, H., & Mead, A. (2008). The sixteen personality factor questionnaire (16PF). In G. Boyle, G. Matthews, & D. Saklofske (Eds.), *The SAGE handbook of personality theory and assessment: Vol. 2. Personality measurement and testing* (pp. 135–160). London, England: Sage.

Duda, J. L. (Ed.). (2000). *Advances in sport and exercise psychology measurement* (2nd ed.). Morgantown, WV: Fitness Information Technology.

Gillet, N., Vallerand, R. J., Amoura, S., & Baldes, B. (2010). Influence of coaches' autonomy support on athletes' motivation and sport performance: A test of the hierarchical model of intrinsic and extrinsic motivation. *Psychology of Sport and Exercise, 11,* 155–161. http://dx.doi.org/10.1016/j.psychsport.2009.10.004

Hays, K. F. (2012). The psychology of performance in sport and other domains. In S. Murphy & P. Nathan (Eds.), *The Oxford handbook of sport and performance psychology* (pp. 24–45). New York, NY: Oxford University Press. http://dx.doi.org/10.1093/oxfordhb/9780199731763.013.0002

Hughes, L., & Leavey, G. (2012). Setting the bar: Athletes and vulnerability to mental illness. *British Journal of Psychiatry, 200,* 95–96. http://dx.doi.org/10.1192/bjp.bp.111.095976

Maniar, S. D., Carter, J., & Smith, L. (2003, October). Characteristics of university student-athletes seeking sport psychology services, Part I. In S. D. Maniar (Chair), *Getting creative with university-based sport psychology services: Typical issues in an atypical field.* Symposium presented at the 17th annual meeting of the Association for the Advancement of Applied Sport Psychology, Philadelphia, PA.

Maniar, S. D., Curry, L. A., Sommers-Flanagan, J., & Walsh, J. A. (2001). Student athlete preferences in seeking help when confronted with sport performance problems. *The Sport Psychologist, 15,* 205–223.

Meeusen, R., Duclos, M., Foster, C., Fry, A., Gleeson, M., Nieman, D., . . . the American College of Sports Medicine. (2013). Prevention, diagnosis, and treatment of the overtraining syndrome: Joint consensus statement of the European College of Sport Science and the American College of Sports Medicine. *Medicine and Science in Sports and Exercise, 45,* 186–205. http://dx.doi.org/10.1249/MSS.0b013e318279a10a

Millon, T., Millon, C., Davis, R., & Grossman, S. (2006). *MCMI–III Manual* (3rd ed.). Minneapolis, MN: Pearson.

Morey, L. C. (1991). *The Personality Assessment Inventory professional manual.* Odessa, FL: Psychological Assessment Resources.

Neal, T. L., Diamond, A. B., Goldman, S., Klossner, D., Morse, E. D., Pajak, D. E., . . . Welzant, V. (2013). Inter-association recommendations for developing a plan to recognize and refer student-athletes with psychological concerns at the collegiate level: An executive summary of a consensus statement. *Journal of Athletic Training, 48,* 716–720. http://dx.doi.org/10.4085/1062-6050-48.4.13

Pinkerton, R. S., Hinz, L. D., & Barrow, J. C. (1989). The college student-athlete: Psychological considerations and interventions. *Journal of American College Health, 37,* 218–226. http://dx.doi.org/10.1080/07448481.1989.9939063

Prochaska, J. O., Norcross, J. C., & DiClemente, C. C. (1994). *Changing for good: A revolutionary six-stage program for overcoming bad habits and moving your life positively forward.* New York, NY: Avon Books.

Schwab Reese, L. M., Pittsinger, R., & Yang, J. (2012). Effectiveness of psychological intervention following sport injury. *Journal of Sport and Health Science, 1,* 71–79. http://dx.doi.org/10.1016/j.jshs.2012.06.003

Simon, J. E., & Docherty, C. L. (2014). Current health-related quality of life is lower in former Division I collegiate athletes than in noncollegiate athletes. *The American Journal of Sports Medicine, 42,* 423–429. http://dx.doi.org/10.1177/0363546513510393

Sports Psychology Professor. (n.d.). Retrieved from http://mastersinpsychologyguide.com/careers/sports-psychology-professor

Tenenbaum, G., Eklund, R., & Kamata, A. (Eds.). (2012). *Measurement in sport and exercise psychology.* Champaign, IL: Human Kinetics.

Voelker, R. (2012, November). Hot career: Sport psychology. *gradPSYCH Magazine.* Retrieved from http://www.apa.org/gradpsych/2012/11/sport-psychology.aspx

*Pamela Rutledge*

# Media Psychologists 18

A media psychologist is a psychologist who specializes in applying psychological science to understand and predict how people interact with and are affected by media and technology. Whereas other disciplines related to media and technology focus on the what, media psychology looks at the why of how individuals and society use, develop, produce, and distribute media. There are two common misconceptions about media psychology. The first is that *media* means mass media. The second is that being a media psychologist implies you are a psychologist who appears in the media. Neither is accurate.

Pamela Rutledge, MBA, PhD, is faculty of media psychology at Fielding Graduate University, and developer of the Brand Psychology and Audience Engagement certificate and concentrations. Dr. Rutledge consults with organizations on a variety of media properties and applications, applying cognitive science and narrative theory to media behaviors, product development, research, and marketing strategies. She has published both academic and popular work, blogs for *Psychology Today*, and is an expert source for journalists on the psychology of media and technology use and popular culture.

http://dx.doi.org/10.1037/15960-019
*Career Paths in Psychology: Where Your Degree Can Take You, Third Edition*,
R. J. Sternberg (Editor)

The field of media psychology reaches far beyond any single medium, and although media psychologists may appear in the media as clinicians or experts, these appearances are not part of the training nor are they the goals of media psychology. Media psychology is a discipline that uses psychology to study and understand mediated experience—any interaction in which technology facilitates or filters human experience.

Media psychology is an applied field. The ubiquity of technology means the application of media psychology plays a significant role across multiple industries. The purpose of this chapter is to demonstrate the breadth of the field and highlight the potential career choices.

## *Why Media Psychology?*

The rapid spread of technology over the past fifty years has left few places on earth untouched by technology. The social and economic consequences have been dramatic. The cell phone is the most rapidly adopted consumer technology in world history, making communication technology both personal and mobile. In the United States, not only has cell phone ownership among U.S. adults long passed the 90% mark (Rainie, 2013), but also 75% of mobile subscribers have smartphones, enabling mobile video, music, and social network consumption (Sterling, 2015). In sub-Saharan Africa, 60% of the population now has mobile phone coverage and rural farmers in Ghana are able, for the first time, to access the prices of corn and tomatoes before making the more than 200-mile trip to market (Aker & Mbiti, 2010). Citizens from around the globe participate in political and social events as they ripple across the world, real time, on social media. We have smartphones, smart cars, smart houses, and, before long, smart cities. Mobile networks provide access to social groups, education, entertainment, health and social services, and career and commercial opportunities; they allow us to offload our daily tasks with the click of a button. These implications of these issues just skim the surface of media psychology.

Media psychologists study the underlying psychological dynamics of how people interact with media and technology to find solutions and innovations across multiple fields. Media psychologists work in industries across almost every domain, from academia to high-tech businesses and from health care to entertainment. Following is a glimpse of some of the research and applied questions media psychologists deal with in different industries.

- In game and virtual reality development:
  - How does virtual game play impact individual beliefs about self-efficacy, resiliency, or social dynamics?
  - How can we create compelling nonlinear narratives?

- In marketing, fundraising, and brand development:
  - What are the elements that allow us to attract and engage attention and emotion when the audience moves from screen to screen?
- In education:
  - How do I effectively support learning styles using technology?
  - How do I create appropriate boundaries when my students want to friend me on Facebook?
  - How do I communicate the value of digital citizenship or prepare students to find and evaluate good information?
- In nongovernmental organizations and nonprofits:
  - How can I effectively leverage technology to deliver social services to diverse populations?
- In governments:
  - How can we construct and use media technologies that promote positive social values?
- In business:
  - How do we establish appropriate social media and communication guidelines for our employees?
  - How should we communicate with our customers in a social environment?
- In entertainment:
  - How can we create immersive environments by developing multiplatform strategies?
  - How do social technologies disrupt traditional business models and what can we do to protect ourselves from extinction?
- In health care:
  - How can we create a mobile app that meaningfully supports a patients' health?
- In technology development:
  - What is it that people are trying to do where technology can make it better, easier, or faster?

If you are intrigued or inspired by any of these questions, then media psychology may be the perfect path for you.

## History of the Field

Media psychology is a relatively new field of academic study. Early proponents of media psychology founded the American Psychological Association Division 46 for Media Psychology (now the Society for Media Psychology and Technology) in the 1980s. Their goal was to create a collaborative space where scholars, researchers, and practitioners working in disparate fields could come together to understand the implications of the increasing integration of technology across society. The first doctoral degree in media psychology was offered in 2003, introduced by Fielding Graduate University. The rapid integration of the Internet and social media continues to amplify the need for studying human behavior in the context of media technologies.

## EDUCATIONAL BACKGROUND NEEDED FOR MEDIA PSYCHOLOGISTS

Media psychology starts with the study of psychology. Psychological theory provides the lens for the array of activities that are enabled by media technologies. Early media effects theories viewed people as passive victims of media. In fact, people still talk about what "the media" does as if it were a one-directional process with an agenda of its own. We now recognize that life with technology is not nearly as simple as those early models. Our relationship with media technologies and its structure, content, and context is mutually influential. Media psychology addresses this complex interrelationship as the media environment and people evolve.

The foundation for media psychology ideally should give you a mental map of psychology—including the range of subfields and some familiarity with major theories and theorists within each. This will allow you to do several things:

- Gain a sense of the tools available so you have the ability to shift perspectives, apply the most relevant psychological theories, and know where to find something when you need it.
- Develop some depth of expertise without losing sight of its context in the field as a whole. This is especially important, as time (and research) tend to break down barriers among subfields.
- Open doors to multiple career paths as you focus your interests.
- Make theoretical sense of observed human behavior and develop hypothesis about what people will do in response to other media and technological experiences and changes.

Several areas of study are relevant to media and technology, depending on the context and goal. Major subfields include cognitive psychology, social psychology, developmental psychology personality and individual differences, narrative psychology, positive psychology and research methodology and design.

As of 2015, few schools had dedicated media psychology graduate programs. An increasing number of media psychology courses are available, however. If you are interested in pursuing a career in media psychology and are looking beyond the dedicated programs available, you can build your own.

- Find faculty in a psychology department who are interested in applying psychological theory to media and technologies. You can find them by searching online for some media psychology topics and research papers and seeing where the authors teach.

■ Find faculty in one of the many related programs, from communications to political science, who are open to the inclusion of psychology as the grounding perspective. This path can be slightly more difficult because psychology is not the preferred theoretical lens in other disciplines; however, people studying media and technology tend to be fairly open-minded.

At the risk of being repetitive, the heart of media psychology is psychology—the study of human behavior. With new media and technology appearing every day, it is easy to be distracted by the bells and whistles. The tools, platforms, apps, and programming will continue to change. Something new and potentially disruptive—whether it's the next Facebook, self-driving cars, or something we can't yet imagine—is around every corner. As we know from neuroscience and evolutionary psychology, human behaviors and emotions are largely the same as they were thousands of years ago. Technologies come and go. Psychological theory is transferable to the next new thing.

## FINDING YOUR PATH

Many students come into a media psychology programs with clear ideas of their interests and what they want to do in a career, but an equal number do not. Students come to a graduate program in media psychology with a variety of backgrounds. Some have lots of psychology but no media experience; others come from film, marketing, or education and have no psychology experience. My experience teaching media psychology suggests that students benefit from the cross-collaboration of varied background and experiences and from being open-minded. Many of my students and colleagues have found their career paths taking unexpected and exciting turns enabled by the pursuit of media psychology. One woman came in a documentary filmmaker and left with a passion for teaching media literacy. Another came in working in a digital agency and left to make interactive children's media. Others decide to apply their degree training to raise awareness and support causes about which they care passionately, such as domestic violence or antibullying.

One conundrum you face in the 21st century is that many of the careers options you will have in 4 or 5 years—the amount of time it takes to earn a doctoral degree—don't exist yet. The crux of media psychology— the ability to apply a breadth of psychological theory in the context of the evolution of technology—teaches critical thinking and the ability to ask good questions, and opens new visions of potential for creating the adaptive and innovative solutions we need to solve 21st-century problems.

## Applications for a Degree in Media Psychology

The question of "what does a media psychologist do?" is not an easy one to answer. It's more instructive to describe the advantages and disadvantages of the field. Media psychology does not have a prescribed path. Like many careers in the social sciences, it is about translating and applying scholarship in the real world. Media psychology combines two areas of mastery—psychological science and media technologies—and employs that integrated body of knowledge to address specific problems and questions in research and practice.

### THE ADVANTAGES

The advantage of a career in media psychology is that the range of applications is literally limitless. Media psychology is applicable to any place human behavior intersects with media technologies. This flexibility allows media psychologists to pursue careers in almost every field imaginable, from health care and education to marketing and entertainment. This is quite exciting. As technology continues to evolve, media psychologists develop increasingly more ways to make a difference.

### DISADVANTAGES

The disadvantage of media psychology is that there is no specific job for a media psychologist. Do not expect recruiters searching for a media psychologist on LinkedIn or job postings on Monster.com. In spite of the wide applicability, the burden is often on job seekers to show how their training can be valuable to an employer or to a field.

## Training Needed to Work as a Media Psychologist

Given the breadth of media psychology, it won't be surprising to learn that every specialized career focus within the field will require a different emphasis in training and preparation, just like any other career in psychology.

As you gravitate to certain areas within media psychology, you will begin to focus on specific subfields and theories that are particularly relevant. Some examples follow. Initial doctoral studies are an excellent time to explore and begin to identify some more specific interests. Later coursework, as well as the dissertation and research phase of a doctoral degree, will allow you to target the area where you want to develop the theoretical and applied depth that will help you establish a career path. Students with specialized interests and goals often supplement their training with particular proficiencies and experiences, such as learning specific software platforms or analytical tools, attending relevant conferences to meet current practitioners, and looking for internships and research opportunities that expose them to particular practices and industries, such as media production, marketing, or social advocacy.

According to feedback from colleagues and former students, pursuing a degree in media psychology was a life-changing experience. A common response is that it developed their ability to assess the continually changing media environment and provided them with a solid foundation for evaluating the emerging research. Most important, the uniqueness of the field opened doors to new career opportunities. The following examples demonstrate some of the applications of media psychology in different domains.

# Education

## TEACHING AND RESEARCHING MEDIA PSYCHOLOGY

Many media psychology graduates stay in academia, teaching and performing research in media psychology and related fields. Because there are few dedicated media psychology programs at colleges and universities, there are opportunities to introduce innovative programming and courses within other related departments and disciplines. Teaching media psychology as a topic requires a facility with range of subfields in psychology as well as the acquisition of teaching experience, which often can be gained as a graduate student. More advanced media psychology courses drill down within a subfield of psychology, allowing scholars to apply their specific areas of expertise to media technologies. For example, social psychology can form the foundation for learning about online behaviors, social networks, and crowdsourcing.

Most media psychologists in academia pursue research interests and publish either independently or with student research teams. There is a wide range of journals now interested in the wide range of topics related to media psychology. Areas under examination in some of our research teams include the social impact of technology on rural communities, personal growth in fan communities, perceptual consistency in augmented reality applications, sporting events as immersive experiences, identity stigmas among gamers, empathy and emotional release in social media attacks on corporations, brand integrity and the role of archetypes, gender roles in fan blogs, and engagement factors across transmedia stories.

## INTEGRATING ONLINE TOOLS IN EDUCATION

Although media psychology can be taught as a subject, it is also valuable to anyone who wants to create media-based content to support teachers in other disciplines. Areas in cognitive psychology, such as learning theory, schemas and mental models, and information processing, and in social psychology, such as social validation and peer pressure (social proof), imply psychological and behavioral implications of design decisions and platform choices when integrating media and technology into a curriculum or learning experience. Media psychologists help educators determine which tools, such as blogging, wikis, Twitter, presentation tools, video, search tools, digital portfolios, and online data access and survey development, can be used to supplement traditional and online education in different situations and with different populations (e.g., Dabbagh & Kitsantas, 2012).

## TEACHING ONLINE

Media psychology also informs a range of skills that enhance online learning in any field, such as creating dynamic, interactive online learning spaces that can support synchronous and asynchronous teaching. As with integrating technology into face-to-face curriculum, the fields of cognitive, developmental, and social psychologies inform different aspects of design and organization of course content, ensure ease of navigation, and create a structure that is conducive to creating meaningful relationships in a virtual space.

Online teaching offers tremendous flexibility to both faculty and students who are otherwise geographically constrained by family, work, and other obligations. There are advantages and disadvantages to online teaching. The online environment challenges traditional methods of establishing authentic relationships, requiring new processes and skills to deliver and receive feedback and to express yourself effectively without the advantage of body language and facial expressions.

The advantages, however, are plentiful. People who have never taught or taken a course online will be surprised by how quickly they feel connected to the others in the course. Online environments solicit participation from even the most introverted students, allow for both asynchronous and synchronous contact, and make education available to people who would not have the ability or opportunity to attend traditional educational institutions.

# Media Literacy and Digital Citizenship

As technology becomes more intertwined with daily life, learning how to use it well becomes a critical issue. The digital divide is no longer about access; it is about the skills to navigate the digital world. The need for improving media literacy is creating a variety of opportunities for media psychologists to pursue careers.

Media psychologists often work as consultants to train people of all ages to effectively navigate the digital world, from understanding digital etiquette and ethical behaviors to mastering tools to access information and communication. Some media psychologists create and deliver digital citizenship programs for students and educators within school systems as well as employees and managers in organizations. Others work with parents and community groups to educate people in how to safely and effectively use digital tools to participate fully in society.

The application of psychology provides a broader view of concepts, such as media literacy. Although many people focus on narrow segments for specific populations and needs, such as Internet safety or cyberbullying, psychologists also have the ability to step back and see the larger picture, such as how developmental issues, social goals, personal growth, cognitive capabilities, and cultural perspectives intersect with the capabilities and use of media technologies. This allows a media psychologist to frame technology use in terms of social and developmental norms.

Media literacy draws on areas within cognitive psychology, social psychology, and developmental psychology and is informed by theories such as self-schema, self-efficacy, and agency, and developmental appropriateness—all of which influence the adoption rate and use of technology. Equally important is the ability to use cognitive frameworks to simplify and communicate media literacy in a way that is accessible to worried parents, blasé students, and a fearful public.

# Marketing, Advertising, and Branding

Psychology has always played an important role in marketing through consumer psychology and much of the research done in the marketing would qualify as media psychology. While psychologists working in marketing is covered elsewhere in this volume (see Chapter 21), I'd like to draw attention to some areas in marketing and engagement in which media psychology is a particularly vital field.

## THE SOCIAL SPACE: COMMUNITY BUILDING AND SOCIAL MEDIA MANAGEMENT

With consumers becoming more empowered, companies now realize they need a new way of interacting with customers—one that develops relationships. This shift has created a new set of careers opportunities around community and social media management and consumer engagement. These careers combine knowledge of social media and community structures with aspects of social psychology, such as networked behaviors, social identity, and social connection. Media psychology makes it easier to recognize and adapt to behavioral trends and support the types of community behaviors that influence consumer engagement.

## BRAND PSYCHOLOGY

The importance of branding, brand strategy, brand personality, and brand storytelling has never received more attention and has never been more social. Brands are now in the business of forming relationships and creating emotional connections and need a strategy that integrates the consumer's brand schema at multiple levels. Brand psychology draws on expertise in storytelling, narrative identity, and brain science in developing brand strategies that tap into unconscious meaning, emotion, and images that frame the larger brand experience.

## AUDIENCE PROFILING

Marketers, companies, governments, and political campaigns have the ability to gather a dizzying range of data on human behavior, from online behavior to our physical locations via mobile devices. These technological developments have created a new range of career opportunities for media psychologists to construct research and perform analysis on consumer behavior to identify and measure psychological drivers, extending the psychographic models at use in 21st-century marketing. Such psychographic models represent a hybrid of analysis of demographics and lifestyle analysis.

Media psychologists working in these capacities must have solid skills in research and analysis and familiarity with the methods and criteria used to calculate and predict valued interactions and track consumer engagement. The value added of media psychology is in understanding the influence of network structures on behavior. Skills in this area include the ability to create research projects, construct methodologically sound surveys, conduct focus groups, and maintain a fluency in analytical tools for evaluating and interpreting qualitative and quantitative data.

## Social Impact: Nonprofits and Social Entrepreneurship

Media and technology for positive social impact draw on the same psychological theories and skill sets that would be employed in other marketing, branding, and persuasive applications. Additional attention, however, is placed on the integration of positive psychology tenets to guide media for social change campaigns, social entrepreneurship, and corporate social responsibility programs. These media experiences are constructed to gain not just the audience's attention but also their trust to further a cause, influence public policy, solicit support, or inspire behavior change. Thus, media psychologists consciously integrate the promotion of constructs such as altruism, self-efficacy, resilience, hope, and optimism in the media they produce. Measurement evaluation moves away from traditional return on investment toward estimates of increased empathy and responses to various calls to action.

Media psychologists are involved in a number of efforts to harness the power of media for social betterment. These include (a) creating best practices for effective collaborative philanthropy and crowdsourced funding, such as Kickstarter.org, that encourage broad-based and grass roots participation; (b) using social technologies to allow low-cost message distribution through audience participation and sharing; (c) developing mobile technologies that can deliver content, such as literacy programs and health information worldwide; (d) creating information systems to support social phenomenon, such as identifying areas of conflict, providing birth registration, and developing low-literacy interfaces for mobile transfer of funds; and (e) developing entertainment media based on entertainment-education models that address social problems, such as domestic violence or family planning, in culturally digestible ways (e.g., Singhal & Obregon, 1999).

### HEALTH CARE AND BEHAVIOR CHANGE

The ability to influence behavior through media is an exploding field. Media psychologists work a number of ways to support positive health and lifestyle behaviors and establish new social norms for improved subjective well-being.

## ROBOTICS

Mediated experience occurs through all kinds of technology. A wide range of career opportunities is available for those who combine psychology with a background in robotics and engineering. Ongoing research in applied robotics at many universities relies on the fundamentals of psychology to create successful products. These types of robotic applications integrate knowledge across cognitive and developmental psychologies as well as robotics, for which key issues in effective design are not just functionality and usability but also user perceptions of human qualities that allow for engagement and trust.

### Mobile Apps and Wearables

One of the most visible emerging technologies is the use of personalized technology, such as mobile apps and wearable devices, that track wellness and medically related behaviors, from movement to blood-sugar levels. Wearables, such as fitness trackers and smartwatches, have created a category known as the *quantified self*, where self-knowledge comes from self-tracking.

According to Pew Research, 69% of U.S. adults track at least one health indicator, particularly those with chronic health concerns, and more and more of these adults are moving to technology (Fox & Duggan, 2013). Psychologists have long known that manual tools like mood journals and weight logs contributed to significant improvement in reaching health goals. The availability of well-designed technology increases adoption—and accuracy. Even the regular use of something as simple as a pedometer increases physical activity and improves health (Bravata et al., 2007), but this emerging field is ripe for new research. The psychological factors are critical, however, because they work only if you use them. Thus, media psychologists are looking at the full range of psychological drivers beyond usability, compliance, sustainability, comprehension, user perceptions of value, cognitive constraints of different screen sizes, literacy levels, and technology adoption across different populations.

## HEALTHY ENVIRONMENTS

Moving from the small to the large, media psychologists study the impact of holistic media environments, from closed-channel media with soothing music and imagery for hospitals to virtual world and augmented reality applications created for therapeutic interventions. Psychologists at the University of Southern California, for example, have been developing virtual reality applications for the U.S. Army that build resiliency and overcome posttraumatic stress disorder (Rizzo, Difede, Rothbaum, Daughtry, & Reger, 2013).

# *Media Creation*

Media creation is not just about the arts, like film and music. It applies to a vast array of activities centered around the ease of creating, using, and sharing things like medical records, business documents, transportation logs, training protocols, video games, and software programs. Media creators include course designers, filmmakers, game developers, app and web developers, journalists, photographers, and systems and product designers of all kinds. Their products include everything from traditional media to emerging technologies, such as virtual reality and augmented reality. Each of these occupations demands specialized technological skills and all of them are enhanced by the application of psychology.

## INTERACTIVE MEDIA AND GAMES

Many students are fascinated by the use and popularity of interactive media and, particularly, video games. Media psychologists working with these industries following two paths: (a) working within companies that design and development different types of interactive media and games, and (b) researching interactive media and gaming experience and impact.

Some media psychology graduates have taken an interest in cognitive and positive psychologies and brain science and have gone to work for companies designing and marketing interactive children's media, such as digital books. Others have gone to work for companies that create software programs for applying gamification principles to online training and gaming platforms. Media psychologists focusing on making and playing games generally supplement their foundation with game dynamics and game design, such as feedback loops, logic, and problem solving, which provide context for applying psychology (e.g., Salen & Zimmerman, 2004).

## CHILDREN'S MEDIA

Interactive children's media marries good storytelling, and intuitive and developmentally appropriate interface design with learning and literacy. Media psychologists can work for children's media developers and producers or they can work as consultants, advising on the myriad issues surrounding the interactive experience, from the quality of the interface to how the parent and child interact with each other while using the media.

## EDUCATIONAL TECHNOLOGY

In a fundamental way, all technology supports learning, whether it's mastery, socialization, or problem solving (Gee, 2007). Educational technology, however, refers to technology design with specific content to target educational goals. In some cases, media psychologists have adapted existing technology to meet learning and developmental needs, such as off-the-shelf games that can be used to teach social skills and attention development, such as for autism spectrum and attention-deficit disorders (e.g., http://www.LearningWorks.com). In other cases, media psychologists have created new technology applications that supplement educational curriculum, such as the many games and apps available that teach reading, math, and fine motor skills.

Several of our media psychology graduates have gone to work for companies in the educational technology field, producing interactive books and games to promote literacy, creating technology-based lessons that follow current content requirements, or creating materials that demonstrate how to easily integrate existing video, presentation, collage, and writing tools in their current lesson plans.

## WEB-BASED DESIGN, USER EXPERIENCE, AND EXPERIENCE DESIGN

Many media psychologists enter one of the fields related to web-based design and user experience. User experience (UX) focuses on the quality of user experience in the creation of design solutions. It involves users' behaviors, attitudes, motivations, emotions, and integrated meaning-making or holistic interpretation of the experience. It draws on the full range of psychological science, from neuroscience to narrative. The focus is on creating a valuable experience for the user. Where usability focuses on the ease of use of technology, such as navigating a website or easily working the controls on a car, user experience is a larger concept.

Experience design extends the concept of user experience to designing processes. Experience design considers all aspects of the user or consumer's journey and looks for ways to enhance experience, provide value, and increase engagement. Media psychologists contribute to this field by understanding the psychology behind the experience of attention, engagement, motivation, and needs.

## DESIGNING FOR TECHNOLOGY CONSTRAINTS

Media design varies not just by the consumer but also by the distribution channel. Cognition, perception, and meaning are key features in designing content for different screen sizes and other technology attributes. The prevalence of smartphones means that apps, games, and web content must be accessible and impactful from the small screen. Media psychologists work with designers to test the use and comprehension of content and the likelihood of interaction and sustained engagement.

## ENTERTAINMENT MEDIA

The entertainment industry is often alluring to new media psychology students. As entertainment media becomes more fluid, moving across multiple platforms, there are many more opportunities to get involved in careers that are part of, or support, the creation, production, and promotion efforts of entertainment properties. Many students come to media psychology from the media, music, and film industries with a desire to learn how to better engage their audiences, create media with more social value, or encourage positive change in some aspect of the entertainment industry. A number have returned to those industries, working in screenwriting, production, and promotion; integrating positive psychology and transmedia strategies; and creating innovative approaches to evaluating media impact as vehicles of social change.

Appearing in the media is not, in and of itself, a part of media psychology. For ethical reasons, it is important to make that distinction. Although some clinicians are media psychologists, being a media psychologist does not qualify someone to do clinical work.

Media psychology is an applied field, but it is not a clinical field. Media psychology curricula do not include clinical training, as you would receive in a clinical psychology program. If your interest is in applying clinical psychology in the media, you are ethically bound to acquire the appropriate expertise in addition to studying media psychology, whether giving advice on YouTube or designing mental health intervention apps. Media psychology curricula also do not include performance training. If you want to be a media personality, media psychology is not the field for you.

The field of media psychology is relevant to the psychological information distributed in the media in the following five ways:

1. Media psychologists routinely deal with moral issues surrounding human welfare and the media, and this includes the ethical presentation of psychology and psychological advice.
2. Media psychologists study how different media channels influence message perceptions and consumption patterns and how distribution choices influence content.
3. Psychology is a complex field. Research can seem impenetrable to the general public. Media psychologists can provide valuable guidance in translating information in ways that are readily accessible but accurately represent research results.
4. Media psychologists educate journalists about the impact of their coverage, particularly during crisis situations, to maximize information without heightening public fear, anxiety, and uncertainty. This role marries an understanding of the journalistic demands placed on media outlets as well as some clinical

training to anticipate cases in which information can exacerbate fear and anxiety and how to best provide guidelines for information delivery.

5. Telepsychology is a rising issue in clinical psychology. The ethical and therapeutic issues in mental health care are challenged by the many ways people communicate on a regular basis. Telepsychology is an area where the line between clinical and media psychologist cross. Any application, however, that includes the delivery of mental health services or interventions must be ethically considered to be clinical in terms of training and licensure requirements.

## Pay Range of a Media Psychologist

Estimating the income of a media psychologist is nearly impossible, given the breadth of the field and all the other factors that weigh in, such as location and level of experience. The U.S. Bureau of Labor Statistics (BLS, 2014) lists psychologists as having an annual mean wage of $75,790 with a range of $42,000 to $114,000. Media psychology will be equally if not more variable, given the range of industries to which media psychology can be applied. For example, the BLS estimates that market research analysts and marketing specialists average approximately $68,700, but media and marketing communications careers run the gamut, averaging from $40,000 to $127,000 per year. There is a similar variability for research scientists, which the BLS estimates range from $53,000 to $120,000 per year. Technology fields also offer many career options, too numerous to mention.

Teaching in higher education has a similar range to that of psychologists. Online teaching, however, can be much more variable. People who are interested in teaching online should be prepared to begin as adjunct faculty. These positions tend to be contracted by the class or by the number of students enrolled in the class and the pay rates vary by institution. Some institutions offer short 6- or 8-week courses, while others will contract for a 12- or 15-week term. A common salary range for online postsecondary instructors is $1,500 to $3,500 per semester-long course.

Although some online adjuncts work for one institution on a part-time basis, it is common for people to work as adjunct faculty teaching multiple courses at several schools, creating the equivalent of a full-time teaching job. According to GetEducated.com (n.d.), some online adjuncts working at multiple institutions report earnings in $100,000-plus range. Online teachers can supplement their incomes with course development, earning $1,000 to $3,000 per course.

# The Future of Media Psychology

The increasing integration of new technologies into every aspect of daily live argues that media psychology will become more, rather than less, valuable and opportunities will grow. Given the breadth of applications, media psychology is not dependent on government funding or insurance reimbursements for a healthy future, like some psychology careers. Media psychology relies on the continued value placed by media producers, businesses, institutions, and health care on how people use, create, and experience media and technologies.

Few would have predicted the technology-enabled behaviors that have quickly become social norms, such as online shopping and dating, selfies, on-demand programming, crowd-sourced philanthropy or cars that park themselves. These only scratch the surface of the ways in which media technologies will continue to affect our daily lives. These advances also suggest that although the field of media psychology may struggle with a specific definition of what a media psychologist does, there will be plenty of work to do.

# References

Aker, J., & Mbiti, I. M. (2010). Mobile phones and economic development in Africa. *Journal of Economic Perspectives, 24,* 207–232. http://dx.doi.org/10.1257/jep.24.3.207

Bravata, D. M., Smith-Spangler, C., Sundaram, V., Gienger, A. L., Lin, N., Lewis, R., . . . Sirard, J. R. (2007). Using pedometers to increase physical activity and improve health: A systematic review. *JAMA, 298,* 2296–2304. http://dx.doi.org/10.1001/jama.298.19.2296

Dabbagh, N., & Kitsantas, A. (2012). Personal learning environments, social media, and self-regulated learning: A natural formula for connecting formal and informal learning. *The Internet and Higher Education, 15,* 3–8. http://dx.doi.org/10.1016/j.iheduc.2011.06.002

Fox, S., & Duggan, M. (2013). Tracking for health. *Pew Research Center Internet, Science & Tech.* Retrieved from http://www.pewinternet.org/2013/01/28/tracking-for-health/

Gee, J. P. (2007). *What video games have to teach us about learning and literacy* (Rev. & updated, 2nd ed.). New York, NY: Palgrave Macmillan.

GetEducated.com. (n.d.). *The definitive guide to teaching online courses.* Retrieved from http://www.geteducated.com/teaching-online-courses/253-online-teaching-opportunities

Rainie, L. (2013). Cell phone ownership hits 91% of adults. *Pew Internet & American Life Project.* Retrieved from http://www.pewresearch.org/fact-tank/2013/06/06/cell-phone-ownership-hits-91-of-adults/

Rizzo, A., Difede, J., Rothbaum, B., Daughtry, J. M., & Reger, G. (2013). Virtual reality as a tool for delivering PTSD exposure therapy. *Military Behavioral Health, 1,* 52–58.

Salen, K., & Zimmerman, E. (2004). *Rules of play: Game design fundamentals.* Cambridge, MA: The MIT Press.

Singhal, A., & Obregon, R. (1999). Social uses of commercial soap operas: A conversation with Miguel Sabido. *Journal of Development Communication, 10,* 68–77.

Sterling, G. (2015, February 9). Report: U.S. smartphone penetration now at 75 percent. *Marketing Land.* Retrieved from http://marketingland.com/report-us-smartphone-penetration-now-75-percent-117746

U.S. Bureau of Labor Statistics. (2014). Retrieved from http://www.bls.gov

*Judith S. Blanton*

# Consulting and Organizational Psychologists

**19**

W hen I was in graduate school, I had no idea that psychologists did what I ended up doing—consulting to organizations. Most of my colleagues in the field also came to this work in a roundabout way. In fact, a number of senior people have moved into consulting from other fields (Leonard, 1999). For example, in my own career, when I completed my doctorate in social-developmental psychology within an educational psychology department, I took a job evaluating a large government program within the Bureau of Indian Affairs. This job required site visits to various tribal schools across the country, where I clarified program objectives, identified measures, and attempted to assess the impact of the program on

Judith S. Blanton, PhD, ABPP, is an organizational consultant in private practice in Pasadena, CA. Previously, she was a partner with RHR International, LLP, a management-consulting firm of psychologists. She received her doctoral degree from the University of Texas at Austin and worked in private industry and academia before beginning her consulting career. She has served as president of the Society of Consulting Psychology (Division 13 of the American Psychological Association) and received its Outstanding Service Award in 2005.

http://dx.doi.org/10.1037/15960-020
*Career Paths in Psychology: Where Your Degree Can Take You, Third Edition,*
R. J. Sternberg (Editor)

academic performance and other variables. Quickly, I became interested in trying to make the programs better rather than merely documenting what was wrong, and this interest evolved into action research. My colleagues and I involved tribal councils, Native American parents, and Bureau of Indian Affairs employees, encouraging these different groups to work together to develop useful programs. Over time, I moved from evaluating programs to broader kinds of consulting. My focus shifted from working with education and social service organizations to consulting with businesses and corporations.

There were no opportunities for formal academic training in the field when I began this work, and there are few opportunities now. Most in the field have had to create our own path. This chapter provides an overview of what the career entails. My hope is to assist those who are considering working in the area decide whether this is the path for them. I will describe what consulting psychologists do, the skills involved, ways of preparing for this career, financial compensation, disadvantages of the career, and attributes for success. In addition, I will offer a number of examples from my own career, including why I chose it and a description of a typical day.

## What Is Consulting Psychology, and Where Do Its Practitioners Work?

Such assistance is advisory in nature and the consultant has no direct responsibility for its acceptance.[1] Consulting psychologists may have clients who are individuals, institutions, corporations, or other kinds of organizations.

---

[1]Is consulting a particular application of psychology skills or a separate and distinct profession or discipline? The question is controversial, and debate continues. Dr. Ellen Lent (personal communication August 5, 2011) has suggested that it is not a distinct field at all, but more a matter of context: "It is easier," she observes, "to describe the activities and settings where consulting psychology takes place" than it is to categorize it. Regardless of how it is classified, as the field matures, we learn more about the methods, techniques, and skills that make consulting effective, and a growing body of knowledge and literature in this area has emerged. I think of it this way: Occasionally, most psychologists consult with colleagues, clients, and patients by providing technical assistance and information. However, for consulting psychologists, consulting becomes the primary focus of their work. The consulting psychologist is not so much a content expert on the client's business (although content about the client and business helps) as an expert on methods to facilitate development and positive change in individuals, teams and organizations.

In short, consulting psychologists use their knowledge and skills to increase organizational effectiveness and improve individual performance. Careers in consulting psychology cover a wide range of activities within a broad range of environments. They may specialize in an industry (e.g., provision of services to retail companies) or types of organizations (e.g., government agencies, not-for-profit organizations, and education institutions). Others provide a specific service (e.g., assessment, coaching, team building).

Consulting psychologists may work independently as solo practitioners. They also may join forces when a project demands multiple consultants, an arrangement that seems to be an increasing trend. Additional options include working in a boutique consulting company or as part of a larger firm that may involve professionals from outside the field of psychology (e.g., masters of business administration, human resource professionals). Consulting psychologists also work internally within an organization providing services to individuals, teams, or functional units within that company, university, or agency.

A consulting career can be a part-time or full-time profession. Some consulting psychologists work part time as a consultant to supplement their day job. This method can provide a solid professional base while one is building a practice. For example, a substantial number of academics consult part time as an adjunct to their teaching and research. Other psychologists combine a consulting and a clinical practice. For example, a colleague of mine sees clinical patients but also works with corporations doing team development and coaching of senior executives.

# What Consulting Psychologists Do

The practice of consulting requires not only skills in doing the work but also skills in getting the work and managing the work and clients, and (for those in independent practice) managing the consulting business. The following sections discuss these three clusters of skills with an emphasis on the work itself.

## SKILLS IN DOING THE WORK

In the late 1990s, the Society of Consulting Psychology (Division 13 of APA) began to clarify competencies for the organizational side of consulting psychology. This ambitious project culminated in the creation of the "Guidelines for Education and Training at the Doctoral and Postdoctoral

Level in Consulting Psychology/Organizational Psychology" (APA, 2007). The competencies were clustered into three broad domains of expertise: individual, group, and organizational. Clearly, these are not neatly separate categories; they overlap and interact. Effective practice often requires work at all three levels simultaneously. Certain areas of competencies are critical at all levels—for example, assessment, process skills, research, and evaluation. Still, this division into three domains can be useful in discussing the kinds of work and kinds of skills needed. The following subsections provide examples of work that consulting psychologists do at the individual, group, and organizational levels. The examples are merely that; they are weighted in terms of my experience. My hope is that they will provide a picture of the broad scope of the field (for another view, see Kasserman, 2005).

## Work With Individuals

Consultants, like clinical psychologists and others, work with individual clients. Typically, however, they are hired by the business or corporation rather than by the individual himself or herself. The task may be to assess someone for hire or promotion, help a faltering employee, or help an individual develop as an effective leader.

### Employee Selection and Appraisal

Many consulting psychologists in the business community focus their work in the areas of employee selection and appraisal. This activity involves assessing a candidate's suitability for a particular job. The consultant generally begins with a careful analysis of the kinds of knowledge, skills, and attitudes related to success in that job. For lower or midlevel jobs, the consultant may assess a number of employees who have been highly successful and compare their scores or performance with those who have had average- or below-average success. Candidates whose profiles are more like successful employees presumably would be better hires. A number of standardized tests are available that can be used to rate applicants on specific skills or additional dimensions related to the job. Consulting psychologists also construct and run assessment centers in which a candidate performs tasks that simulate activities he or she would perform on the job.

For a more senior level executive position, the consulting psychologist needs to understand the knowledge, skills, and attitudes necessary for that job in that business at that point in time. For senior positions, however, it is usually not possible to norm the tests on incumbents or predecessors because the numbers are too small and because future job requirements are likely to be different from earlier job demands. If standardized tests are used, it is important to determine whether they assess dimensions that reflect the culture and qualities required by that particular organization. Typically, for higher level positions, interviews supplement any tests that are given. A good interview can focus on the unique demands of a particular company and job and get at nuances that a standardized test cannot. In most cases, the consulting psychologist provides a written report. In addition, he or she may discuss the strengths and weaknesses of the individual with the potential boss (or human resources person). Suggestions for development are sometimes included. Generally, the consulting psychologist also provides the candidate with oral feedback. If he or she accepts an offer, the feedback can be used to plan his or her integration into the company and improve the likelihood of successful on-boarding. Such an integration program would typically involve coaching.

### Executive Coaching

Executive coaching is one of the fastest growing areas within the consulting psychology field. Although many nonpsychologists are executive coaches, consulting psychologists who can combine their deep knowledge of human behavior with knowledge of the business culture can be particularly effective when working with business or corporate executives. Executive coaching is different from therapy or counseling in a number of ways. Most of the people receiving coaching are high-functioning individuals for whom the focus is on enhanced professional development rather than addressing personal problems or pathology. Executives may receive coaching because they are valued employees but are plateaued or are having difficulties because of a specific behavior, such as abrasiveness or communication problems. Coaching is also used when an organization wants to accelerate development for individuals identified as having high potential. In both cases, the focus is on professional development within the workplace and does not address the kinds of personal issues typically dealt with in counseling or therapy. The company typically pays for coaching and expects a return in the form of improved or accelerated job performance. The time frame for coaching varies greatly. Coaching can be short term (3 months); other assignments take 6 to 9 months and some coaches require a commitment of a year.

### 360-Degree or Multirater Surveys

The *360-degree survey* is designed to obtain feedback from all those around an individual on leadership style or some other variables. It entails gathering data from the individual, his or her boss, subordinates, and peers.

Sometimes customers or representatives from key constituencies with whom the subject of the survey interacts also are involved. The consultant may use any one of many standardized surveys. Alternately, he or she might create a customized survey or gather the data through interviews. The consultant compiles the results and presents them graphically in a way that shows the similarities and differences in the responses of the various groups. The consultant then debriefs the individual about the findings and, typically, creates a development plan based on the feedback. Often, the 360-degree survey process is included as part of an executive coaching effort.

### Process Consultation and Being a Trusted Advisor

Consultants often develop a strong personal relationship with a senior executive or manager and may have an ongoing relationship that is more like serving as a trusted advisor or sounding board than doing formal coaching. "It's lonely at the top" may be a cliché, but it is also true, and some executives use consulting psychologists as an honest and objective source of feedback and as a sounding board to try out ideas or just discuss difficult topics.

## Work With Teams and Groups

Consulting psychologists do not work only with individuals. They also can work with the executive team (the chief executive officer and his or her direct reports), a departmental team, or other kinds of groups. This work can take a number of directions, and the following paragraphs provide a few examples.

### Assessment and Development of Teams

Consulting psychologists work with new teams, helping them cohere and get direction, or with existing teams to help them plan and work together more effectively. For example, as part of my work with the leaders of an information technology department, I interviewed each member of the team individually to gain background information and to identify what was working and what was not. I also used a questionnaire that measured various team dimensions. Using this information, I planned a retreat at which we addressed issues that had been identified, set goals, and did exercises to clarify values what would be helpful in reaching those goals. We then held follow-up meetings after 3 and 6 months to assess progress. In one follow-up meeting, my colleague and I helped the team clarify its roles and responsibilities and addressed a few residual conflicts.

### Team Conflict

Group members do not always work well together. As part of team building, I have had group members take a test that measured how they deal with conflict. I summarized the data from the instrument and presented it graphically as a way of kicking off a discussion of conflict management. In coaching, I sometimes have held joint meetings with the coachee and his or her boss to discuss how they could deal with their conflicts.

Recently, I was asked to intervene when two engineers from different departments had stopped speaking to each other although they needed to work together to develop a product. At that point, they were communicating only by e-mail, and this was affecting their work and slowing down product development. They were from different countries and cultures, which complicated their communication. Each was convinced that the other was the total cause of the problem. My task was to get them focused on the way their behavior was affecting the work. I was able to convince them that they did not need to be friends but did need to behave in a more professional manner and to fully share information.

Teams also can get into difficulty when they suppress conflict. I have worked with groups to develop rules of engagement to help them develop a culture that surfaces and deals with problems in a direct and constructive manner.

### Family Businesses

A number of consulting psychologists specialize in working with family businesses. This is a particularly challenging area because it requires an understanding not only of business issues but also of family dynamics. The consulting psychologist needs to have a good understanding of the individuals and how they interact within this particular setting and how their personal relationships affect their business goals. Issues of sibling rivalry, long-standing resentments, and favoritism can greatly complicate a business. One of my colleagues who practices in this area said that although he is not doing family therapy, his earlier training in this area has been an asset.

### Intergroup Management in an Organizational Context

Race, gender, and ethnic group membership can have a powerful impact on how a group works (or does not work) together. Certain consulting psychologists focus on helping diverse groups work effectively together. I have a particular interest in organizations that span time zones, countries, and languages. As organizations become global and diverse, they need to find better ways of communication. One of my colleagues specializes in working with global companies and cross-national teams. He described the difficulty a cross-national team with members from Japan, France, and the United States had coming to decisions and then implementing them. He found that when the Japanese did not verbally object to an idea or statement, the Americans were assuming that they agreed. It never occurred to the Japanese that their silence represented a commitment to a course of action, however, and they were surprised when the Americans were upset when their Japanese colleagues did not implement their suggestions after the meeting. My colleague used his facilitation and team-building skills to have the group discuss what silence meant and agree on what *agreement* meant. Both morale and follow-up action improved.

Consulting psychologists also help organizations improve their virtual teams. Such teams involve a group of geographically dispersed people who rely primarily or exclusively on electronic forms of communication to work together. I have worked with managers who were trying to develop skills in supervising employees who were nine time zones away and with whom they mostly interacted through e-mail, phones, teleconferencing, and various computer technologies. More and more managers now supervise groups of individuals who seldom or never meet but who must solve problems and develop products as a team. This is a challenging and exciting new area for research, technology, and consulting.

## Work With Organizational Systems

In their work with individuals, teams, and groups, consulting psychologists are highly attentive to the larger organizational system. They also may undertake projects that focus on the system itself.

### Survey Development and Analysis

Consulting psychologists (along with industrial–organizational psychologists) often develop and implement attitude, satisfaction, or climate surveys for organizations. A company may want to know about their employees' concerns and what they like or dislike about their working situation. Many standardized instruments have been created for use in this area, and consulting psychologists need to identify which tools might be appropriate and how to interpret findings. One advantage of psychological training is to be able to evaluate the many tests that have proliferated on the Internet and may be poorly designed and normed. Some psychologists may customize or develop a new survey from scratch. The skills needed to develop a new survey are complex and require substantial effort to ensure that the tool is both reliable and valid for its purpose. Consulting psychologists usually don't merely administer the survey or supply summary data; instead, they work with the organization to understand the findings and, often, to develop strategies for dealing with problems that surfaced in the process. Although survey development and analysis is an important and complex skill, most consulting psychologists see this activity as a means to an end (organizational improvement) rather than an end in itself.

## Management of Change and Transitions

Consulting psychologists may take on a broad variety of organizational issues under the heading of managing change, including helping a company implement a new system or initiative, deal with the need to downsize, adapt to rapid growth, or smooth the merger or acquisition process. For example, consulting psychologists may get involved early in the due diligence process of an acquisition, in which they assess the management or senior leadership team in the business being acquired. Other tasks might involve the development and implementation of a communication plan. Surveys or interviews often are used to understand the cultures of the companies that are merging. After the merger or acquisition, the consulting psychologist can help the two organizations address the differences in their cultures or operating procedures.

The boundary between individual and organizational systems work is fluid. For example, I have been involved as part of a consultant team in the selection of the new management team following a merger. Part of the work was on the individual level (executive assessment) but deeply linked to the organizational transition. Initially, I was concerned that employees would be threatened by being interviewed and evaluated by an outside person. I was surprised to find that most of the managers and executives were supportive of the process because they saw our consultant team's involvement as providing an objective third-party perspective and clarifying criteria for positions. Employees were scattered over multiple states, and some were in another country. They had been concerned that the senior executives would pick only managers they knew from the acquiring company. With our involvement, all appropriate managers had an opportunity to be considered in terms of clear criteria based on the needs of the newly merged company. We did not make the decisions, but our assessments provided key data and were instrumental in the identification of qualified individuals. In the merger process, we also were involved in coaching key executives as they moved through this challenging process.

The book *Big Change at Best Buy* (Billings & Gibson, 2003) described a complex management-change process implemented in this well-known retail firm. The company had spent a great deal of time and money developing standard operating procedures but found that the various stores were not implementing them. The book provided a case study of actions taken to engage employees and managers in making and sustaining the needed changes. It also demonstrated how a team of consulting psychologists worked together and how they partnered with an internal team of Best Buy employees assigned to this project. The consulting psychologists not only helped with the change process but also built the internal capacity of the organization to do this.

### Human Resource Systems Development

Consulting psychologists also get involved in developing and implementing various human resource systems, such as a performance management or succession planning system, a leadership or high-potential development program, or an employee retention plan. The objective might be to increase internal capacity, provide input on best practices, or evaluate the organization's current program and make recommendations for improvement. To implement such initiatives successfully, a consulting psychologist would need to partner with internal human resources or a variety of company employees.

## SKILLS IN GETTING AND MANAGING THE WORK

To do the work, you must first get the work. This is particularly important if you are in a solo practice. You need skills in networking, developing marketing materials, and promoting sales. In addition to being able to write a good proposal, you need to be able to develop a realistic time frame and estimate the costs of doing the work. How many days will it take? What sort of materials or tests will be needed, and what will they cost? These generally are not skills one learns in graduate school, and early in my career, I found that I consistently underestimated time and costs. I forgot to account for unforeseen interruptions and problems. I might be ready to go, but I might have to wait on someone else to do her task before I could proceed. Luckily, I had a knowledgeable colleague who would add 20% to whatever my initial estimate was and that was generally on target.

Then, once you have the project, you must manage it and the client. If you have a complex project, particularly one that requires you to direct other consulting psychologists, skills in project management are necessary. My previous firm believed this skill set was so important that it developed an internal course in this area. Numerous software programs now exist that are useful in project planning and management—

for example, helping to construct Gantt charts, tracking expenditures, and scheduling.

## SKILLS IN MANAGING THE BUSINESS

Business management skills are not important if you are an employee, but if you want to create your own private practice, it would be useful to cultivate the kinds of business skills needed by anyone starting and running a small business. If you plan to go it alone, be prepared to wear the following hats in addition to being a consultant: secretary, receptionist, controller, health benefits administrator, accountant, accounts receivable clerk, accounts payable manager, tax auditor, insurance agent, office manager, travel agent, information technology help desk, marketing vice president, director of sales, event planner, retirement fund administrator, president, chief executive officer, and chief financial officer. For those who plan to employ other consultants on a part-time or full-time basis, additional challenges arise. You need to deal with issues of selection, salaries, bonuses, performance management, and quality control.

Obviously, the decision to enter private practice takes careful consideration. I have colleagues who started their own firms and enjoy the flexibility and freedom it provides. Others, however, became highly frustrated because they vastly underestimated the time it took to manage the business when they wanted to concentrate only on consulting.

# Preparation Needed for the Career

The "Guidelines for Education and Training at the Doctoral and Postdoctoral Levels in Consulting Psychology/Organizational Psychology" developed by APA Division 13 (APA, 2007) provides an excellent and highly detailed description of the training required to be a consulting psychologist. The first graduate program to offer a degree in consulting psychology was Alliant University in 1999. Since then, other graduate programs have begun to offer coursework or some sort of concentration in consulting. Most people in the field still receive their education from graduate programs in industrial–organizational, counseling, clinical, social, or other psychology field and then broaden their skills through self-study, on-the-job experience, mentoring, continuing education courses, and internal training offered by various consulting firms.

As noted, the Society of Consulting Psychology (APA Division 13) guidelines stress training in the individual, group, and organizational or systems levels. In addition, Division 13 stresses the necessity for knowledge in research and evaluation:

> The behavioral sciences are most clearly distinguished from fad and "pop" psychology by their discipline of research and evaluation. Consulting Psychologists need to learn methods of evaluating their organizational interventions to assure that clients are maximizing their return on investment. (Lowman et al., 2002, p. 222)

In addition to an understanding of both quantitative and qualitative evaluation methods, the guidelines suggest that consulting psychologists should have practical experience in real-life projects. Supervision is particularly important in providing this type of experience. There are several models of supervision in consulting graduate training programs (Blanton, 2014). Finding good supervision can be difficult, particularly for those who seek to be licensed (Blanton, 2014). A final area of training has to do with practical professional issues, such as ethics, confidentiality, license requirements, and legal issues. Because consulting psychologists operate in the turbulent world of organizations, these practical professional issues are particularly salient. Even seasoned consultants may seek shadow consulting from other consultants to continue their professional development.

Two organizations provide excellent resources for those interested in learning more about consulting and improving their skills in that area. The Society of Consulting Psychology (Division 13 of APA) typically includes workshops and sessions appropriate for psychologists who want to move into consulting at its midwinter meeting. *The Consulting Psychology Journal: Practice and Research*, the official journal of the division, publishes many articles that provide theory and case examples useful to both newcomers and senior consultants. The Society for Industrial and Organizational Psychology (Division 14 of APA) is another excellent resource. Its annual meeting offers a wide range of sessions on topics relevant to consulting, including the latest research in related areas and workshops that offer continuing education credit.

In terms of the training needed for consulting work, my own postdoctoral experience and training provide an example. I did (and continue to do) a great deal of independent reading in the area of process consultation, organizational change, and business. In addition to reading the psychological literature, I read the *Wall Street Journal*, *Harvard Business Review*, and other business magazines. Because I had grown up in an academic and not-for-profit world, early in my consulting career, I enrolled in a program in the Business School at the University of Southern California that offered a certificate in management with a mini-MBA curriculum. This program enabled me to understand not only the business jargon but also the way that business people think about things. Just learning a few buzzwords used in business and expecting that you can work in this environment is like just learning the words *id*, *ego*, and *superego* and thinking that you can provide psychoanalysis. One must learn not only a new language but also a new conceptual system.

Furthermore, I was fortunate enough to join a consulting firm that invested a great deal of time and money in training its consultants. When I joined the firm, I took a number of internal courses taught by my senior colleagues. I shadowed fellow consultants as they worked and sought out feedback and advice on projects in which I was involved. One of the advantages of working in a consulting firm is the opportunity to get feedback on complex issues and address such issues as the genuine needs of the client, how to evaluate progress or success, the quality and impact of current efforts, and what we might need to do differently to add more value. Another excellent learning tool is to debrief (with coworkers, colleagues, or a shadow consultant) an intervention after it is completed. This postmortem can be used to learn from our successes and failures. Whatever one's training, as a consulting psychologist, it is critical to continue to hone one's skills on an ongoing basis.

## Why I Chose Consulting as a Career

Because consulting is a multifaceted field, I can offer many reasons why I chose this work. Let me give five.

First, I find the work itself inherently interesting and intellectually stimulating. Even what may look like a routine assessment of a job applicant can be enormously challenging if you take seriously your assignment to understand the complexity of the individual and his or her fit with a new role. This variety presents an opportunity (even a necessity) to apply everything you have learned in school (and elsewhere).

Second, consulting also provides a great opportunity to learn about new things. Like an anthropologist, the consulting psychologist enters into many different cultures. In my career, I have worked with Fortune 100 companies, small family businesses, Native American tribal councils, and college administrators. By working within them, I have learned about the operations of newspapers, the television and movie industry, and the challenges in developing spacecraft. I found out that it is much more difficult than one would imagine to manufacture what looks like a simple bolt. I've had backroom knowledge of scientific laboratories, insurance companies, and electronic equipment retailing.

Third, I like the fact that, at times, one must improvise and operate without a safety net. Often I have planned a clear agenda for an intervention, such as a team-building retreat, with a specific timetable and maybe even a PowerPoint presentation, only to throw it out to take a completely different direction because I sensed that the group needed to probe more deeply into a topic or found that a new issue surfaced that needed to be addressed quickly and directly. In spite of the initial dizziness that this kind of challenge creates, successfully negotiating the difficulties allows for creativity and is personally rewarding.

Fourth, I enjoy working with smart, competent people. Many of our clients are highly impressive people who have accomplished a great deal professionally, and I have had the honor of learning about the life histories of those I assess and coach. I usually work not at the remedial level, but rather at helping effective people become even more so. It is also stimulating to work with bright colleagues who are psychologists and with whom I can share and learn.

Finally, I derive great satisfaction from helping to make situations, individuals, and organizations better. Seeing an executive who was struggling with his or her boss feel positive about that relationship, having a dysfunctional team begin to work together collaboratively, or helping smooth a difficult organizational change provides enormous satisfaction, because I have made a positive difference.

## Financial Compensation

Financial compensation in consulting psychology ranges wildly. It can be one of the highest paying areas of psychology, yet many need to supplement their consulting with other work because they are unable to develop a solid practice. The 2009 APA salary survey (Finno, Michalski, Hart, Wicherski, & Kohout, 2010) did not specifically include consulting psychology as a category but included it in the summary of data on applied psychology under the classification industrial–organizational psychologists. Only licensed psychologists were included in the survey. Although these data do not specifically deal with consulting psychologists, and the number of valid responses was low (162), they do provide a rough idea of salary levels. The average salary cited in the survey was $143,469 and the median was $120,000. These salaries were the highest of all the subcategories of psychologists, but the range of salaries was quite high, indicating great variability in income.

For people who are used to getting a regular salary, the compensation structure for consultants, particularly those working independently, can arouse anxiety. One's ability to do the work is not the same as one's ability to get the work within a highly competitive environment. Many in the field make more income than would be possible in academia or clinical positions. Entrepreneurial individuals often can make well above the average reported in the APA survey, but others struggle or leave the field. The self-employed consulting psychologist with a substantial level of billing must consider overhead expenses; he or she may enter a state of shock when comparing gross income with net profit after the checkbook is balanced.

As an example of how income may fluctuate, a consulting psychologist might be dependent on a major client, and when his or her contact within that company leaves, the entire contract may evaporate. The psychologist's billing can go from hundreds of thousands of dollars to zero almost overnight, and it may take time to find an equally lucrative client.

Even the salaries of those who work within a consulting firm can vary a great deal from year to year, depending on the individual's billing and the overall success of the firm. Consulting firms generally pay a good base salary but provide opportunities for bonuses that can double (or more) that income if the individual is highly productive. In consulting, income variability is likely to be linked to productivity rather than seniority.

## Disadvantages of the Career

Consulting provides a number of advantages, which I mentioned when I described why I chose the profession. However, the field has disadvantages as well. Travel can be fun and glamorous but also fatiguing. In some cases, you might be on the road from 50% to 80% of your time. Such schedules can put strains on family life. The high-functioning clients are exciting to work with but also can be challenging and demanding. Few of these clients are in awe of the doctoral degree, and they can be intimidating to a novice consultant.

Because most consultants are self-employed or work for a consulting firm, the pressure of business development is always present. The independent consultant who does not sell, does not eat. In a consulting firm, your bonus, your promotion, and even your job itself are affected by the degree to which you can generate work for yourself and your colleagues.

## *Attributes Needed for Success in the Career*

Your personal characteristics are at least as important as your competence as a psychologist.[2] Students often ask, "What specific classes should I take to be successful?" As noted earlier in this chapter, certain knowledge areas are important, but this is only the ticket for admission. In the long run, personal style, professional presence, and interpersonal abilities are the elements that differentiate the highly effective consulting psychologist. You need to be able to relate to and have credibility with your client group. For example, if working with line staff, consulting psychologists cannot be seen as too academic or theoretical, or they will be dismissed as ivory tower. If you want to work with senior leaders, you must be able to interact comfortably and credibly with assertive, demanding, fast-paced executives. Those intimidated by such individuals do not do well. The ability to establish rapport and trust rapidly is a necessity. Communication skills are important; business people are not patient with long, complex, jargon-laden explanations. Both verbally and in writing, the consulting psychologist needs to be articulate without being pretentious. Communication needs to be crisp, focused, and to the point.

Stamina and energy are critical. I have seen excellent people leave the field because they found the pace to be too fast or grueling. A consulting psychologist is likely to spend substantial time in a car driving to meet a client or in an airport waiting for a plane to go home. It is not necessary to be an extravert when doing consulting, but if you are an introvert, you need to find ways to replenish your energy after long periods when you need to be on. For example, if you are facilitating an off-site retreat, you would probably be expected to have dinner (and perhaps drinks) with the participants late into the evening. Then, when the participants have gone to bed, you might be up late with your colleagues debriefing and revising plans for the next day's events. Even informal social activities are work for the consultant. Because

---

[2]The 2004 Guidelines for Education and Training that were developed by the Society of Consulting Psychology offered this formal definition of the consulting psychologist's role:

[T]he function of applying and extending the special knowledge of a psychologist, through the process of consultation, to problems involving human behavior in various areas. A Consulting Psychologist shall be defined as a psychologist who provides specialized technical assistance to individuals or organizations in regard to the psychological aspects of their work. (American Psychological Association, 2007, p. 980)

everything is data, you are on duty even during recreational activities such as golf. It is in these less-structured times that you can learn a great deal about the dynamics of the group and the operating styles of its members.

In terms of intellect, good consulting psychologists must not only be smart but also have high learning agility. That is, the successful consulting psychologist is a sponge who absorbs useful ideas and skills rapidly but also can switch gears with ease. Good work requires the ability to think systemically—that is, the capacity to view an organization as an interconnected system in which intervention in one place affects functioning in others. Flexibility in thinking is important to incorporate different perspectives as needed. My colleagues and I talk about successful consulting psychologists as having *helicopter thinking*: they are able to operate at both a conceptual and a practical level—to see the big picture—but then to drop down to examine and handle the details.

Highly successful consulting psychologists are achievement motivated, set high standards for themselves, and are competitive. Those who work within a firm also need to be able to work well as part of a team and not always be the star. Good colleagueship requires individuals to have an interesting blend of self-sufficiency and independence while also being highly collaborative. Tenacity and drive are important, particularly in doing business development. Successful consulting psychologists generally have a strong customer service orientation and take great pride in going the extra step for their client. At the same time, they should not have a high need for approval. Often the job of the consulting psychologist is to speak the truth to a powerful individual who may not be pleased with the information. It is okay to want to be liked, but if you need to be liked, you should get a springer spaniel rather than go into consulting.

The best consulting psychologists I know are self-aware: They are attuned to their impact on others. They also are perceptive, able to pick up subtle cues from those around them, and skilled in applying their understanding of individuals when dealing with varied situations and styles. The consulting psychologist needs to be able to read the audience and adjust to diverse situations and people.

Personal qualities such as follow-through and good organization are critical. A lack of attention to detail, such as misspelling a key executive's name or making a mistake on a bill, can be deadly. I have had colleagues falter because they were unable to juggle the multiple demands, the constantly changing schedules, and the torrent of phone calls and e-mails. The use of technology (e.g., smartphones, laptop computers with sophisticated office management software packages, and all sorts of apps) has made handling the logistics easier, but the consulting psychologist must still organize and prioritize a flood of information.

# A Typical Day in the Life of a Consulting Psychologist

One of the things I like about consulting psychology is that I never have a typical day. Everyone's practice is different, and my own has changed from year to year and even day to day. Those who work internally, those who work for government groups, those who work independently, and those who work as part of a large firm have quite different experiences from mine. For example, for me, business development might take up entire days doing such things as taking a potential client to lunch, giving a talk to raise awareness about my work, or developing marketing materials. Although no day is typical, I will give an example of a day that is not unusual.

I start early, checking my e-mails and voice mail before breakfast to make sure I have not had a cancellation or a major change in schedule. (Many schedule changes are a fact of life.) I will be assessing a candidate for chief operating officer for a client company this morning, so I spend a few minutes reviewing notes I made last week after interviewing the chief executive officer and senior staff members about success factors for that job. While I drive across town to a client's office, I make calls on my (hands-free) cell phone, returning a call I had received on my voice mail and checking in with my assistant about some administrative work. When I arrive at the client's office, I enter a conference room, where I meet the candidate and get a last-minute briefing from the human resource vice president about areas where they would like me to probe. (Although this meeting was in the client's office, we might well have met in my office or in an airport lounge.)

After the interview, I check my voice messages again and perhaps return a call or two. On the way back to the office, I pick up a sandwich that I eat while I check my e-mail. In the afternoon, I meet with a colleague at his office to finalize the plan for an off-site retreat scheduled for the coming weekend for a dozen members of a marketing department. When we are done, I check with my assistant, who is putting together materials for the off-site retreat to make sure that everything has been copied. I decide to add one more handout, and I photocopy it while my assistant makes packets for the participants. I reschedule a meeting that has been canceled (for the second time) with a potential client. I begin to fill out my expense form (my least favorite part of the job but critical for keeping track of things such as mileage and meals). I then review the client's scores on the instrument that I gave this morning as part of the assessment process. I begin work on the assessment report because I want to get back to the client tomorrow to give verbal feedback. Depending on my schedule tomorrow, I might work on the report tonight on my laptop. Before bedtime, I check e-mail and voice mail and my schedule for tomorrow one last time. It looks as if I have breakfast on the other side of town at 8:00 a.m. with an executive I have worked with before and who has just taken a job at a new company. This means I will need to set the alarm early.

## Conclusion

A career in consulting psychology offers the option of part- or full-time work that is varied, stimulating, and demanding. Becoming a consulting psychologist is a professional option for a wide range of psychologists who are willing to broaden their initial training in another area of psychology. The consulting field is growing as psychologists seek to apply their skills outside of the mental health and health fields. Consulting provides the opportunity to use one's psychological skills to make a difference in a broad range of settings, including businesses, corporations, government agencies, academic institutions, and the not-for-profit world.

## Recommended Resources

American Psychological Association, Society of Consulting Psychology: http://societyofconsultingpsychology.org
American Society for Training and Development: http://www.astd.org/
Center for Creative Leadership: http://www.ccl.org/Leadership/index.aspx
Human Resources Planning Society: http://hrps.org/
The Frances Hesselbein Leadership Institute (formerly the Peter F. Drucker Foundation for Nonprofit Management): http://www.hesselbeininstitute.org/
Society for Human Resources Management: http://shrm.org/
Society for Industrial Organizational Psychology: http://siop.org/

## References

American Psychological Association. (2007). Guidelines for education and training at the doctoral and post-doctoral levels in consulting psychology/organizational psychology. *American Psychologists, 62*, 980–992. http://dx.doi.org/10.1037/0003-066X.62.9.980

Billings, A., & Gibson, E. (2003). *Big change at Best Buy.* Palo Alto, CA: Davis-Black.

Blanton, J. (2014). Supervision practices in consulting and Industrial-Organizational psychology doctoral programs and consulting firms. *Consulting Psychology Journal: Practice and Research, 66,* 53–76. http://dx.doi.org/10.1037/a0035681

Finno, A. A., Michalski, D., Hart, B., Wicherski, M., & Kohout, J. L. (2010). *2009: Report of the APA Salary Survey.* Retrieved from http://www.apa.org/workforce/publications/09-salaries/index.aspx

Kasserman, J. (2005). Management consultation: Improving organizations. In C. J. Habben, T. L. Kuther, & R. D. Morgan (Eds.), *Life after graduate school in psychology: Insider's advice from new psychologists* (pp. 183–195). New York, NY: Psychology Press.

Leonard, H. S. (1999). Becoming a consultant: The real stories. *Consulting Psychology Journal: Practice and Research, 51,* 3–13. http://dx.doi.org/10.1037/1061-4087.51.1.3

Lowman, R., Alderfer, C., Atella, M., Garman, A., Hellkamp, D., & Kilberg, R. (2002). Principles for education and training at the doctoral and postdoctoral level in consulting psychology/organizational. *Consulting Psychology Journal: Practice and Research, 54,* 213–222.

*Bruce L. Bobbitt*

# Psychologists in Management

20

O n the following pages, I describe my career as psychologist working in management in a large corporate sector corporation. As I noted in the second edition of this book (Bobbitt, 2007), I found myself doing work that was different from my graduate and undergraduate career goals. In short, after both teaching and practicing psychology, I started working in managed health care in the area of quality improvement. When I was first in the corporate setting I was not sure whether I was a good fit for the organization given that I had been trained in psychology and not in business. I liked what I was doing, however, and realized that I had found

Bruce L. Bobbitt, PhD, LP, is senior vice president of Behavioral Health Quality at Optum. A graduate of Cornell University, Bobbitt received his PhD from the Institute of Child Development at the University of Minnesota and has been licensed for independent practice in the State of Minnesota for the past 32 years. Bruce worked in community mental health, hospital psychology, and private practice. He served the profession as American Psychological Association Council Representative from Minnesota and served for 16 years on the Executive Council of the Minnesota Psychological Association.

http://dx.doi.org/10.1037/15960-021
*Career Paths in Psychology: Where Your Degree Can Take You, Third Edition,*
R. J. Sternberg (Editor)

an unexpected niche in corporate America. I have now been working in managed health care in a management capacity for more than 20 years. Not only did I like what I was doing, I found that my background and training in psychology provided me with a core set of skills that I have used throughout my career.

My purpose in these pages is to describe what it means to be in management in a large corporate sector business and how my background and training as a psychologist helped me enjoy an interesting and fulfilling career. To put my own work in perspective, I begin by outlining the core features and variations that define corporate sector businesses. This is followed by a discussion of management. As with many areas of psychology, what appear to be deceptively simply concepts (business, management) are revealed to be complex concepts with multiple meanings. For example, there is a continuing and ongoing debate about what defines *leadership* as opposed to *management*.

Following these level-setting sections, I review what managers do, how managers do what they do, and the importance of understanding the concept of leadership. Throughout, I rely on my own experience in management with one of the nation's largest health care companies and one of the country's largest corporations (Fortune 500: The Lists, 2015). In the last edition, I described my work in managed health care as an unexpected career. In the decade since those comments were published, I have continued my work in managed care quality with greater levels of management responsibility. Currently, I oversee a quality department of more than 200 employees focused on behavioral business. In this role, I have experienced both the rewards and challenges that accompany a high-level management position and a corporate sector business. I use these experiences to describe the types of skills and individual attributes that are needed to be successful in this type of setting. Overall, although psychology has provided a good base for my career, I needed to acquire other skills and content knowledge on the job to be successful. I note these as well as the advantages and disadvantages of this type of career to help you make decisions about how to chart your own career with a basic background in psychology.

## Business

Business activity is an integral part of our culture and country. So much so that unless we are engaged in the formal study of the topic, we rarely think about what they are and what they do. In short, corporate sector businesses are organized entities that provide goods and services to consumers and purchasers that are not part of the government. As covered in this volume, there are also nonprofit organizations that are similar to for-profit businesses. Additionally, a class of organizations referred to as nongovernmental organizations (NGOs) are difficult-to-define organizations that generally operate as advocacy organizations. My focus in this chapter is on for-profit businesses. Profits, sometimes referred to as margin, are the funds that a business retains after all expenses and taxes are paid. Businesses can be owned by a private individual or by groups of individuals. These businesses are referred to as privately held companies and are contrasted with publicly held companies. Publicly held companies are owned by shareholders who purchase shares on stock exchanges.

Businesses also vary in size. In general, small businesses usually are owned by private individuals. Many, but not all, large corporations are publicly traded entities. The company that I work for is a publicly held corporation and is listed on the New York Stock Exchange. Cargill is an example of a large corporation that is privately held. You can choose to buy shares in a publicly owned company, but privately owned companies do not have shares that the public can purchase. In almost all cases, large corporations have boards of directors that oversee the operations of the business.

It is important to understand these distinctions as you consider using your skills and training in the corporate sector. The organizational dynamics are different across different types of corporate sector businesses. In all cases, profits are earned and retained by owners. In the case of large publicly traded businesses, the shareholders are key stakeholders in the operation of the businesses. Shareowners invest in the company with the goal of receiving a financial return that comes either in the form of an increase in the stock price or a dividend paid by the company. As such, shareholders exercise influence on the company in two ways. Shareholders can sell shares if they think the organization is not performing in the way they need it to—either the stock price is not appreciating in value or the company does not provide a sufficient dividend. The second way to influence the company is to vote on the composition of the board of directors and on resolutions put forward by the board.

The facts are all well and good, but the daily operation and success of a business is primarily determined by the joint performance of the company's management and the oversight provided by the board of directors. Successful companies have outstanding management teams that both run the day-to-day operations of the business and chart the strategic direction of the business.

## Management

The previous description provides that backdrop for understanding what management is and what it means to be a manager. This section provides a structural and operational definition of management. The following sections address what it means to be a manager and also a leader.

Management is the team within a company that is responsible for organizing the different functions and ensuring that all functions operate properly. Business functions vary by type of business but generally include business strategy, sales, marketing, product development and research, information technology, human capital, operations, project management, quality and finance. All businesses have different levels of management, with higher levels of management having accountability for broad functions and profit and loss responsibility. Executive management is defined differently in different businesses. In large corporations, high-level executives can be in charge of functional areas with or without responsibility for profit and loss.

Staff who are responsible for a task or set of tasks and who do not have direct reports generally are not part of management. Some of these individuals, however, may be responsible for complex tasks. In health care companies, employees without direct reports are often responsible for highly complex tasks. As an example, my company employs highly trained researchers with doctorates (some of whom are psychologists) who complete complex projects. In the business world, these people may be referred to as individual contributors to differentiate them from management. Again, management is responsible for the operations of the organization.

Management as a concept and a process is chronicled in multiple publications, including newspapers and magazines as well as countless popularized treatments that are available through online retailers and are readily available in bookstores. *The Wall Street Journal* is a good place to start learning about management process and the current worldwide business climate. I also recommend Jim Collins's (2001) classic book on what makes good companies become great companies. Finally, Chan (2009) has provides an entertaining review of business school training.

## BEING A MANAGER—WHAT MANAGERS DO

The previous description is helpful in understanding the architecture of business organizations, but it does not capture what managers do or how they do it. It is important to understand both what managers do and how managers behave in achieving results. In this section, I describe what managers do. In the next section, I focus on how managers do what they do and introduce the concept of leadership.

Managers oversee both processes and people. For example, most sales and services organizations have call centers that receive telephone calls from consumers or providers. As a first example, a member covered by an insurance plan can call the insurer to get answers about their benefit plan or about whether a particular provider or hospital is in the credentialed provider network. The process in question is how the call is routed to the right employee to provide the answer to the question. Behind the scenes, numerous other processes allow the person who answers the phone to have the right information on the computer terminal. In all companies with call centers, a variety of measures are followed to indicate how well the process is working. In addition, it is sometimes the case that calls are recorded (callers are informed of this possibility) to ensure that the people answering the phone are managing the calls properly.

In the previous example, a manager oversees the work of the people answering the phone. The manager is responsible for understanding the process and understanding how the employees are doing at the task. The manager makes use of reports, team meetings, and individual meetings with the employees to ensure that the process is working as designed. The process in this case has some degree of variability because the people who make the call may have any of a number of different questions. The person answering the phone has to be able to answer all of the questions that may come in or in rare cases direct the call to a different part of the organization. The process for the employee, however, is standardized as much as possible to ensure that all callers are treated consistently and that the quality of the interaction is positive. The manager in this case is overseeing and managing a process that occurs many times throughout the day and the task is to ensure that calls are answered in a timely way and that the employee provides the caller with accurate information and that the interaction is positive. The manager also is involved in reviewing and selecting employees for the job. The people who become managers in these types of roles often begin their career answering calls—they become subject matter experts.

Although I do not directly manage the call center, I supervise a call center that takes a particular type of call. I also have a significant amount of contact with the senior managers who oversee this process in other parts of our organization. The goal in the process is to have a stable and repeatable process.

My second example is a complex process that takes place over many months and requires coordination across many departments. The National Committee for Quality Assurance (NCQA) publishes industry standards and accredits managed behavioral health organizations (NCQA, 2014). My department is responsible for preparing and managing the entire process. Preparing and completing this type accreditation requires identifying the standards that we need to meet and ensuring that we have processes in place across the organization to meet all of these standards. In this case, the outcome of the process is the completion of the survey. Unlike the phone example, the scope and process of this type of project is broad and requires work over a long period of time. Because organizations have processes in place to meet the standards, some work is ongoing to ensure that the standards continue to be met and also to put new processes in place when standards change (NCQA has a process for adding new standards and raising the bar for managed behavioral health care organizations based on input from stakeholders across the health care spectrum). The activity of the manager of this project includes leading meetings from staff across different departments to ensure progress, reviewing documentation, auditing files, and forming initiative action plans if an area or process is in need of improvement. As different levels of management become involved in the process, the most senior manager role changes to one of oversight and ensuring that the right staff members are in place and the necessary resources are available to be successful. A good overview of basic manager skills can be found in Stettner (2014).

## BEING A MANAGER—LEADERSHIP AND CULTURE

Compared with the structural definition of management (the group or team that is responsible for running the operations of the company) outlined previously, the description of management activity begins to bring the role to life—but only partially and inadequately. Being a manager is a living experience that requires deep involvement with people, especially the people who report to you. Until now, I have only used the words *management* and *manager.* Most managers are involved with people as well as processes. Therefore, it is important that managers understand people and have the skills to work with a wide variety of individuals in the workplace. What I have not discussed is leadership. I have done this purposefully to build on the concepts of managing processes and managing people. With the introduction of the leadership concept, however, the story becomes ever more real and enlivened.

What is a leader? A leader is a person who influences others to follow. As author John C. Maxwell simply notes, "The true measure of leadership is influence—nothing more, nothing less" (2007, p. 16). This definition does not require that a leader have a large department or even have direct reports—they may be individual contributors. Leaders influence others by how they do what they do.

Within the business literature, there has and most like will be a continued dialogue about the similarities and differences between leaders and managers. I have read much of this literature and found much of it compelling and helpful (cf. Bossidy & Charan, 2002; Friedman, 2008;

Goleman, 2000; Maxwell, 2007). These writings, however, have made more sense to me upon reflection and to the degree that I have had experiences similar to some of the situations described in these and other publications. The debate about management and leadership is sometimes framed in the same way as well-known dichotomies in psychology—nature–nurture and personality traits–situational determinants of behavior. As with the psychology debates, we now know that the concepts are not true dichotomies but useful heuristics that help outline more accurate and nuanced views of human behavior.

My own experience has led me to the following conclusions on the relationship between leadership and management. The two concepts are highly related but are not the same, and the people who are good at certain types of management may not be great leaders; conversely, great leaders may not be good process managers. However, even if the process being managed is relatively defined (such as answering the phone properly and within defined standards), it is necessary for a manager to be an effective leader of people.

In large organizations, it is important that executives who run major areas and departments have excellent leadership skills. Although a senior leader may not manage a microprocess, they need to have clear understanding of all of the business processes in their area. Good leaders will know as much as they can about what their staff do on a daily basis even if they have not done the same task as part of their job in the past. In addition to a thorough understanding of the content knowledge, good leaders influence others in a positive way that promotes employee engagement with the mission of the department or organization. The best executive leaders who I have worked with influence others by communicating a clear vision for accountability and results coupled with a positive and employee-centric style. They are not coercive or negative.

The third concept in this section is culture. The culture of a business is the ether that determines how employees treat each other. Although culture is always difficult to define, its impact is obvious to all employees in all organizations. Some companies have negative and coercive cultures—good employees do not stay in organizations with negative cultures. The culture is in the air. UnitedHealth Group is an example of a company that a number of years ago engaged in a systemic effort to identify and put into language its core values as they defined its core employment and customer values. UnitedHealth Group identified five core values that defined its business values and its business processes: integrity, compassion, relationships, innovation, and performance. As a list of words, these values appear straightforward and to some even obvious. It is what UnitedHealth Group has done with them, however, that makes them valuable both to its business and to its managers and a leaders. It is important to reinforce and teach the values daily to build a culture. The culture starts with the leaders of an organization as established by their example.

I have emphasized leadership and culture because these key concepts drive how we manage the company and how our managers behave. Culture and leadership become the lifeblood of an organization. Leaders who inspire others are successful—and they and their teams get a lot done, which leads to business success. Thus, being part of management is far more than holding a position with a title at the top of a particular organizational chart. It is a responsibility to work with people in a way that brings out the best in them that results in the business meeting its objectives.

## Attributes and Preparation Needed for Success as a Manager and Leader

As noted, there are large literatures on both management and leadership. These literatures are found in the popular press as well as in research journals. This section reviews what successful managers and leaders are like, noting both the literature and my own experience in the corporate sector. I previously outlined the importance of culture in determining work performance and behavior. Other aspects of private-sector businesses are also important to understand. Even though I have not highlighted it explicitly, my review on management, leadership, and culture make use of psychological principals. I draw on some of these principals here as well.

In contrast to some settings that employ psychologists, successful private-sector businesses, especially large corporations, all share similar characteristics. I am certain that my own experience is similar to those of others in large organizations. In addition to our formal culture, my organization has a bias for getting things done. The pace is extremely fast. Although always focusing on strategic goals, we define activities quickly and track accomplishment. Reflection, review, discussion, and debate occur to get things done—rarely do we linger on broad philosophical or historical issues for long. We are always thinking about the future and getting things done that affect our future success. Successes are celebrated appropriately but briefly. When we encounter a bump in the road, we learn from it and move forward. We are practical—we adopt solutions that work and can be repeated.

Our view of human nature and the characteristics of our employees is positive. Even when people struggle with work issues, they are not seen in a negative light, and we do everything we can to identify strengths and skills as opposed to weaknesses and deficits. People are not seen as having psychopathology, even if they are experiencing challenges. In this way, we have adopted many of the tenets of positive psychology even if we do not always describe this approach using these two words.

Given the previous description coupled with the earlier reviews of culture and leadership, what are the attributes or characteristics that define successful managers and leaders? Successful managers and leaders focus on the strengths of others, support others, communicate clearly and effectively, and inspire others to achieve. Successful managers and leaders like to get things done and enjoy working with people—they are both available and disciplined. Time is used wisely. They understand others—a trait that is referred to as emotional intelligence (see Goleman, 2000). Having superior intellectual skill is a baseline requirement for top managers and executives. What is really important, however, is how managers and leaders understand other people and are sensitive to them.

In addition to these personal characteristics, managers and leaders need to have working knowledge and skill in areas that normally are not part of a psychology curriculum. These include understanding all of the core features of a business that were mentioned earlier: business strategy, sales, marketing, product development and research, information technology, human capital, operations, project management, quality, and finance. Of these, I mention two that have become integral parts of modern corporate sector businesses. The first is project management. Project management is a technical field that has grown rapidly in recent years. Project managers can achieve a certification of proficiency (cf. Project Management Institute, 2013). The second is quality improvement processes. Quality processes are used in all major organizations and increasingly are being adopted in health care organizations (cf. Bobbitt, Cate, Beardsley, Azocar, & McCulloch, 2012, for a review and for additional references). If you are aspiring to work in management in the corporate sector, a working understanding of these concepts is essential.

Because I do not have a business degree or a masters of business administration, I learned about these parts of business on the job. I was fortunate that I was able contribute to the organization as I learned. Even though I did not think about it at the time, I have at least a sufficient number of the characteristics outlined in this chapter to achieve some degree of success in my work as a manager at UnitedHealth. My background in psychology was extremely helpful, and I find that I am able to draw on that background in my role as a manager.

So, the good news is that psychology is a good background for a career in management. Things have changed, however, in the last couple of decades. The industry is far more sophisticated and the pace of change is rapid. Twenty-first-century managers and leaders must have excellent technological skills that I did not have when I came into the business. It is less likely that a psychologist could move into this industry and become successful without additional formal training in business. If you want to become a manager or hold an executive position in the corporate sector, I recommend that you take at least one business course to find out whether you have both an aptitude for business and the personal skills needed to become a manager.

The second recommendation is one that you will find in virtually any book or essay on management and leadership. You need to understand yourself. Managing and leading other people is an intense and demanding environment that requires self-knowledge and a high degree of resilience. Do you like to understand what you do well and what you don't do well? In addition to the focus on other people that I have outlined, it is important that you be able to be assertive and manage conflict successfully. You need to be able to communicate clearly and succinctly to a wide variety of audiences. In short, you really need to understand yourself and your skills.

## Advantages and Disadvantages of a Career in Management

I have thoroughly enjoyed the work I have done in management over the past 21 years. I found that I had abilities and skills that allowed me to succeed in an interesting yet demanding environment. The people I work with are remarkable human beings. They live a rich and full life and at the same time push our organization forward. I have learned so much from them. I have become a better and more understanding person as a result of working as a manager and a leader. I have been humbled by the skills and personal characteristics of my peers and my team. I have never been bored. Not once.

The disadvantages of my career are the flip side of the advantages. There are many long days and long hours. Although the intensity and the focus are exhilarating, at times it is a challenge to keep perspective given the demands for excellence and intense interpersonal relationships in this work setting. These drawbacks are more than compensated for by the advantages.

One of the ways that I help myself in my unexpected career is to remain active in psychology. I have done this through involvement with APA and my local state psychological association (the Minnesota Psychological Association). In addition, I know that I learn best by writing and teaching. I have given many presentations on managed health care both locally and nationally. I helped mastered my business skills by writing about key issues in the field (Bobbitt, 2006; Bobbitt & Beardsley, in press; Bobbitt et al., 2012; Bobbitt, Marques, & Trout, 1998; Bobbitt & Rockswold, 2016). It was important for me not only to experience my profession but also to understand it. Writing about it has helped with that process.

## Compensation

My comments on compensation are not based on a formal study of business compensation—nor are they based on any proprietary company information. I have worked long enough that I have some understanding of the range of compensation available in the corporate sector. Depending on the scope of the position, managers can make $50,000 to $70,000 on the low end and many hundreds of thousands, even millions on the high end. If you do well, you get paid more. If you take risks and attempt to perform at higher level, the financial reward can be great.

## Future Prospects for Psychologists in Management

Unless something goes really wrong in the United States and the rest of the world, there will always be corporate sector businesses. The corporate sector draws entrepreneurs who take risks to build businesses; many of these entrepreneurs do not succeed, but the ones who do always will require skilled and competent leaders and managers. A background in psychology can be helpful for this type of career. This background alone, however, is not sufficient. If you want to get advanced training in psychology, you need to add additional skills by training in business and other technical areas to be successful. If you have good business skills and solid training in business, training and education in psychology can help you significantly as you develop your career in business.

## References

Bobbitt, B. L. (2006). The importance of professional psychology: A view from managed care. *Professional Psychology: Research and Practice, 37*, 590–597. http://dx.doi.org/10.1037/0735-7028.37.6.590

Bobbitt, B. L. (2007). A psychologist in managed care: An unexpected career. In R. S. Sternberg (Ed.), *Career paths in psychology: Where your degree can take you* (2nd ed., pp. 329–342). Washington, DC: American Psychological Association.

Bobbitt, B. L., & Beardsley, S. D. (in press). Quality improvement and population behavioral health. In W. T. O'Donohue & A. Maragakis (Eds.), *Quality improvement and behavioral health.* New York, NY: Springer.

Bobbitt, B. L., Cate, R. A., Beardsley, S. D., Azocar, F., & McCulloch, J. M. (2012). Quality improvement and outcomes in the future of professional psychology: Opportunities and challenges. *Professional Psychology: Research and Practice, 43,* 551–559. http://dx.doi.org/10.1037/a0028899

Bobbitt, B. L., Marques, C. C., & Trout, D. L. (1998). Managed behavioral health care: Current status, recent trends, and the role of psychology. *Clinical Psychology: Science and Practice, 5,* 53–66. http://dx.doi.org/10.1111/j.1468-2850.1998.tb00135.x

Bobbitt, B. L., & Rockswold, E. (2016). Behavioral health service delivery, managed care, and accountable care organizations. In H. S. Friedman (Ed.), *Encyclopedia of Mental Health* (2nd ed., Vol. 1, pp. 150–155). Waltham, MA: Academic Press. http://dx.doi.org/10.1016/B978-0-12-397045-9.00029-X

Bossidy, L., & Charan, R. (2002). *Execution: The discipline of getting things done.* New York, NY: Crown.

Chan, E. (2009). *Harvard Business School confidential: Secrets of success.* Singapore: Wiley (Asia).

Collins, J. (2001). *From good to great.* New York, NY: HarperCollins.

Fortune 500: The Lists. (2015, June 15). Largest U.S. corporations. *Fortune, 171,* F1–F22.

Friedman, S. D. (2008). *Total leadership: Be a better leader: Have a richer life.* Boston, MA: Harvard University Press.

Goleman, D. (2000). Leadership that gets results. *Harvard Business Review, 78,* 78–90.

Maxwell, J. C. (2007). *The 21 irrefutable laws of leadership.* Nashville, TN: Thomas Nelson.

National Committee for Quality Assurance. (2014). *2015 Standards and guidelines for the accreditation of MBHOs.* Washington, DC: Author.

Project Management Institute. (2013). *A guide to the project management body of knowledge (PMBOK guide)* (5th ed.). Newtown Square, PA: Author.

Stettner, M. (2014). *Skills for new managers* (2nd ed.). New York, NY: McGraw Hill.

*Anne E. Beall*

# Consumer Psychologists 21

W
e live in a world in which we make purchasing decisions all
the time. We make decisions about where we want to live,
what clothing we want to wear, what food we will eat, and
what entertainment we will buy with our hard-earned dollars. When we're not actively buying things, we often are
shopping for or thinking about products and services that we
believe will make our lives better. In many ways, we endorse
products and services every day of our lives. The world is full
of brands vying for our attention and our attachment, and
we respond to this clamor through our purchasing decisions.

Businesses are constantly trying to get a better understanding of how consumers make their purchasing decisions.
As a result, businesses are the primary employer of consumer

Anne E. Beall, PhD, is the CEO of Beall Research, Inc., a strategic market
research firm located in Chicago. She has held positions at The Boston Consulting Group (BCG) and National Analysts. Anne received her MS, MPhil,
and PhD degrees in social psychology from Yale University. Anne specializes in
conducting large-scale, complex strategic studies for Fortune 500 companies.
She is the author of *Strategic Market Research: A Guide to Conducting Research
That Drives Businesses* and several other books and articles.

http://dx.doi.org/10.1037/15960-022
*Career Paths in Psychology: Where Your Degree Can Take You, Third Edition*,
R. J. Sternberg (Editor)

psychologists. Consumer psychology is the study of how people make these decisions and how companies can better serve and retain their current and potential customers. Our work involves answering major questions that businesses have about understanding consumers' thoughts and behaviors. The answers to these questions help these organizations do a better job attracting and retaining customers. Some examples of the questions that we answer in our profession include the following:

- What advertising is most persuasive and why?
- How likely are consumers to consider a specific company's product?
- Who is likely to buy a new service that is being considered?
- How well do current products meet consumers' needs?
- Are there unmet needs that consumers have in a certain area?
- What features of a product cause the greatest satisfaction or dissatisfaction?
- How likely are consumers to buy a product or service again and why?

We answer these questions by conducting primary research using a variety of tools, and employing both qualitative and quantitative research methods. The types of research we conduct depend on the nature of the question and the amount of research that has been conducted already. Sometimes very little research has been conducted on a specific question, and a large amount of exploratory work is needed before any specific elements or variables can be isolated for specific measurement. In these cases, qualitative research is the best place to begin.

So what is it like to be a consumer psychologist? In this chapter I discuss the various research methodologies that are employed, the roles and day-to-day responsibilities, the preparation and attributes needed to succeed, and the future outlook for the field.

## Qualitative Research

Qualitative research seeks to understand why and how consumers make the decisions that they do. It often involves guided discussions with consumers, in which the researcher will ask broad, exploratory questions, followed by detailed, probing questions to examine in greater detail what led to the consumers' initial responses. Following are the most widely used types of qualitative research methodologies:

- *Focus groups.* A trained moderator guides a group of approximately eight respondents in a structured discussion to understand a variety of thoughts and behaviors on certain issues and to get reactions to brands, products, services, or new ideas.

- *Creative consumer groups.* A group of individuals who screened for being creative thinkers engages in a structured group discussion with a trained moderator to brainstorm new ideas, products, or services, or to improve existing ones.
- *Shop-alongs.* A researcher accompanies a consumer on a shopping trip, observing what is purchased and how the consumer is influenced by the retail environment.
- *In-depth interviews.* An interview that can occur in a variety of settings, including the consumer's home or a research facility. These interviews involve an in-depth exploration of what matters to the consumer, how decisions are made, and the response to current or potential products or services.
- *Observational research.* Research that can occur in a consumer's home, research facility, or retail environment. This methodology involves having a researcher observe consumers using a particular product or service to understand how the product meets the person's needs and what the individual likes and dislikes about it. This type of research often is used to improve products and services.

## Quantitative Research

Quantitative research involves surveying large samples of people on a specific topic. It is numerical by nature. Some typical methodologies include the following:

- *Mail surveys.* Respondents answer a questionnaire that is mailed to them.
- *Telephone surveys.* Surveys conducted over the phone.
- *Internet surveys.* Respondents answer a survey online.
- *App surveys.* Respondents fill out a survey through an app on a smartphone or tablet.
- *Intercept surveys.* Respondents are intercepted after performing an activity (e.g., shopping, going to a movie, going to an amusement park) to obtain their reactions to the experience right after it has occurred.
- *In-person product usage research.* Research can occur in a consumer's home, research facility or retail environment; consumers use the product and then answer an in-person or electronic survey.
- *Digital listening.* The analysis of open-ended content often posted online about products and services (e.g., customer reviews, product

reviews, messages on social media pages, etc.). This content is analyzed in terms of words, phrases, and themes most often mentioned as well as the emotional nature of the postings (e.g., anger, happiness). This type of analysis helps companies understand what consumers say about them online and how it differs from other companies.

## Statistical Analysis

Another area of work that consumer psychologists do is statistical analysis. We analyze data to help clients determine the relationships between real-world results, such as revenue, number of customers, and investments in marketing. For example, we can determine whether a relationship exists between spending on advertising and the number of consumer phone calls to retailers and eventual sales. We recently conducted a large analysis to determine whether a company's investment in advertising on the Internet was related to their actual sales. We found that although they had increased their advertising expenditures, they did not achieve an increase in the number of customers or in their total revenue over a substantial period of time. Statistical analyses like these help organizations get a clear picture of whether or not their investments are paying off.

## What Consumer Psychologists Do

As consumer psychologists, our first goal is to understand what the major business issue is from the client's perspective and the major questions that need to be answered to address that issue. We then determine which research methodology is most appropriate to answer those questions. For example, if a client is losing market share and is interested in understanding whether their new advertising is effective with consumers of different ages, we might design a study where we conduct focus groups with people in different age-groups. We would show the client's advertising and discuss what messages each age-group receives from the ad and what impression they have of the brand or product being advertised. We would then understand whether these impressions lead potential customers to consider this company for purchasing in the future.

If a client wants to determine the size of a market for a new product, we would conduct quantitative research to identify how many Americans are likely to purchase this new product, what price they would pay for it, and what they perceive the major benefits of the product to be. We also would look at whether this product is unique and if other products could be substituted for it less expensively. The answers to these questions will help us determine the potential size of a market.

The nature of a consumer psychologist's daily activities depends on whether they are a qualitative researcher, a quantitative researcher, or both. Qualitative researchers frequently engage in the following activities:

- Design the study (i.e., determine the best research methodology, the number of groups/interviews to be conducted, and the type of respondent who will participate in the study)
- Write a brief questionnaire that will be used to "screen" for people who qualify for the study
- Create a discussion guide that will be used to guide the conversation and probe on specific issues that are important for answering the major research questions of the project
- Conduct the interview, focus groups, shop-along, or observational research, and videotape or audiotape it
- Observe or listen to the interview, focus group, or shop-alongs while taking notes on consumer responses and major findings
- Identify the major patterns that emerge (e.g., older people tended to like the advertising more or younger people tended to take less time when shopping with children, the majority of people like the product but think it's too expensive)
- Write a report that describes the major findings of the research, and identifies key recommendations for how the client can use the findings to increase the success of their business

Quantitative researchers frequently engage in the following activities:

- Design the study (i.e., determine the number of surveys or in-person intercepts to be conducted, and type of respondent who will participate in this research)
- Write a survey that is administered online or via an in-person or telephone interviewer
- Oversee programmers who code the survey (if it is administered via online, telephone, or tablet) and then test the final survey to ensure that it is working properly
- Monitor the data as it gets collected and ensure that quota groups are being filled (quotas are requirements that a specific number of surveys be completed for certain demographic, attitudinal, or behavioral groups)

- After data are collected, remove the survey respondents who provided bad data—those who gave answers to questions that are logically inconsistent, answered the survey too quickly, or who gave nonsense answers to open-ended questions
- Tabulate the data and identify the major findings
- Conduct statistical analyses to determine the relationship between certain variables
- Write a report that answers the major strategic questions, identifies the major takeaways, and describes how they can be used to increase the client's revenue; the goal is to provide *strategic* recommendations based on the data collected that the client can implement within its organization

The nature of a consumer psychologist's activities also depends on the type of company one works for as a researcher. Most consumer psychologists work for market research companies or market research departments within large consumer-goods and retail companies. Market research firms conduct research for their clients, which are these larger companies. Typically, these two types of companies form a partnership. Within this partnership, the research design, surveys, and discussion guides often are created by individuals at the market research firm with assistance from the professionals within the corporate research department. Data usually are collected and analyzed by individuals at the market research firm, who compile the findings into a report for the consumer-goods company. The market research industry ebbs and flows in terms of which tasks are completed internally by a market research department and which ones are done by an external market research firm. At various times in my career, I have seen numerous companies try to limit the use of external suppliers and do it all in house. And at other times, I have seen corporate research departments downsize and try to do as much of their research as possible through external suppliers.

A consumer psychologist's responsibilities also vary by the size of their company. In large market research firms, people often have specialized functions and perform a job that is related to only one aspect of the research. For example, some specialize in programming surveys, others specialize in tabulating the data, and still others conduct the statistical analyses. In smaller market research companies, one person may be charged with performing all of these tasks. In most market research firms, however, generally certain people manage quantitative studies and a different group manages the qualitative research. People who do both qualitative and quantitative research are rare. Luckily, I have hired a couple of people in my firm who can work in both areas. In corporate market research departments, the larger the department, the more likely there are to be specialists who have expertise in a certain type of research or a certain type of product.

In market research departments at consumer-goods companies, responsibilities vary by the size of the department and the specific tasks that are outsourced to market research companies. Consumer psychologists generally will help to design studies; manage research partners; and review final discussion guides, surveys, and reports. They will attend qualitative research such as focus groups and will help to interpret what consumers are saying so that their colleagues can use the information to make changes within the business. They also will present final research findings to senior managers within the company.

Not surprisingly, one's level within a market research organization also determines the nature of one's activities. Early in one's career, you will be responsible for learning the basics of this work. The first qualitative projects I worked on involved listening to focus group tapes, taking detailed notes, and drafting report that was later significantly revised by the more senior person who had moderated the focus groups. In the beginning of my career, I was mostly a support person who assisted the senior project manager in understanding how to analyze the data that were collected. As my career progressed, I eventually learned how to manage a project from start to finish and to supervise others as they did the work for different pieces of the project. Generally, entry-level individuals in market research firms will be identified as either having a qualitative or quantitative research focus, and they will learn the different aspects of each type of research. As one's career progresses, one will be expected to manage others as they complete the tasks for various aspects of a study. At the higher levels of an organization, one typically is expected to either have an area of specialization or to be a salesperson and generate revenue for the market research company. In market research departments within major consumer-goods companies, entry-level people often will learn how to manage their market research partners, whereas the more senior-level people will tend to be involved in ensuring that the strategic objectives of the work are met and often will meet with senior people in their firm to ensure that the findings are used to drive major decisions.

As the owner of a successful strategic market research firm, my responsibilities involve generating revenue for the firm, managing the overall operations of the company, and determining how many staff we have, what projects we take on, how they are completed, and the final product that is delivered to clients. The people who report to me manage the day-to-day aspects of the work, and the next level within the organization includes the people who specialize in the different aspects of the work.

## A Typical Consumer Psychologist's Day

One of the great things about this career is that there is no typical day. My staff and I like the fact that on any given day, we could be conducting focus groups, analyzing quantitative data, writing reports, reviewing psychological theories, or presenting results to clients. In the 20-plus years that I've been doing this work, I've never been bored. That engagement is probably because no day is really the same, no project is exactly the same as the last one, and consumer problems are intrinsically stimulating.

The events of a consumer psychologist's day at a market research firm will depend on where one is in a project, and the type of team one works with along with the degree of client interaction one has in one's job. For example, early in a focus group project, we will be talking with the client about what their specific questions are, what they want to learn from the project, and what type of consumer they want to have in the focus groups. After writing a screening questionnaire, we will be writing a discussion guide that will be used for the focus group that will guide the conversation. We often will work with the client and create several versions of this guide. The day of the focus groups, one of the members of my firm will moderate the focus groups, while others take detailed notes.

Afterward, we will have a lengthy discussion with the clients about the major takeaways. We will be answering questions such as, Does the new product look promising or not? Are there any issues with the advertising? Do consumers seem likely to pay a premium for this service or not? The clients will be looking for help in understanding the consumers' reactions to the discussion and what they should tell their larger organization.

Quantitative work is different in terms of the specific tasks that one conducts, but the overall objective is the same: Identify the most appropriate methodology, conduct the research, and then explain to the client what the data mean and how they can be used to help drive the business or organization.

## Advantages and Disadvantages of a Career in Consumer Psychology

One of the major advantages of this type of work is that one's research is used to help major companies around the world. Our work has been used to develop new products, change television advertisements, and alter the way that companies interact with their customers. Our clients come to us with a genuine interest in doing a better job attracting and retaining their customers as well as providing superior products and services. Our research has had a huge impact on organizations. It's always rewarding to see a commercial on television that our company has tested (including several Super Bowl commercials), to see companies changing existing products and services, or to see a new product launched as a result of our research.

Another major advantage of this career is the degree of teamwork that occurs on most projects. Unlike some research careers, market research is not an isolated pursuit punctuated by weekly laboratory meetings. There are always people in my firm to brainstorm potential solutions, help solve difficult problems, or edit a major piece of work. The many people that I have worked with over the years—both within and outside of my organization—have been one of the highlights of my career. Many of my colleagues at Beall Research have taught me a great deal, and many of the individuals we have worked with at client companies have helped us understand industries and educated us tremendously.

Another major advantage is that the career is intellectually stimulating and the business problems we address aren't trivial. As a result, the work isn't easy, which is an advantage in my opinion because it's always challenging. The large variety of industries and problems we address is another advantage in that it leads one to be intellectually engaged and infrequently bored.

But as with all careers, there are disadvantages. One of the major things I had to get used to when I joined the field was that I wasn't selecting the problems that I would solve. As a graduate student, I had always selected the questions that I would research. But in this field, the client provides us with the business problem, we translate that into a set of questions, and then we use research to answer them. So if you have a specific desire to solve a certain problem that you have selected, this career is not for you.

Other disadvantages relate to the fact that this is a service business. There can be long hours, unrealistic deadlines, and demanding clients who don't understand the nature of research and the need to take time to do it properly. Qualitative researchers can travel extensively and spend nights moderating focus groups because evening time periods are generally the time when consumers are available. In contrast, quantitative researchers typically travel little and can spend long hours immersed in large data sets trying to make sense of a large array of numbers.

In addition, the environment in which you work can play a major role in determining the opportunities and challenges that you will face. There are typically trade-offs depending on whether you work in a large or small organization, within a market research firm or a market research department at a consumer-goods company side. Most of my career, I have worked in small research firms where I have gotten to know most of my colleagues quite well. I have found that working in a small firm tends to offer more reasonable hours, more varied responsibilities, more appropriate—or at least more negotiable—deadlines, and clients with whom I have been able to forge strong, lasting relationships. Smaller research firms, however, tend to eschew formal training and mentoring programs for more informal, individually driven, on-the-job training. In larger research settings, job responsibilities tend to be defined narrowly and work hours tend to be longer. The rigid structures of larger firms, however, also tend to come with greater name recognition and more formal advancement paths.

There are also trade-offs depending on whether one works in a market research firm or in the market research department of a larger company. Individuals who work in a corporate research departments generally commission research in a specific product or service area and manage the study's progression. As a result, those working in corporate research departments often are involved only in research on one specific type of product (e.g., mattresses). On the other hand, consumer psychologists in market research firms typically conduct research across a variety of products, services, and industries. Because corporate researchers are the ones commissioning the majority of research from market research firms, they tend to be more involved with implementing the strategic findings within a company. To the extent that these two types of researchers develop strong relationships, both groups can help one another tremendously.

## Preparation Needed for a Career in Consumer Psychology

At my firm, we hire individuals who have an undergraduate or master's degree in one of the social sciences. We typically look for someone with strong writing skills who can think analytically and solve a problem. If we are hiring a qualitative researcher, we also look for someone who has done some interviewing and has strong interpersonal skills, which are essential for doing any type of moderation of focus groups and in-depth interviews. If we are hiring a quantitative researcher, we look for someone who has a strong understanding of statistics and has analyzed data using programs such as SPSS, Stata, or other statistical software.

In general, we don't expect entry-level people who are right out of college to have experience in the market research industry. If they have conducted class projects or independent research utilizing some type of research technique, we will take that experience into consideration. It is more important that they demonstrate sound critical thinking in the interview and show that their interest is in understanding human behavior and helping businesses. We recommend that any undergraduate or graduate student interested in consumer psychology take classes in research methods and statistical techniques as well as any class that teaches theories of human behavior (e.g., social psychology).

## Attributes Needed for Success in a Career in Consumer Psychology

The best consumer psychologists have an uncanny ability to see the strategic implications of data while paying attention to the details of a data set. They can see the individual trees within the forest as well as the overall size and shape of the forest itself. The most successful colleagues that I have known have been able to translate reams of data into a clear story that has specific implications for a client. These same individuals also can see specific weaknesses in a data set by knowing when numbers don't make sense, identifying inconsistencies that indicate an underlying data problem, or determining when an analysis isn't appropriate.

Interpersonal skills are critical to succeeding in a market research career, because it is a socially intensive industry that involves communicating seamlessly with colleagues, clients, and consumers. As you move up the ladder, being able to manage those who report to you is an important skill. For individuals who make their living selling market research, being able to translate a client's concerns into a research project and then providing recommendations for the business is a key part of being successful in this field.

In our firm, we prize specific attributes and we hire people who exemplify them. These attributes are *smart, nimble, hard-working, helpful, confident, passionate,* and *funny*. We have found that our business requires people who are intelligent, able to change direction easily, and hard working. It is also important to be helpful and responsive to client requests while maintaining a degree of confidence in one's interactions with others. We also believe that being passionate about the work with a certain degree of humor is essential. We have found that people with these attributes have the greatest fit with our organization and the highest degree of success.

## Pay Range for Consumer Psychologists

Pay ranges differ depending on the type of company where one works, the amount of experience one has, and the nature of one's responsibilities. As mentioned, consumer psychologists typically reside in either market research firms or in large corporations that have a market research department and are called *market researchers.*

Quirks, one of the largest professional resource portals for market research professionals, conducted a compensation salary survey in 2014 of approximately 3,000 market research professionals. They found that the average annual salary is $122,955 in corporate research departments and $129,293 in market research firms. Table 21.1 lists the base salaries of the different jobs within market research companies and corporate departments (Quirks, 2015).

Of course, these are the base salaries, and compensation can include bonuses and other benefits such as dividends and commissions. Individuals

**TABLE 21.1**

**Base Salaries Within Corporate Research Departments and Market Research Companies**

| Title | Corporate research department | Market research company |
|---|---|---|
| Research analyst | $62,602 | $51,677 |
| Senior research analyst | $75,182 | $64,472 |
| Project manager | n/a | $61,594 |
| Senior project manager | n/a | $79,113 |
| Group head manager | n/a | $82,366 |
| Director of research | n/a | $98,682 |
| Customer insights manager | $97,759 | n/a |
| Market research manager | $99,210 | n/a |
| Market research director | $134,419 | n/a |
| Senior vice president or vice president of research | $172,369 | $143,761 |
| Owner/partner/president/CEO/COO | n/a | $120,546 |

*Note.* Data from Quirks (2015).

who work in sales functions within market research firms typically also earn commissions for selling market research projects.

## Future Prospects for the Market Research Industry

Current demand for consumer psychologists is strong. The market research industry is currently a $16 billion a year industry (Gold, 2014). As shown in Figure 21.1, the total revenue for research services among the top for-profit firms in 2013 was $10.7 billion with the top 50 market research firms making $9.8 billion in revenues (Gold, 2014). Nonprofit firms that conduct market research make up a small part of the industry and had market research revenue of approximately $1.5 billion.

The term *market research industry* is somewhat of a misnomer, given that market researchers can be found in industries throughout the economy. In 2012, approximately 415,700 market research analysts were employed in the United States, a number that is expected to grow 32% between 2012 and 2022, far beyond the 11% average growth projection for all occupations (Bureau of Labor Statistics, 2014). Additionally, *U.S. News & World Report*'s "Best Business Jobs" (2016) ranked market

**FIGURE 21.1**

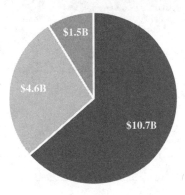

■ Top For-Profit Firms (196 Firms)   ■ Additional For-Profit Firms   ■ Non-Profit Firms

Total annual revenue (in billions of dollars) in 2013.
Data from Gold (2014).

research analyst the 11th best business job. These rankings take into consideration an occupation's 10-year projected growth volume, 10-year projected growth percentage, median salary, job prospects, employment rate, stress level, and work–life balance.

The industry is slowly starting to grow again since the recession of 2008. Figure 21.2 shows the annual growth rate since 1988. As shown in the figure, the average growth rate for the top 50 firms after gross domestic product adjustment (adjusting for inflation) was 2% in 2013 (Gold, 2014), which is lower than the prerecession growth rates of 5–8% growth among these firms.

Despite relatively slow growth compared with prerecession years, the market research industry is poised for major changes as a result of an explosion of new technologies. There are an ever-increasing number of ways to better replicate the actual situations in which consumers make their purchasing decisions, allowing researchers to rely less heavily on self-reported data. Technologies such as Google Glass, webcams, and smartphones are changing how respondents communicate their thoughts and feelings to researchers. For example, some researchers now ask respondents to take photos of retail environments and answer short surveys while shopping, which gives insight into how the person is thinking and feeling at the very moment they are in a specific retail environment. Another major shift is occurring

**FIGURE 21.2**

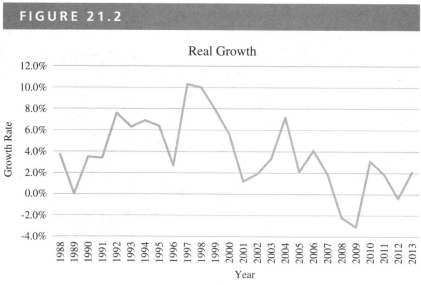

Annual growth rate for market research industry after GDP adjustment. Data from Honomichl (2008, 2009, 2010, 2011, 2012, 2013).

in the flexibility and depth of the online research being conducted. Usability studies previously gauged respondents' reactions to a website by presenting the website to them in a focus group setting. Now, many of these groups have been replaced by usability studies that take place online within the respondents' homes. Researchers can now evaluate how consumers respond to a website by recording what they see and do on their computer screens. Traditional focus groups sometimes are replaced by online focus groups and online discussion forums because they are less expensive and allow the researchers to talk to a variety of people around the country. Consumer psychologists increasingly are being asked to analyze what consumers post online to understand what they tell friends and family members about certain brands or products.

Traditional methods of research still remain strong, however. Good research design sometimes uses a combination of methods to ensure that we understand the consumer as fully as possible. An in-store survey that is a couple of minutes long can be augmented with focus groups with people who shopped at this same store to understand thoughts, feelings, and behaviors at the moment along with long-term thoughts after buying the product.

I am excited about the future of the market research industry. It's an industry with a great deal of promise and potential for growth. As long as businesses have questions they need to answer, I believe there will always be a need for consumer psychologists. I look forward to the next several decades.

## Recommended Readings

Aaker, D. A. (2001). *Developing business strategies* (6th ed.). New York, NY: Wiley.

Ariely, D. (2009). *Predictably irrational, revised and expanded edition: The hidden forces that shape our decisions.* New York, NY: HarperCollins Publishers.

Beall, A. E. (2010). *Strategic market research: A guide to conducting research that drives businesses* (2nd ed.). Bloomington, IN: IUniverse.

Feinburg, F. M., Kinnear, T., & Taylor, J. R. (2013). *Modern marketing research: Concepts, methods, and cases* (2nd ed.). Mason, OH: South-Western.

Lindstrom, M. (2010). *Buyology: Truth and lies about why we buy.* New York, NY: Broadway Books.

McQuarrie, E. F. (2015). *The marketing research toolbox: A concise guide for beginners.* Thousand Oaks, CA: Sage.

# References

Best business jobs. (2016). Market research analyst. *U.S. News & World Report.* Retrieved from http://money.usnews.com/careers/best-jobs/market-research-analyst

Bureau of Labor Statistics. (2014). Market research analysts. *Occupational outlook handbook: 2014–15 edition.* Retrieved from http://www.bls.gov/ooh/business-and-financial/market-research-analysts.htm

Gold, L. N. (2014, June). The 2014 AMA Gold top 50 report. *Marketing News,* 28–105.

Honomichl, J. (2008, June 15). Honomichl 2008: Top 50 business report of the U.S. marketing research industry. *Marketing News,* H1–H69.

Honomichl, J. (2009, June 30). 2009 Honomichl top 50. *Marketing News,* 12–72.

Honomichl, J. (2010, June 30). 2010 Honomichl top 50. *Marketing News,* 14–73.

Honomichl, J. (2011, June 30). 2011 Honomichl top 50 report. *Marketing News,* 11–66.

Honomichl, J. (2012, August 31). 2012 Honomichl global top 25. *Marketing News,* 12–40.

Honomichl, J. (2013, June). 2013 Honomichl top 50 report. *Marketing News,* 26–100.

Quirks. (2015). *Market research salaries by job title.* Retrieved from http://www.quirks.com/jobs/research-salaries/Market-research-salary-by-title.aspx#CRJT

*Gary R. VandenBos and Rosemarie I. Sokol-Chang*

# Psychologists in the Publishing World

22

P ublishing is at the core of any psychologist's career: it is the means by which research and knowledge is transmitted and received—and aids intellectual change. It is a record of how the discipline evolves and grows. Some psychologists are actively involved in publishing by authoring articles, book chapters, books, and more; others are involved as readers of

As the former APA publisher and the executive director of the American Psychological Association's Office of Publications and Databases, Gary R. VandenBos, PhD, was responsible for developing the premier program for the dissemination of psychological knowledge worldwide. VandenBos began his career at Michigan State University as research coordinator of the Michigan State Psychotherapy with Schizophrenics Research Project. He has maintained a clinical practice since 1974.

Rosemarie I. Sokol-Chang, PhD, is Publisher of the American Psychological Association Journals Program. Sokol-Chang has held faculty positions at Skidmore College and SUNY New Paltz, and leadership positions in the NorthEastern Evolutionary Psychology Society and Feminist Evolutionary Perspectives Society. Sokol-Chang received her bachelor's degree from Kentucky State University and her doctorate from Clark University, both in psychology.

http://dx.doi.org/10.1037/15960-023
*Career Paths in Psychology: Where Your Degree Can Take You, Third Edition*,
R. J. Sternberg (Editor)

psychological content. Thus, as either recipients or active participants, all psychologists are engaged in publishing.

## Nature of an Editor's Career

Although few psychologists work solely as editors as their full-time professional work, many psychologists are engaged in editorial work as part of their career. They work on newsletters, blogs, listservs, journals, or books as editors because they enjoy the evaluative and critical work of providing constructive feedback to help shape effective and efficient communication. These activities often complement their full-time careers, and can be used as a measure to evaluate their work, such as by university departments.

The fundamental nature of an editor's work is to facilitate the recruitment, selection, and development of the highest quality intellectual property for effective communication to the reader.

## Kinds of Activities in Which Editors Engage

We will detail the routine activities in which a journal editor is engaged. Although there will be overlap for editing other types of material, some aspects are unique to journal editing. An academic journal is focused on a general or specific topic (e.g., experimental psychology or creativity) and is described in its editorial coverage statement—the short description that explains what type of content the journal publishes, and in what format, such as review or experimental articles.

The two broad functions of a journal editor are (a) to determine the material that is eventually published, while eliminating material that is not of sufficient quality or appropriate focus on the coverage mission of the journal; and (b) to enhance the quality of scientific writing.

Basic activities of the editor involve author recruitment, manuscript recruitment, review of manuscripts, development of manuscripts, selection of manuscripts, and grouping articles into a journal issue. Additionally, journal editors are responsible for the recruitment and training of reviewers, without whom no scholarly publication can maintain a high standard.

# AUTHOR AND MANUSCRIPT RECRUITMENT

Editors are involved in recruiting psychologists to submit manuscripts for publication. The extent to which manuscripts are actively recruited is determined by the reputation and coverage area of the journal. Has the journal been launched recently or is it well established? Is the journal covering a broad general area or a specialized area? In general, more established journals that cover a broader area will include those that psychologists know about and consider to be outlets for their work. Newer or more specialized titles will attract a smaller subset of psychologists.

General reputation will influence the nature and type of the editor's role in author recruitment. For example, many institutions require their employees to submit to journals that have an impact factor. An impact factor is a ratio of how often articles in a journal are cited to how many articles are published during a certain time frame. It is calculated by measuring the citations in other reputable journals indexed in one of the Thomson Reuters databases. Because of the cycle required to measure impact in this way, it takes a journal at least 3 years to receive an impact factor; many journals take much longer, and some are never issued impact factors. The higher a journal's impact factor, the more likely an editor will not need to recruit authors for submissions.

In general, editors encourage the submission of manuscripts as opposed to inviting submissions, as the latter has the implication of guaranteeing eventual acceptance. All high-quality scholarly journals use peer review, and all submissions face the risk of rejection. Editors encourage submissions through personal communications, in face-to-face meetings, and through calls for submission in journals, posted on listservs or as mass mailings.

# REVIEW AND SELECTION

An editor's first read of a new submission determines whether the manuscript is in the domain of the journal coverage and whether the manuscript is of sufficient quality to survive the review process. After the initial read, the editor will determine whether the manuscript will be sent for peer review or will be rejected without external review.

The peer-review process involves engaging reviewers to read the manuscript and consider the content for quality and applicability to the journal's readers (Figure 22.1). Review request letters are sent to two or three individuals seeking assistance to assess and evaluate the manuscript. If the selected reviewers decline the invitation, the editor must identify additional potential reviewers.

**FIGURE 22.1**

| Author submits a manuscript to a journal. | Editor reads the manuscript, and decides whether or not to send it for peer review. | If sent for peer review, two or three reviewers read the manuscript and offer feedback and a recommended decision. | The editor rereads the manuscript and the reviewer feedback, and issues a decision, as well as specific feedback if offered the chance to revise. | Editor receives revised manuscript and decides whether to send it for peer review again, or issue a decision on the editor's reading. | Once a manuscript is accepted, editor decides how to group the article into a journal issue with other articles. |

Peer-review process.

The editor monitors the progress of the peer review and reminds reviewers of upcoming deadlines and overdue reviews. Once the reviews are received, the editor rereads the manuscript, reads the review commentaries and formulates an editorial decision in terms of rejection or a request for revision. Depending on the journal, between 30 and 50% of the manuscripts will be rejected after the first round of review. Those not rejected will be invited to revise. The invitation to revise is not an acceptance of the manuscript, as some percentage of revised manuscripts will be rejected on further review.

The editor of the journal typically directs and manages the peer review process. With some small journals, editors may coordinate all reviews themselves; with medium sized journal, they may work with a manuscript coordinator who handles the administrative and clerical aspects.

With larger journals, the editor may have a team of associate editors, such that the editor needs to decide which manuscript to process him- or herself and which to assign to an associate editor, and which associate editor to assign it to if several are available. Associate editors are often expert in a specific content area within the journal's coverage. Once an associate editor receives the reviews and writes a draft letter recommending a decision, the editor reviews the decision letter, makes edits as needed, and sends the decision to the author.

## EDITORIAL DEVELOPMENT

Manuscripts that have been invited for revision are essentially in the editorial development phase. A core editorial activity is crafting the editorial feedback letter about the revision and enhancements that the editor seeks from the author. The simplest letter merely asks the author to revise in a manner responsive to the comments and criticisms of the peer reviews. More detailed editorial feedback might be a page long in which the editor articulates the two or three desired editorial improvements along with a reminder to respond to the peer reviewer's commentary.

Editorial action letters may be two or three pages long, in which the editor describes the desired changes along with rational and information about what the editor is attempting to achieve with these changes. This letter might include requests to delete or reduce content as well as requests for additions and expansions.

Although reviewer commentaries are important in the review process, an editor renders the final decision. With two or three separate reviewers providing feedback on a manuscript, it is possible that the advisory suggestions will be different. One reviewer might recommend that a manuscript be rejected, whereas another recommends the same manuscript be sent back to the author for revision. The editor's role is to make a decision based on the readings of the editor and reviewers; ultimately, it is the editor's role to decide what is most likely to appeal to the journal's readers.

## ARTICLE ASSIGNMENT AND GROUPING

Once manuscripts have been accepted for publication in a journal, an editor decides how to group them into an issue. Articles that have a similar theme might be grouped into a special issue or a special cluster on the topic. Articles might be grouped into sections within the journal, such as brief reports and longer articles or merely by the date of acceptance. Generally, editors are thoughtful about article placement in an issue. Often readers will first look at a table of contents listing the article title and authors before looking at a journal issue in more detail.

## REVIEWER RECRUITMENT AND TRAINING

Most journals have an editorial board composed of 30–50 individuals who have agreed to be regular reviewers with a commitment to handle 6–12 reviews for the journal in a timely manner.

When an editor assigns reviewers, the editor typically will select one or two reviewers from the editorial board and one or two ad hoc reviewers who have relevant expertise but who do not have a formal commitment to review on a regular basis. The journal editor sets the standards for reviewers' performance, including the tone of the reviews and the level of detail expected. With the editorial board members, the editor may send a letter of invitation to serve on the board that included instructions for performing reviews for the journal. With ad hoc reviewers, the editor may mention a few expectations in the review request letter for a manuscript, but in most cases will assume that the ad hoc reviewers understand the function, customs, and behavior expected of reviewers. If reviews come back that fail to meet those expectations, such as writing in an unprofessional tone or providing a review that lacks sufficient detail, the editor may have to edit the review commentary as well as work on the reviewer's development as a reviewer.

## A Typical Day of an Editor

Being a journal editor is not a full-time job. The size of the journal is the major determinant of whether one does editorial work on a daily basis or less frequently. Journals are defined as small, medium, and large in overlapping ways, such as the number of new submissions per year and the number of published articles per year, and indirectly by the number of pages published per year.

Small journals might receive 60–120 manuscripts per year, and publish 25–30 articles per year. A medium-size journal may receive annual submissions ranging between 150–300 manuscripts per year and publishes between 50 and 100 articles per year. A large journal typically processes between 400 and 1,000 and more submissions per year and publishes 100–300 articles per year.

The editor of a small journal without associate editors generally will perform duties once or twice a week, spending 4–8 hours per week. Medium-size journals require some attention on a daily basis. The editor might work 1–2 hours per day or devote 2 to 3 half-days per week engaged in editorial activities. With a large journal, the workflow of incoming submissions and outgoing editorial action letters requires the editor to work on the journal daily.

The editor needs to engage in some activities that do not make up a typical day but that do fit into the typical year. An editor may give two to three talks per year at relevant professional meetings about the journal and its editorial focus to publicize the journal and attract submissions. The editor might also present a workshop at a meeting about how to publish an article in a journal or how to review a manuscript.

# Advantages and Disadvantages of Being an Editor

## ADVANTAGES

Being selected and appointed to be a journal editor is a career-marking event. It confers public and professional acknowledgment of your expertise and standing in the scholarly community. Journal editors are viewed as a foremost expert in the area that the journal publishes. Often, editors will be asked to participate in other field-shaping events, such as joining task forces related to publishing psychological science, serving as members on a council of editors, or participating as a panel member to talk about psychology publishing or the subfield an editor represents.

Being a journal editor also brings further visibility and professional recognition. Institutions that value service beyond one's college or university recognize the value that serving as an editor brings to a faculty member and the institution. As a result, some institutions offer course releases or other forms of support to allow the editor to immerse her- or himself into the task. After having shepherded a journal for 4–6 years, the editor is often a foremost expert in the field, which might open the door for book opportunities that might not have existed before the editorship.

As an editor one has both the opportunity (and duty) to read all submissions, and thus, has access to a wide range of prepublication material in the journal's area of expertise or specialized focus. An editor has the broadest awareness of the full range of work being done and written and often is well positioned to see the potential links between disparate research findings. Personal advantages also include a sense of providing service to the field, giving back and mentoring, and the overall positive sense that one is contributing and preparing for the next generation of scholars.

## DISADVANTAGES

Editorial work takes time, and the amount of recognition for the editorial time is not always parallel to the recognition one could have received from personal research or publishing. Performing the tasks of an editor often detracts from time that could have been spent on additional research studies, building or shifting the focus of a research lab and service at one's institution. As with many parts of an academic lifestyle, being an editor is often a labor of love.

Most editors receive some honorarium for their service; however, editorial work is not generally conceptualized as salary. Rather, an honorarium is a modest financial reward to offset the professional activity of editing. Honoraria may be shared with associate editors, used to buy out courses, or even used to fund a portion of one's research lab.

Editors are often put in the unpleasant role of rejecting manuscripts from colleagues and friends. Editors reject manuscripts for a myriad of reasons; most people consider it a reflection on the quality of a manuscript, yet a manuscript might instead be outside of the scope of a journal, cover a topic that has been published extensively in the journal already, or just be beyond the cut of the number of manuscripts that reasonably can be published in the journal. The more junior editor of a journal may have to reject the manuscript of a mentor, as well. This situation is particularly stressful, as editors might wonder whether this decision will affect their careers.

Editors have to address the challenging issues of plagiarism and potential fraud, both relatively rare but legitimate stressors of the position. Plagiarism occurs intentionally or unintentionally, and thus needs to be handled delicately. Issues of potential data fraud that occur during manuscript evaluation—or after an article's publication—require extensive analysis as the outcome can have a very real impact on the author's future.

Finally, some authors react negatively and strongly to editorial decisions or specific reviewer comments. It is hard for some authors to separate feedback on the particular study reported, or what is included in the manuscript as background and interpretation, from her- or himself personally. Occasionally, this results in the author writing hostile and critical letters to the editor. Being an editor requires thicker skin even than being an author as well as knowing what resources are available to aid in such appeal processes.

## Preparation Needed To Be an Editor

In a sense, any individual seeking an advanced degree is engaged in the initial preparation for a career as an editor. A career in psychology assumes the development of expertise, whether clinical or research. One aspect of having particular expertise involves the communication and sharing of that expertise—whether it is about routine knowledge and practice, knowledge generation, or theory development. A significant number of psychologists write or present information about their activities and expertise at conferences and in newsletter columns, reviewed journal articles, or books. This is prerequisite and essential step in preparation to become an editor.

Few psychologists step immediately into the role of editor. More typically, the arc begins as an author and reviewer. Many graduate students are afforded the opportunity to engage in the peer-review process, first as authors, and some later as reviewers. Most people who become editors go a step further in their development by serving as an associate editor of a journal or serving as a guest associate editor of a special issue.

Some individuals may move from being an associate editor of a small journal or newsletter to becoming an associate editor of a more prestigious journal before becoming an editor. Others may be an associate editor of a medium-size journal before becoming editor of a small specialized journal or before moving on to become the editor of a larger journal. Editing one or more books may be part of some individual's editorial careers but not others.

## Attributes Needed for Success as an Editor

Editing a scholarly journal in psychology is an extremely challenging and demanding job. The pace of submissions and revisions can be brisk, and an editor often has no formal training in editorial work. Editors are most successful when they can manage time effectively, keep a balanced evaluation of material, and demonstrate leadership capabilities to form the current vision of the journal and direct a team of associate editors and reviewers.

Being a journal editor requires the ability to evaluate effective and efficient communication; communication that not only has enough depth to inform the reader but also is not overly detailed for the less expert reader. An editor must adopt the reader's perspective and consider what a reader will expect so that the reader will be able to assimilate and use the information being conveyed.

An editor must have attention to detail, but not at the expense of seeing the larger picture. A journal editor needs to read through the manuscript section by section, while maintaining the organization as a whole. The editor evaluates whether the parts are in the right place as well as drills down to a sentence level to consider whether the sentence is conveying the intended message.

Editors need to have broad exposure in some area. A journal editor needs to be reading 2–4 journals regularly in a specific research domain or 10–12 journals regularly when the content is more general. An editor is familiar with the breadth and depth of an area and the awareness of emerging questions. This allows an editor to evaluate what a particular manuscript is adding to the literature and whether the reported research is current, using up-to-date methods.

Some personal qualities that aid an editor include being fair-minded intellectually. The editor needs to evaluate and nurture sound research from multiple perspectives and theoretical orientations, without introducing bias. Having the ability to absorb negative or hostile feedback without malice or retribution is helpful. Writing in a diplomatic manner is essential; an editor must be able to acknowledge the strengths and weaknesses of a manuscript, and provide critical but constructive feedback.

## Pay Range for an Editor

An editor of a small journal may receive nothing or any sum up to $2,000 per year; medium-size journals generally offer an honorarium between $1,000 and $5,000; and larger journals offer $5,000–$10,000 per year. A small number of editors of long-standing and highly prestigious journals may receive honorariums of $15,000, $20,000, $25,000, or more per year. The typical editorial term is 3–6 years. Short terms are often renewable.

## Future Prospects for Editors

The future of scholarly journals is changing, as some journals move to an online-only format, reshaping how readers interact with journals. There is no good substitute, however, for the peer-review process for deciding which content to publish in a journal. As such, as long as scholarly content is produced to forward communication and advancements in psychology, there must be editors who can ensure intellectual standards and professional excellence of published material and who can enhance the quality of scholarly communication.

*Laura E. Berk and Sean W. Wakely*

# Psychologists Writing Textbooks 23

Our collaboration originated nearly two decades ago, when Laura was crafting the earliest editions of her child and life-span development textbooks and Sean became her editor. When we contemplated the opening of this chapter, we immediately realized Laura's story was typical for many academics who found their way into the career of textbook writing after

Laura E. Berk, PhD, is a distinguished professor of psychology at Illinois State University. She is the author of twenty-six editions of four textbooks: *Child Development*; *Infants, Children, and Adolescents*; *Development through the Lifespan*; and *Exploring Lifespan Development*, published by Pearson Education.

Sean W. Wakely, BA, is founder and principal adviser at Academic Author Advisers, a literary consulting group that helps textbook authors and educational technology companies successfully navigate the rapidly evolving higher education publishing environment.

We are deeply grateful to the 56 textbook authors who responded to our survey, providing rich information about authors' perspectives and experiences.

http://dx.doi.org/10.1037/15960-024
*Career Paths in Psychology: Where Your Degree Can Take You, Third Edition*,
R. J. Sternberg (Editor)

establishing their professional reputations as excellent teachers, researchers, and scholars. As Laura recalls,

> Having reached mid-career, I sought a wider reach than was afforded by the research articles, book chapters, and course assignments reflected on my vita. Fortuitously, one of Sean's predecessors dropped into my office one day and boldly asked: "Had I ever considered writing a child development textbook?"
>
> I was both intrigued and daunted by the prospect. A passion for writing nurtured from an early age by inspiring teachers; a love of teaching; intense fascination with the field of human development; and a desire to convey a vision of that field soon outweighed my initial ambivalence. Three months later, I signed a publishing contract and embarked on the three-year journey of writing my first textbook.
>
> I won't begin to claim my early experience with textbook writing was without unexpected drawbacks. For example, the time and effort involved soon exceeded other professional obligations. It required, among other things, unremitting library research to keep pace with a rapidly evolving subject; wide-ranging reading across hundreds of topics; a "thick skin" in the face of conflicting feedback from scores of scholarly reviewers; and intense self-discipline to meet deadlines. When long work hours intruded into family time, I sometimes revisited the wisdom of my text-authoring decision. But as each successive chapter took shape, I felt an increasing sense of fulfillment in writing for undergraduate students. Today, as a veteran author of 26 editions disseminated around the globe, I'm convinced that grappling with the challenges and enduring the sacrifices has all been "worth it"—yielding peak professional and personal gratifications.

Similarly, other textbook authors, in reflecting on the meaning of their work, often mention impact—a unique chance to influence hundreds of thousands, even millions, of college and university students during a crucial period in their development. When asked why they write, authors frequently cite deeply satisfying messages from students and instructors, like these:

> I was fortunate enough to have a professor teaching with your textbook. That book is one of the reasons why I am a . . . psychologist today. So first of all—thank you for an amazing book! Secondly, I am now going to be teaching my first course. I would love to use your book.

> I wanted to tell you thank you. Thank you for this gift of understanding [psychology] better than I did before. . . . Just wanted to say thanks for this contribution to the world to make it a better place.

This chapter addresses the career of writing college and university psychology textbooks (although much of our discussion applies to writing textbooks in virtually any field). Creating influential textbooks is a collaborative activity, necessitating a mutually supportive relationship between author and publisher. This chapter's coauthorship encompasses both sides of this essential collaboration—Laura as the author of three successful textbooks and Sean as an educational publishing executive with more than 30 years of industry experience. We feel enriched and rewarded by the professional and personal relationship we have formed over many years.

To ensure that our discussion of textbook writing broadly represents authors' experiences and opinions, we asked 146 psychologists writing for large undergraduate courses to respond anonymously to an online survey (Berk & Wakely, 2015). Fifty-six agreed to participate—a response rate of 38%. Our respondents resemble a balance in conventional gender identification (56% male and 44% female) and in courses represented—introductory psychology (31%), child and life-span development (24%), social psychology (18%), abnormal psychology (15%), biological psychology (5%), and other fields (13%).[1] Respondents' longevity as authors is impressive: Eighty-five percent have been writing for more than a decade and one third for more than three decades. Most are tenured or emeriti professors; few are younger than 50 years old. In fact, the majority (57%) are in their 60s and 70s, with two in their 80s! Like other professional endeavors requiring synthesis of extensive knowledge, textbook authoring is associated with career maturity (Sasser-Coen, 1993).

Before considering just what text authors do and the gratifications and challenges of their craft, let's consider what a textbook is in the 21st-century's increasingly digital world of educational publishing.

## What Is a Textbook?

Just about anyone who has experienced formal schooling is familiar with textbooks. Still, it's important for readers to understand that when we refer to *textbooks* throughout this chapter, we consider them to be categorized as follows:

### COURSE NARRATIVES

Textbooks are teaching narratives that reflect a typical organization or scope and sequence for a specific courses (in which *scope* is the range and depth of topics taught and *sequence* is the order topics are covered).

---

[1]These percentages add to more than 100 because many authors—in fact, nearly half of our survey respondents—have written more than one textbook, typically for related courses.

Online course narratives that form the core of comprehensive digital learning produces are sometimes called *learning paths.* In the increasingly complex digital environments currently under development, the learning path's pace and direction is directly affected by meaningful, ongoing interactions with the learner's performance—even anticipating a learner's needs based on a personalized profile developed by the adaptive learning system (Tyton Partners, 2013).

Instructors and students rely on textbooks or course narratives to serve as a compendium of course content. Thus, instructors are freed from covering every detail in lectures, because the course narrative provides a readily accessible and accurate learning reference for students.

## SYNTHETIC BY NATURE

Textbooks are didactic works that draw from and synthesize existing scholarship and teaching practices; textbooks rarely, if ever, result from original research. Textbook writing is a distinct genre, with a unique structural logic and specialized writing conventions, generally rooted in pedagogical or learning frameworks. Understanding the genre, and how it is responding to emerging digital contexts, is crucial to textbook authors' successful evolution into online learning content experts and developers.

## EVOLVING INTO DIGITAL FORMS

Textbooks can be delivered in print, digital, or hybrid (print plus digital combination) formats. Digital textbooks range from flat versions of print books featuring little user interactivity to fully online experiences leveraging the capabilities of algorithmically driven, adaptable, and personalized learning.

There is great uncertainty about the future of print textbooks at the present time. In *Words Onscreen: The Fate of Reading in a Digital World*, American University linguistics professor Naomi S. Baron speculates that "the future of publishing seems headed for a hybrid model," although she holds out the possibility that nonfiction works requiring deep reading, such as textbooks, may remain largely in print for some time to come (Baron, 2015, p. 222). Supporting the likelihood of ongoing hybrid product models are results from a survey of more than 2,900 faculty at 2- and 4-year colleges and universities, sponsored by the Independent College Bookstores Association (ICBA) and the Campus Computing Project (CCP; Green, 2016). As noted in the report summary, "while the movement in course materials in colleges and universities is clearly from print towards digital, the survey data suggest it will be a slow process" (Green, 2016). For example, only 16% of the ICBA survey's respondents confirmed the core course materials they assigned in fall 2015 were primarily digital, and nearly one quarter of the respondents (24%) indicated the majority of the course materials they assign would never be fully digital (Green, 2016, p. 1). Consequently, the next generation of textbook authors needs to be fully comfortable with constructing course narratives that can be delivered in both print and digital contexts. No one can be sure how long it will take to fully transition to digital learning models, but all indications point to many years, if it happens at all.

## FULL TEACHING AND LEARNING PACKAGES

Most print textbooks, especially at the introductory level, are accompanied by an array of teaching support materials and student learning aids.

- Teaching supplements may include instructor's manuals with sample syllabi, teaching tips, and lecture summaries; test items and answer keys for use in preparing quizzes and exams; and Power-Point slides, digital illustrations, video clips, and simulations to populate lectures and online assignments.
- Student supplements include online quizzes and flashcards, homework assignments, practice tests, interactive simulations, and other strategies to help students better learn the material.

Supplement packages can play an important role in faculty members' textbook selections (known as *adoptions*). Therefore, it behooves authors to participate in the development of their textbooks' supplements or at least to scrutinize them before publication to ensure quality.

Digital or hybrid products often integrate teaching and learning aids, such as quizzes and interactive simulations, into the underlying, online course narrative, thus blurring the lines between learning pedagogy and assessment, practice, and homework. Creating seamless, unified learning solutions is an area of great experimentation at present. Exciting opportunities exist for textbook authors and content experts to envision and construct content for fully integrated and robust online learning solutions. In particular, psychologists' rich understanding of how learning occurs provides psychology majors with distinct advantages in mapping out the successful future of online learning.

On the basis of what we can learn from experienced textbook authors and anticipating the skills necessary to construct evolving digital course narratives, what does it take to write a successful textbook or develop effective online learning experiences?

## *What Do Textbook Authors Do?*

A textbook author's main task is to write, and the most successful authors compose on a regular schedule—generally, every day. Those who rely primarily on sabbatical leaves or summer breaks for writing time are typically less productive than those who make writing part of their daily routines.

## WRITING BEGINS WITH RESEARCH

Authors embarking on a textbook project do not just sit down and instantly begin to write, of course. A textbook must competently reflect the classic and current knowledge base in a major area of psychology or the field in general. As a result, most of our survey respondents report spending significant amounts of time preparing to write. Textbook authors must thoroughly and continuously search the scholarly literature, judiciously select from it, and engage in extensive background reading. It is not a surprise to hear authors observe that while they began their textbook writing careers as specialists, they eventually developed into generalists.

The time demands of textbook writing are great, and respondents to the survey we conducted noted resulting sacrifices in other career areas—most often in original contributions to research. Many authors make such sacrifices willingly, perhaps because their first loves are teaching and writing. Some moderate their textbook writing commitments by teaming with others—for example, approximately 50% of our survey respondents write with a coauthor, and nearly 25% share the work with two or more authors. Still, some solo authors can manage a prolific research career while also writing one or more textbooks.

Whichever arrangement they choose, authors are more likely to write successful texts when they have at least a modest history of conducting original research: Accurately explaining, critiquing, and applying empirical evidence, along with instilling in students an appreciation of the research process, is at the heart of textbook writing.

## TEACHING EXPERIENCES INSPIRE
## THE BEST TEXTBOOKS

Textbook writing is usually a second career, superimposed on regular faculty obligations of teaching and research. Consequently, authors typically lead especially full professional lives. Most, however, say they draw vital sustenance and inspiration from their mainline career pursuits. In keeping with this observation, 55% of our survey sample view their teaching experiences as indispensable to successful text writing, and they rely heavily on their rich classroom experiences to inform their prose.

For example, the most effective textbook authors replace the technical voice used in scholarly writing with a student-friendly narrative designed to capture a novice's interest and promote understanding of the field. Therefore, the best authors learn how to introduce key topics effectively and to craft understandable explanations from years of trial-and-error experiences and close interactions with students. By the same token, first-hand encounters with students' learning challenges can prompt helpful pedagogical strategies authors can integrate into text narratives, online learning solutions, and teaching and learning supplements. Teaching also can awaken a would-be author to the limitations of available textbooks, thereby kindling a new approach to the subject: One survey respondent asserted that inspiration for her textbook writing strategy came from "looking through bad textbooks and seeing what I didn't want to do!"

## HOW DO I BECOME A TEXTBOOK AUTHOR?

All successful textbooks start with a vision, or mission, generally stimulated by a combination of teaching insights, knowledge of the discipline, and sense of how to improve on competing titles. Once a vision solidifies, the next step is to prepare a project proposal (an explanation of the planned work and its key features, a table of contents, a description of the intended audience, and an analysis of the competition) and then submit it to one or more publishers along with a writing sample (typically one or two chapters). If the project meets a market need and is well presented, the author may be offered a publishing agreement. The terms of the agreement spell out the timetable for completion of the manuscript, publishing rights, royalty rates, and other aspects of the author–publisher relationship.

Many authors find the author–publisher partnership interesting and gratifying. Astute editorial advice and publisher-solicited manuscript reviews from scholars and experienced instructors are enormously helpful in guiding authors as they write and revise. Often publishers help a new author refine and execute her vision by conducting marketing research through focus groups and surveys. Publishers also may supply a development editor, who facilitates the writing process by coaching authors on how to better organize and revise their work.

On average, it takes 2 to 3 years for the first edition of single-authored, large-market manuscript to reach completion. Once it is accepted for publication, the author works closely with the publisher's production personnel as chapters are copyedited (checked for grammar, spelling, and consistency). Next, the print text is laid out in pages, which a proofreader, members of the production staff, an editor, and the author review for accuracy. Authors also may work with the publisher's media and technology staff to select photos, design print and digital illustrations, develop interactive simulations, and build content for online learning paths. Production work can take as little as 2 to 3 months, although it typically takes 6 to 9 months, and occasionally longer for complex or first-edition titles. Shortly after publication of the printed text, the online version is pushed live along with any associated teaching supplements. Even for an experienced author, nothing beats the thrill of seeing the published textbook in print and online for the very first time.

## Am I Cut Out To Be a Textbook Author?

What are the most important attributes and skills textbook authors need to possess? What experiences best prepare them for their craft? When asked these questions, our survey participants were in remarkable agreement.

### AM I A STRONG WRITER?

First and foremost, respondents emphasized a talent for lucid, engaging writing. Just over two thirds mentioned essential qualities of written communication: clarity, liveliness, freedom from unnecessary jargon, information distilled into the most accessible form without sacrificing accuracy and rigor, compelling stories and other examples, and occasional flashes of humor. Respondents also noted the importance of conveying a consistent viewpoint and key takeaway messages—features that make text content purposeful, useful, and memorable.

One third mentioned the value of previous writing experiences, including preparation of literature-review articles, book chapters, and pieces for lay audiences, along with regular practice at such writing. One respondent elaborated,

> The demands for crystal clear writing are intense. Anyone who aspires to textbook writing should write every day. I blog, which is good practice, and responses to my blog tell me which topics catch people's attention and which do not. I also freelance for a number of websites as an "expert writer." This keeps me writing in between editions and revisions.

### DO I UNDERSTAND STUDENTS?

The majority of respondents regarded a keen understanding of students as crucial. A participant explained, "Writing for students means that the author must constantly scrutinize the text from a teaching perspective. During a revision, when I add something, I imagine teaching it. That helps me determine how to write about it." As noted previously, teaching is the experience our survey sample viewed as the best preparation for text writing.

## HOW DO I RESPOND TO CHALLENGES?

With respect to personality traits, half of our sample cited self-discipline, perseverance, and patience. One amplified, "[It's] a long process. It doesn't happen overnight. It can be frustrating. There are days when you'd rather be doing something else."

One third pointed to strong organizational and integrative skills plus attention to detail. The ability to filter and synthesize masses of information so the end product contains the right material at the right length is basic to the task.

Just as many emphasized the ability to work well with others, especially coauthors and editors. They noted that being receptive to suggestions and criticisms while staying true to one's authoring goals requires determination and a skillful capacity to compromise: "Our colleagues are often brutal when they write reviews, and you have to get past the emotional response. At the same time, you have to realize that you can't please everyone." Another explained, "[You need] political skills to deal with textbook editors who often want you to make changes you don't want to make." The challenge is to use feedback from editors constructively.

## DO I HAVE A PASSION FOR LEARNING?

One fifth of our sample referred to open-mindedness—intellectual curiosity, imagination, and being a lifelong learner. In the words of one: "I have a hard time sticking to one subject for very long. I want to know everything! This is not a great characteristic for a researcher, but I've found it to be very helpful for textbook writing." The usefulness of a broad knowledge base in psychology and related fields may explain why nearly 30% of survey participants viewed their academic training as significant. Some mentioned a high-quality undergraduate liberal arts education; others credited graduate studies that required them to develop extensive knowledge of research across the discipline.

## DO I HAVE A MENTOR?

Finally, 27% of survey respondents described relationships with mentors as key to becoming a skilled textbook author. For a few, this involved assisting a professor with textbook-preparation tasks while in graduate school. As one remarked, "I hit the jackpot by having a PhD advisor who cared enough about me to teach me how to love the writing life . . . and to embrace a strong work ethic." More often, experienced lead authors mentor new coauthors whom they have invited to join an author team.

Mentoring also can be indirect. For example, one respondent started by writing instructor's manuals, which immersed her in the world of authorship. These experiences familiarized her with the wide breadth of topics covered by the best textbooks in her field.

A complex combination of personal attributes and experiences contributes to the development of a text author. When these factors coalesce, authors are poised not only to succeed but also to experience their work as deeply satisfying.

## What Do Textbook Authors Like Most About Their Craft?

As a group, textbook authors are impressively devoted to and enthusiastic about their work, describing it with passionate expressions like: "I love the process of making difficult topics accessible." "It's a 'flow' experience for me." "I feel a sense of calling and meaning." "It's the best thing I'll ever do professionally." Five intrinsic satisfactions are especially salient in their responses:

### ENHANCED KNOWLEDGE

Just over 70% of our survey sample cited constructing a "big picture" of their chosen field and keeping up to date on its progress as enormously satisfying. This wider, deeper knowledge improves their teaching and research. It also better equips them to discuss psychological topics with people they encounter in everyday life. In the words of two participants: "Writing motivates me to broaden my knowledge of topics that I probably would not explore if I were motivated only by my own personal interests. . . . [It] has made me a better teacher and psychologist." "It improves my communication with everyone about what I do and what we know (and don't know)."

### REACHING A WIDE AUDIENCE

Fifty-five percent mentioned textbook authors' unique opportunity to reach vast numbers of students, and some referred to a significant impact on colleagues adopting their texts as well. Many respondents seem awestruck at attaining such a great reach, reporting that it engenders a weighty sense of responsibility: "It's humbling to think that my words are shaping the way students approach psychological science." Another wrote, "My text has been translated into about a dozen languages. I hope that I have provided a rigorous introduction to the field to students all around the world. Few people get that privilege." And yet another explained,

> I feel like what I write for the textbook will be read by many, many more people than my journal articles, so of course it's very important to consider what ideas and studies are reviewed and highlighted for the next generation of scholar/citizens.

## THE WRITING EXPERIENCE

A few survey respondents said the satisfactions an author derives from writing are so obvious they need not be mentioned. About one third expounded on their love of writing, and some noted that the writing process is itself a source of new learning and discovery: "I found that working with the material . . . led me to develop new ways of presenting it, new examples, and new demonstrations that I might not have otherwise developed." "I had to be open to creative ways to pass on content to students." "I enjoy the challenge of creating narrative frameworks for each topic in the field." In reflecting on their efforts to write in innovative, engaging ways, our survey participants—though mindful of untold hours of challenging work—nonetheless characterized their experience as "creative," "joyful," and "a lot of fun."

## SENSE OF ACCOMPLISHMENT AND PURPOSE

About one fourth of our sample spoke of the fulfillment they derive from attaining a goal that is "unimaginably difficult and time-consuming." They often referred to a sense of mission: "a strong desire to pass on the discipline," "teaching students to think critically and creatively," and "playing a part in how people understand themselves, others, and the world."

## GRATIFYING RELATIONSHIPS

From the outside looking in, textbook writing seems like a self-contained, even lonely, process. Yet one fifth of our survey participants challenged this stereotype: They ranked interactions with "wonderful and interesting people" as among their craft's greatest pleasures. Some referred to unusually simpatico coauthors with whom they had forged cherished, enduring relationships. Others described rewarding ties with publishing personnel—editors, marketing managers, and sales representatives. Widely recognized authors mentioned invitations to speak at conferences (especially ones devoted to the teaching of psychology). Those serving courses with the largest enrollments reported frequent campus visits to support their texts—travels that spurred professional growth. One related,

> I'm able to interact with smart, exciting, and hard-working people . . . often instructors and students who have used the book and want to share their experience. Whether [those interactions are] positive or negative, I grow as a writer and educator.

Overall, textbook authors feel honored to be entrusted with their task and deeply fortunate to engage in a labor of love. For most, the satisfactions of their career overshadow its drawbacks.

## What Key Challenges Do Textbook Authors Face?

Survey respondents suggested a number of disadvantages or challenges that textbook authors face, but three themes were mentioned most often: time commitment, the publishing environment, and lack of respect.

### TIME COMMITMENT

The greatest challenges identified in our survey are the time and attention demanded by textbook projects—an unwelcome surprise to many new authors. More than 75% highlighted the significant workload and the long hours it entails as the key disadvantage they experience: "It's easy to underestimate how much time and effort it takes to write a textbook. During the most challenging parts of that process, one can easily lose track of one's own research. It's tough to maintain that balance." Another explained,

> In order to do the job right, you have to devote enormous amounts of time to it, and to persist in doing so for years at a time . . . This is why I always advise potential textbook authors to consider carefully the question of whether they have the time, the energy, and the motivation to devote to writing a book, but also to consider their personal and family situations. I suggest that they ask themselves whether they are willing to give up their evenings and weekends, and perhaps some of their vacations, family events, and other social activities for years at a stretch. It is not an easy question to answer, but it must be addressed honestly if one is to avoid having a book create personal, financial, or worst of all, family strife.

## THE PUBLISHING ENVIRONMENT

Pressing deadlines go hand in hand with long hours spent researching, evaluating, and preparing content—and a plethora of deadlines sorely test an author's coping abilities. One author recounts frustrations working with publishers "who set many deadlines and make many demands on authors but are not so conscientious about keeping the schedules they set or their commitments to the authors."

In fact, the general nature of educational publishing, the wrenching changes the industry is experiencing, and disagreements with their own publishers are the second-most mentioned set of challenges (60%). Many authors are troubled by their publisher's unrealistic or capricious expectations: rushed revision schedules; contract issues; extensive busy work, such as finding acceptable photographs or tracking down elusive third-party permissions; time invested in contributing to marketing materials and engaging in promotional activities (yet having little control over publishers' marketing or sales efforts); and constant, high turnover of publishers' staff. In *Markets From Culture: Institutional Logics and Organizational Decisions in Higher Education Publishing*, Patricia Thornton (2004) presents a fascinating case analysis of the evolution of the higher education publishing industry from the 1950s through the 1990s that supports respondents' frustrations with the current publishing environment. She notes that family-owned publishing firms committed to the profession and to creating high-prestige books have been replaced by international corporations whose decision making is instead focused on exploiting markets and publishing high-profit titles.

Many respondents who mentioned publishing challenges are concerned with rising costs of higher education and textbooks, diminishing textbook quality standards, students' lack of preparation, industry consolidation, competition from used books and book rentals, digitally enabled piracy and copyright infringement, and competition from online open educational resources. Survey participants also expressed considerable apprehension about successfully navigating increasingly digital teaching, learning, publishing, and distribution models.

Of course, publishing agreements are written by publishers and, therefore, are strongly biased toward the publisher's side—a reality that contributes to the resistance authors often encounter in their attempts to address difficulties with their publishers. Some authors seek the assistance of specialized attorneys in negotiating their publishing agreements, thereby introducing a better balance into the relationship at the front end—a step that can help prevent future conflicts. Retaining an author's agent to advise on the prospectus, sample-chapter development, identification of suitable publishers, and postcontractual problem solving can aid in writing a successful textbook as well. The Text and

Academic Author's Association (http://www.taaonline.net), maintains a directory of such professionals, in addition to providing authors with wide-ranging useful resources and a supportive membership community.

## LACK OF RESPECT

Perhaps the most poignant survey finding (about 25%) is the lack of respect respondents—especially those at Research 1 (R1) universities—report experiencing from colleagues and the academy as a whole. In addition, a number of textbook authors have felt the sharp sting of colleagues' thinly veiled envy of their broad readership and presumed financial success: "I do wish that other faculty had a greater appreciation for the extent of the scholarship that goes into well-crafted textbooks." "Some colleagues believe that I have 'sold my soul' for profit." Others commented,

> I'm not sure writing textbooks leads to much respect from your peers, and can even lead to some jealousy . . . I would caution a tenure-track junior faculty member at a big R1 about writing textbooks. I doubt they would get much credit for this work, and it is extremely time-consuming.

> There are people who dislike, or even despise, textbook authors no matter what other accomplishments an author may have to his or her credit. It is something that we have to learn to accept and cope with.

So why do so many excellent scholars and teachers choose to become textbook authors despite long hours, stressful deadlines, and lack of support from colleagues and institutions? As we discovered from responses to the next question in our survey, the advantages can be compelling, ample, and rewarding.

# What Are the Rewards for Writing Textbooks?

A common notion among their academic peers may be that textbook authors are just "in it for the money." Countering this assumption, a minority (37%) of survey respondents ranked financial rewards among the reasons they enjoy their textbook writing experiences. Broadening and deepening their own knowledge (70%) and reaching and teaching many more students than they could through their own classes (67%) are the primary motivations for our participants. An even richer perspective on the true rewards of textbook writing can be gleaned from considering authors' reactions to whether their textbook writing experiences yield a fair return on time spent.

## WHAT IS CONSIDERED TO BE A FAIR RETURN?

Table 23.1 displays respondents' reactions to the question, "Does your textbook(s) provide a fair return on the time you invest in it (them)? Why or why not?" More than 70% of respondents think the financial rewards are worth the tremendous effort they put into preparing their textbooks, with 22% of the overall sample focusing on the financial rewards alone. These results tell us that, indeed, the financial incentive is strong. One participant's reaction to whether the return was fair was,

> I would say so. The first edition is the most time-consuming and the royalty checks are not huge in the first year, but tended to increase each year after that. The first edition took about three years total to write, the second took one year to update and revise rather substantially, and the subsequent editions have taken only a few months every two to three years. The money continues to grow, so the return is certainly worth the effort.

Royalty-based publishing agreements reward performance on an individual basis, so it's impossible to describe a specific compensation range. Successful textbook authors might earn hundreds of thousands of dollars annually for each title they write, but it should be kept in mind that such sums are exceedingly rare. They are associated with courses featuring only the largest enrollments, such as introduction to psychology, social psychology, or human development, and with a handful of best sellers. Most successful textbook authors can expect to earn a few thousand or several tens of thousands of dollars annually. A popular textbook can be revised and published for decades, however, so over time even modest royalty checks can add up to significant amounts.

### TABLE 23.1

**Survey Participants' Responses to "Does your textbook(s) provide a fair return on the time you invest in it (them)?"**

| Response category | Participants[a] (%) |
| --- | --- |
| Yes, financially/Yes, personally and professionally | 27 |
| Yes, financially | 22 |
| Yes, nonspecific reason | 20 |
| No, financially/Yes, personally and professionally | 10 |
| Undecided/Nonspecific mixed opinion | 8 |
| Yes, personally and professionally | 4 |
| No, financially detrimental | 4 |
| Yes, financially/No, personally and professionally | 2 |
| No, personally and professionally | 2 |
| No, nonspecific reason | 2 |
| No, financially/No, personally and professionally | 0 |

*Note.* Data from Berk and Wakely (2015).
[a]Rounded to nearest full percent.

## ROYALTY CHECKS AREN'T THE WHOLE STORY

We intentionally phrased the question about fair return on time invested so it didn't specifically refer to financial rewards. What's most revealing is how many respondents interpreted the question to include personal and professional returns on their labors—strongly indicating that rewards other than royalty checks are also highly valued.

More than 40% mentioned that personal and professional benefits accruing from their textbook projects constitute a fair return. Of that group, one in four feels that nonmonetary rewards are worth the effort, even when the financial rewards fall short of expectations, as reflected in this typical comment:

> I'm grateful to get paid well to do this work. But the greatest return is not financial. . . . To be able to share my passion for our science with a broad audience is the best return on my investment of time.

Realistically, not every textbook succeeds, and new authors must understand that embarking on any textbook project involves some measure of risk and potential for disappointment. As one participant described his or her experience, "It was so much work to do, and then nobody seemed to care about it. It languished. Sad, really, because it was good."

For bold new authors who accept the risks, are confident they have something important and relevant to add to their audiences' teaching and learning experiences, and are ready to commit the massive amounts of required time and effort, what does the future of higher education publishing look like?

# What Is the Future of Textbook Publishing?

Will this chapter on textbook writing seem quaint or obsolete shortly after its publication? Is the occupation of textbook author doomed to become a casualty of the digital age? Will psychology textbooks as we know them in the first decades of the 21st century even exist a few years from now?

## TEXTBOOKS WILL PERSIST IN SOME FORM

We believe strongly that textbooks and the course narratives they represent will continue to be relevant and vital components of learners' and instructors' educational experiences for many years to come. The dominant print model, however, is gradually evolving to encompass hybrid and fully digital models. In response, so too must textbook authors expand their skills and push the boundaries of the craft they practice. There will always be a role for excellent teachers and scholars to create course narratives that guide students' journey of discovery through the fascinating world of psychology. But how authors compile information, develop pedagogy, and construct learning experiences that successfully support the delivery of instruction certainly will be different from how textbook authors currently do their work.

## HYBRID AND DIGITAL PRODUCT MODELS

What kind of teaching and publishing environments do our survey respondents expect the next generation of psychology textbook authors to encounter? It should come as no surprise the vast majority identified the changing publishing environment and difficulties with publishers (77%) and the ongoing transition to digital learning and publishing models (73%) as the key challenges facing tomorrow's textbook authors.

Conventional wisdom points to an evolving product model that is quickly moving from print to digital. Yet, according to a Fall 2015 Student Monitor survey of 1,200 undergraduate students at 100 four-year universities and colleges, 49% of students polled preferred reading textbooks in print or preferred not to read large amounts of onscreen text. Even more surprising is the finding that of students who previously had purchased or were aware of e-textbooks and who planned to be in school the following term, 39% said they would be unlikely or very unlikely to purchase an e-textbook. Only 34% indicated they would be somewhat likely or very likely to purchase one. In fact, just 12% strongly agreed with the statement "I would prefer to study with an e-textbook than a printed textbook," and another 12% somewhat agreed with it (Student Monitor, 2015).

A glimpse into the preferences of tomorrow's college students based on current technologies is provided by a 2014 survey conducted by Scholastic and YouGov. This study found that 65% of 6- to 17-year-olds agreed "they'd want to read print books even if eBooks were available," an increase from 60% in the 2012 survey (Scholastic and YouGov, 2014, p. 68). These studies and others suggest that a significant number of students will want print textbooks to provide part or all of their courses' narratives for some time to come. Therefore, it is incumbent upon publishers and authors to develop attractive and effective online learning experiences that overcome the current reluctance to fully transition away from print learning resources if they want customers to eagerly embrace those product models.

## WHAT DO TEXTBOOK AUTHORS NEED TO KNOW?

Our advice to future textbook authors is to anticipate a protracted evolution and expect that hybrid product models (print plus digital) will be the norm for many years. For a host of reasons, such as increasingly efficient used book and rental competition facilitated by the web, publishers will push hard to transition from print to hybrid and fully digital product models. Therefore, tomorrow's textbook authors need to think in both print and digital terms, particularly when writing for larger courses that can sustain the substantial investments required to create interactive simulations, adaptive learning content, video, and other online pedagogical tools.

Future textbook authors would do well to learn basic coding, so they can speak to their publishers' increasingly digital development and production teams in vocabulary they understand. Textbook authors also will need to think in terms of digital tools and more visual workflows, such as write-in templates that automatically code content, storyboards, wireframes, and Agile product development practices. Such tools and processes are necessary to create the digital components that in the short run will be integrated with printed textbooks—and that in all likelihood will become the primary means of delivering textbooks or course narratives during the next generation of authors' lifetimes.

## *The Challenge Ahead*

Although a single chapter is unable to do justice to the dynamic and evolving nature of writing higher education textbooks, our survey participants' richly informative responses assisted us in identifying key trends and common themes. Respondents consistently expressed profound, wide-ranging satisfactions even as they described many challenges looming on the horizon. One author's comments sum up particularly well how our survey participants view the uncertain future of textbook writing:

> The biggest challenge is the changing world of publishing. Printed textbooks are no longer the primary product of text publishing, and the changes are unsettling. Publishers seem to be trying all kinds of things to keep their monopoly on the college audience when students have many options to purchasing outrageously expensive texts. Future authors must be tech savvy because publishers are focusing on technology and not on scholarship. I would like for publishers to recognize that media flash is not a substitute for information. Another challenge for textbook authors is the changing world of higher education, specifically the increasing popularity of online instruction. This format does

not lend itself to traditional textbooks, so future authors must adapt to this format to make online instruction more effective than it is currently. I would like to see research (not just opinion) about what makes online courses successful and what detracts from their effectiveness. Another challenge for me as an author is maintaining a cordial and productive relationship with publishers, who are undergoing corporate changes that cause personnel turnover. Although losing an editor has always been an unsettling event, that situation has become so common that I don't know who my editor is at one of my publishers. I would like for this challenge to be resolved by bringing more stability to publishing, but I do not see this outcome in the near future.

Although our survey respondents identified myriad problems and uncertainties, and a few even expressed doubts about the relevance of textbook authors in an increasingly digital era, the message to new textbook authors is still one of encouragement: The best way to be part of the future is to take an active role in helping to build and shape it.

## *References*

Baron, N. S. (2015). *Words onscreen: The fate of reading in a digital world.* New York, NY: Oxford University Press.

Berk, L. E., & Wakely, S. W. (2015). *Textbook writing career survey.* Unpublished manuscript.

Green, K. C. (2016). *Going digital: Faculty perspectives on digital and OER course materials.* Retrieved from http://www.campuscomputing.net/goingdigital2016

Sasser-Coen, J. A. (1993). Qualitative changes in creativity in the second half of life: A life-span developmental perspective. *Journal of Creative Behavior, 27,* 18–27. http://dx.doi.org/10.1002/j.2162-6057.1993.tb01383.x

Scholastic and YouGov. (2014). *Kids and family reading report* (5th ed.). Retrieved from http://www.scholastic.com/readingreport/Scholastic-KidsAndFamilyReadingReport-5thEdition.pdf?v=100

Student Monitor. (2015). *Converting data to insight, fall 2015,* slides 104–106. Retrieved from http://www.studentmonitor.com/f15/f15base.pdf

Thornton, P. H. (2004). *Markets from culture: Institutional logics and organizational decisions in higher education publishing.* Stanford, CA: Business Books.

Tyton Partners. (2013). *Learning to adapt: A case for accelerating adaptive learning in higher education.* Retrieved from http://tytonpartners.com/library/accelerating-adaptive-learning-in-higher-education

*Paul T. Bartone and Ann T. Landes*

# Military Psychologists

24

The military psychology career path includes a wide range of specialties and activities, offering many exciting job opportunities in clinical, research, academic, and consulting areas. Some military psychologists serve in uniform, whereas many others work in civilian positions within the military organization. What unifies them all is a desire to

Colonel (Retired) Paul T. Bartone, PhD, is a professor and senior research fellow at the Center for Technology and National Security Policy, National Defense University. Bartone served as the research psychology consultant to the Army Surgeon General and is a past-president of the American Psychological Association's (APA) Society for Military Psychology (Division 19). He received a BA in psychology from the University of Massachusetts, Boston, and a PhD in human development from the University of Chicago.

Ann T. Landes, PhD, is a psychologist for the Department of Veterans Affairs. As a primary care psychologist and health behavior coordinator, she cares for and provides services to veterans and their families. She serves as an outpatient clinic geropsychologist.

The authors are very grateful to Gerald P. Krueger for his many helpful comments and suggestions on the manuscript. Thanks also to Kathryn T. Lindsey and Gerald P. Krueger for providing their personal career reflections.

http://dx.doi.org/10.1037/15960-025
*Career Paths in Psychology: Where Your Degree Can Take You, Third Edition*, R. J. Sternberg (Editor)

apply psychological knowledge and techniques to improve the lives of men and women serving in the military, as well as veterans and families.

Currently, about 1.38 million men and women are serving in the active duty military in the United States alone, with more than 1.94 million family members, including spouses and children (Department of Defense [DoD], 2010). In addition, more than 848,000 serve in the Reserves and National Guard, with another 1.1 million family members. Military veterans make up an even larger population, with more than 21.5 million veterans living in the United States as of September 30, 2014. Other countries also have millions of military personnel, veterans, and families, many of whom are in need of psychological services.

Military psychologists serve this population in myriad ways, in both clinical and research roles. This chapter provides a snapshot of the major career options available to military psychologists. Many choose to serve as psychologists in uniform, whereas others work as civilians. Military psychologists can be found in state and local government agencies as well as in the private sector. The vast majority of military psychologists in the United States, however, are employed by either the DoD or the Department of Veterans Affairs (VA), and so that will be our focus.

We begin by describing what military psychologists do, both in research and clinical domains. This discussion is followed by practical information on how to prepare for a career in military psychology and about some of the educational opportunities available for students. We next discuss the personal attributes that are valuable for military psychologists and then present some of the pros and cons of this career path. Finally, several personal stories are provided from psychologists who have taken the military psychology path.

# What Do Military Psychologists Do?

Military psychologists can work in the military as either research psychologists or clinical psychologists. Alternatively, they can work in the VA as either research psychologists or clinical psychologists.

## RESEARCH PSYCHOLOGISTS IN THE MILITARY

Research psychologists in the military apply the principles and methods of psychology toward understanding and improving and sustaining the health, well-being, morale, and performance of military personnel and families. Probably every specialty within psychology is represented within military psychology, from neuroscience and physiology to personality and organizational psychology. Major focus areas include the following:

- *Neuroscience and neuropsychology*, including research examining the neuropsychological effects of exposure (and threat of exposure) to chemical and biological weapons; reducing and preventing traumatic brain injury (TBI) and posttraumatic stress disorder (PTSD); exploring the biogenetics of PTSD, TBI, and other mental health problems.
- *Human factors and physiology*, understanding and predicting human performance in extremely harsh environments, effects of sleep and sleep loss, operating complex military equipment and weapon systems.
- *Cognitive psychology*, decision making, basic cognitive processes, sensation, perception, enhancing cognitive processing and decision making under stress.
- *Developmental, social, and health psychology*, identifying the psychosocial effects of stress and how to maximize stress resilience; understanding and preventing suicide; developing more effective leaders; improving morale and psychological well-being.
- *Industrial and organizational psychology*, selection and assessment; social and organizational influences on human performance; cohesion, leadership in organizations; increasing cohesion across diverse organizations, coalitions, interagency operations.

Regardless of specialty, military research psychologists are experts in research methods and statistics, assessment, and developing valid and reliable assessment tools and strategies. They also teach and provide expert consultation and reports to military leaders and policymakers (Bartone, Pastel, & Vaitkus, 2010). Much of military research psychology is conducted in laboratory settings such as the Walter Reed Army Institute of Research in Silver Spring, MD; the U.S. Naval Health Research Center in San Diego, CA; and the U.S. Air Force Research Laboratory near Dayton, OH. But wherever they work, military research psychologists are trained and prepared to deploy anywhere in the world to provide research and support to commanders. Since at least the 1991 Persian Gulf War, teams of behavioral scientists led by military psychologists have traveled to conflict areas to study stress, health, and performance in deployed military units (Krueger, 2010). These studies have led to multiple policy changes to protect health and enhance performance. Military psychologists also study ethical behaviors, seeking to understand and prevent problems such as mistreatment of prisoners and sexual misconduct (Bartone, 2010; McBride, Thomas, McGurk, Wood, & Bliese, 2010).

## CLINICAL PSYCHOLOGISTS IN THE MILITARY

Military clinical psychologists do all of the things that other clinical psychologists do, including diagnosis, treatment, and consultation. The difference is the populations being served: military members and their families. Their work is mainly in military hospital settings in the United States and overseas, most often in multidisciplinary teams that may include psychiatrists, social workers, and psychiatric nurses. Typical assignments last for 3–4 years, followed by new jobs in other locations. This ensures the military clinical psychologist gains a broad range of experiences and skills to better serve the military population.

In addition to diagnostic assessments, treatment, and interventions, military clinical psychologists consult extensively with other health care providers, patients, and family members. They develop and deliver a range of educational programs aimed at reducing mental health problems in the military workforce. The duties of the clinical psychologist are quite similar across the different service branches, although assignment locations and populations served vary with the service. U.S. Navy psychologists work mainly with Navy and Marine personnel, while Army and Air Force psychologists work mainly within their own services. These traditional service boundaries are becoming less rigid, however, as the U.S. military consolidates into more joint structures and operations. It is increasingly common for military psychologists to be assigned to joint facilities such as the Walter Reed National Military Medical Center in Bethesda, MD, where they provide services for Army, Navy, Marine, and Air Force personnel and family members.

Although military clinical psychologists spend most of their time in medical centers and clinics within the United States, they are at times assigned to overseas military facilities in Germany, Korea, Spain, Italy, or the United Kingdom. Psychologists also deploy along with troops on training and operational missions. For example, Navy clinicians may serve as psychologists on board aircraft carriers. Psychologists may deploy as part of mobile medical facilities such as the Mobile Army Surgical Hospital (MASH) or as part of Combat Stress Control (CSC) teams. Psychologists deploying with the troops take on significant responsibility and authority, also gaining valuable experience in addressing the diverse mental health needs of military personnel. Operational deployments normally last for no more than 6 months, although during the Iraq and Afghanistan conflicts some psychologists deployed for longer.

## MILITARY PSYCHOLOGISTS IN THE DEPARTMENT OF VETERANS AFFAIRS

The VA operates one of the nation's largest health care systems, caring for the physical, psychological, emotional, social, and vocational needs of military veterans and families. Most psychologists are employed within the Veterans Health Administration, which includes 150 medical centers and more than 1,400 outpatient clinics, veteran centers, nursing homes, and domiciliaries. As of 2014, more than 9 million veterans were enrolled to receive VA health care services (U.S. Department of Veterans Affairs, 2016a).

VA psychologists are professionally trained and licensed to provide interventions for prevention and treatment of various problems that veterans and their families may experience. Veterans may seek treatment for PTSD, depression, anxiety, TBI, chronic disease and pain management, substance abuse disorders, and adjustment to life transitions The VA psychologist usually is integrated into a health care team within the medical facility. Hence, in addition to mental health clinics, settings include primary care, inpatient psychiatry, and inpatient medical, surgery, rehabilitation medicine, geriatrics, and palliative care.

The VA also provides many opportunities to conduct research. The VA Office of Research and Development (U.S. Department of Veterans Affairs, 2016b) sponsors research focused on health-related issues and health care innovation. Research projects often are joint collaborations with universities, other federal agencies (e.g., DoD), private industry, and nonprofit organizations. Current VA research topics include PTSD treatment and prevention, TBI, Alzheimer's disease, caregiver stress, genomics, homelessness, infectious disease, mental health, women's health, obesity, kidney disease, and complementary and alternative medicine.

## *Preparation Needed*

The typical course of education for a military psychologist begins with a bachelor's degree with a major in psychology or some related field. This is followed by a doctorate degree, which for military clinical psychologists can be a PhD or PsyD in clinical or counseling psychology. For clinical psychologists, the doctorate must be from a program accredited by the American Psychological Association (APA). Also required is a 1-year clinical internship in an APA-approved program, and a current, unrestricted license to practice psychology.

Research psychologists in uniform must hold a PhD from a research-oriented academic program, which can be in any area of psychology, including experimental, social and organizational, developmental, personality, health, or neuropsychology. Whether clinical or research, military psychologists must be U.S. citizens and must be able to meet basic minimum health and fitness standards. A security background check is required, because all officers are granted a secret security clearance. Applicants must be no older than 42 years (waiverable) and must pass a basic health physical and a fitness test. The U.S. military does not discriminate on the basis of race, gender, religion, ethnicity, or sexual orientation. APA and its Division 19 (Society for Military Psychology) provide a number of excellent resources for the prospective military clinical psychologist, available online (APA Division 19, 2016).

## INTERNSHIPS

The U.S. military sponsors a world-renowned predoctoral clinical internship program that prepares students for licensing and practice in all areas of psychology. Internships provide an intensive year-long experience of didactic and clinical training, including rotations in hospital and clinic as well as operational settings. Operational settings can include brief stints on submarines, aircraft carriers, and military training exercises. Interns are trained in the assessment of psychological disorders using multiple methods and learn a variety of therapeutic interventions emphasizing evidence-based and validated approaches. Special attention is given to the development of communication and consultation skills, deemed critical for success in the multidisciplinary military health care environment. Interns learn how to conduct effective emergency consultations, evaluations for personnel actions, and comprehensive mental health evaluations for medical evaluation boards.

The U.S. Army generally offers five 1-year APA-accredited clinical psychology internships, and the Navy offers two. Each internship site sponsors six interns per year. Applicants are usually in their final year of graduate coursework or working on their dissertations at the time of application. Army interns attend a 10-week Basic Officer Leadership Course (BOLC) in San Antonio, TX, during the summer before the internship, and Navy interns attend a 5-week Navy orientation program at Newport, Rhode Island.

The U.S. Air Force provides up to 25 fully funded 1-year internship positions in clinical psychology at three Air Force medical treatment facilities located in Maryland, Texas, and Ohio. All are APA-accredited programs. Air Force interns complete a 5-week basic training course at San Antonio, TX, before starting their internships. All internships are full time, and include a stipend between $75,000 and $83,000 per year depending on location, with about 20% of this amount tax exempt. Interns incur a 3-year military service obligation after their training. Table 24.1 lists the current U.S. military clinical psychology internship sites.

The VA also provides extensive clinical psychology training opportunities, including 598 internships and 390 fully funded fellowship

## TABLE 24.1

**U.S. Military Clinical Psychology Internship Programs**

| Service branch | Location | Website |
| --- | --- | --- |
| Army | Eisenhower Army Medical Center, Augusta, GA | http://www.ddeamc.amedd.army.mil/GME/InterResPrograms/CPIP/ |
| | Walter Reed National Military Medical Center, Bethesda, MD | http://www.wrnmmc.capmed.mil/Research Education/GME/SitePages/Psychology/Army%20Psychology.aspx |
| | Tripler Army Medical Center, Honolulu, HI | http://www.tamc.amedd.army.mil/offices/Psychology/training.htm |
| | Madigan Army Medical Center, Tacoma, WA | http://www.mamc.amedd.army.mil/education/graduate-medical-education/internships/clinical-psychology-internship.aspx |
| | Brooke Army Medical Center, San Antonio, TX | http://www.bamc.amedd.army.mil/staff/education/allied-health/behavioral-medicine/clinical-psychology-internship-program.asp |
| Navy | Walter Reed National Military Medical Center, Bethesda, MD | http://www.wrnmmc.capmed.mil/Research Education/GME/SitePages/Psychology/Internship.aspx |
| | Naval Medical Center, San Diego, CA | http://www.wrnmmc.capmed.mil/Research Education/GME/SitePages/Psychology/NMCSDInternship.aspx |
| Air Force | Malcolm Grow USAF Medical Clinic, Joint Base Andrews, MD | http://www.79mdw.af.mil/shared/media/document/AFD-150126-015.pdf |
| | Wilford Hall Ambulatory Surgical Center, Lackland Air Force Base, TX | http://www.59mdw.af.mil/About/Education-Training/ClinicalPsychologyInternship.aspx |
| | Wright-Patterson USAF Medical Center, Wright-Patterson Air Force Base, OH | http://www.wpafb.af.mil/shared/media/document/AFD-151002-034.pdf |

positions each year (U.S. Department of Veterans Affairs, 2016d). VA internships emphasize developing professionals who can accurately assess and diagnose patient problems, employ evidence-based treatments, conduct research, teach, and supervise, while upholding ethical and professional standards. Clinical skills are enhanced by working with people from different cultures, under the supervision of experienced clinical experts. Interns experience rotations in behavioral medicine, gerontology, substance abuse treatment, trauma and rehabilitation psychology, couples and family therapy, neuropsychology, palliative care, and homelessness rehabilitation.

Stipends for interns and fellows are competitive, and adjusted for local cost of living rates. Currently, annual stipends range from $23,974 to $28,382 for interns, and from $42,239 to $52,709 for fellows. Intern and fellow appointments are full time for a 12-month period (U.S. Department of Veterans Affairs, 2016c). Federal holidays, annual, and sick leave are provided for all trainees within the VA system (for more information on how to qualify, see U.S. Department of Veterans Affairs, 2016d; or search using keywords "VA Psychology Training").

## HEALTH PROFESSIONS SCHOLARSHIP PROGRAM

Each military service offers generous scholarships to psychology students under the Health Professions Scholarship Program or HPSP. Qualifying students receive full paid tuition, plus a generous monthly stipend of more than $2,000. The Navy awards five of these scholarships each year, and each provides 3 years of support. For more on the Navy HPSP program, see their scholarships guidance (Walter Reed National Military Medical Center, 2012b).

The Air Force also provides awards under the HPSP. Terms and eligibility criteria are similar as for the other services (for more information, see U.S. Air Force, 2016). Details on the Army's HPSP program also are available online (U.S. Army, 2016).

## UNIFORMED SERVICES UNIVERSITY OF THE HEALTH SCIENCES

Within the USUHS, the Medical and Clinical Psychology program offers PhDs in both medical research psychology and clinical psychology. The program is designed primarily for students who are already in the military and wish to become psychologists. As commissioned officers, students continue to receive their military pay and benefits while attending the 4–5 year program, and their university tuition is paid by their individual military service. A small number of civilian students also are admitted to the program each year. For these students, tuition is also paid, and there is no service obligation.

The USUHS medical and clinical psychology program combines psychology with an emphasis on biomedical and health sciences. Basic and applied approaches to health psychology and behavioral medicine are emphasized. The goal is to train scientist—practitioners with a broad understanding of the psychosocial, psychobiological, and behavioral factors involved in mental health and adaptation. Courses cover topics in the etiology, prevention, and treatment of illness, substance abuse, and mental health, as well as links between physical and mental health. Applications are welcome from Reserve and National Guard enlisted personnel as well as civilians. Most students are commissioned as officers before coming to USUHS. Each service admits around three or four new students to the program each year. As entry requirements differ somewhat across the services (Army, Navy, Air Force), the best starting point is to contact the medical recruiting office of the respective service. More information about medical and clinical psychology and prospective student admissions is available at on the USUHS site (2016a, 2016b).

## POSTDOCTORAL FELLOWSHIPS

Each of the services offers postdoctoral fellowships or residencies that allow military clinical psychologists to prepare for licensing exams while enhancing their knowledge and skills in particular areas, including clinical neuropsychology (Walter Reed National Military Medical Center and Tripler Army Medical Center), clinical health psychology (Tripler Army Medical Center), clinical child/pediatric psychology (Tripler Army Medical Center), and forensic psychology (Walter Reed National Military Medical Center). Fellowships are available to active-duty psychologists who have completed their doctoral degrees and obtained a state license.

The Navy offers two postdoc fellowships at Portsmouth, VA. Training emphasizes assessment and treatment of PTSD, depression, TBI, chronic pain, family issues, and substance or alcohol abuse. Experience is also provided in dealing with severe mental health conditions requiring inpatient psychiatric treatment in a military context. More information is available online (Walter Reed National Military Medical Center, 2012a).

## LICENSED DIRECT ACCESSION PROGRAM

Clinical and counseling psychologists who are already licensed can enter the military through the Licensed Direct Accession Program. Candidates must meet the same age and fitness standards as other military officers.

To learn more about Direct Accession, contact a medical program officer recruiter or visit the Walter Reed National Military Medical Center website (n.d.).

## Attributes Needed for Success

What do you need to succeed as a military psychologist? Of course, you should be well trained and knowledgeable in your profession, whether clinical or research psychology. You also should have a desire to work with the military. Military personnel, veterans, and family members can experience the full gamut of life adaptation and mental health challenges. Military psychologists in uniform must be willing to deploy alongside military personnel, assuming many of the same hardships and risks.

A basic level of physical fitness is needed to go where military personnel go and to demonstrate acceptance of the values and standards of the organization. This is especially important for uniformed military psychologists, who will work directly with troops. An appreciation of variety is helpful because military psychologists typically encounter such a wide range of situations and problems. They also may have to change jobs and locations fairly often. It is important to be able to work well with other professionals because psychological services usually are provided as part of an integrated health team. Researchers usually work in collaborative teams.

Military psychologists must adhere to the morals and ethics of the psychology profession. As recognized experts in human behavior, they are role models in upholding the highest ethical standards for the humane treatment of the troops, coworkers, peers, and family members as well as enemy combatants, noncombatants, and prisoners of war.

Essential qualities for success as a VA psychologist are similar. First, one must meet the educational and training standards for doctoral-level clinical practitioners or researchers. Other valuable attributes include a commitment to providing quality care for veterans and family members, curiosity, flexibility, adaptability, and a desire for continual learning.

The ability to communicate with people from various backgrounds and educational levels, both as a provider of services and as a team member within the workplace, is a valuable attribute. Furthermore, because of the diversity of the veteran population and their needs, the capacity to practice as a generalist is important. Successful VA psychologists are guided by strong ethical and moral codes of conduct.

## Pros and Cons of Being a Military Psychologist

The major benefits of working as a military psychologist are intrinsic. As a military psychologist, you have the satisfaction of knowing that your professional work is making a positive difference in the lives of thousands of military people and their families. And you get to see the results of your work, in the faces of the young men and women who are helped by your interventions, and sometimes in policy changes informed by your research. It is also great to be working as part of a team. Wherever you are assigned, you can expect a great deal of support from those around you, peers and supervisors. You also have the satisfaction of knowing that your work is contributing to national and global security. As Etzioni (2007) reminds us, security is the first and most essential human right.

In addition to the highly competitive salary, both uniformed and civilian military psychologists receive excellent benefits, including 30 vacation days per year, low-cost life insurance, and regular cost-of-living increases. The military pays for all job-related moving expenses. Uniformed psychologists may retire after 20 years of service regardless of age, and civilians at 65 years old. In addition to the pension, civilians and uniformed psychologists also have the option to contribute to a Thrift Savings Plan, with matching employer contributions. Free medical and dental care is provided to uniformed military psychologists and their families. Civilian psychologists also receive low-cost health and dental insurance. Military personnel, family members, and retirees have access to an excellent global network of military commissaries and on-post or on-base department stores where groceries and other items can be purchased at cost savings. Uniformed psychologists also have available first-class fitness facilities and other recreational resources. Most military organizations pay expenses for travel to professional meetings, and facilitate publication of research in refereed journals. Clinicians are sponsored in obtaining continuing education credits.

There are some disadvantages to being a military psychologist. Whether uniformed or civilian, military psychologists work within hierarchical, bureaucratic organizations, and the bureaucracy at times can impede the work. Permission usually is needed to travel for a professional conference, and the chain-of-command is sometimes slow to respond. Also, most papers and manuscripts must undergo a security review, which sometimes can delay publication.

An additional drawback for uniformed military psychologists is that one cannot always choose your assignment locations or timing of job moves. But it is possible to negotiate for new assignments and professional development opportunities. Another disadvantage is that as a federal government employee, you may be restricted from accepting outside employment such as consulting or part-time teaching. However, teaching in your official capacity is generally encouraged. Another drawback is that in some settings, military rank still trumps professional expertise, so your recommendations may be overruled by a nonpsychologist (e.g., a medical commander) who happens to outrank you.

Finally, when military psychologists deploy on training or mission activities, they can be exposed to the same stressors and dangers as the military personnel they serve. These stressors include separation from family; long working hours; and the risk of injury, disease, or death. Military psychologists working as civilians and in the VA generally don't face these deployment-related risks.

Choosing to serve veterans and their families within the VA system brings numerous rewards as well. First and foremost, you are helping to make lives better in the wake of major life changes, such as reintegration into civilian life, or recovery from traumatic injuries. The VA psychologist has the advantage of working in an environment free from the pressure of insurance-related issues and costs. Additionally, because of the multidisciplinary teams and comprehensive services available either onsite or through virtual interventions, you have multiple options for ensuring that veterans and family members can obtain the support services needed.

As with any job, there are drawbacks. The VA is a big government organization, and psychologists must deal with many bureaucratic procedures and regulations. Insufficient federal funding can result in staff shortages and inadequate office space, equipment, and administrative support. VA psychologists also may be asked to relocate to underserved areas.

## Salary Range

Military psychologists earn excellent pay, generally more than other psychologists. All uniformed psychologists are commissioned as officers, most often at the O-3 rank because of their advanced degrees (captains in the Army and Air Force; lieutenants in the Navy). Basic pay is the same for research and clinical psychologists and is tied to rank and years of service. In 2015, the annual base pay at this beginning level is $46,944. Additional pay for housing adds another $24,000 (tax free) on average depending on assignment location and marital status. New military psychologists therefore can expect to earn about $71,000 per year. This grows to around $86,000 after 4 years of service. After 10 years of service and promotion to the O-5 level, the pay is around $108,000 per year. Most military clinical psychologists also receive specialty pay of $2,000 to $5,000 per year and may receive additional incentive pay depending on assignment location (Defense Finance and Accounting Service, 2016). In some years, generous recruitment and retention bonuses also are offered to psychologists.

Following the Iraq and Afghanistan conflicts, there was a marked increase in military personnel and veterans seeking psychological services, and a shortage of clinical military psychologists. This has led to additional job opportunities for civilian psychologists working with active duty military personnel as well as veterans. For DoD positions, the government civilian pay grade ranges from GS-12 to GS-13, with a salary of $86,000 to $111,000 depending on experience. Civil pay rates for VA positions are comparable, ranging from GS-11 to GS-13, or $57,000 to $119,000 (based on a search of https://www.USAJobs.gov). Benefits vary with the position, but generally include a generous pension plan and employee-sponsored health and dental insurance.

# Personal Reflections

To provide a better flavor for the life and career possibilities offered by military psychology, four personal stories are presented in the following sections. In addition to the chapter authors, we include accounts from two distinguished military psychologists. Kathryn T. Lindsey served as a clinical psychologist for the U.S. Navy and is a past-president of APA Division 19, Society for Military Psychology. Gerald P. Krueger was a research psychologist for the U.S. Army and is past-president of APA Division 19, Society for Military Psychology; APA Division 21, Applied Experimental and Engineering Psychology; and the Human Factors and Ergonomics Society, Potomac Chapter. Both are now retired from military service but continue to work actively in the field.

## KATHRYN T. LINDSEY

I completed my undergraduate work as a psychology major at Iowa State University, with a scholarship from the Naval Reserve Officers Training Corps (NROTC) program. The NROTC program covers full tuition costs, books, and fees and also provides a small monthly living stipend. In return, NROTC students serve in the military for 4 years after graduation. I was attracted to the Navy, and had a desire to serve. My father was in the Navy, and from him I learned the value of service to country. My two sisters had also served, one in the Navy and one in the U.S. Marines.

Upon graduating in 1988, I was given an officer's commission. I served the next 12 years in a variety of interesting jobs, including as Protocol Officer in Italy, Administrative Department Head in London, and Manpower Planner in the Bureau of Naval Personnel in Arlington, VA. During this time, I attended the Naval Postgraduate School (NPS) in Monterey, CA, receiving a master's degree in management in 1998. My master's research looked at the psychological factors associated with extremism and gang membership among military prison inmates. Results were used to inform Congressional investigative panels on gangs in the military.

I always wanted to be a clinical psychologist, and so I applied to the USUHS in Bethesda, MD, and was accepted into the Medical and Clinical Psychology program. USUHS was a fantastic developmental experience. In addition to coursework, I gained supervised clinical experience in personality and neuropsychological assessment, diagnostic interviewing, mental status exams, treatment of phobias, anxiety disorders including PTSD, depression, seasonal affective disorder, substance abuse, and marital and family therapy. I had the opportunity to work in diverse settings, including the National Naval Medical Center (Bethesda, MD), the Walter Reed Army Medical Center (Washington, DC), U.S. Naval Academy (Annapolis, MD), Baltimore VA Hospital, and the Northern Virginia Psychiatric Group in Fairfax, VA. My clinical internship at the Naval Medical Center included rotations providing a range of services to active duty service members, wounded warriors, family members, and retirees. I finished my PhD in 2005 and left USUHS well prepared to take on the challenges of a Navy clinical psychologist.

Next was a postdoc as the director of the Navy's Substance Abuse Rehabilitation Program (SARP) in Naples, Italy. My later assignments included Head of the National Naval Medical Center's Behavioral Health Department in Bethesda, MD; director of the Midshipman Development Center at the Naval Academy, Annapolis, MD; assistant psychology professor at the Naval Academy, and head of the Mental Health Department at the Naval Health Clinic, Annapolis, MD. In all of these assignments, I was a respected partner on the Navy health care team, delivering valued psychological services and support to Navy Academy midshipmen, active duty men and women, family members, veterans, and retirees. On reflection, my career as a Navy clinical psychologist brought many rewards, but the best is knowing that my service made a positive difference in so many lives.

## GERALD P. KRUEGER

I earned my psychology BA and an ROTC commission in the military police at the University of Dayton. In my first active duty assignment at the Human Engineering Laboratory at Aberdeen, MD, I examined performance of soldiers operating new equipment systems. Later, I served in Vietnam at DoD's Advanced Research Projects Agency (DARPA) in Saigon, where I mentored Vietnamese officers testing new materials and equipment. That fascinating experience convinced me military research psychology was right for me.

Under the U.S. Army Medical Service Corps' graduate psychology program, I spent 3 years at Johns Hopkins University, receiving MA and PhD degrees in experimental psychology. After graduation, I served in assignments at several Army Labs doing research or directing others doing experiments in the lab, in simulators, or during operational field studies aimed at examining and predicting soldier performance under stressful working conditions. For example, at the Aeromedical Research Lab, Fort Rucker, AL, I studied performance of helicopter pilots while wearing chemical protective suits, wearing night vision goggles, conducting sustained flight operations, carrying out map-of-the-earth flights, and testing new forms of antihistamines. It was thrilling to collect pilot performance data while I was seated in the rear of helicopters on such missions.

At the Walter Reed Army Institute of Research (WRAIR), I directed studies on effects of soldier sleep deprivation during sustained operations. Colleagues and I studied specialized aviation teams, tank crews, infantry troops, and security guards at nuclear storage sites. I developed an international network of more than 500 researchers and military strategists in nine nations to inform North Atlantic Treaty Organization's (NATO) doctrine for sustained and continuous military operations. It was here as a headquarters staff officer that I learned how to manage research programs effectively and to disseminate results as recommendations to improve military policy at the highest levels.

After some success and promotion to the rank of colonel, I was chosen to serve as commander and technical director of the U.S. Army Research Institute of Environmental Medicine (USARIEM) in Natick, MA. Our mission was to help "sustain and enhance the health and performance of military forces in training or in combat" (USARIEM, 2016). We integrated psychology and physiology research principles into multidisciplinary studies of soldier performance under environmental stressors, including high heat, extreme cold, high altitude, and sleep deprivation. We also evaluated advanced military nutrition products and the biophysics of uniform design and made advances in neuroscience and exercise physiology. Studies examined the harshest missions of Army Rangers, Special Forces, airborne parachutists, and light infantry and also gave special attention to the performance of women soldiers.

USARIEM psychologists led the development of soldier-friendly medical guides aimed at preventing psychological, performance, and health-related problems during deployments. We created pocket hand-books used by thousands of Army, Navy, Marine Corps and Air Force personnel deployed to the Persian Gulf War (1990–1991), and later to Somalia, Bosnia, and Haiti. The institute received many accolades for making research findings available in understandable form. My 25-year career as a uniformed Army research psychologist was always exciting, challenging, and quite rewarding intellectually and professionally.

## PAUL T. BARTONE

After finishing my PhD at the University of Chicago in 1984, I began the job hunt. After much looking and several interviews, I had three attractive offers. One was from the Walter Reed Army Institute of Research (WRAIR), which had posted an ad in the APA Monitor. I chose the Walter Reed job, expecting that my research on stress and health would be applied there, as opposed to so much academic research, which seems to just sit on the shelf. I was surprised to learn that before starting work at Walter Reed, I would have to attend a 3-month officer basic training course at Fort Sam Houston, TX. But this struck me as an interesting challenge. So I accepted a direct commission as an Army Captain, with a 3-year service obligation. My thinking at the time was that the Army would provide an unusual postdoc experience before moving on to a more traditional academic research position.

Just as I arrived at the WRAIR, a major disaster struck the Army. A plane carrying soldiers home from peacekeeping duty crashed near Gander, Newfoundland, killing all 248 onboard. I joined a research team to study the after-effects of this tragic loss and spent most of the next 6-months embedded with the affected Army unit at Fort Campbell, KY. Our team conducted multiple studies on the psychological sequelae of this event for individuals, families, and units, work that led to a series of improvements in how the military prepares for and responds to trauma (Ursano, McCaughey, & Fullerton, 1995). For example, research on Army survivor assistance officers (assigned to help family members after the death of a service member) identified organizational shortfalls that contribute to increased psychological problems for survivors, shortfalls that were later addressed with significant policy changes (Bartone, Ursano, Wright, & Ingraham, 1989). I found the work interesting, challenging and relevant. I was hooked.

In the end, I spent 25 years on active duty in the Army, conducting field studies on soldier stress and adaptation around, from Alaska to Kuwait, Saudi Arabia, Croatia, and Bosnia—anywhere soldiers went. While a research psychologist, I received training to parachute out of airplanes and to rappel from helicopters. I have interviewed soldiers in the Mojave Desert and in the scrub hills of Grenada. I also had the opportunity to teach at the Army's Military Academy at West Point, NY, and the National Defense University in Washington, DC; to command a research lab in Heidelberg, Germany; and to provide psychological training to Albanian, Bulgarian, and Polish military forces under NATO's Partnership for Peace program. I've pursued my research interests in psychology and seen the results applied to improve the health and welfare of military personnel and families, not only in the United States but also in many allied countries. Along the way, I have made lifelong friends and colleagues from around the world. The military psychology career path is not for everyone. But for those who choose it, the rewards are great.

## ANN T. LANDES

I was born in Saigon, Vietnam, and immigrated to the United States in 1971, after my widowed mother married an American soldier. Our first home in the United States was on the beautiful grounds of the VA Medical Center in Tuscaloosa, AL. I essentially grew up around military folks—my stepfather, grandfather, uncles, family, and friends—and the values that embody service and love for country.

Looking back, it is surprising that when choosing a career, I never considered a job devoted to caring for veterans and their families. So how did I become a VA psychologist? It all started when my stepdad was dying from multiple complications related to Agent Orange exposure, a chemical defoliant widely used in the Vietnam War. At that point, I had been working as a chemical engineer for several years, and realized that what I was doing in life lacked meaning for me. After much prayer and discussion with my husband, I quit my job and returned to school for what I believe was a calling: counseling. I completed my master's degree and entered the counseling psychology doctoral program at Georgia State University. During the second semester, my stepdad died. I have heard it said that death can often usher in unexpected new beginnings. In that sense, his death was both devastating and clarifying. I knew that what I wanted most was, in words attributed to Abraham Lincoln, "to care for him who shall have borne the battle and for his widow and his orphan."

Upon completion of my doctoral classes, internship, and fellowship, I entered employment at the Malcom Randall VA. I began as a primary care psychologist and transitioned to Health Behavior Coordinator, my current position. In the former job I worked directly with primary care staff, providing mental health services to veterans presenting in the clinics. A typical day there begins with me consulting with staff on various patient issues. I then see scheduled patients and answer calls from primary care staff related to emergent patient concerns. Additionally,

I facilitate various groups focused on issues such as depression, PTSD, smoking cessation, insomnia, and chronic illness. Additional duties include program development, supervision of psychology trainees, and program evaluation.

As health behavior coordinator my clinical role with primary care patients is focused on health promotion and disease prevention. Examples include: chair yoga, weight loss, women's health, and healthy living skills. The administrative aspect involves the development and provision of various training programs to primary care staff to enhance patient care. Training includes motivational interviewing, patient and clinician health coaching, and team development.

Every day is different. I can honestly say that serving veterans and their families never grows meaningless and continues to invigorate me. For those days that seem somewhat challenging, I am constantly reminded through the selflessness and gratitude expressed by the veterans how fortunate I am to be among them, providing care and assistance.

## Future Prospects for Military Psychology

Throughout the last decade, the United States deployed large numbers of military personnel to serve in the Iraq and Afghanistan conflicts. Thousands returned carrying psychological wounds, often along with severe physical wounds, and are in need of psychological, social, and vocational support. Many of these people now are veterans seeking care through the VA. Others remain on active duty and rely on the military medical system for treatment and services. Military families also have been affected by the stressors of war and need professional support. The demand is high for both research and clinical military psychologists to serve this population.

Although U.S. military engagement in Iraq and Afghanistan has decreased substantially, the world remains unstable, with many areas of conflict. The United States and its allies recognize a continuing requirement to maintain credible military forces to deter conflict and to be able to respond to a range of emergency situations and humanitarian crises around the globe. The demand for military psychologists and other behavioral health professionals thus likely will not end soon. For now and the foreseeable future, the need for military psychologists is significant, the work important, and the rewards unmatched. Come join us!

# Recommended Readings

Bartone, P. T., Johnsen, B. H., Eid, J., Violanti, J. M. & Laberg, J. C. (2010). *Enhancing human performance in security operations: International and law enforcement perspectives.* Springfield, IL: Charles C Thomas.

Britt, T. W., Castro, C. A. & Adler, A. B. (2006). *Military life: The psychology of serving in peace and combat.* Westport, CT: Praeger.

Kennedy, C. H. & Zillmer, E. A. (2012). *Military psychology: Clinical and operational applications.* New York, NY: Guilford.

Laurence, J. H. & Matthews, M. D. (2012). *The Oxford handbook of military psychology.* Oxford, England: Oxford University Press.

Mangelsdorff, A. D. (2006). *Psychology in the service of national security.* Washington, DC: American Psychological Association.

Matthews, M. D. (2013). *Head strong: How psychology is revolutionizing war.* Oxford, England: Oxford University Press.

Moore, B. A. & Barnett, J. E. (2013). *Military psychologists' desk reference.* New York, NY: Oxford University Press.

National Center for Post-Traumatic Stress Disorder. (2004). *Iraq War clinician guide* (2nd ed.). U.S. Department of Veterans Affairs. Online only. Retrieved from http://www.ptsd.va.gov/professional/materials/manuals/iraq-war-clinician-guide.asp

Rumsey, M. G., Walker, C. B. & Harris, J. H. (2013). *Personnel selection and classification.* Hillsdale, NJ: Erlbaum.

# Additional Resources

American Psychological Association, Division 19. (2016). *Becoming a military clinical psychologists.* Retrieved from http://www.apadivisions.org/division-19/students-careers/becoming/index.aspx
Provides detailed information on scholarships, internships, and post-doctoral fellowships available from the U.S. Army, Navy, and Air Force.

American Psychological Association, Division 19. (2016). *Student affairs committee.* Retrieved from http://www.division19students.org
Contains useful information, opportunities, and advice for students interested in military psychology.

U.S. Air Force. (2016). *Specialty: Clinical psychologist.* Retrieved from http://www.airforce.com/careers/detail/clinical-psychologist/
This U.S. Air Force clinical psychology recruiter website provides information about clinical psychology programs, opportunities, and how to apply.

U.S. Army. (2016). *Careers & jobs: Clinical psychologist (73B)*. Retrieved from http://www.goarmy.com/careers-and-jobs/amedd-categories/medical-service-corps-jobs/clinical-psychologist.html
U.S. Army clinical psychology recruiter website.

U.S. Army. (2016). *Careers & jobs: Medical Service Corps officer (67)*. Retrieved from http://www.goarmy.com/careers-and-jobs/browse-career-and-job-categories/medical-and-emergency/medical-service-corps-officer.html
U.S. Army Medical Service Corps recruiter website.

U.S. Army. (2016). *Careers & jobs: Research psychologist (71F)*. Retrieved from http://www.goarmy.com/careers-and-jobs/amedd-categories/medical-service-corps-jobs/research-psychologist.html
U.S. Army research psychology recruiter website.

U.S. Department of Veterans Affairs. (2015). *Psychology training*. Retrieved from http://www.psychologytraining.va.gov/
Describes training opportunities for psychologists, including internships and fellowships available.

U.S. Navy. (2016). *Clinical psychology*. Retrieved from http://www.navy.com/careers/healthcare/clinical-care/clinical-psychology.html#ft-key-responsibilities
U.S. Navy clinical psychology recruiter website.

U.S. Navy. (2016). *Research psychology*. Retrieved from http://www.navy.com/careers/healthcare/healthcare-sciences/research-psych.html#ft-key-responsibilities
U.S. Navy research psychology recruiter website.

Walter Reed National Military Medical Center. (2016). *Overview of the department of psychology and internship program*. Retrieved from http://www.wrnmmc.capmed.mil/ResearchEducation/GME/SitePages/Psychology/Army%20Psychology.aspx
Provides an overview of U.S. Army clinical psychology programs and requirements.

## References

American Psychological Association, Division 19. (2016). *Becoming a military clinical psychologist*. Retrieved from http://www.apadivisions.org/division-19/students-careers/becoming/index.aspx

Bartone, P. T. (2010). Preventing prisoner abuse: Leadership lessons of Abu Ghraib. *Ethics and Behavior, 20*, 161–173. http://dx.doi.org/10.1080/10508421003595984

Bartone, P. T., Pastel, R. H., & Vaitkus, M. A. (2010). *The 71F advantage: Applying Army research psychology for health and performance gains*. Washington, DC: National Defense University Press.

Bartone, P. T., Ursano, R. J., Wright, K. M., & Ingraham, L. H. (1989). The impact of a military air disaster on the health of assistance workers. A prospective study. *Journal of Nervous and Mental Disease, 177*, 317–328. http://dx.doi.org/10.1097/00005053-198906000-00001

Defense Finance and Accounting Service. (2016). *Military pay charts, 1946–2016.* Retrieved from http://www.dfas.mil/militarymembers/payentitlements/military-pay-charts.html

Department of Defense. (2010). *Demographics 2010 report.* Retrieved from http://download.militaryonesource.mil/12038/MOS/Reports/2010_Demographics_Report.pdf

Etzioni, A. (2007). *Security first: For a muscular, moral foreign policy.* New Haven, CT: Yale University Press.

Krueger, G. P. (2010). U.S. Army research psychologists: Making a difference, yesterday, today and tomorrow. In P. T. Bartone, R. H. Pastel, & M. A. Vaitkus (Eds.), *The 71F advantage: Applying Army research psychology for health and performance gains* (pp. 1–44). Washington, DC: National Defense University Press.

McBride, S. A., Thomas, J. L., McGurk, D., Wood, M. D., & Bliese, P. D. (2010). U.S. Army mental health advisory teams. In P. T. Bartone, R. H. Pastel, & M. A. Vaitkus (Eds.), *The 71F advantage: Applying Army research psychology for health and performance gains* (pp. 209–246). Washington, DC: National Defense University Press.

Uniformed Services University of the Health Sciences. (2016a). *Medical and clinical psychology.* Retrieved from https://www.usuhs.edu/mps/

Uniformed Services University of the Health Sciences. (2016b). *Prospective student admissions.* Retrieved from https://www.usuhs.edu/graded/prospectivestudents

Ursano, R. J., McCaughey, B. G., & Fullerton, C. S. (1995). *Individual and community responses to trauma and disaster.* London: Cambridge University Press.

U.S. Air Force. (2016). *Career development.* Retrieved from https://www.airforce.com/careers/specialty-careers/healthcare/training-and-education

U.S. Army. (2016). *Army medicine.* Retrieved from http://www.goarmy.com/amedd/education/hpsp.html

U.S. Army Research Institute of Environmental Medicine. (2016). Retrieved from http://www.usariem.army.mil

U.S. Department of Veterans Affairs. (2016a). *National center for veterans analysis and statistics.* Retrieved from http://www.va.gov/vetdata/Quick_Facts.asp

U.S. Department of Veterans Affairs. (2016b). *Office of research & development.* Retrieved from http://www.research.va.gov/default.cfm

U.S. Department of Veterans Affairs. (2016c). *Psychology training: Stipends and benefits.* Retrieved from http://www.psychologytraining.va.gov/benefits.asp

U.S. Department of Veterans Affairs. (2016d). *Psychology training: VA fellowships and internships.* Retrieved from http://www.psychologytraining.va.gov/index.asp

Walter Reed National Military Medical Center. (2012a, July 19). *Navy post-doctoral fellowship in clinical psychology: APA-accredited.* Retrieved from http://www.wrnmmc.capmed.mil/ResearchEducation/GME/Shared%20Documents/Psychology/Post-Doctoral%20Fellowship%20Updated%2019July2012.docx

Walter Reed National Military Medical Center. (2012b, June 28). *Scholarships: Navy Health Professions Scholarship Program for Clinical or Counseling Psychology.* Retrieved from http://www.wrnmmc.capmed.mil/ResearchEducation/GME/Shared%20Documents/Psychology/HPSP%20Revised%2028%20June%2012.docx

Walter Reed National Military Medical Center. (n.d.). *Licensed psychologists.* Retrieved from http://www.wrnmmc.capmed.mil/ResearchEducation/GME/Shared%20Documents/Psychology/LICENSED%20DIRECT%20ACCESSIONS.docx

*David M. Corey*

# Police and Public Safety Psychologists | 25

W ithout doubt, law enforcement is an exciting career. It is also dangerous, stressful, and—at times—deeply fulfilling. The risks of police work extend far beyond those to which the police officer is exposed. They include risks to the suspects and criminals the police pursue as well as risks to ordinary citizens and the trust communities place in their protectors.

Publicized accounts of inexplicable violence by police officers against unarmed and nonthreatening citizens raise important questions about the prevalence of racial profiling and bias, unnecessary force, and the ways that police agencies respond to citizen complaints about the police. The U.S.

Dr. David M. Corey, PhD, ABPP, is a practicing psychologist at Corey & Stewart in Portland, Oregon, and an ABPP board-certified specialist in police and public safety psychology and forensic psychology. He is the founding president of the American Board of Police and Public Safety Psychology and a fellow of the American Psychological Association. Dr. Corey is coauthor with Yossef S. Ben-Porath, PhD of the MMPI–2 Restructured Form (MMPI–2–RF) *Police Candidate Interpretive Report*. He is a faculty fellow at Fielding Graduate University, Santa Barbara, California.

http://dx.doi.org/10.1037/15960-026
*Career Paths in Psychology: Where Your Degree Can Take You, Third Edition*, R. J. Sternberg (Editor)

Department of Justice conducts special investigations of police agencies whose officers display a pattern of violating civil rights, which indicates that these injustices are usually the result of deep flaws in the recruitment, selection, training, supervision, investigation, and disciplinary procedures of its officers. In all of these areas, and more, police psychologists play important roles.

Psychologists have worked to improve the quality of American policing since as early as 1916 when Lewis Terman administered intelligence tests to help select police officer and firefighter applicants in the city of San Jose, California. Following the civil unrest and race riots of the 1960s, the President's Commission on Law Enforcement and Administration of Justice called for the use of psychological tests to measure the personal characteristics that contribute to effective policing. As of 2016, 98.5% of all police agencies serving communities of 25,000 or more, as well as the majority of even smaller departments, require that police applicants undergo a preemployment psychological evaluation to determine their suitability to perform the functions of a police officer (Bureau of Justice Statistics, 2010).

In addition to helping to decide which police applicants to hire, police psychologists also help detectives solve crimes, improve organizational functioning and management effectiveness, provide therapy, and develop and implement programs to enhance officer health and resilience. Psychologists perform similar services with other first responders and public safety agencies, including fire departments, jails and prisons, and 911 call centers. In fact, the significance and impact of this work are so well established that the American Psychological Association (APA) now recognizes police and public safety psychology as a specialty in professional psychology (APA, n.d.-b). It is formally defined this way:

> Police and public safety psychology is concerned with assisting law enforcement and other public safety personnel and agencies in carrying out their missions and societal functions with effectiveness, safety, health and conformity to laws and ethics. It consists of the application of the science and profession of psychology in four primary domains of practice: assessment, clinical intervention, operational support, and organizational consultation. (APA, n.d.-a)

Most police and public safety psychologists work in only one or two of these "domains of practice." Some go on to become specialists who do this work full time, and others perform more limited services while engaged in a general clinical practice. Regardless of the path, all of the work of police and public safety psychologists is clustered in these four practice domains, as described next. This chapter discusses these four domains, along with other considerations for this career.

# The Assessment Domain

Psychologists use the terms *evaluation* and *assessment* interchangeably, so the assessment domain in police and public safety psychology has to do with evaluating individuals for some purpose. For the most part, these evaluations are for one of two purposes: either to help decide whether a particular applicant is psychologically capable of doing the job safely and effectively (this is called *preemployment screening*) or to help decide whether a police officer or other public safety employee (such as a fire-fighter, correctional officer, or 911 dispatcher) is having psychological problems that prevent him or her from continuing to do the job (this is called a *fitness-for-duty evaluation*).

## PREEMPLOYMENT SCREENING

Not everyone is cut out to be a cop, and the same can be said for being a firefighter, correctional officer, probation officer, emergency communications dispatcher, and other emergency service positions. In their world of work, things can be routine or slow at one moment and, in a split second, catastrophe can strike and they're expected to respond immediately and correctly. Although most of us move away from danger, they move toward it. Doing this kind of emergency work well requires a certain kind of person: someone who is emotionally stable; able to withstand high levels of stress (interspersed with periods of boredom), work as a member of a team, and follow orders and rules; capable of quickly taking control of situations without abusing authority or over-reacting; and willing to have their split-second decisions scrutinized after the fact by internal investigations, grand juries, the press, and public opinion.

But the work of a police officer in a rural small town is far different than that of an officer in the inner city or a large metropolis, so police and public safety psychologists also have to be adept at figuring out whether any unique job demands or working conditions for a particular position may require other psychological traits or abilities, or cause them to be weighed differently. This involves a process called *job analysis* and it is used to determine the standard for assessing whether a person is psychologically qualified for the position.

Police and public safety psychologists who conduct preemployment screening have to be skilled at reading research literature to stay informed about the psychological characteristics necessary for a police officer or other emergency worker to be successful. They must know how psychological testing, personal background information, and clinical interviews—the three sources of information psychologists rely on when conducting these evaluations—can be used to assess suitability for these positions and to predict problems.

## FITNESS-FOR-DUTY EVALUATIONS

When conducting preemployment screening, all applicants for the position must be given the evaluation or none can be given it. That's the law, and it's intended to keep employers from discriminating against applicants on the basis of their mental health history. In other words, an employer can't decide to require psychological evaluations of only those applicants with a history of depression or who have taken antidepressants. The demands and consequences of the position must justify a psychological evaluation for all applicants or none.

Conversely, when it comes to *incumbent employees*—people who are already in the position—the reverse is true. An employee generally is assumed to be psychologically suited to do the work unless there is a reasonable basis for believing that something has changed and the employee is no longer able to safely and effectively do the job. In that case, an employer can require that the employee submit to a fitness-for-duty evaluation.

Police and public safety psychologists who conduct fitness-for-duty evaluations have to be knowledgeable about all of the same things required for preemployment screening (such as the qualifying standards, psychological testing, interviewing), but they also have to know a lot about the law. Employees have certain legal rights that applicants don't, and a psychologist who is unaware of these laws and how the courts have interpreted them can unknowingly violate the employee's rights and also expose the employer to liability. Because employees who are deemed unfit for duty may lose their jobs, a good deal of litigation often follows. For these reasons, many police and public safety psychologists who conduct fitness-for-duty evaluations also are trained in forensic psychology.

## The Intervention Domain

Police and public safety psychologists who treat or counsel police officers and other public safety workers work in the intervention domain. As one would expect, however, psychologists who treat employees can't ethically evaluate those same employees' fitness for duty, too. This is what psychologists call a *multiple relationship* that gets in the way of professional objectivity and presents a conflict of interest. So, most often, psychologists who work in the assessment domain either don't do intervention or treat only employees who work in agencies that don't do assessment. Multiple relationships and conflicts of interest are something that psychologists are always on the lookout for, but they can be especially problematic when working in paramilitary organizations.

Psychologists who provide therapy and counseling for police officers and other emergency responders play an enormously important role. It is not easy for these employees to trust outsiders; their experiences can lead them to become suspicious and cynical. So when they do take the initiative to seek help from a professional, their initial experience is all-important.

Intervention psychologists who work well with these employees respect them as professionals and do not judge them. They are not voyeurs who seek the vicarious thrill of a front row seat to the police officer's recitation of trauma, despair, fear, guilt, stress, and the panoply of other emotions, thoughts, and behaviors that sometimes can plague emergency responders, particularly after years of exposure to human suffering, abuse, and neglect. Psychologists who provide effective treatment to these workers and their families are knowledgeable about the common and unusual stressors in public safety work, normal and abnormal adaptation to occupational stress and trauma, research related to resilience and recovery in public safety personnel, and the critical importance of confidentiality.

Some police and public safety psychologists specialize in providing certain modalities of treatment, such as cognitive behavioral, group, or psychoanalytic treatment. Others specialize in treating certain kinds of conditions like posttraumatic stress disorder, substance use disorders, or depression. Still others focus their work on certain kinds of specialized interventions, commonly including postshooting debriefings (in which police officers who have been involved in on-duty shootings meet with a psychologist to receive help, advice, or information about normal and abnormal reactions) and disability recovery (for employees who have developed disabling conditions that prevent them from working in their regular duty assignments).

# The Operational Support Domain

Police and other public safety work is highly operational, meaning that they execute functions requiring coordinated action and that are designed to protect public safety, maintain or restore order, or apprehend criminals. When psychologists perform services intended to help with these functions, they're providing operational support.

Police and public safety psychologists who work in the operational support domain have no autonomous role. They provide services that help the operational team do their jobs more effectively. For example, a police negotiator who is trying to talk to an armed, barricaded, and homicidal subject into surrendering peacefully may seek the assistance of a specially trained consulting police psychologist who can make observations and suggest strategies to accomplish the objective. Police psychologists rarely would be involved in talking directly to the barricaded subject; instead, their focus is on providing psychological expertise that helps the operational specialists do their jobs successfully.

Because psychologists are committed to a strict code of ethical principles and standards of conduct, police psychologists are careful to avoid allowing their knowledge and expertise to be used in a way that violates those ethical principles and standards. This is especially important when consulting to the police on matters involving interrogation of people held in custody. It is never ethical for psychologists to participate in the violation of human rights.

## The Organizational Consultation Domain

When police and public safety psychologists perform services intended to improve the organization's effectiveness, they are working in the organizational consultation domain. Such services might include designing and implementing a multirater or 360-degree feedback program to enable individual leaders in a police agency to know how they're being viewed from different segments of the organization and community. They also may include consultation to an individual supervisor to assist in resolving a longstanding personnel problem or efforts to mediate conflict between a labor group and management. As in the operational support domain, psychologists working in the organizational consultation domain are providing services designed to improve the functioning of the department so that the employees can perform their duties more effectively.

## Where Police and Public Safety Psychologists Work

The majority of police and public safety psychologists work in private practice settings and contract with agencies to provide their services. Some police departments, especially large ones, have behavioral science or psychological service units staffed with full-time psychologists. In some agencies, like the Los Angeles Police Department, psychologists in these units are assigned only to roles in the intervention, operational support, and organizational consultation domains, whereas services in the assessment domain are allocated to other psychologists working either on contract or in other city departments. In others, such as the New York City Police Department, department psychologists are deployed to perform services in all four domains.

# Preparation for a Career in Police and Public Safety Psychology

The specialty of police and public safety psychologists is built first and foremost on the foundation of knowledge, skills, and abilities of clinical, counseling, or industrial–organizational psychology. Because the specialty did not earn official APA recognition until 2013, few APA-accredited doctoral programs in psychology offer education in police and public safety psychology as a major area of study. Instead, to the extent that they exist at all, doctoral programs offering coursework in this specialty are limited to a small number of courses that provide an emphasis on, experience with, or exposure to this area.

Most police and public safety psychologists acquire the education and training needed to be competent in the specialty though postdoctoral training. A few large police and public safety psychology consulting firms, and some psychological service units in large urban police agencies, offer postdoctoral fellowships or residencies intended to provide comprehensive preparation in all four specialty domains.

A unique aspect of the specialty, however, is the requirement that psychologists working in this specialty be knowledgeable about the essential functions of police and public safety organizations and personnel, and the working conditions unique to their respective positions. This kind of knowledge is best, and most easily, obtained through exposure to a variety of different police, fire, and other public safety organizations and by conducting ride-alongs (or sit-alongs in the case of 911 emergency communications centers), which allow for a rich introduction to the tasks, settings, demands, working conditions, stressors, hierarchy or chain-of-command, and culture of these unique work settings. Some psychologists choose to become reserve police officers and receive the formal academy and field training necessary to be sworn law enforcement officers, and a growing number of police and public safety psychologists enter the specialty after first serving for a number of years as a full-time police officer, firefighter, or other public safety worker.

# A Typical Day for a Police and Public Safety Psychologist

As you might expect, the average day for police and public safety psychologists depends on where they work (such as in private practice or in a police department), what domains they work in, and whether they perform these specialty services exclusively or as just one part of a more general clinical practice. My own practice is fairly typical for police and public safety psychologists who work in a private practice setting.

I have a consulting firm with another full-time police and public safety psychologist, two administrative assistants, and a part-time research assistant. This last position may be somewhat unusual for the typical specialist, but I was educated in the tradition of the scientist–practitioner who is committed both to evidence-based practice and to a practice that contributes to the empirical literature. As a result, a typical day for me looks like this:

I'm usually in the office by 6:30 a.m., and I almost always find my associate already at his desk. We'll discuss aspects of the day's calendar that may require collaboration or consultation with one another, and we then move on to our individual routines. E-mail and various administrative responsibilities (financial, personnel, and others) occupy the remaining of the morning before the administrative staff arrives at 8:00 a.m., after which time my attention turns to the day's scheduled appointments.

More often than not, I will have a fitness-for-duty evaluation scheduled for 9:00 a.m., which requires preparation and file review starting about 8:00 a.m., unless the case includes a large numbers of records that would require starting much earlier. At 9:00 a.m. I'll meet with the employee or examinee to ensure that he or she is able to give informed consent to the evaluation, and then I'll begin the interview. During the next 3 hours or so of the interview, the administrative staff will be administering written testing to, on average, six police or other public safety candidates in a large conference room. The candidates complete no less than two written psychological tests each as well as a set of personal history questionnaires.

After I complete the morning interview, the fitness-for-duty examinee usually takes a lunch break. I'll do the same (regrettably too often done at my desk while I catch up on more e-mail and phone calls), after which time the fitness-for-duty examinee will begin written testing, and I begin evaluating the preemployment candidates. Once these evaluations are complete, I review the psychological testing of the fitness-for-duty examinee and follow-up with remaining interview questions. This process usually ends at about 3:30 or 4:00 p.m., after which I write up the reports of the preemployment evaluations I conducted. Most often, the fitness-for-duty evaluation report is written either the next morning (if I don't have another fitness evaluation scheduled) or on Friday, which I reserve to catch up on reports, phone calls, correspondence, research activities, and carrying out work associated with the various professional boards and committees on which I serve. My formal day will end around 6:00 p.m., although my evenings typically include an additional round of e-mail correspondence, writing, and journal reading. In my practice, I rarely get called after hours or on the weekends. Little work in the assessment domain constitutes an emergency.

My colleagues who work full time in police departments, however, rotate being on-call to handle a wide range of emergencies associated with the intervention or operational support domains. Their days are filled with such tasks as treating a suicidal police officer, counseling an officer and her spouse, and visiting officers at various precincts or on ride-alongs during which a good deal of informal intervention occurs. They may receive an urgent call to consult on a hostage negotiation or to debrief an officer who was involved in an on-duty shooting incident. They may be called to a chief's office to help solve pressing organizational issues, to help redesign a training program, or to confer about a personnel matter. For the in-house psychologist, days that are fully scheduled rarely end without a change and days with holes in the schedule rarely remain unfilled.

## Motivation to Seek a Career in Police and Public Safety Psychology

The reasons for seeking a career in this specialty are likely to be as varied as the psychologists who choose it. But many of my specialist colleagues chose this career for reasons for similar to my own: opportunity, resonance, and meaning.

Because police and public safety psychology only recently became recognized as a specialty, most practicing police and public safety psychologists became involved in this field because they trained with someone who was doing it, worked in a practice in which another psychologist was performing services in one or more of the specialty domains, or had the good fortune of being asked by a police chief, fire chief, or other public safety administrator to provide services. In other words, the opportunity presented itself, and they took it.

I became involved in police psychology as an undergraduate student when a professor I worked for as a teaching assistant invited me to work with him on a study of the impact on police officers of favorable stereotype-violating exposures to racial minorities. This was followed soon after by an opportunity to be a paid research assistant for a firm that was conducting research with the San Diego Police Department, and I was completing my master's degree in San Diego. While completing my doctoral degree in clinical psychology, I worked as a psychological assistant for a psychologist who performed services in all four specialty domains. All of this was the result of pure opportunity—opportunity that I was drawn to and took advantage of.

But the work and the individuals also resonated with me, as is also true for my colleagues. Police officers, firefighters, correctional officers, and 911 dispatchers are, as a group, earnest, caring, empathetic, sensitive, smart, brave, and service oriented. They're also usually quite funny with a tendency toward dark humor, which helps them get through horrific experiences by finding irony in unexpected elements of these events. When you work with people who you think about at the end of the day, and look forward to working with them again, that kind of resonance is itself a source of motivation and satisfaction.

Finally, the work is meaningful and, therefore, rewarding. It is nearly always a bad day when a person has to call 911 to summon a police officer or firefighter. But to be the one who the police and fire departments call when they need help is an awesome and heady responsibility. Providing that help in a way that solves a serious problem, accomplishes an important goal, or makes a meaningful contribution to the work of a police or other public safety officer is immensely rewarding.

Occasionally, we get to save lives, too, and often we contribute to making individuals and communities healthier and safer. It is important and responsible work when deciding whether a candidate is psychologically qualified to be a police officer, firefighter, correctional officer, or dispatcher. Such decisions require reliable and valid evidence, and the ability to defend the decision on its merits. It is important and rewarding work to assist a police negotiator in persuading a barricaded subject to release a hostage or to surrender himself without shots being fired. Designing and conducting training programs that teach police officers how to interact more effectively with the seriously mentally ill, or how to monitor and challenge their decision making to avoid the consequences of implicit or automatic racial bias, affects not just the lives of the officers you train but countless unnamed citizens as well.

Oh, and one more thing. You often are given a badge to get you through security checkpoints. (You have to admit, that's a nice perk.)

## Challenges of a Career in Police and Public Safety Psychology

To be sure, police and public safety psychology involves important, meaningful, and rewarding work, but it also includes challenges. It is nearly impossible to work with first responders without being exposed, at least vicariously, to the stressors that affect their lives. Repeated vicarious or direct exposure to others' trauma can have negative effects on the psychologists retained to help and leads to this type of work being termed psychology *in extremis*. Psychologists who practice in this specialty require strong support systems, resilient personalities, an insatiable interest in learning, and the self-confidence necessary to stand up to authority when necessary.

Police and public safety psychologists who work in the intervention and operational support domains in particular are apt to be called at odd hours and may be subject to 24/7 on-call availability. Unless properly managed, this can have negative effects on personal health and family life.

## Future Prospects for a Career in Police and Public Safety Psychology

Future prospects for a career in police and public safety psychology are excellent. Many police psychologists began their careers in the 1970s and 1980s, when the momentum to use psychologists to select and train police officers accelerated. This cohort of police psychologists is quickly reaching retirement age, and the need for younger psychologists to replace them is evident. Preemployment screening of police officers is now the norm, and in most states it's also required by law. The benefits accrued to the public and the police departments have persuaded many fire departments, corrections institutions, and 911 centers to require preemployment evaluations of their applicants, too. As a result, the demand for preemployment screening of police and public safety applicants is strong for the foreseeable future.

Police and public safety employees have become so accustomed to talking to psychologists that little skepticism or cultural reservations inhibit their readiness to seek counseling when needed. Many police and public safety agencies routinely provide postincident debriefing to their employees in the wake of a significant on-duty trauma, and some states have enacted laws that require postshooting debriefings of police officers by a psychologist immediately after the event and a follow-up visit within a year. Coupled with federal health insurance parity laws, which require mental health insurance benefits to match those for physical conditions, the prospects for utilization of intervention services is also strong.

## References

American Psychological Association. (n.d.-a). *Police and public safety.* Retrieved from http://www.apa.org/ed/graduate/specialize/police.aspx

American Psychological Association. (n.d.-b). *Recognized specialties and proficiencies in professional psychology.* Retrieved from http://www. apa.org/ed/graduate/specialize/recognized.aspx

Bureau of Justice Statistics. (2010). *Local police departments, 2007.* Washington, DC: Author. Retrieved from http://www.bjs.gov/content/pub/pdf/lpd07.pdf

*Lonnie R. Sherrod*

# Psychologists Giving Grants Through Nonprofits

# 26

am a developmental psychologist. Across the past century, philanthropy has become an important force influencing the development of children, families, and communities. It has been influential in the development of applied developmental science and in furthering the new view on developmental science that aims to promote positive development in children and youth. Hence, it was not unusual for a developmental psychologist to work for a foundation. Few foundations fund research, however, so it is more unusual for a scientist to work in philanthropy; I was lucky in being able to work for a foundation that funded research, the William T. Grant Foundation, making it even more appropriate for me to do this

Lonnie R. Sherrod received his PhD in psychology from Yale University (1978), an MA in biology from University of Rochester (1976), and a BA from Duke University (1972). He is executive director of the Society for Research in Child Development (SRCD) and Distinguished Lecturer in Fordham University's Applied Developmental Psychology Program, where he was a professor of psychology. He has edited *The Social Policy Reports* and has served on the editorial boards and coedited special issues of numerous journals.

http://dx.doi.org/10.1037/15960-027
*Career Paths in Psychology: Where Your Degree Can Take You, Third Edition,*
R. J. Sternberg (Editor)

work. This chapter describes what it is like to work for a foundation, addressing the nature of the work, the required skill set, the career trajectory, the advantages and disadvantages of this type of work, and how you decide to do this type of job and prepare for it.

## A Brief History of Philanthropy

I begin with a brief history of philanthropy and its relationship to science because the mission of the foundation is relevant to the work a psychologist can do there.

For 10 years, I was vice president of the William T. Grant Foundation (first program vice president, then executive vice president). The Grant Foundation is a private, independent foundation, founded in the 1930s by Mr. Grant, who ran a chain of five and dime–type department stores. Because his jobs were entry level, many of his employees were young people, and he noticed that their development was compromised by a variety of problems relating to mental health, family functioning, and so forth. He therefore established this foundation to understand how to help youth live up to their full potential (Cahan, 1986). This mandate has always been interpreted as funding research.

In this regard, the Grant Foundation is an unusual foundation. The current situation of philanthropy and its relative separation from science has not always been the case, however. Philanthropy originated early in the 20th century (Wisely, 1998). At the turn of the century, a variety of charities existed. Their goal was to relieve the suffering of the poor, affirmed, and otherwise unfortunate. The industrialization of the early 20th century generated a number of wealthy men who wanted to use their business sense and accumulated wealth to address society's problems. They saw the existing charities as providing temporary relief by treating symptoms. These new philanthropists wanted to "solve" social problems by identifying core causes and treating them. Several of the currently most visible private foundations arose early in this century: the Russell Sage Foundation in 1907, the Carnegie Corporation in 1911, the Rockefeller Foundation in 1913, the Commonwealth Fund in 1918, and the William T. Grant Foundation in the 1930s, for example.

Because of the interest in identifying core causes of social problems, these new philanthropists looked to science with its ability to separate causes and effects as providing tools for their efforts. Science with its clear distinction of cause and effect provided a strategy for approaching the *solution* of social problems by identifying core causes that could be addressed as opposed to alleviating symptoms or temporarily providing relief (Cahan, 1986; Karl & Katz, 1981). Although most of these new foundations did not fund much science, the appreciation of science as a tool provided a funding context in the first half of the 20th century that fueled the growth of the social behavioral sciences and the universities in which they became housed (Prewitt, 1995; Sherrod, 1998, 1999). Because most social problems involve human behavior, there was also a clear role for psychology, although it was not explicitly articulated.

What this approach to philanthropy meant was that foundations funded a lot of programs oriented to individual improvement—for example, to giving individuals and families the ability to improve their lives: educational programs, libraries, family support, treatment of and cures for diseases. Thus, this work had a psychological bent even if implicitly. Beginning about in the 1960s, at the same time as a variety of other social movements, such as civil rights and the anti–Vietnam War effort, foundations began to question this past strategy. In fact, they had not been successful at solving social problems or improving the overall status of human well-being. Although the success of their efforts can be debated at length, problems such as poverty did not disappear. Furthermore, as one problem was reduced, a new one arose. Hence, philanthropy came to believe that widespread social change was needed, and its efforts changed. It began to orient its efforts to systematic social reform (Gregorian, 2000; Wisely, 1998), to eliminate poverty and racism, and to promote international cooperation, and in this shift, its relation to science was lost (Sherrod, 1998).

At the same type that the nature of philanthropy was changing so, too, was its size and importance (Gregorian, 2000; Nason, 1989). Both the number of foundations and their absolute worth has growth substantially during the last half of the previous century as well as the 21st century. The number of private foundations has doubled since the 1970s, and the total assets of these foundations has doubled even after controlling for inflation (Renz & Lawrence, 1993).

In addition to growth in absolute numbers and asset value, foundations in this country also have become increasingly diverse in their structure and mode of operations. The foundations that originated early in this century are private or independent foundation; however, four other types of foundations have arisen over the past few decades. The one type that has grown the most is the community foundation. These foundations operate like independent foundations except that their mandate is to serve a particular community; the New York Community Trust and the Chicago Community Trust are examples of this type of foundation.

Three other types of foundations are family, corporate, and operating foundations. Family or corporate foundations function as direct arms of the family or corporation that founded them. These types of foundations vary in their mode of operation. These newer types of foundations have represented a substantial portion of the growth of philanthropy in the last half of the 20th century. Predictions are that local philanthropic activities such as community foundations will represent the most intense area of future philanthropic activity (Hall, 1988; Nason, 1989).

Hence philanthropy continues to provide important job opportunities for psychologists as well as others. Furthermore, while our social strategy for using charity to attend to social problems has changed over the past century, the role of behavior in contributing to social problems does not change. Therefore, psychologists in working for a foundation will always have a role to play.

## The Nature of the Career

I am not sure how to address the nature of the career except in a somewhat autobiographical fashion. I was always book oriented and interested in scholarship, so it is not surprising that I initially chose to pursue an academic career. I went to graduate school in psychology and had every intention of pursuing an academic career. I liked the certainty of the career track moving from a postdoctoral position to junior and finally senior faculty. When I finished my PhD in psychology, however, I was anxious to get on with my career because I previously had been in biology graduate school and thought it was time to move to a job. Most opportunities available to me were postdoctoral positions, which felt like still being in school.

Just as I was deciding on a specific postdoc, an opportunity arose to work with the Social Science Research Council (SSRC), an independent nonorganization that does research planning. It functioned a lot like the National Academy of Sciences, planning and building areas of research in the social behavioral sciences. I was the only psychologist on staff and so I worked on related topics—life-span development and giftedness, for example. I went to SSRC with the idea of using it as a postdoc to learn about funding and the social structure of science. I really liked the work, however, and thought I was better at it than most of my academic colleagues would have been. Hence, I stayed in this job almost 10 years.

During my tenure at SSRC, I had received funding from the William T. Grant Foundation (WTG) for one of my programs on biosocial science. This program used biological perspectives to address certain social problems such as child abuse and teen pregnancy. WTG was then focused on stress and coping in school-age children so that child abuse and teen pregnancy were of keen interest to them. The President, Robert

Haggerty, was a pediatrician and so he liked the biological approach. Hence, I got a 3-year grant from WTG for my SSRC biosocial science program and got to know the foundation through that grant.

Dr. Haggerty felt limited in his work by a lack of program staff with advanced training in areas of interest to the foundation. Hence, he hired several scholars in different fields to be part-time program staff. He knew me from my grant with them, so I was the first person he hired as one of these senior program associates. Then, years later, when his program vice president retired, he asked me if I was interested in the job. I accepted and began my tenure as a foundation vice president.

There are two important points: First, there is no career path as such; most moves from one position to the next are opportunistic. Second, as a result, one does not prepare for this career; instead, one employs the skill set used in each job as well as that acquired in one's training. I did not plan or prepare for my work at WTG; it just happened. Although there are relevant training programs in, for example, nonprofit management or public policy, a degree in psychology is equally relevant and useful.

## Professional Development

These comments lead naturally to a consideration of professional development. Although it may not be necessary or even possible to plan for a career working for a foundation, every field has professional development opportunities, and this means there are associations geared to professionals in the respective field. For foundation employees, this is the Council on Foundations, a professional association for foundation staff, much like the American Psychological Association (APA), for example. The Council on Foundations has an annual meeting and other benefits, and your involvement as a foundation employee is always fully covered by one's employer. Depending on the foundation, all staff or only the most senior staff participate. At WTG, the president rarely participated in the Council on Foundations so I saw it as my responsibility to represent WTG in these circles, in part to promote the importance of philanthropic funding for research.

Increasingly, even in my field of developmental science, professional development associations have emerged to focus on specific topics, such as infancy or adolescence and cognitive development or developmental psychopathology. The same is true for philanthropy. Children, youth, and families has been and continues to be a major concern of philanthropy. Grantmakers for Children, Youth and Families (GCYF), a special interest group of foundations concerned with children, youth, and families, began as an affinity group of the Council on Foundations, but became independent and now functions just like the Council (e.g., holding an annual conference). Many major foundations, including corporate ones, are members and attend the annual meeting because most large foundations have some concern for children, youth, and families.

GCYF attempts to help members with professional development, covering topics such as how to make grants, insurance coverage for small organizations, and so forth. But more important, it covers program-relevant information. It has an annual 2- to 3-day meeting that brings together well-known speakers from academic, business, nonprofit, government, and other sectors. It organizes groups of members around topics to constitute learning circles, and it publishes a newsletter. This professional organization for grantmakers concerned with children and youth is as important as such organizations as the Society for Research in Child Development are to child development researchers. GCYF was my major professional association while I worked at WTG; it provided important opportunities for networking and for program development on foundation funding for children and families, including the role of research.

There are also regional associations just as there are in psychology. The New York Regional Association (NYRAG) was also important to my work at the Grant Foundation and provided an opportunity to address issues affecting children, youth, and families in the New York metropolitan area.

These professional associations are important to the psychologist's role working for a foundation. They establish contacts in the field relevant to doing a good job and also contribute to identifying possibilities for future employment in the field. Thereby, they offer multiple professional development opportunities. The Foundation Center, a library on philanthropy, keeps job postings at foundations, from president to administrative assistant.

## The Nature of the Work for a Foundation

Most psychologists are trained either as scientists pursuing a research or academic career or as clinicians who offer different forms of treatments for individuals with psychological problems. To some extent, the latter is more similar to working for a foundation, but problems are addressed at an individual level in therapy rather than at a population or societal level. I was trained as a scientist and the nature of scientific work is quite different.

## RECEIPT AND REVIEW OF APPLICATIONS

The daily activities and responsibilities depend on the nature of the foundation's program. Because WTG funded mainly research, it functioned a lot like a current federal research funding organization such as the National Science Foundation (NSF) or the National Institutes of Health (NIH). One major set of responsibilities was to manage the review process for submitted applications.

When I worked for WTG, it funded investigator-initiated proposals. That is, investigators submitted applications in line with the overall program; we did not seek them. These applications were subjected to a scientific peer review as at NSF or NIH. One of my responsibilities was to oversee this review process. I received the application, selected reviewers, and then used the reviews to decide which applications to submit to the foundation's board. The foundation had a two-phase board review. The scientists who sat on the board constituted a program committee who first considered these applications and their reviews, and I managed these meetings. The committee decided which applications to recommend to the full board, which consisted of an equal number of business professionals who managed the foundation's assets.

The scientists were interested mainly in scientific merit attending to the characteristics that define good science, sampling, and measures as well as theory and significance. The business professionals didn't really understand or care much about these qualities, although they did want to fund good science. Instead they were interested in how the information gained from the study could be used to help children and families.

Handling these responsibilities required a detailed understanding of science as well as appreciation for how particular types of science could help us address social problems affecting children. Before working for WTG, my research interests had been relatively basic, that is, based in theory and intellectual ideas rather than in social problems and how science could address them. As a result of my experience at the foundation, I became much more interested in applied research, that is, research grounded in social problems and how it can be useful, and in how to use research to design social policies to help children and families. I am now executive director of the Society for Research in Child Development (SRCD), perhaps the premier professional association in developmental science. And while I was at WTG, I (along with others) convinced this organization to attend to policy and communications as well as research, which it continues to do in a major way to this very day.

This aspect of the job—managing the review and decision making of applications—was rather straightforward and easy given my training as a scientist. Although WTG funded projects in fields other than psychology, my work at SSRC had acquainted me with developmental science across disciplines. Two aspects of this work were difficult. The first was selection of reviewers. Although science portends that its scientific review process is fully objective, in fact, selection of reviewers has a big impact on final outcome. Some reviewers are just easier than others or may emphasize particular aspects of the proposal such as its statistics, either of which can bias their final opinion of the proposed study. My goal in these reviews was to undercover as many potential criticisms of the application as possible so that there were no surprises at the program committee meeting. The worst thing that could happen was for a serious flaw to be identified only at that meeting. I often elected to present imperfect study proposals with a justification for why they should be funded (e.g., from the perspective of usefulness), but one did not want surprises at the meeting.

The second aspect of this process that was difficult was the inevitable idea of a promissory note. Applicants were required to submit a preproposal asking whether we'd receive a full proposal for review. On the one hand, potential applicants would tend to argue with you if you wanted to discourage an application. On the other hand, although we funded about only half the applications we received, applicants would interpret willingness to receive a full application as a promissory note for funding. This occurred despite the fact that we would inform folks that our process was exactly like the federal agencies, such as NIH, and no one expected all of those applications to be funded.

## PROGRAM DESIGN AND DEVELOPMENT

The other aspect of work at the foundation involved program development or design, that is, deciding the broad areas for which the foundation will direct its funds. Generally, this is the president's job, but Dr. Haggerty and I, as the only program staff, worked together on most things. This was the most interesting aspect of the job for me.

Dr. Haggerty had focused the program on stress and coping in school-age children. Before his arrival, WTG focused on infancy. Dr. Haggerty believed school-age children had been ignored, yet they faced numerous stressors. What this program meant was that we funded research, for example, on the impact of divorce, of living with a mentally ill parent, of child abuse, and of teen pregnancy. When I arrived at the foundation, adolescent research was growing, and we funded a number of longitudinal studies of teens; we decided to continue to fund many of these studies into young adulthood, and I think made a contribution to the emergence of the now-thriving field of young adult development that has documented the delay in the transition to adulthood and the changing life span of the younger generations.

WTG also had a major impact on the field of youth development by publishing a report in the mid-1980s entitled *The Forgotten Half.* This report described the disproportionate amount of federal funding and services for that half of the population that attends college. This report was one of WTG's most visible activities; the task force that produced it included a number of powerful public figures, such as Hillary Clinton, who was then wife of the Arkansas governor. Although this report was produced before I joined the foundation, we continued to attend to and promote its recommendations during my tenure. Hence, for example, it provided some justification for increasing our research focus on the transition to adulthood (Hamburg, 1993).

WTG also had a young investigator's program, Faculty Scholars, that provided 5 years of support to allow junior scholars in clinically oriented fields such as medicine to make a commitment to a research career. As a result, all our applications for this grant came from psychology, pediatrics, or child psychiatry. I knew from my work at SSRC that there was good child development research in social behavioral science fields, such as anthropology, economics, and sociology so we added scholars from these fields to the selection committee, and the program became fully multidisciplinary.

These are just two examples of the power of foundation funding for research in shaping a field. Hence, it was perfectly appropriate, even quite interesting, for me as a research psychologist to work for the foundation. WTG was unusual, however, in its funding of research and particularly in its decision-making processes (just described) about which projects to fund. WTG continues to fund mainly research, but it has since become more like other foundations in that it does not just receive investigator-initiated proposals. The foundation now strategically selects research projects that contribute to its overall mission, which is currently to reduce inequality.

## TRAVEL AND TALENT SCOUTING

Working for a foundation can involve regular travel. Travel serves two purposes: monitoring grantees and talent scouting. The nature of the travel is dictated by the foundation's program. WTG, for example, rarely funded projects outside the United States, so most of my travels were domestic. We did fund one grant on the one-child-only policy in China, which did require a trip to China. I previously had been to China, but as a senior representative from a U.S. foundation, I was treated royally, which was quite nice. Generally, such trips involved meeting with the grantee and their team as well as an occasional dean or other university administrator in the grantee's school. Such meetings often involved a program evaluation component as described in the next section.

The other major reason for traveling was to attend a variety of different meetings of professional associations, such as APA and SRCD, as well as of organizations such as SSRC and the National Academy of Sciences. The purpose of these travels was to identify innovative new areas of research that the foundation should consider funding as well as promising young investigators who might apply to the foundation. These trips of course contributed to program development, which I have described. Most program staff at a foundation do both types of traveling, but only the most senior do the latter.

## Program Evaluation

Program evaluation was the hardest part of the job, and I never felt we handled it successfully. Grantees provided both program reports and financial reports throughout the term of the grant as well as at its end. Hence, we could determine whether as a grantee they actually did what they promised to do in their application. This was almost always the case. Sometimes, grantees would need a change in budget or more time to complete the project, and I handled all such decisions. They were rarely problematic. The harder questions were impact on science and even harder the impact on children and families.

We did at various times look at indicators of scientific contribution regarding number of papers the grant produced and even entertained the idea of looking at the impact factor of the papers resulting from grant. We also formed consortia of grantees in particular areas, such as adolescent health or child abuse and neglect; these consortia would meet periodically to share findings or develop collaborations. Our faculty scholars almost always became leaders in their field. Hence, I think that one generally could argue that we made few mistakes in the specific project we chose to fund. And I have given examples of possible impacts on the field—becoming more multidisciplinary and extending the developmental framework up through young adulthood (now called the third generation of life).

One constraint on doing more evaluation of our program was the lack of program staff. You needed some expertise to do this type of program assessment, but I was the only staff person other than the president who really had the expertise to do this type of work. Because managing the application review process had to take priority, there was rarely time to do much in evaluating grants. So we'd usually do so only if we were worried about a particular grant or saw it to be especially important for some reason.

I once did a review of the Faculty Scholars program by meeting with university deans and other administrators at universities where we had a Faculty Scholar grantee. Our goal was to get their input on the details of the program. As a result of these visits, we did revise the amount of that program as well as aspects of its review process.

Assessing impact on the well-being of children and families was even more difficult than evaluating impact on science. There are two issues here: impact of research on policy generally and impact specifically of the projects we funded. At best, research generally has a relatively small impact on policy; the goal in bringing research to policy is to ensure that it is one of many variables on the table. It is rare that it will have a major impact because other factors like cost and budget as well as ideology are going to be more important. It is also difficult to assess the impact of a single study. So many variables affect children's development, it is difficult to identify how one variable, covered in a specific study, makes a contribution. There are exceptions, for example, research on adolescent work influenced the amount of time we allow teens in school to work; WTG funded some of this work. Scientific knowledge is cumulative, so it is unlikely a single study will alone be unusually important. I think this is one reason foundations shy away from funding research.

## New York City Service Programs for Children

WTG had a small program, approximately $500,000 a year, to fund programs servicing children in the New York metropolitan area. The funded programs had to relate to the foundation's overall program, but it did not have to involve research. We tried to encourage these program to collect more information than they otherwise might have done, for example, on participants, but their goal was to serve, not to study. We also looked for programs for which research might justify their approach, even if they did not acknowledge that approach. Because of this program, we had quite a bit of interest in program evaluation, so I learned a lot about this field as a result of working for WTG. In fact, after my time at WTG, I joined the faculty of Fordham University's Applied Developmental Psychology program. Fordham was interested in me in large part because of my expertise in program evaluation and social policy, both of which I acquired through my work at WTG.

At WTG, we often tried to help launch evaluations of social programs, some of which we funded, but this was not a requirement. We helped to launch several of these evaluations by bringing together program staff with relevant researchers. And some of these were among our most successful grants by helping a program develop into one that was appropriate for replication and dissemination or by promoting a researcher moving into a new line of research that helped to build their career.

## OFFICERS' DISCRETIONARY GRANTS

The service program grants were called officers' discretionary grants (ODF) because the officers (Dr. Haggerty and I at WTG) made the decisions. These grants were reported to the board but they did not influence the decisions what to fund. We also made ODFs for research and research-related purposes. WTG spent $500,000 on each program, and grants were capped initially at $10,000, which we later raised to $25,000. I managed both programs and always checked with Dr. Haggerty.

# Required Skill Set for Working at a Foundation

I will use academics as my comparison point. Any professional position requires certain skills and abilities, such as analytical skills, communication skills, ability to work with other people, and ability to learn quickly. The biggest difference between a research and a research planning job, as at a foundation, is the level of focus of one's attention. Research requires focusing on specific topics with keen attention to details. Working for a foundation requires being a generalist, being able to attend to the broad outlines of a topic or area, and identifying where there are gaps that the foundation can help fill.

## WORKING WITH PEOPLE RATHER THAN IDEAS

People skills are important for foundation work. Although science increasingly consists of large collaborative projects, it still involves a large component of individual investigator attention. Foundation work, on the other hand, is much more about working with people: applicants, grantees, reviewers, board members, and staff at other foundations.

Managing one's board is perhaps the biggest task of this aspect of working for a foundation. Boards vary in how active they are; some rubber stamp what the staff brings to them. This was not true at WTG. The program committee only approved about half of what we brought; the full board approved more but not 100%. With an active board, you have to prepare for meetings by anticipating what the reaction is likely to be to specific proposals and preparing for that reaction. You can do this based on what you know of individual board members, and their views relevant to the proposals; or you can try to get preliminary reactions before the meeting. The bottom line is that you need to be prepared for your board meetings; you don't want any surprises. And this involves interpersonal or political skills.

## Recognition for One's Work

Generally, one's work as a psychologist is easily acknowledged and recognized. This is much less true for working at a foundation. One needs to have a bit of self-confidence to work at a foundation. It is harder to assess one's individual contribution, and even if it can be determined, it is not publicly recognized. In science, one's contribution is quite clear and can be easily indexed through grants, publications, awards, and appointments; there are also specific indicators of these contributions, such as the citation index, which assesses the actual impact of one's work in terms of the number of times others cite it in their own work. Even in collaborations, one is a first author or principal investigator or not. In therapy, the success of one's patients can be assessed.

Working at a foundation does not offer such clear-cut roles nor evaluation of them. Furthermore, often one does not get direct credit for one's work. You work behind the scenes to make things happen as part of a team, and even to try to evaluate one's individual contribution would be seen as presumptuous. For example, I have noted that we diversified the WTG Faculty Scholars Program across disciplines by making the selection committee multidisciplinary.

This is my view, but it is not publicly acknowledged or recognized as a contribution I made. Some might even disagree, but I am sufficiently confident in my work and what I have brought to each job that I do not need this public acknowledgment of the role I played. Others may need more public recognition for their work than I do to keep motivated and remain on task.

The advantage of this is that one does not need to worry about individual indicators of success, such as publications and grants, as do faculty members who have to attend to such indicators for tenure and promotion. The disadvantage of this is that the criteria for salary and promotion are not always clear. I got one promotion at WTG from program vice president to executive vice president, but this had less to do with my job performance than with an internal staff reorganization to clarify that I was the second in command for all areas of foundation funding, not just programming.

## Advantages and Disadvantages
## of Working for a Foundation

The biggest advantage of working at a foundation is that it carries the funding of your work, unlike science, which requires constant fund raising. Funds are never unlimited, however, so foundation work requires making hard choices about how to use limited resources. There is always more that could be funded than there are funds. I think it is easier and less stressful to sell your ideas to funders than it is to decide how to spend money. I decided to leave WTG before I had a next job. Interestingly, jobs that involved heavy fund raising were the major opportunities that arose because folks assumed giving away money qualified you to raise money. In fact, just the opposite is the case. As I have said, I think raising money is easier than giving it away, which might be why folks considered if I had done the latter, the former would be easier.

The United States is a good country for foundation work because the donor receives tax benefits, making it advantageous to set up and fund a foundation. Foundations therefore have an initial value represented by the size of the gift made by the donor that founded the foundation. WTG was a medium to small foundation. Its current assets are about $300 million, which means they gave away less than $20 million per year. In the United States, foundations are required to spend annually at least 5% of their total assets. So if the foundation has $100 million, it has to spend at least $5 million per year; WTG has around $300 million, so it spends more than $15 million annually. The expenditures, however, have to represent gifts or grants, not administration. And most foundations are concerned about the ratio of grants to administration, wanting to keep the ratio as low as possible.

Foundations tend to be part of the wealthy institutions in a society. This means resources, although not unlimited, are never seriously limited. The resources you need to do your job are always freely available. I moved from the foundation to an academic job and was shocked at how limited resources were. Even Xerox paper was in short supply. In fact, one almost had to have grant funds to obtain the resources you needed to do your job. The resources you need to do your job, including professional development as well as grant making, are always freely available at a foundation. This is a big plus making philanthropy an attractive sector for which to work. And unlike in the private sector, one does not have to constantly demonstrate one's worth in terms of something like profit.

One disadvantage of working at a foundation is that they are dependent on the economy. Their assets are invested in the market, as is all other wealth. Hence, when the market is strong, they have lots of money to spend. When the market collapses, as in 2008, they have less money to spend. Sometimes, they can fund only current commitments and cannot make any new grants. Of course, they could decide to spend more than the required 5% of their assets, but this is rarely done. In this way, they are more like the private sector.

Not surprisingly, salaries are better as well; depending on your level at the foundation, salaries are probably 10–25% higher than in an academic job. And benefits like travel funds are much less limited; I had a virtually unlimited travel budget at WTG, for example. Furthermore, practical job benefits like health insurance and retirement are also generally quite good. Although clearly in the nonprofit sector, foundations are also more like the private sector in these regards.

## Choosing a Career Path and Preparing for It

As I have said, working in philanthropy is not a career like research or clinical practice for which there are training programs and clear steps for progress through one's career. It is nothing like medicine and law. Even fields like medicine and law, however, have undergone change in these regards in recent decades. We live in a rapidly changing world, so that any career requires constant updating of one's knowledge and skills as well as an ability to go with the flow and adapt to constantly changing work conditions. As a result, a career that does not promise such certainty in terms of needed preparation and distinct career trajectory may be more adaptive in the 21st-century's changing world than one that offers the illusion of certainty in these regards. Practicing medicine or clinical psychology these days is different than it was decades ago.

## Conclusion

I highly recommend philanthropy or other nonprofits as a career or at least as a one-time job for psychologists. I would not, however, recommend going to school in psychology for that purpose; once you are a research or clinical psychologist, I definitely recommend considering philanthropy as a possible career choice. It need not be lifelong, as was true in my case, but in the rapidly changing world, few careers are lifelong!

# References

Cahan, E. D. (1986). *William T. Grant foundation: The first fifty years, 1936–1986*. New York, NY: William T. Grant Foundation.

Gregorian, V. (2000). Some reflections on the historic roots, evolution, and future of American philanthropy: Report of the President. *Annual Report of the Carnegie Corporation of New York*. New York, NY: Carnegie Corporation.

Hall, P. D. (1988). Private philanthropy and public policy: A historical appraisal. In R. Payton, M. Novak, B. O'Connell, & P. Hall (Eds.), *Philanthropy four views*. New Brunswick, NJ: Transaction Books.

Hamburg, B. A. (1993). President's report: New futures for the "forgotten half:" Realizing unused potential for learning and productivity. *Annual Report of the William T. Grant Foundation*. New York, NY: William T. Grant Foundation.

Karl, B. D., & Katz, S. N. (1981). The American private philanthropic foundation and the public sphere 1890–1930. *Minerva, 19*, 236–270. http://dx.doi.org/10.1007/BF01096567

Nason, J. (1989). *Foundation trusteeship: Service in the public interest*. New York, NY: The Foundation Center.

Prewitt, K. (1995). *Social sciences and private philanthropy: The quest for social relevance*. Essays on Philanthropy, No. 15. Series on Foundations and their Role in American Life. Indianapolis: Indiana University Center on Philanthropy.

Renz, L., & Lawrence, S. (1993). *Foundation giving: Yearbook of facts and figures on private, corporate, and community foundations*. New York, NY: The Foundation Center.

Sherrod, L. R. (1998). The common pursuits of modern philanthropy and the proposed outreach university: Enhancing research and education. In R. Lerner & L. Simon (Eds.), *Creating the new outreach university for America's youth and families: Building university-community collaborations for the 21st century*. New York, NY: Garland Press.

Sherrod, L. R. (1999). An historical overview of philanthropy: Funding opportunities for research in applied developmental science. In P. Ralston, R. Lerner, A. Mullis, C. Simerly, J. Murray, & C. Fisher (Eds.), *Social change, public policy, and community collaboration: Training human development professionals in the twenty-first century* (pp. 121–129). Norwell, MA: Kluwer Academic Publishers.

Wisely, S. (1998). The pursuit of a virtuous people. *Advancing Philanthropy, Winter 1997–1998*, 14–20.

*William M. P. Klein, Rebecca A. Ferrer, and Sally S. Dickerson*

# Psychologists Giving Grants Through Government Organizations

27

W hen one is working through an undergraduate or graduate program in psychology, it is uncommon for there to be much discussion about government jobs—or for that matter, discussion about any jobs outside of the traditional academic setting. But the three authors of this chapter

William M. P. Klein is associate director of Behavioral Research at the National Cancer Institute (NCI). He received his PhD in social psychology at Princeton University in 1991 and served on the psychology faculty at Colby College and the University of Pittsburgh before coming to NCI.

Rebecca A. Ferrer is a program director in the Basic Biobehavioral and Psychological Sciences Branch of the National Cancer Institute. She received her PhD in social psychology at the University of Connecticut in 2009.

Sally S. Dickerson served as a rotating program director at the National Science Foundation from 2012–2015. She is now the Associate Provost for Sponsored Research and a Professor of Psychology at Pace University. Dr. Dickerson completed her PhD in social psychology at the University of California, Los Angeles in 2004.

http://dx.doi.org/10.1037/15960-028
*Career Paths in Psychology: Where Your Degree Can Take You, Third Edition*, R. J. Sternberg (Editor)

are clear examples of how a psychology degree can be put to use in government agencies. We all majored in psychological fields and then went off to get our PhDs in social psychology. When we finished our PhDs, none of us expected that ultimately we might end up working at a government agency. William M. P. Klein was a faculty member in a psychology department for 18 years before moving to the National Institutes of Health (NIH) to lead the Behavioral Research Program at the National Cancer Institute (NCI). Rebecca A. Ferrer moved directly into a postdoctoral position at NCI after graduate school and then took a full-time position as a program director there (a position we will define momentarily). Sally S. Dickerson just completed a term as a rotating scientist at the National Science Foundation (NSF) and has now returned to her academic position. Despite not having any idea when we were in graduate school that such positions were in our futures, we have all found them highly fulfilling.

Our jobs have many interesting features, but a principal one—and the one we focus on in this chapter—is to provide funding for scientists to do their research. As any psychology major knows well, research in psychology has contributed many lessons to our understanding of human behavior. What you may not realize is that much of this research is expensive. Equipment such as laptop computers and medical devices such as blood pressure monitors must be purchased and maintained. Laboratory staff must be paid salaries and benefits. Graduate students working in a laboratory must be compensated for their efforts as well as have their tuition covered. The human participants in psychological experiments often must be paid as well (and if the participants are animals, they must be purchased and maintained in an animal laboratory). More complicated research—such as projects that involve collecting data from multiple sites or from samples for which access is difficult (e.g., patients with a particular diagnosis, or homeless individuals who by definition do not have a contact address)—can cost even more. In some research settings, researchers are expected to seek funds that cover a significant portion of their own salaries.

How are all of these costs covered? Most institutions such as universities rely on their research staff—usually faculty—to apply for grants outside the institution. These grants can help pay for the expenses of the

We thank the many scientists (most of them psychologists) who have served as mentors for us throughout our careers and who all have played a role in helping us develop the skills to succeed in our current positions. Special thanks to Ross Buck, Robert Croyle, Robyn Dawes, Julie Downs, Jeffrey Fisher, Geoffrey Fong, Shelly Gable, Paige Green, Kara Hall, Margaret Kemeny, Ziva Kunda, Jennifer Lerner, John Levine, Jamie Pennebaker, Amber Story, Shelley Taylor, Neil Weinstein, Mark Weiss, and Edward Yeterian.

research (or what are called *direct costs*) as well as expenses incurred by the institution during the conduct of the research, such as building maintenance and administrative support (called *indirect costs*). Institutions and research staff pursue many places for grant funding. One common source is philanthropic foundations, which pool contributions from donors to support specific research priorities. For example, the Bill and Melinda Gates Foundation provides extensive funding for researchers developing methods to reduce infectious disease in developing countries. But the most common source of funding for researchers at institutions in the United States is the executive branch of the U.S. government. The two most well-known federal funding sources are the NIH and the NSF. A notable proportion of funding at both agencies supports work in the behavioral and social sciences, including psychology, anthropology, sociology, and economics.

That's where we come in. For these agencies to have a good sense of what to fund in psychology and other behavioral and social sciences, it is essential to have scientists with expertise from these fields at the table when making funding decisions. Fortunately, that is the case—usually in the form of scientists with doctoral degrees in some area of psychology who have decided to use their degree for public service. The most common role for these individuals is that of a program director or PD (also known as a program official or program officer). As we will explain, PDs oversee grants in a particular area of science related to their expertise. Many PDs are in relatively permanent positions, meaning that they are working full time for a funding agency and would not concurrently hold other positions in academia or industry (with the exception of adjunct faculty positions). Other PD positions, including many at NSF, are rotating, such that individuals take leave from their position and work as a PD on a terminal basis, typically for 1–3 years. These positions are valuable for the rotating scientist, as they provide an opportunity to learn about the other side of the grants process and develop insights into grantsmanship. It can be valuable to the agency to have fresh, different perspectives to inform funding priorities and emerging areas of research. Someone with a background in psychology might fill other positions besides PDs at a funding agency, and we will mention those briefly as well, but most of this chapter's focus will be on the job of the PD.

Before we explain this role, however, we begin with a short description of how the grant-funding process works to provide some context for what we do on a day-to-day basis in our jobs. Different agencies of the government have different research priorities. At the National Cancer Institute, for example, we are interested in why people smoke, how to get them to stop smoking (or not start in the first place), and how to inform regulations designed to protect people from secondhand smoke. The National Institute of Diabetes and Disease of the Kidneys

(NIDDK) is interested, like many other institutes at NIH, in how to decrease obesity—a major risk factor for diabetes and other diseases. The NSF tends to support more basic behavioral research, such as how emotion and emotional regulation influence behavior and how they develop over the life span. The Department of Defense might be interested in the understanding of how cultural differences in the expression of nonverbal behavior might facilitate recognition of aggressive motives. Or the Department of Education might want to see grant applications that address optimal strategies for helping underrepresented minorities perform better in school.

PDs with psychology degrees at these agencies often are involved in helping set priorities for research in the behavioral and social sciences. To help inform these priorities, these PDs might hold workshops that bring together expert researchers to focus on identifying pressing research questions within a specific area of need (like one on emotion and palliative care organized by Ferrer). Or they might visit research institutions around the country to talk with scientists in the area and collect their input about scientific gaps. It is incumbent on the PD to engage a diverse set of scientists and perspectives to generate novel ideas that go beyond the ideas often generated by individual investigators or labs.

## The Role of Program Directors During Grant Review

A primary responsibility of PDs is to help researchers throughout the grant application process. Researchers interested in obtaining grant funding for their work typically are called principal investigators or PIs, for short. Before submitting a grant application, they are strongly encouraged to contact PDs to talk about their ideas and get advice on how to handle their submissions. In these conversations, PDs can help potential applicants understand current research priorities at the agency and whether or not the ideas being proposed are aligned with those priorities. PDs also can advise the applicant on the priorities of the different subsections of the funding agency. For example, at NIH, PDs might be able to help an applicant think through which of the 27 NIH institutes and centers might be most appropriate for this particular research proposal. Every grant is assigned to a PD, and at NIH, if the applicant has had contact with a particular PD, that individual can be requested in the cover letter to the application as well. Additionally, at NSF, proposals can be reviewed by multiple programs (e.g., co-review) if the research falls at the intersection of two areas (e.g., a proposal on social development could be co-reviewed by Social Psychology and Developmental and

Learning Sciences). In this case, the PDs from the two (or more) programs would work together throughout the proposal's review process.

Most grants actually are reviewed by peers—that is, other researchers with expertise and qualifications similar to that of the applicants. Depending on the agency, PDs attend and sometimes even lead peer review discussions of grants and take notes during the discussion, which then can be used to provide feedback to the applicant about concerns that can be addressed or how to improve the application if it is resubmitted. Ultimately the applicant will receive a summary of the review, and the PD can help with interpretation of that summary.

If a grant is not reviewed well, PDs might advise the applicant on how it might be improved. If it does do well, the PD often must make a judgment about whether it is worthy of funding by the PD's home institute (at NIH) or program (at NSF). At some NIH institutes, there is a *payline*, such that all grants achieving a particular score or percentile—relative to other grants that were reviewed—are nearly automatically funded, assuming the PD considers the grant worthy. At that point, the PD becomes the formal overseer of that grant during its life—typically 4–5 years. For grants that are close to this payline but just missed it, the PD often has the opportunity to pitch the grant to his or her superiors at the institute. Every institute has its own process for reviewing these kinds of grants, but in most cases the PD's opinion of the grant is important in moving it forward.

The process is somewhat different at NSF. There is not a payline or percentile cutoff that determines funding. Instead, PDs use the information provided by the different reviewers and panel discussion to evaluate each proposal and make a decision about which ones to recommend for funding. Certainly, the panel's perspective and evaluation is weighed heavily in the decision-making process, but the PDs take into consideration a number of other factors, including factors such as portfolio balance (ensuring a diversity of different topics, methods, and approaches are represented in the funded awards).

## Role of Program Director After a Grant Is Funded

PIs who are successful at receiving grant funding for their research are expected to complete a progress report at the end of each year of the grant indicating what has and has not been accomplished as well as any changes in personnel, study aims, and research plans. PDs review these progress reports and inform their institutes whether they think adequate progress is being made on the project—an essential precondition to getting funding for the next year of the research project unless the grant was paid in one lump sum. PDs will review the final report that PIs must submit at the end of the last year of the project.

During the project itself, the PD might help the PI with any problems or questions that have arisen during the course of the project, such as how to handle delays, or problems with recruiting participants. The PD might help the PI think about funding mechanisms that might be appropriate for their next grant submission, building on the currently funded project. Some grants are specifically designed to facilitate the PI's training in a particular area of research, and in this case, the PD might advise PIs on how their training grants might be leveraged to develop a new research-based grant.

PDs typically have a portfolio of grants in a given area of science, and from time to time, they might be asked to conduct a portfolio analysis of all of their grants to identify areas of strength and weakness in research areas being funded by their institute. Such analyses can help PIs to provide support for other grants that are close to the payline, because those grants may center on a particular area of research not yet funded in their portfolio or in the portfolios of other PDs with similar expertise.

# A Typical Day in the Life of a Program Director

It is a cliché to say that every day in the life of a PD is different, but that is certainly the case. On an average day, PDs attend many meetings with other staff to discuss new initiatives and ideas, communicate with possible and current grantees, and respond to a wide variety of requests, including invitations to review articles for journals. PDs talk with grantees by phone or e-mail them with answers to their questions, read grantees' short summaries of their research ideas and provide feedback, and give advice about many aspects of the process (e.g., when to submit, what study section to recommend in a cover letter). PDs also might attend invited talks; there are many at any given time on the NIH campus and at NSF, just as there are on a university campus. Before a given application deadline, PDs are likely to be spending time with potential grantees to help them through the application process. The pinnacle of a given cycle is the peer review meeting, which PDs often attend or lead. Decisions to fund a grant may involve portfolio analyses and dialogue with other units in the agency who might provide cofunding for a grant of mutual interest.

Of note, many PDs publish position papers and commentaries that discuss new areas of research and directions for the field, and some conduct their own research. For example, NCI conducts a periodic national survey of people's engagement with and attitudes about health information related to cancer (the Health Information National Trends Survey, see Rutten, Moser, Beckjord, Hesse, & Croyle, 2007), and many PDs at NCI have published interesting articles reporting analyses of those data. It is also possible to conduct research with secondary data or to carry out meta-analyses, neither of which requires having one's own research laboratory to collect primary data. Publishing research articles helps PDs maintain their credibility as scientists despite not currently working in traditional academic settings, and it also strengthens their qualifications for academic positions if they have an interest in moving to another job in the future. Some types of grant mechanisms actually mandate collaborative work between outside PIs and the PDs for those grants, based on expertise and the needs of the funding agency. Rotators at NSF—like Dickerson—are given *release time* to facilitate their continued connections with their home institutions and their scholarly activities, including publishing, collecting data, and mentoring their students. Rotating PDs can preserve strong working relationships with students and collaborators through the use of virtual technology (e.g., holding lab meetings via Skype) and periodic visits to their colleges or universities.

On any given day, one might find PDs working on a draft of a funding announcement or a manuscript, reading some recent journal articles to keep up to date on progress in relevant scientific areas, meeting with a research fellow (such as a postdoctoral fellow) to provide mentoring on a project, or meeting with their supervisor about a new project idea or, on at least a yearly basis, about their performance. PDs also can be involved in working groups for special topics or initiatives and other agency-wide activities, in which they are able to interact with PDs from other areas. PDs are called on to represent their institutes or agencies at larger meetings. Like people in many jobs, the average day of a PD is filled with the challenge of managing e-mail.

PDs also travel as part of their jobs. They often attend professional conferences, where they might give presentations about funding processes and priorities (or about their own research) and meet with current and potential grantees about their research ideas and progress. Large grants require site visits by PDs as a way of ensuring that projects are making sufficient progress and that the agency's funding is being used prudently. And PDs might visit universities and other research institutions—often by invitation—to meet with their research faculty and to discuss agency priorities for funding.

# Rewards of Being a Program Director (and Some Drawbacks)

The job of being a PD is clearly quite different than being a practicing clinical psychologist, a psychology professor, or a conventional researcher doing psychological research. In traditional academic settings such as universities, the primary goal is to build an area of science by conducting one's own research and becoming recognized by the field; there is often little integration of research priorities in a given department or program. Conversely, the primary goal for government funding agencies is to take a broader and more integrated role in moving science forward. Given their control over the purse strings, staff at federal funding agencies have a hand in directing science. And at many agencies, they are doing so in way that addresses major societal problems like violence, disease, abuse, and terrorism. The opportunity for engaging in public service is often what draws individuals to these kinds of positions.

There are other rewards to consider. Depending on the agency, for example, psychologists are able to advance the science in their own way by mounting national surveys; conducting major reviews of the literature that outline broad future directions for a field of research, which might coincide with agency priorities (often resulting in what are called position papers or white papers); and summarizing the outcomes of meetings and other events hosted by their agencies. Many psychologists in government positions come from academic positions, where they have already built their own research programs, and they want to try something new. Working at a government agency can help these psychologists develop a big-picture view of a discipline, and science more generally; learn about scientific communication and science policy (and interaction of science and government); and collaborate with and learn from people in other disciplines. For example, Dickerson has had interactions with linguists, anthropologists, and others leading to many interesting conversations about big cross-cutting questions across disciplines.

Working for the government opens a window into how the U.S. government functions—that is, how it sets priorities and aims to meet them. Many PDs are called on to participate in important national activities, particularly within the executive branch of the government. For example, Klein serves on a committee of behavioral scientists across multiple agencies of the government, under the aegis of the National Science and Technology Council in the executive branch. This committee has contributed to revisions of the Common Rule (which is used by institutional review boards [IRBs] to assess the ethics of human subjects research), developed several reports and surveys of broad interest to federal agencies (such as one on language and communication), and evaluated various aspects of science policy.

The salaries of PDs are reasonably competitive, particularly for junior scientists. The government hires staff into 1 of 15 salary levels (each with 10 steps). For example, a GS-9/5 represents someone at level 9, step 5. A psychologist with a PhD coming in as a PD is likely to enter at least at the GS-12 level, which as of 2015 translates to a salary in the range of $75,000–$98,000. Rotators at NSF can come in on several different types of contracts; with one type of contract (Intergovernmental Personnel Act), they are simply paid their own salary from their home institution while they complete their time-limited tenure as a PD.

Importantly, these salaries cover all 12 months of the calendar year, not just the academic year as is typically true of salaries in academic jobs. Remember that some researchers have to apply for grants to cover a significant portion of their salary; that is not a concern of PDs because they are the ones providing funding for grants, not getting grants themselves. Government benefits (e.g., health, insurance, retirement) are also relatively good. Perhaps most important, after a 1-year probationary period, government positions are about as stable as any job could possibly be. Finally, most government funding agencies are in Washington, DC, a thriving city with ample access to museums, fine arts, and great restaurants, and a diverse and heterogeneous population. Philadelphia is only 2 hours away (and New York City is 4 hours away—easily reached on an inexpensive shuttle if so desired). Three airports in the Washington, DC, area make it possible to get anywhere by air.

Of course, no job is perfect—a job like this has some drawbacks as well. As alluded to earlier, being in this kind of position involves greater efforts at the larger scientific and national level, which can make it more challenging to make specific individual research contributions. Also, the U.S. government maintains a more hierarchical structure than academic institutions, with rules and protocols that must be followed and that can deter progress on some kinds of efforts. Most intramural research pursuits, for example, must be reviewed not only by an IRB as would be the case at an academic or other research institution, but also by the Office of Management and Budget, an office that reviews a wide range of government activities to minimize burden on the U.S. public and maximize efficiency. This is the office that approves Internal Revenue Service tax forms, for example. Also, at any given time, a scientist in the government could be called away to address another priority, as happened with staff at the Centers for Disease Control and Prevention in 2014 when the Ebola outbreak became a national priority. Of course, these unique opportunities also can be construed as a benefit of the job. And, finally, government employees are negatively affected by Congressional budget standoffs; for example, we had to cope with the effects of sequestration and a government furlough in 2013 and 2014.

## Preparing for a Job as a Program Director

How might one prepare for a position as a PD? A PD typically needs to have a doctoral degree (PhD), perhaps with postdoctoral experience. At NSF, PDs are required to have at least 6 years of experience past the time their PhD was granted. At NIH, it helps (although is not required) for some of the postdoctoral experience to be at NIH itself. Ferrer is a good example of that—she completed her PhD in social psychology, then came to the National Cancer Institute as a postdoctoral researcher and stayed in that position for 2 years before being hired as a PD. She now oversees a growing portfolio of grants in the areas of emotion, decision making, and health behavior, facilitated greatly by her postdoctoral work. In addition to scientific expertise, it helps for a PD to have good communication skills and to be able to work well with others. It also helps to have a passion for public service—knowing that one is making a difference without doing it in a way that is particularly visible.

Importantly, people with psychology backgrounds hold other positions in funding agencies, and they do not all require a PhD in psychology. For example, public health advisors might manage large projects or work hand in hand with PDs to evaluate the portfolio of funded research in a given research area. NIH also supports research fellows who come to do research or administrative work for a short period of time before moving on to graduate school or other opportunities. At NSF, people with a bachelor's or master's degree can serve as science assistants. Science assistant positions are temporary and provide an excellent way for recent graduates to gain first-hand experience with different aspects of the grants process and science policy. They provide support to PDs and division leadership, and they are involved in all types of grants-related activities, including assisting with panel meetings, conducting portfolio analysis, and communicating research findings to the public.

Some psychologists at NIH serve as scientific review officers (SROs)—people who coordinate and oversee peer review of grants. The SRO is charged with developing a sophisticated understanding of science in the review group's topic area and recruiting a broad range of scientists who together have the expertise necessary to review applications that are likely to come into that review group. The SRO also compiles the summary statement for each grant, including a written summary of the key points of the discussion. SROs almost uniformly have doctoral degrees, affording them the necessary expertise to interpret the comments of the peer reviewers and communicate them in the review summaries. Their expertise also positions them well to select peer reviewers to serve on the review panel and to help the panel understand the scientific context of the grant.

Finally, people with degrees in psychology also might secure positions in human resources at funding agencies or in communications. A government funding agency has many of the same needs as a corporate organization, and many of these needs are met by psychologists. For example, psychologists may help with increasing diversity in the workplace, developing employee surveys, or assisting with communication of research priorities and the availability of resources, such as toolkits. Organizational psychologists are sometimes called on to run training sessions and workshops to increase workplace efficiency and enhance leadership skills.

## Conclusion

As the chapters in this book illustrate, individuals with a background in psychology can pursue many interesting careers. This chapter elaborated on one such interesting career—one that offers the opportunity to have a great deal of influence over the direction of science in the United States, not to mention the opportunity to help leverage that science to address real problems, such as poor health, poverty, violence, and terrorism. A PD at a U.S. funding agency can motivate new areas of research, become well versed in many areas of science, work with potential grantees to help them polish their research ideas, and even make many of their own scientific contributions. They can do so while drawing a steady salary in a setting in which jobs tend to be stable. Given the numerous areas of science related to human behavior, a psychology background is useful as a PD—particularly one who might be overseeing a portfolio of behavioral research at their agency. We hope this overview of the position offers a clear picture of what it might be like to use a psychology background in this innovative way.

## Reference

Rutten, L. F., Moser, R. P., Beckjord, E. B., Hesse, B. W., & Croyle, R. T. (2007). *Cancer communication: Health Information National Trends Survey.* Washington, DC: National Cancer Institute.

*Wayne J. Camara*

# Psychologists in Educational Testing and Measurement Organizations

28

American students may be among the most tested students by the time they enter college according to several international comparisons. Most children first encounter standardized testing around the age of 4 years old, when they are assessed for kindergarten readiness. At that early age, educators often complete structured social and developmental history inventories with parents, assess children's motor and social skills with structured ratings, and assess cognitive skills with other tests. The No Child Left Behind Act (NCLB, 2002) mandated testing in grades 3 through 8 in reading and math, as well as high school, with assessment

Wayne J. Camara, PhD, is senior vice president of research at ACT® and held a similar position at the College Board for two decades. He is former president of the National Council of Measurement in Education, Association of Test Publishers, and Division 5 of the American Psychological Association. His research has focused on college admissions, test validation, college readiness, and standards and practices in the use and development of assessments.

http://dx.doi.org/10.1037/15960-029
*Career Paths in Psychology: Where Your Degree Can Take You, Third Edition*,
R. J. Sternberg (Editor)

in science at three grade levels. More than 40% of students in 27 states completed assessments given by two consortia[1] in 2014–2015, which required 8–10 hours of testing time. Most states administer additional tests in one or more subjects (e.g., social studies, health) and many school districts require additional tests (Salazar, 2014). One study found that up to 19 school days are consumed by state-mandated testing, interim assessments, and test prep activities (Nelson, 2013). These estimates do not include various other types of assessments commonly administered in schools.

The pace of educational testing continues unabated in high school, particularly for students who plan to attend college. In addition to state- and district-mandated testing and preparation for such tests, college-bound high school students generally take preadmissions tests in their sophomore and junior years to qualify for scholarships and to prepare for the ACT® or SAT® and Advanced Placement® (AP) Exams. Additional psychological and educational tests are administered to identify students who may have special needs (e.g., learning disabilities) or talents (e.g., gifted). Even individuals who don't complete high school eventually take a high school equivalency test or other assessments to qualify for a vocational program or a credential for employment. Finally, students will often complete career interest inventories during their K–12 education, such as the Armed Services Vocational Aptitude Battery during high school, which is used both to gather career information and to identify students who may qualify for military service.

Just as the use of educational testing has increased dramatically, so, too, have opportunities and demand for psychologists who have completed graduate school training in research, statistics, testing, and measurement. Different types of psychologists, as well as other professionals, spend much of their careers working in organizations that develop and administer educational and psychological assessments and in organizations that conduct educational research.

This chapter describes the different paths leading to this career, attributes and training required for success, the work settings and environment in educational testing organizations, and financial compensation for psychologists. It begins with a brief discussion of my own career path in educational testing organizations.

---

[1]Partnership for Assessment of Readiness for College and Careers (PARCC) and Smarter Balanced Assessment Consortium (SBAC) are two multistate assessment consortia.

# My Career Path
# in Educational Testing

Like many undergraduate students, I entered college without a clear choice of a major or a career goal. I was soon drawn to the study of human behavior and chose psychology as a major (my fourth!). In my junior year, I enrolled in an elective course, Psychological Testing, which used the classic text authored by Anastasi (1976). I came to understand how information from standardized tests, when used appropriately, could supplement professional judgment and provide a means of comparing individuals to other individuals (a normative purpose), to themselves (a longitudinal purpose), or against a set of established criteria or standards (a criterion-related purpose). In addition, tests could reduce the individual biases we each hold and provide important information for descriptive and inferential purposes. Anastasi (1976) also demonstrated how tests are used in a variety of settings, such as industrial, clinical, vocational counseling, and education settings.

I earned a master's degree in educational measurement and then a certificate of advanced graduate study in school psychology, working as a psychologist in K–6 schools where I assessed students for learning and behavioral issues with a range of cognitive, personality, and projective tests. Although I enjoyed the testing, measurement, and diagnostic aspects of the work, I quickly understood the limitations that face individuals trained in psychology who do not possess a doctoral degree.

In 1987, I completed a PhD program at the University of Illinois at Champaign-Urbana. My course of study included a combination of foundation and quantitative courses in both educational measurement and industrial/organizational psychology (I/O psychology). Again, my primary interests were the efficacy and validity of tests and assessment in decision making. My master's thesis evaluated a variety of predictors used in employment selection, and my dissertation involved developing an adaptive screening assessment for applicants to the state civil service. Coursework and research focused on personnel selection, validation, educational testing, computer-based testing, and measurement theory. However, I also completed a number of required courses in statistics and quantitative psychology, and required proficiency across a variety of statistical software programs (e.g., SAS, SPSS, LISREL) outside of formal coursework.

My first postdoctoral experience was as a research scientist at the Human Resources Research Organization (HumRRO), where I worked on a number of research and development (R&D) projects, conducting job analytic studies, identifying personality traits and other noncognitive factors that were associated with success in entry-level managers, examining the validity of the military's testing program, and conducting research related to the development of a biographical inventory (biodata) for personnel selection. As an entry-level research scientist, I was responsible for working with several small teams on different research projects, each of which was managed by a more senior research scientist. I devoted a substantial amount of time to writing responses to federal and state government requests for proposals (RFPs), which are the primary sources of funding for many educational research and testing organizations. I gained an enormous amount of practical experience in budgeting, staffing, and pricing of research and technical services, areas that are not taught in graduate programs. My training in research design, sampling, and research methodology were invaluable for this type of work. The primary deliverables of all educational research organizations are written reports and oral presentations.

I have been employed at not-for-profit educational testing organizations for the past 21 years. First, at the College Board in New York City, as a research scientist, then as a psychometrician, and eventually as vice president of R&D, to my current position as senior vice president of research at ACT in Iowa City, IA. Both organizations are globally recognized for the quality and popularity of major assessment programs (e.g., ACT, AP, SAT, Workeys), as well as research and innovation in measurement, assessment, and educational success. There are many additional testing organizations in the United States. Many organizations, such as Educational Testing Service, Pearson, Inc., or CTB/McGraw Hill, design and deliver state and district assessments, whereas other testing organizations primarily develop and deliver assessments in fields with licensure or credentials. A third group of organizations sponsors and delivers a single assessment for their profession.[2] Finally, several major research universities house centers dedicated to testing and measurement, which employ psychologists in nonteaching professional roles and relies on external contracts and grants for funding.[3]

## PSYCHOMETRICIANS AND RESEARCH SCIENTISTS

Professionals who develop and conduct research on tests are commonly referred to as *psychometricians*. *USA Today* described them as "a small but growing group of elite researchers who do little else but think about standardized tests. . . . Trained in both psychology and statistics (they) make sure standardized tests actually test what kids know, quickly,

---

[2]For example, the American Institute of Certified Public Accounts produces the AICPA assessment and the Laws School Admissions Board produces the LSAT assessment.

[3]For example, Center for Research on Evaluation, Standards, and Student Testing at UCLA, the Linguist Center for Iowa Testing Programs at the University of Iowa and the Center for Testing and Evaluation at the University of Kansas.

fairly, and accurately" (Toppo, 2004, p. D1). In actuality, psychologists who work in testing usually are classified in one of two related career paths—either as research scientists or psychometricians. The American Psychological Association's Division 5, Evaluation, Measurement, and Statistics (2010), proposes a minor distinction between psychometricians and quantitative psychologists, but these positions (as well as statisticians) focus on statistical modeling, statistical programming, and data and also on how test items or tests perform. Psychometricians generally have completed doctoral training in an educational measurement program, statistics or evaluation program, or quantitative psychology.[4] Psychometricians are concerned with measuring educational and psychological characteristics, such as achievement, abilities, skills, and other factors. Other professionals, working as research scientists, may evaluate educational programs; conduct research on educational problems, such as literacy and gender differences in learning; or design and analyze surveys or research studies. They often attempt to answer education questions that strive to improve teaching and learning. For example, they may examine issues such as test anxiety, gender differences in science achievement, or the types of instruction that result in greater reading achievement among elementary students.

Research scientists or other measurement professionals working in testing organizations may focus more on the psychological constructs, measurement theory (e.g., validity), learning and cognition, personality traits, or evaluation. Such positions still require a significant knowledge of statistics, research design, and assessment, but often the day-to-day activities require less skill in statistical programming, data manipulation, and higher level statistical processes. Educational psychologists, as well as psychologists from other specialties, will compete with graduates from educational measurement and evaluation programs for such positions. A recent study (Packman, Camara, & Huff, 2010) of testing and measurement professionals found that just under 40% were employed in academia, 40% in research or testing organizations, 10% employed in government agencies (e.g., state department of education), and about 10% were employed in other organizations (e.g., consultant, director of research). The most popular job titles of measurement and testing professionals working in testing and research organizations included research scientist (17%), psychometrician (17%), test developer (14%), program manager (11%), director of research or psychometrics (11%), and research associate or analyst (9%). The same study also found that 73% of professionals in such organizations hold a doctorate degree, with 22%

---

[4]Some psychometricians may be trained in other areas such as economics, I/O psychology, educational psychology, or computer science, but they generally would have significant experience in measurement and statistical applications.

having a master's degree. About half of full-time professionals have been in their current position for 2–10 years.

In an interdisciplinary survey of measurement and testing professionals working in any setting, it was found that they are slightly more likely to be Caucasian (82%) or Asian American (9%) and male (56%). Table 28.1 illustrates the primary work setting from the same survey respondents by type of degree. About 43% of doctoral-level professionals received a degree in psychology compared with 44% who came from education programs and 13% from statistics and other programs outside of education and psychology. Among master's degree professionals, 37% had a degree in psychology, compared with about 32% each for education and statistics/or other programs. Psychologists, however, accounted for 46% of doctoral-level professionals working in research and testing organizations as compared with 39% and 15% of those with degrees from education and statistics/or other departments, respectively (Camara et al., 2010). A survey of measurement professionals who are members of the National Council on Measurement in Education (NCME)

## TABLE 28.1

**Degree Program by Primary Work Setting**

| | Academic | | District | | Research/ Testing | | Other | | Total | |
|---|---|---|---|---|---|---|---|---|---|---|
| | M | D | M | D | M | D | M | D | M | D |
| Counseling/Clinical psychology | 20 | 6 | 4 | 1 | 12 | 3 | 2 | 1 | 38 | 11 |
| Curriculum/Teaching | 20 | 9 | 6 | 4 | 15 | 2 | 5 | 3 | 49 | 18 |
| Educational administration/Policy | 7 | 6 | 5 | 3 | 1 | 2 | 0 | 1 | 14 | 13 |
| Educational psychology | 25 | 34 | 8 | 8 | 29 | 36 | 8 | 7 | 74 | 89 |
| Research, evaluation, measurement | 27 | 91 | 12 | 25 | 43 | 77 | 14 | 29 | 100 | 232 |
| General psychology | 12 | 4 | 4 | 2 | 9 | 1 | 4 | 1 | 29 | 8 |
| I/O psychology | 6 | 4 | 1 | 2 | 5 | 7 | 4 | 1 | 16 | 14 |
| Public policy/Policy administration | 2 | 0 | 3 | 0 | 1 | 2 | 1 | 0 | 7 | 3 |
| Quantitative methods/ Psychometrics | 28 | 62 | 3 | 9 | 29 | 48 | 9 | 13 | 71 | 138 |
| School Psychology | 4 | 3 | 2 | 5 | 3 | 2 | 1 | 0 | 10 | 10 |
| Statistics | 25 | 20 | 2 | 3 | 25 | 15 | 7 | 5 | 61 | 44 |
| Other | 36 | 8 | 8 | 5 | 39 | 15 | 11 | 5 | 97 | 34 |

*Note.* The number of degrees exceeds the *N* because individuals were asked to indicate all graduate or professional degrees. Data from Packman, Camara, and Huff (2010).

reported professionals concentrated in the Northeast and graduate students concentrated in the Midwest and the South. In addition, academics represented the largest career segment (42%) followed by testing organizations (28%), state government (35%), federal government (21%), and other employers (20%; Camara, 2011).

## DIFFERENT PATHS LEADING TO THE CAREER

Psychologists who work in testing organizations (or other educational research organizations) typically have completed graduate training in quantitative psychology, psychometrics, I/O psychology, or educational psychology. However, individuals who have graduate training in other areas of psychology and have demonstrable competencies in statistics, research design and methodology, measurement, evaluation, and testing also may find employment in such organizations. As in most other areas of applied psychology, professionals who have master's degrees do not normally compete for the same positions as doctoral-level psychologists; however, individuals who have accumulated a great deal of experience and recognition for their work despite the lack of a doctoral degree are exceptions to this rule. Psychologists often compete directly with nonpsychologists who possess similar training in research, psychometrics, evaluation, and testing. In fact, the majority of professionals working in educational testing companies are not psychologists; instead, they have doctoral degrees in educational measurement programs or other disciplines (e.g., sociology, economics) that require strong research and statistical skills.

Less than 1% of doctoral-level psychologists who are members of the APA indicate that their primary areas of specialization are in quantitative psychology, psychometrics, or statistics, with another 1.3% who were trained in educational psychology (APA, 2014). In 2010, 29 graduate programs in psychology departments offered specializations in quantitative psychology, quantitative methods, or measurement (APA Division 5, 2010), whereas 84 doctoral programs in educational measurement recently were identified (Gaertner & Kolen, 2015). Approximately half of the 84 programs housed in education appeared to offer the specialized training in psychometrics and educational evaluation that would be required for entry-level positions in most educational testing and research organizations. Kohout and Wicherski (2009) reported that 117 students were enrolled in doctoral programs in quantitative psychology in 2007–2008, with an additional 269 students enrolled in doctoral programs in educational psychology. The field of psychometrics and measurement is intertwined with educational measurement and quantitative psychology and may be located in education departments. Programs that provide comparable graduate preparation may be called "research and statistics" or "research and evaluation" or may be within another specialty in graduate psychology programs (Sireci, 1996).

The NCME identified up to 70 full-time internships for doctoral students enrolled in measurement and quantitative programs and the list of sponsors in Exhibit 28.1 provides a snapshot of the major employers in this field (NCME, 2014). Testing organizations include both for-profit and not-for-profit publishers. This list is not inclusive of research and testing organizations hiring psychometricians and research scientists and omits many organizations involved in employment and clinical testing, credentialing and licensure testing, and university-based testing centers, which also hire psychologists and nonpsychologists with expertise in measurement, statistics, research methods, and assessment.

The competencies required to be successful are common to most professionals working in the testing and measurement. Students interested in pursuing careers in this field should have strong quantitative skills and prior exposure to one or more of the following areas: psychology, education, statistics, computer science, and testing. Coursework in advanced mathematics, such as calculus and matrix algebra, can be helpful in the advanced statistical coursework required in psychometrics and

---

**EXHIBIT 28.1**

**Organizations With Full-Time Doctoral Internships in Psychometrics, Measurement, and Statistics**

---

ACT, Inc.
Association of American Medical Colleges
College Board
CTB/McGraw-Hill
Educational Testing Service
Houghton Mifflin, Riverside Publishing Co.
Law School Admissions Council
Measured Progress
National Board of Medical Examiners
National Board of Osteopathic Medical Examiners
National Center for the Improvement of Educational Assessment
National Conference of Bar Examiners
Pearson, Educational Measurement
Professional Examination Services
RAND
Second Language Testing, Inc.

---

*Note.* Many additional educational research and testing organizations are not included in this list of NCME internships, including employment testing and research organizations that list internships with the Society for Industrial and Organizational Psychology (see http://www.siop.org/IOInternships/toc.aspx), that privately advertise their internships, or that may not have had an internship program at the time of publication. Data from Packman, Camara, and Huff (2010).

quantitative psychology. Graduate coursework typically involves experimental methods, data analysis and interpretation, research design, test theory, and measurement. In addition, individuals pursuing a doctoral degree in psychometrics or quantitative psychology should have coursework in advanced statistical methods, computer programming, statistical software, and measurement theory (Illinois State University, 2005; Sireci, 1996). An informal review of job descriptions from the leading educational testing organizations indicated that nontechnical competencies are also essential for success, including attention to detail, precision, the ability to work independently and in groups, and the ability to explain and communicate statistical information and technical concepts to nontechnical audiences. In addition to oral and written communication skills, psychologists working in educational organizations need to be able to work on different projects simultaneously and to balance priorities, deadlines, and demands among multiple projects. These work environments also require a high degree of personal organization, planning, and logic to develop project plans required for testing and research. Professionals who can speak to and write for a wide variety of audiences, including students, teachers, parents, educational administrators, policymakers, and other researchers, are highly valued because much of the work involves communication and interdisciplinary groups.

The majority of their time may be devoted to designing research, collecting data, conducting statistical analyses, collecting data, programming, and writing results. Increasingly, however, they need to work closely on a daily basis with professionals trained in teaching and learning, business and finance, marketing, law, and technology. Advancement into managerial and executive leadership positions normally will require additional soft skills as well as an ability to work on cross-disciplinary teams. Communication skills are a key requirement for professionals in such organizations, who may be called on to write a technical/or business proposal for a state testing program; explain a score report to the media; or explain to an audience of skeptical educators how results from assessments delivered on tablets, computers, and on paper are statistically comparable. Efficiency in writing is just as important as clarity in communication, and it is not unusual to be expected to produce lengthy technical proposals in a few weeks while managing large research studies. Unlike most graduate school experience, researchers in large testing organizations may work on several different projects with several different teams of professionals under tight deadlines. The ability to present the technical material in oral presentations and to handle questions under fire is essential for success. Finally, although psychologists may not be trained in business, operations, technology, and law, the ability to demonstrate acumen in these areas and address the external environment and internal systems that collectively affect assessment design and delivery are essential for leadership and managerial roles in testing organizations.

## Roles and Responsibilities

Psychologists in testing organizations assist in developing educational tests that are used in schools. The ACT, the Graduate Record Examination (GRE), the Law School Admissions Test (LSAT), and the SAT are examples of admission tests that are developed, administered, and scored by psychologists and psychometricians working in educational organizations such as ACT, Educational Testing Service, the Law School Admissions Council, and the College Board. Educational testing companies also respond to RFPs and are hired by industries to develop certification and licensure tests, or by states and national government agencies to develop educational tests. In 2002, the Public Broadcasting Service estimated revenue from state and district testing ranged from $400 million to $700 million before the implementation of NCLB. The General Accounting Office (2003) estimated that states may have spent an additional $3.9 billion to $5.3 billion on tests mandated under the federal NCLB requirements alone between 2002 and 2008. A 2012 study estimated states collectively spend $1.7 billion dollars on assessments annually. Assessment contracts in grades 3–9 accounted for about $669 million with six vendors owning nearly 90% of this work and per student costs for testing ranging from $13 to $105 (Chingos, 2012). In 2014, more than 4 million AP examinations were taken, and it is estimated that more than 3.5 million undergraduate admissions tests were administered. These figures do not include many other standardized tests administered in schools or to students.[5]

All of this translates into an enormous amount of testing in schools and a demand for more psychologists and psychometricians with the appropriate skills to produce, score, and report results on the increased number of tests. Many testing professionals have joked that the NCLB legislation also leaves no psychometrician behind, as the amount of testing conducted in public schools has at least doubled. States generally contract with large educational testing companies to develop tests designed to assess educational standards for each subject (e.g., math, science) at various grade levels. Testing is tailored to the state's standards, unlike national testing programs, which develop many forms for use each year, or off-the-shelf career interest, personality, and intelligence tests that may use the same one or two test forms across several years.

---

[5]These additional tests would include formative and interim assessments, district achievement tests, tests for special populations (e.g., students with disabilities, English language learners), and career or vocational interest inventories.

Psychologists and psychometricians may work in test development to create a test blueprint that is similar to an architectural blueprint. They consider the construct being measured (e.g., mathematical reasoning, chemistry, career interests); the number and types of questions required to cover the knowledge or skill domain that is being assessed; and other psychometric features that are important in producing a fair, valid, and reliable test. For example, they are concerned with the reliability of tests and with ensuring that when humans score essays or open-ended items, they apply consistent and reliable standards across readers and student responses to ensure that scoring is not biased. Often psychometricians work directly with teachers to review items and scoring rubrics. They conduct statistical analyses once tests scores have been produced; for example, they examine individual test items on achievement tests to ensure that they represent a range of difficulty for each skill or subject and that students have the appropriate amount of time to complete a test without taking more time from classroom instruction than is necessary. On tests such as the ACT, psychometricians equate each form to ensure that scores from all test forms are comparable. They also may work with educational administrators and counselors to ensure that score reports are accurate, clear, and easily understood by schools, students, and parents.

Testing organizations have R&D units that examine a wide range of research questions concerning assessments and gather evidence of validity to support the use of test scores and results for students and schools. Psychologists and psychometricians perform statistical analyses of test results after tests are administered, conduct research to ensure the quality of test results, and evaluate the effectiveness of the testing programs. Psychologists and psychometricians also conduct research on the tests, evaluating educational programs and interventions, investigating individual differences in terms of teaching and learning, examining the impact of testing accommodations, and studying the influence of a variety of different factors (e.g., background, social, cognitive, school, and teacher factors) in these areas. Educational organizations, such as the American Institutes for Research (AIR), HumRRO, the RAND Corporation, Westat Inc., and many others, are involved in conducting research in these areas.

Individuals trained in psychology at the master's level are employed in test development, psychometric, and research units in these organizations. They typically begin their careers coordinating research tasks, such as contacting schools to coordinate data collection from students, writing test instructions, or conducting routine data analyses for doctoral-level professionals. Eventually, with substantial experience and training, some individuals trained in psychology at the master's level are given considerable responsibility in project management and research efforts.

There is no typical day for a research scientist or psychometrician. Each day brings different tasks, different challenges, and different duties depending on the type of organization one works for, the tests one works on or the programs one evaluates, and the specific responsibilities one has. One commonalty is that research scientists and psychometricians across organizations, programs, and jobs work independently on their own projects and analyses, but that work is always incorporated into a group product and team environment.

Developing a test and reporting scores for a small program many involve a handful of staff, whereas developing, delivering, scoring, and reporting scores on assessments for the two major state consortia (i.e., Partnership for Assessment of Readiness for College and Careers [PARCC], Smarter Balanced Assessment Consortium [SBAC]) has involved literally hundreds of professionals across a dozen or more organizations, as well as thousands of educators who proctor the tests, score the essays, and review scores with students in schools. Psychometricians assist organizations and content experts (e.g., reading, math, science) in determining the number and types of items to place on a test. They ensure that items measure all major areas of a construct without overemphasizing one or two areas. They are similarly concerned that students have an appropriate amount of time to complete the test. In addition, they ensure that no item differentially favors a group of students because of irrelevant factors. For example, items that contain terms or focus on content that is not widely known will not appear on national achievement tests, because they could favor a particular group of students on the basis of regional, ethnic, or cultural differences.

In the past several years, state assessments have increasingly moved to digital delivery, with both consortia and several independent state assessments declaring computer-based testing as the preferred, or soon to be only, administrative option available. Schools, however, often lack the technical infrastructure to transition fully to one standardized digital delivery system, and different modes, devices, and testing conditions are present in the state and consortia assessments. Research scientists and psychometricians working on assessments used for student, school, and educator accountability are concerned about the comparability of scores and validity of scores resulting from these differences. They study the impact administration mode (e.g., paper, computer), device (e.g., tablet, laptop), and tools (e.g., spellchecker, on-screen keyboard) have on item rendering, cognitive demand, response times, and performance.

In spring of 2014, the ACT was delivered digitally in school-day testing programs with college reportable scores—the first undergraduate admissions to go online with comparable and official scores for high-stakes uses (Li, Yi, & Harris, 2015). Graduate and professional school admissions tests have been delivered by computer since the GRE was introduced on computer in October 1992 (Schaffer, Steffen, Golub-Smith, Mills, & Durso, 1995). As of 2016, admissions tests for entry into medical school, business school, graduate school, and many other specialty fields (e.g., dentistry, pharmacy) are delivered on computer (Camara, Packman, & Wiley, 2013).

Before including items on tests, psychometricians try them out to determine how students will perform on the items. If the majority of items on a test are easy, the test will not do a good job of differentiating students who are high performers from those who are low performers. Most achievement tests not only cover a wide variety of content and skills in an area (e.g., geometry, biology) but also include a mix of items that are considered easy, medium, difficult, and hard. Psychometricians also oversee the scoring of tests. Many tests include essays or open-ended tasks that require human scorers to be trained to grade them consistently. Psychometricians also examine the difficulty of tests and equate scores from different forms of a test so that scores from one test administration are statistically comparable to scores from an earlier and subsequent administrations. Research scientists are often concerned with examining a number of ways that irrelevant factors can affect scores. They examine test items and responses to detect possible cheating or other irregularities and conduct validity studies that gather evidence of how test scores can be appropriately used. At ACT, research scientists and psychometricians conduct validity studies that examine how accurately the ACT and high school grades predict student achievement in college or specific majors. Some studies focus on group differences (e.g., ethnic, gender) on tests and demonstrate that the same differences often exist on the performance that is being predicted (e.g., college grades, graduation, retention). Other studies examine the effects of coaching, a more rigorous high school curriculum, or family education and wealth on test scores and college performance.

Psychologists employed in educational testing or research organizations may have fewer opportunities than their colleagues in academia to conduct research on their specific areas of interest. Research is often dictated by the types of applied problems or challenges confronting the testing program or the demand to introduce improvements in the assessment or additional evidence of its effectiveness. Larger organizations such as ACT, Educational Testing Service (ETS), and Pearson may be better able than smaller testing organizations to support research that is not directly related to a product or invest in a line of research that may take years of effort before realizing a breakthrough. Many educational testing and research organizations will bid for test development or research contracts, and employees work on the projects that the company is successful in winning. These projects become the priority, and although many professionals conduct some independent research or consultation, it generally is not a first priority.

Psychologists in an educational organization are also likely to work with many teams, and they need to be willing to compromise and to understand that marketing, business, and customer demands may be just as important to the success of a project as the scientific or statistical expertise they represent. Psychologists trained in research programs value objective information and empirical facts. They are trained to have a healthy dose of skepticism about conclusions or diagnoses that are based solely on professional judgment. These differences will often put such psychologists at odds with many of their colleagues who have worked in clinical and educational settings and who rely on expert judgment as the foundation for much of their interventions. Successful researchers and psychometricians who work in testing companies combine superb technical skills and organizational abilities, amazing amounts of drive and personal motivation, and an ability to communicate with non-researchers to explain technical and complex issues in clear and simple language. In addition, they enjoy solving problems in a practical and applied environment and can balance a large number of projects and responsibilities.

Packman et al. (2010) conducted a survey of testing and measurement professionals to ascertain tasks they perform in different organizational environments. Two hundred (37%) respondents who worked in educational testing or research organizations reported the mean percentage of time devoted to specific activities. Results from Table 28.2 illustrate that three major types of activity account for about 85% of their work—psychometric work on operational testing programs, administrative tasks (e.g., project management, vendor management), and conducting research. A separate study of testing professionals reported that they spend 25% of their time on statistical or psychometric analyses and programming, followed by research (18%) and project and contract management (18%; Camara, 2011).

## Employment Opportunities

According to Packman et al., "There has been widespread acknowledgement that the demand for professionals in educational measurement, assessment, and psychometrics has exceeded the supply" (2010, p. 15). As noted earlier, much of the demand can be traced to the increase in mandated testing under NCLB, a similar increase also has occurred in assessments used for admissions, college readiness, certification, and licensure

## TABLE 28.2

**Mean Response for Categories and Tasks in the Research/Testing Organization Setting**

| Category<br>Task | Mean |
|---|---|
| Operational Testing Procedures | 30.5% |
| Working with content experts on test design/item writing/ review | 2.3 |
| Psychometrics | 3.1 |
| Conducting meetings with stakeholders or customers | 2.5 |
| Preparing reports for stakeholders or customers | 2.9 |
| Evaluating testing policy decisions | 2.2 |
| Explaining operational procedures to nontechnical audience | 2.5 |
| Conducting Research | 27.5% |
| Data collection | 2.2 |
| Data analysis | 3.0 |
| Planning or designing research study | 3.0 |
| Proposal/manuscript preparation for presentation/publication | 2.7 |
| Securing external or internal funding | 2.0 |
| Professional Development and Service | 10.3% |
| Conference attendance and presentation | 2.4 |
| Continuing education or training | 1.8 |
| Organizational committee work | 1.8 |
| Service to professional association | 1.6 |
| Editing or reviewing a proposal or manuscript | 1.9 |
| Administrative Tasks | 27.7% |
| Project management | 3.5 |
| Recruiting, hiring, evaluating personnel | 1.9 |
| Vendor management | 1.8 |
| Working on budgets or finances | 2.0 |
| Other Tasks | 9.7% |

*Note.* Number of respondents for each category and task ranged from 134 to 193 ($M = 171$). From "A Snapshot of Industry and Academic Professional Activities, Compensation, and Engagement in Educational Measurement," by S. Packman, W. J. Camara, and K. Huff, 2010, *Educational Measurement: Issues and Practice, 29*, p. 21. Copyright 2010 by John Wiley and Sons. Adapted with permission.

(Packman et al., 2010). In 2004, four for-profit testing organizations accounted for about 70% of state testing contracts, but as of 2016, many smaller organizations now account for the remainder of the state testing market, which has continued to increase. Large not-for-profit educational testing organizations that develop their own national testing programs, such as the ACT, College Board, and ETS, as well as other organizations that either bid on customized assessments (e.g., AIR, CTB/McGraw-Hill, Measured Progress) or bid on research projects (e.g.,

RAND, HumRRO, Westat), have increased their footprint in the K–12 assessment arena.

In 2014, more than 65 positions were advertised in measurement, testing, evaluation, and research at the placement center during the American Educational Research Association's annual convention, compared with 50 positions 10 years earlier. NCME (2016) career center and LinkedIn (2016) searches returned more than 50 results for a search of psychometric positions with well over half of those in educational or assessment organizations. Most positions required a doctoral degree and more than 60% of the openings were with not-for-profit educational testing and research organizations, or sponsors of certification and licensure tests. An estimate of 100 to 150 advertised vacancies for psychometricians, statisticians, and measurement and testing professionals in a year is probably quite accurate. It has become common practice for headhunters to recruit experienced professionals among the major testing companies. In response to the increased demand and competition for skilled measurement professionals, salaries, signing bonuses, and greater flexibility in work locations have become more common for psychometricians and measurement professionals working in testing organizations. For example, several companies have opened up satellite offices specifically to recruit and retain researchers and psychometricians in more attractive and less costly geographic areas. The greatest change, however, is in professionals working remotely from their homes, which is often available for experienced professionals in some testing organizations.

## Financial Compensation

Compensation is difficult to gauge across educational testing organizations. In 2007, an interdisciplinary survey of testing professionals was conducted that showed the median income for doctoral-level respondents was $90,000–$109,999, while the median income for master's level respondents was lower at $70,000–$89,999. Those employed at testing and research organizations, however, had slightly higher compensation levels associated with tenure and managerial positions. Nearly 40% of professionals working in testing and research organizations report receipt of bonuses, with more than 35% reporting bonuses of $10,000 or greater. Ordinal regressions showed controlling for years of experience had no significance in salaries based on gender or ethnicity (Packman et al., 2010). Managerial and executive-level salaries in these fields may range from $150,000 to beyond $300,000. After interviewing testing company officials, Toppo (2004) reported that "new psychometricians can often command $100,000 salaries, more than twice as much as in most other academic disciplines" (p. 3). Toppo noted that many psychometricians have competing offers from firms before they complete their course-work; quoting testing officials who noted that the high demand for psychometricians and researchers, combined with the limited supply of new PhDs, has resulted in many positions that cannot be filled in the foreseeable future.

# Conclusion

This chapter began with a discussion of the role of psychometricians and researchers, who develop, administer, score, and conduct research on tests. The job tasks may appear to be statistical, but the challenges and work are much broader and more complex than those associated with accounting or many other quantitative arenas. Tests are samples of human behavior or performance, and they never tell the entire story. Psychologists are one of the few professionals who may spend as much time cautioning the public and customers about the limitations of their products (tests) and the tentativeness of their reports (test scores) as they do in advocating for their use.

One's choice of career should rest not only on the intrinsic properties of the career but also on the broader social context to which the career contributes (Vroom, 1997). Psychologists who work in educational research and testing can contribute to increased learning in students and to increased efficacy for schools and organizations. They use scientific principles, research methods, and advanced statistical and programming skills in test development and research. These professionals understand that behavior is driven from many factors, several of which are not measured on a test. Psychologists apply their skills to solve problems in education while keeping in mind the range of social, cultural, academic, and other influences that influence achievement and success in education; this is one way their work is fundamentally different from that of many other quantitative professionals.

# References

American Psychological Association. (2014). *APA member profile*. Washington, DC: Author. Retrieved from http://www.apa.org/workforce/publications/14-member/index.aspx

American Psychological Association, Division 5. (2010). *Psychometrics, measurement, evaluation, quantitative psychology and research methods doctoral programs.* Retrieved from http://www.apadivisions.org/division-5/resources/doctoral.aspx

Anastasi, A. (1976). *Psychological testing* (4th ed.). New York, NY: Macmillan.

Camara, W., Packman, S., & Wiley, A. (2013). College, graduate, and professional school admissions testing. In K. F. Geisinger (Ed.), *APA handbook of testing and assessment in psychology* (Vol. 3, pp. 297–318). Washington, DC: American Psychological Association. http://dx.doi.org/10.1037/14049-014

Camara, W. J. (2011, April). *Uncovering educational and assessment professionals: Demographics, education, experience and engagement.* NCME Presidential Address. NCME Annual Meeting, New Orleans, LA.

Camara, W. J., Packman, S., & Huff, K. (2010). *Data tables: Appendix to a snapshot of industry and academic professional activities, compensation and engagement in educational measurement.* Unpublished manuscript.

Chingos, M. M. (2012). *Strength in numbers: State spending on K–12 assessment systems. Brown Center on Education Policy at Brookings.* Washington, DC: Brookings Institution.

Gaertner, M., & Kolen, M. J. (2015). *Programs in educational measurement and related areas: 2014 Update.* Madison, WI: National Council on Measurement in Education. Retrieved from http://www.ncme.org/ncme/AsiCommon/Controls/BSA/Downloader.aspx?iDocumentStorageKey=aab26b90-eb44-4e83-bd90-4ad0bdb8098b&iFileTypeCode=PDF&iFileName=Program%20Descriptions

General Accounting Office. (2003, May). *Title 1: Characteristics of tests will influence expenses: Information sharing may help states realize efficiencies* (GAO Report No. 03-389). Washington, DC: Author.

Illinois State University. (2005). *Preparing for graduate study in quantitative psychology.* Retrieved from http://my.ilstu.edu/~mshesso/quant_grad_prep.htm

Kohout, J., & Wicherski, M. (2009). *2009 Graduate study in psychology: Faculty and student data discussion of results.* Washington, DC: American Psychological Association. Retrieved from http://www.apa.org/workforce/publications/09-grad-study/report.pdf

Li, D., Yi, Q., & Harris, D. (2015). *Spring 2014 ACT test mode comparability study.* ACT working paper (2015-05). Iowa City, IA: ACT Inc. Retrieved from http://act.org/research/papers/pdf/WP-2015-05.pdf

LinkedIn. (2016). Psychometrics positions listed in a LinkedIn search of the US. Retrieved March 24, 2016 from https://www.linkedin.com/vsearch/j?type=jobs&keywords=psychometrics&orig=GLHD&rsid=210572571458851577069&pageKey=voltron_job_search_internal_jsp&trkInfo=tarId%3A1458851502155&search=Search&locationType=I&countryCode=us&openFacets=L,C&page_num=4&pt=jobs

National Council on Measurement in Education. (2014). *Internships.* Madison, WI: Author. Retrieved from http://www.ncme.org/ncme/ AsiCommon/Controls/BSA/Downloader.aspx?iDocumentStorageKey =157f4d17-2069-423c-999b-6ba85690533e&iFileTypeCode=PDF& iFileName=Internships

National Council on Measurement in Education. (2016). Psychometric positions listed in the NCME Career Center. Retrieved March 24, 2016 from http://www.ncme.org/ncme/NCME/Resource_Center/ Career_Center/Professional_Opportunities/NCME/Resource_Center/ CareerCenter/Position_Listings.aspx?hkey=f7cdd6c2-326a-4b6d-9092-649eb44109d1

Nelson, H. (2013). *Testing more, teaching less: What America's obsession with student testing costs in money and lost instructional time.* Washington, DC: American Federation of Teachers.

No Child Left Behind Act (NCLB) of 2001, Pub. L. No. 107-110, 115 Stat. 1425 (2002).

Packman, S., Camara, W. J., & Huff, K. (2010). A snapshot of industry and academic professional activities, compensation and engagement in educational measurement. *Educational Measurement: Issues and Practice, 29,* 15–24. http://dx.doi.org/10.1111/j.1745-3992.2010.00180.x

Public Broadcasting Service. (2002). *Frontline: The testing industry's big four.* Retrieved from http://www.pbs.org/wgbh/pages/frontline/shows/ schools/testing/companies.html

Salazar, T. (2014, November 18). *50 ways to test: A look at state summative assessments in 2014–15.* Washington, DC: Education Commission of the States. Retrieved from http://www.ecs.org/clearinghouse/ 01/16/06/11606.pdf

Schaffer, G. A., Steffen, M., Golub-Smith, M. L., Mills, C. N., & Durso, R. (1995). *The introduction and comparability of the computer adaptive GRE general test.* ETS Research Report 95-20. Princeton, NJ: Educational Testing Service. http://dx.doi.org/10.1002/j.2333-8504.1995.tb01655.x

Sireci, S. G. (1996, August). *Psychos and psychometrics: Careers in quantitative psychology.* Paper presented at the annual meeting of the American Psychological Association as part of the Psi Chi/Division 2 Symposium Nonclinical Degrees and Careers in Psychology, Toronto, Ontario, Canada.

Toppo, G. (2004, October 12). An answer to standardized tests. *USA Today.* Retrieved from http://usatoday.com/news/education/2004-10-12-tests-usat_x.htm

Vroom, V. H. (1997). Teaching the managers of tomorrow: Psychologists in business schools. In R. J. Sternberg (Ed.), *Career paths in psychology: Where your degree can take you* (pp. 49–68). Washington, DC: American Psychological Association.

*Mary S. Barringer and Shantina R. Dixon*

# School Psychologists 29

T he American Psychological Association (APA) Division 16, School Psychology, defines school psychology as follows:

> A general practice and health service provider specialty of professional psychology that is concerned with the science and practice of psychology with children, youth, families; learners of all ages; and the schooling process. The basic education and training of school psychologists prepares them to provide a range of psychological diagnosis, assessment, intervention,

Mary S. Barringer, PhD, LSSP, is retired from Bryan Independent School District and currently provides consultation, assessment, and staff development. She earned a BS from the University of North Texas in 1985 and a PhD from Texas A&M University in 2000. Her interests include early childhood assessment and autism spectrum disorders.

Shantina R. Dixon, PhD, LSSP, is a coordinator of special education. She is employed by Bryan Independent School District. She earned a BA from Xavier University of Louisiana in 1998, an MA from Xavier University of Louisiana in 2000, and a PhD from Texas A&M University in 2008. Her interests include counseling, behavior disorders, and autism.

http://dx.doi.org/10.1037/15960-030
*Career Paths in Psychology: Where Your Degree Can Take You, Third Edition*, R. J. Sternberg (Editor)

prevention, health promotion, and program development and evaluation services with a special focus on the developmental processes of children and youth within the context of schools, families and other systems. (American Psychological Association, 2016)

The National Association of School Psychologists (NASP) further describes school psychologists as follows:

Uniquely qualified members of school teams that support students' ability to learn and teachers' ability to teach. They apply expertise in mental health, learning, and behavior, to help children and youth succeed academically, socially, behaviorally, and emotionally. School psychologists partner with families, teachers, school administrators, and other professionals to create safe, healthy, and supportive learning environments that strengthen connections between home, school, and the community. (NASP, n.d.-c)

To understand the need for school psychologists, it is important first to understand the scope of emotional and behavioral challenges faced by children and adolescents in the 21st century, some of the factors that increase student risk status, and some of the barriers to receiving mental health services in other settings. Approximately 20% of adolescents have a diagnosable mental health disorder, and between 20% and 30% of adolescents have a major depressive episode before they reach adulthood (Schwarz, 2009). Suicide is the third leading cause of death in adolescents and young adults, with between 500,000 and 1 million young people ages 15 to 24 years old attempting suicide each year. Some, but not all, students with mental health problems meet eligibility criteria to receive special education services. In the 2011–2012 school year, 373,000 students in the United States received special education support services for serious emotional disturbance (U.S. Department of Education, National Center for Education Statistics, 2015).

Family factors that contribute to a child's risk for developing mental health problems include family violence, negative interactions, abuse, criminality, substance abuse, parent psychiatric disorders such as depression, long-term parental unemployment, and poor supervision (Walker & Shinn, 2002). Community and cultural factors, including socioeconomic disadvantage, neighborhood violence and crime, media portrayals of violence, and social and cultural discrimination also contribute to a child's risk for developing emotional and behavioral problems (Walker & Shinn, 2002). Unfortunately, 25% to 30% of adolescents do not receive the mental health care they need (Schwarz, 2009) because of factors such as lack of adequate insurance, lack of access to qualified specialists in adolescent mental health issues, lack of stable living conditions, and lack of confidentiality. Untreated mental health problems among adolescents often result in negative outcomes such as poor school performance, school dropout, strained family relationships, involvement with the child welfare or juvenile justice systems, substance abuse, and engaging in risky sexual behaviors. An estimated 67% to 70% of youth in the juvenile justice system have a diagnosable mental health disorder (Schwarz, 2009). But students with emotional disturbance and other mental health problems are not the only ones who are in need of psychological services in school settings. In the 2011–2012 school year, 455,000 students received special education services for autism, and another 26,000 for traumatic brain injury. When all disability categories are combined, over 6.4 million children and adolescents aged 3 to 22 years were served through special education (U.S. Department of Education, National Center for Education Statistics, 2015).

Now for the good news. The U.S. Department of Health and Human Services includes among its protective factors for youth: academic achievement and intellectual development, high self-esteem, emotional self-regulation, good coping skills and problem-solving skills, and engagement and connections in two or more contexts, such as school (Youth.gov, n.d.).

School psychologists are trained to provide direct services, such as social skills and problem-solving training, and indirect services, such as consultation with teachers and parents, to meet the needs of youth in both general education and special education settings. Evidence that school-based mental health programs are effective in preventing youth violence, drug abuse, and mental disorders, and in promoting positive youth development, continues to accumulate (Graczyk, Domitrovich, & Zins, 2003).

## *Professional Settings*

Most school psychologists (81%) work in public school settings, typically within departments of special education. Most provide direct and indirect psychological services, but some pursue administrative roles, such as director of special education, director of psychological services, director of student services, and director of support/intervention services (NASP, 2011). Licensed, doctoral-level school psychologists can also work in private practice providing evaluations, individual and family therapy, and consultation and training for school districts. The juvenile correctional system employs school psychologists to serve incarcerated youths. School psychologists also work for test-publishing companies as assessment consultants and educational researchers in test development. Doctoral-level school psychologists working within university systems conduct research and provide training for undergraduate and graduate students.

# Working in School Settings: The Role of School Psychologists in Tiered Models

Within school settings, school psychologists act at multiple levels. Primary prevention activities (also referred to as *universal interventions*) are those proactively provided to all students in a population and focused on creating healthy individuals, classrooms, schools, and communities. Secondary prevention activities are provided to students identified as at risk for negative outcomes, such as school failure. Tertiary interventions are intensive services provided to a small group of students already identified as having disabilities or as exhibiting severe emotional, behavioral, or academic problems.

## PRIMARY PREVENTION

Although all students do not arrive at school equally prepared for school success, all are expected to meet grade-level standards and pass grade-level state assessments. If a student is to be held to a standard, then the academic and behavioral skills required to achieve that goal must be taught directly. A school system using a preventive model allocates the majority of its resources (time, money, and staff) to primary prevention activities, with the goal of preventing problems from emerging and giving all students equal opportunities for success.

Establishing districtwide classroom management expectations for teachers and providing skills training to enable students to meet those expectations are examples of primary prevention activities. Others include establishing clear rules and routines for all students in the system and developing a positive behavior support system. The behavior support system includes direct instruction in the rules as well as instruction, practice, and reinforcement of the skills needed to follow the rules. Primary prevention activities also include promoting effective instruction to prevent learning problems, establishing bullying prevention programs, and teaching students mediation skills to prevent school violence.

So what is the role of the school psychologist in primary prevention? Because the goal of primary prevention is to provide positive interventions for all students in a system, and because school psychologists are in short supply, training campus staff to implement interventions is a critical and cost-effective activity. Examples of staff training that can be provided by school psychologists include training in positive behavior support to new employees, training parents in effective behavior management, training general education teachers in strategies to support students with autism, and crisis intervention and safe restraint training.

Another efficient method of service provision is consultation. School psychologists can conduct system-level consultation to administrators such as superintendents, principals, and program directors. The client in system-level consultation is almost always a large organization or department, rather than an individual student, and the intervention may include, for example, developing and implementing programs to increase parent involvement, improving services to students with limited English proficiency, or the promotion of effective teacher communication at a specific campus. School psychologists also can participate in program evaluations and needs assessments to help administrators identify the strengths and weaknesses of specific programs or departments, identify goals, develop plans for improvement, implement plans, and evaluate program processes and outcomes.

## SECONDARY PREVENTION

Most students benefit from primary prevention activities, but some do not benefit enough to prevent the emergence of emotional, behavioral, or academic difficulties. It is important to have a plan in place to monitor the primary prevention program and identify students who are not responding in the desired manner so that secondary interventions can be implemented. The school psychologist can be instrumental in creating and supporting effective monitoring plans.

Secondary prevention is an intermediate-level prevention activity for students who continue to experience academic and behavioral difficulties despite consistent implementation of primary prevention activities. The emphasis in secondary prevention is on early identification and intervention before problems become severe. Secondary interventions are provided to a much smaller population of students (approximately 15%), usually in groups.

A typical secondary intervention for a student with persistent behavior problems is the development of a behavior contract. Because all behavior serves a purpose (has a function), school psychologists conduct a functional behavior assessment, which consists of identifying a measurable behavior and collecting information about how, when, and where the behavior occurs to identify its function. Once the school psychologist has collected the information, he or she helps create a plan to teach the student positive, effective, replacement behaviors that serve the same function. Interventions may include additional training for teaching staff, modifications to the classroom or school environment, and direct skills training for the student, usually in a small group with other students who have similar behavior problems.

Other examples of secondary interventions include assigning adult or peer mentors for the student, changing instructional strategies, providing additional tutoring, and providing counseling groups for students with anger management difficulties or specific social skills deficits. Secondary interventions are adequate to meet the needs of most students referred. Again, monitoring the effectiveness of the intervention and making adjustments along the way are crucial components of secondary prevention activities that may require the support of the school psychologist.

## TERTIARY INTERVENTIONS

Tertiary interventions build on, rather than replace, primary and secondary prevention activities for a small group of students who exhibit severe, persistent, academic or behavioral problems. Tertiary interventions are individualized and intensive. They can also be intrusive, expensive, and perceived by the student as stigmatizing, which is why schools must ensure that all primary and secondary prevention activities are implemented with fidelity before tertiary interventions are considered. Tertiary behavior interventions are required when the student's emotional and behavioral difficulties are so extreme as to interfere with learning or threaten the safety of the student or others, and they usually include counseling and a more intensive behavior plan. Interventions also may include services to the student's family and intensive case management to coordinate services provided at school with services provided in the community. Academically, tertiary interventions are indicated when the student fails to respond to research-based instructional interventions.

Tertiary interventions focus on the student, rather than the classroom or the school, and some tertiary behavior interventions require removal of the student from the home campus to an alternative setting where the environment is highly structured and behavior can be managed more safely. Students requiring tertiary interventions often, but not always, are identified as requiring special education support services. Because of the severity of the problem, school psychologists usually are involved in assessment, planning, and intervention for students in tertiary behavior interventions.

## SERVICES TO STUDENTS WITH DISABILITIES

In most, but not all, school systems, school psychologists work directly with students who are identified as eligible to receive special education support services. This means that in addition to the skills and knowledge required of all psychologists, school psychologists must have training in education and a thorough understanding of the federal and state laws protecting people with disabilities and regulating the provision of special education services in schools. In the past 40 years, the practice of school psychology has been influenced significantly by Public Law 94-142, the Education for All Handicapped Children Act of 1975 (now known as the Individuals With Disabilities Education Act [IDEA]), which was created to ensure that all children with disabilities are provided a free, appropriate, public education and to protect the rights of these students and their families. The act specifically addresses eligibility, mandating that all states make an active effort to find and evaluate all students who may have a disability and be eligible for special education support services. Historically, school psychologists have been involved in the implementation of IDEA, primarily by identifying students who are eligible to receive special education services. School psychologists assess students who are suspected of having a wide array of disabilities, including emotional disturbance, learning disabilities, intellectual disabilities, traumatic brain injuries, and autism as well as those who come from diverse cultural and linguistic backgrounds. They also serve as members of multidisciplinary teams that develop and implement intervention plans for these students.

Although they may assess students for many different special education eligibilities, including intellectual disability, learning disability, other health impairment, and traumatic brain injury, school psychologists almost always take the leading role in evaluations for emotional disturbance and autism. They also usually are included in multidisciplinary teams evaluating preschoolers with severe disabilities or multiple disabilities. The school psychologist's role in evaluation for these students typically includes reviewing referral information; interviewing parents; consulting with teachers; planning and conducting individual assessments; interpreting results; and writing reports that include recommendations for planning, implementing, and evaluating interventions to meet the needs identified by the assessment. Because there are different types of emotional disturbance, the assessment procedures for this disability vary from student to student. Instruments are selected based on the specific referral question and the student's age and developmental level. Assessment procedures typically include parent and teacher ratings of the frequency of specific behaviors; interviews with parents and school staff; classroom observations; and individual assessment of the student, including an interview, self-report measures, standardized measures of intelligence and academic achievement, measures of adaptive functioning, and projective measures when appropriate. A school psychologist has significant autonomy in selecting measurement tools and strategies.

As members of the individualized education plan (IEP) team, school psychologists contribute to the development of education plans for students in special education. The role of the school psychologist is to interpret assessment data to assist the team in determining eligibility and creating appropriate academic and behavioral supports, modifications, accommodations, and interventions. The IEP team uses assessment data to develop specific, measurable, annual learning objectives and a schedule of services for implementing the IEP goals in the least restrictive environment (LRE). The LRE requirement emphasizes the importance of educating students with disabilities, to the maximum extent appropriate, with peers without disabilities to prevent their being isolated and stigmatized because of their disabilities. Multidisciplinary IEP teams include a parent or adult student, general education teachers, special education teachers, assessment professionals, administrators, and related services providers. Related services providers and other professionals serving on IEP teams can include occupational and physical therapists, school nurses, music therapists, counselors, autism specialists, adapted physical education teachers, and assistive technology specialists, among others.

After the IEP is developed, the role of the school psychologists in its implementation varies considerably. For some students, the school psychologist may continue to be involved in providing individual psychological services, ongoing parent and teacher consultation and training, and implementation of the behavior intervention plan. For other students, all services in the IEP may be provided by campus-based professionals with little involvement by the school psychologist. Should problems arise, however, the school psychologist usually is called, particularly when the problems involve behavior and discipline.

## Academic Preparation for a Career in School Psychology

By completing advanced coursework in developmental and social psychology, learning, effective instruction, and effective parenting, school psychologists learn to understand children's development from multiple theoretical perspectives and to implement research-based interventions to alleviate cognitive, behavioral, social, and emotional problems, particularly within the school setting (APA, 2016). School psychologists also complete advanced training in measurement theory, test construction, and statistics. They learn how to assess and intervene effectively with individuals from culturally or linguistically diverse backgrounds. To be effective at the system level, school psychologists complete advanced coursework in design and evaluation of classroom programs, comprehensive and integrated service systems, and educational and psychological interventions (APA, 2016).

### DOCTORAL TRAINING AND LICENSURE

The APA School Psychology division sets the minimum standards for the doctoral-level preparation of school psychologists. Since 1988, NASP has credentialed school psychologists at the specialist and doctoral levels through the Nationally Certified School Psychologist (NCSP) certification. Most doctoral programs in school psychology follow the scientist-practitioner model. A doctoral degree requires a minimum of 4 years full-time (or equivalent) graduate study, a dissertation based on original research, and a full-time internship of at least 10 months. The APA accredits doctoral training programs in school psychology and institutions that provide internships for doctoral students in school psychology. The National Council for Accreditation of Teacher Education and NASP also are involved in the accreditation of advanced degree programs in psychology. NASP requirements for doctoral programs include a minimum of 4 years (90 graduate semester hours) of full-time study (or the equivalent) at the graduate level, at least 78 hours of which are exclusive of credit for the supervised internship and dissertation, and a minimum of 1 academic year of doctoral-supervised internship experience consisting of a minimum of 1,500 clock hours (NASP, 2010).

## SPECIALIST-LEVEL TRAINING AND CREDENTIALS

NASP requirements for specialist-level training include a minimum 3 years (60 credit hours) of full-time study at the graduate level, or the equivalent if part-time. An internship of 1 full school-year is required.

Thirty states use the NCSP as part of their standard for certification. Although many states do not formally acknowledge the NCSP within credentialing documents, individuals who meet training requirements for the NCSP generally meet or exceed the training requirements for initial credentialing in most states (NASP, n.d.-d). NCSP certification requirements include completion of 60 graduate semester hours through a program of study that is officially titled School Psychology. At least 54 graduate semester hours must have been completed exclusive of credit for the supervised internship experience. Additionally, completion of a 1,200-hour internship in school psychology, of which at least 600 hours must be in a school setting, is required. Applicants must pass the Praxis National School Psychology Examination (NASP, n.d.-a).

## OPPORTUNITIES FOR SPECIALIZATION

School neuropsychology is a specialization that incorporates brain behavior relationships, contemporary neuropsychological theory, assessment techniques, and evidence-based interventions (NASP, 2011). Additional training as a school neuropsychologist typically occurs after completion of graduate-level training, with certificate programs ranging from about 10 months to 2 years. Certified or licensed school psychologists who have had specialized coursework and supervisions may be eligible to apply for the Diplomate in School Neuropsychology from the American Board of School Neuropsychology (ABSNP; NASP, 2011).

School psychologists commonly serve on multidisciplinary teams for students with autism and emotional disturbance. These significantly impaired students require highly skilled professionals to guide their assessment and intervention planning, and specializations have emerged to meet these needs. School psychologists with specialized training in behavior analysis and intervention can serve as behavior specialists/ consultants and autism specialists, conducting functional behavior assessments and developing, implementing, and supervising behavioral and academic interventions. As the number of students identified with autism spectrum disorders in schools continues to rise, an increasingly popular credential is board-certified behavior analyst (BCBA), which requires specialized graduate coursework, additional supervised fieldwork, and a board examination.

The number of students in the United States who are limited English proficient continues to rise rapidly, creating a high demand for bilingual school psychologists specially trained to provide culturally and linguistically appropriate services to these students. School psychologists who are fluent in American Sign Language and familiar with deaf culture are in short supply and are needed to provide appropriate assessment and intervention to the sizeable population of students with auditory impairment. Because early identification of disabilities is essential to positive outcomes, public schools are required by IDEA to find and assess children with disabilities, and to offer school-based services for eligible students, beginning on their third birthday. This requirement has created a demand for school psychologists who specialize in developmental disabilities and early childhood evaluations and interventions. At the other end of the spectrum, schools serve adolescents and young adults with severe disabilities through the school year in which they reach the age of 22 years old. In meeting the needs of these students, school psychologists work with teams to facilitate the transition from school-based services to life after public school. Transition activities include identifying student and parent expectations for how and where the student will live, work, and socialize and providing training to support the transition process.

## Financial Compensation

School psychologists employed in public and private school settings usually work under contracts for a specified number of days per year, typically between 180 and 220 days. According to the most recent NASP membership survey (Castillo, Curtis, & Gelley, 2012) the mean salaries of NASP members who were employed as full-time, school-based practitioners in the 2009–2010 school year were $64,168 for practitioners with 180-day contracts, and $75,452 for practitioners on 220-day contracts. The mean salary for university faculty was $77,801. Salaries vary significantly across schools, districts, states, and regions and also vary by level of education. According to the 2009–10 survey (NASP, n.d.-b), the mean daily (per diem) salary for master's level (specialist) practitioners in public school settings was $330.36, and the mean per diem salary for doctoral-level school-based, NASP members was $409.42. According to the Bureau of Labor Statistics, the median annual wages for clinical, counseling, and school psychologists as a group in May 2012 was $67,650 (Bureau of Labor Statistics, U.S. Department of Labor, 2014).

## Employment Opportunities

According to the Occupational Outlook Handbook, while employment of psychologists is projected to grow at the same rate as the average for all occupations (about 12% from 2012 to 2022), prospects are best for those with a specialist or doctoral degree in school psychology or a doctoral degree in another applied specialty (Bureau of Labor Statistics, U.S. Department of Labor, 2014). The Bureau of Labor Statistics projects that 16,400 new school psychologist jobs will be added during that decade.

In his recent message to NASP members, Dr. Stephen Brock (2015) notes that school districts around the nation are reporting a higher demand for school psychologists than can be filled with the current applicant pool. Citing the research of Castillo, Curtis, and Tan (2014) and Curtis, Grier, and Hunley (2004), Dr. Brock forecasts between a 2% and 4% shortage of school psychologists over the next decade as a result of a combination of factors, including retirement and failure of universities to produce enough new professionals to meet the demand.

## Personal Attributes Required for Success

To complete a training program in school psychology, you need to have strong writing skills and you will have to develop skills in organizing your time. Self-discipline in time management and organization will serve you well. Personality characteristics are equally important. Successful completion of the training program will require you to have the self-confidence to hear constructive criticism from faculty without becoming defensive.

Once you are on the job, you must have patience and flexibility. Being effective in a school system requires that you understand that children's problems are often symptoms of system problems, and systems do not change easily or quickly. Believe it or not, some staff and parents will not immediately jump at the opportunity to act on your recommendations. Persistence is crucial. Given the size and complexity of most school systems and the increasingly multicultural aspect of many communities, your ability to communicate effectively and respectfully with individuals of different ages and developmental levels, as well as from a broad range of cultures, socioeconomic status, and educational backgrounds, will in a large part determine your effectiveness.

## Why Dr. Dixon Became a School Psychologist

I developed an interest in school psychology during my fourth year as a teacher. I was teaching science at a school district's disciplinary alternative education program (DAEP) in Houston, TX. Several of my students who attended the DAEP were in special education. It bewildered me that so many special education students were being sent to DAEP. My investigation into the reason behind the placements revealed that most of these students were sent for noncompliance and fights on campus. As a result, I became interested in the correlation between behavior and academic demands.

I graduated with a master's in curriculum and instruction from Xavier University of Louisiana before teaching in Houston, TX. During a trip to New Orleans, I visited with my husband's mentor, who was a professor at Xavier University, to discuss pursuing a career in counseling. During that meeting, we discussed my interests and concerns for student success. The professor informed me that a career in school psychology would more than likely be fulfilling for me. I started researching school psychology and APA-accredited universities with school psychology programs. In the end, I chose Texas A&M University to further my studies.

My graduate studies at Texas A&M University thoroughly prepared me for a career as a school psychologist. The research projects and practicum experiences I completed as a student were invaluable. After graduating with my PhD in 2008, I felt invigorated and motivated to advocate for children.

My advice to those considering school psychology as a career is to first work with children with special needs. This will help you gain practical experience with this population of children while deciding whether you want to pursue a career in this area.

## *A Day in the Life of a School Psychologist: Dr. Dixon*

I am in my seventh year practicing as a licensed specialist in school psychology (LSSP) in my school district. It is also my second year as a coordinator of special education. In addition to coordinating special education services for 15 elementary campuses, I supervise interns, trainees, and Texas A&M University school psychology doctoral students.

On one typical day, I start work at 8:00 a.m. with a meeting with doctoral-level practicum students from Texas A&M University. We discuss counseling, assessments, report writing, consultations, and crises. Each student is allocated time to present his or her cases and receive feedback. The goal is to make sure their experience is beneficial to them and, ultimately, supportive to our students.

At 9:05, I check e-mails and return some of the many phone calls I've received. These e-mails arrive from a variety of stakeholders. As a coordinator, I receive e-mails from principals, parents, central office administrators, teachers, and others. While I was an LSSP most of my e-mails were from teachers. Timely communication in a school district is critical to the overall health of the position.

At 9:30, I attend a staffing for a student on one of the elementary campuses. Staffings are held when staff on campus wants to discuss how to best educate a student. At this staffing, we discuss whether or not to recommend a more restrictive setting for a student who is struggling behaviorally within the classroom setting. We discuss the pros and cons of moving the student to a more restrictive setting. We also discuss strategies that could be used within the current classroom setting to keep the student on his campus. These strategies are then discussed with the IEP committee charged with oversight of the student's IEP.

At 10:45, I conduct walkthroughs within three special education classes on an elementary campus. These walkthroughs help to ensure that teachers are following all district procedures and to provide teachers with support and feedback. Most teachers follow all district procedures and policies without difficulty.

While at the school, I may be stopped in the hallway by the principal to discuss a student who is verbally or physically aggressive toward peers and teachers. We discuss strategies in the behavior intervention plan that could be used with the student before outbursts. I also request that a staffing be held to refresh teachers on the student's behavior intervention plan.

By 12:30 p.m., I am back in my office to prepare for my next meeting. While preparing, I continue to receive calls. For example, I receive a call from a school principal. We discuss programming for one of the self-contained classes on campus and schedule a time to discuss interventions.

At 1:00, I meet with the director of special education and the secondary coordinator of special education to problem solve issues in the programs. During this particular meeting, we discuss the need to open additional Life Skills classrooms (classrooms for students with severe developmental disabilities). Our current elementary and middle school Life Skills classes are close to being overcrowded.

By 2:30, I leave the executive leadership team meeting early to supervise one of the interns. Although I enjoy all aspects of my job, this is one side of the job that I particularly enjoy. We discuss counseling cases, assessments, admission review and dismissal (ARD) meetings, and anything else that the intern would like to discuss.

At 3:30, I drop by the principal's office to discuss a situation that was brought to my attention by the intern. We discuss the issues raised. The principal informs me that she will investigate the situation and get back to me.

At 3:40, I check e-mails and make a phone call before departing for another campus.

By 4:00, I am at another building. I meet with another intern to discuss items on her weekly agenda. The intern has been struggling with teacher implementation of reinforcement systems. One recommendation that was provided to the intern is to include teachers in the creation of reinforcement systems so that teachers are more likely to buy in to them.

Although this describes my typical day and the various activities, each day is different. On some days, as a school psychologist, I may provide teacher consultation, do counseling, or complete an assessment. Moreover, a crisis in a school building or with a given student takes precedence over the day-to-day responsibilities.

# Advantages and Disadvantages of a Career in School Psychology

The advantages of a career in school psychology are many. School psychologists have high levels of job satisfaction (Worrell, Skaggs, & Brown, 2006) and report being most satisfied with the social service, independence, and values aspects of their jobs. They are also satisfied with their coworkers and job activities. School psychologists typically have control over their daily schedules and practice with a significant level of autonomy. They commonly move between several settings within a day, interacting with a diverse population of individuals and engaging in a broad array of activities from individual assessment and intervention to developing and evaluation programs for system change at the highest level.

School psychologists have the opportunity to collaborate with other professionals, including occupational and physical therapists, speech therapists, counselors, and other psychologists in private practice or clinics. Medical professionals rarely have a thorough understanding of the provision of services under the educational model, and school staff rarely understand the medical model. School psychologists are in a unique position to serve as the critical link between pediatricians and psychiatrists providing pharmaceutical interventions and school-based teams providing educational interventions for the same student.

Continuing education, in addition to being required for an annual renewal of the psychologist's license in most states, is strongly encouraged in most employment settings. School districts and departments of special education usually budget for psychologists and other professional staff to attend local, regional, state, or national conferences to obtain specialized training, which allows school psychologists to obtain required continuing education credits at reduced personal expense. Another advantage of the profession is that many school psychologists employed in public and private schools have contracts that roughly approximate the number of days students are in attendance, allowing freedom either to enjoy substantial vacation time or to engage in other professional activities during summer breaks.

On the down side, school psychologists who work within departments of special education often find their daily activities driven by timelines established by federal regulations and state boards of education. They may find that they spend an inordinate amount of time completing evaluations, managing paperwork, and conducting IEP team meetings. Some school psychologists are assigned large caseloads, allowing limited time to devote to each student. Although NASP recommends a case load of one school psychologist to between 500 and 700 students, in reality, caseloads are commonly closer to 1:2,000 and even as high as 1:3,500 in some states (Wier, 2012). Large caseloads are the result, in part, of diminishing budgets. A significant source of frustration for many school psychologists is the deterioration or elimination of systemic, proactive, and preventive activities that predictably results from unmanageable caseloads. School psychologists must have good training, strong skills, and the confidence to advocate both within their school districts and at the state and national level to protect the integrity of their work and define their roles.

## Conclusion

Like most people who have found a career that matches their strengths, personality, and values, we take immense pleasure in our work. A career in school psychology offers variety, autonomy, and personal satisfaction. No career path is without challenges, and school psychology is no exception to this rule. If you think you are interested, your first stop should be to volunteer in a public school. Many children need additional adult support, and even if you decide not to pursue a career in school psychology, your time will have been well spent.

## References

American Psychological Association. (2016). *School psychology.* Retrieved from http://www.apa.org/ed/graduate/specialize/school.aspx

Brock, S. E. (2015). President's message: Where are the school psychologists? *Communiqué, 43,* 2. Retrieved from https://www.nasponline.org/publications/periodicals/communique/issues/volume-43-issue-8/where-are-the-school-psychologists

Bureau of Labor Statistics, U.S. Department of Labor. (2014). *Occupational outlook handbook, 2014–15 edition, psychologists.* Retrieved from http://www.bls.gov/ooh/life-physical-and-social-science/psychologists.htm

Castillo, J. M., Curtis, M. J., & Gelley, C. (2012). School psychology 2010: Demographics, employment, and the context for professional practices—Part 1. *Communiqué, 40,* 28–30.

Castillo, J. M., Curtis, M. J., & Tan, S. Y. (2014). Personnel needs in school psychology: A 10-year follow-up study of predicted personnel shortages. *Psychology in the Schools, 51,* 832–849. http://dx.doi.org/10.1002/pits.21786

Curtis, M. J., Grier, J. E. C., & Hunley, S. A. (2004). The changing face of school psychology: Trends in data and projections for the future. *School Psychology Review, 33,* 49–66.

Graczyk, P. A., Domitrovich, C. E., & Zins, J. E. (2003). Facilitating the implementation of evidence-based prevention and mental health promotion efforts in schools. In M. D. Weist, S. W. Evans, & N. A. Lever (Eds.), *Handbook of school mental health: Advancing practice and research* (pp. 301–318). New York, NY: Kluwer.

National Association of School Psychologists. (2010). *Standards for the credentialing of school psychologists.* Retrieved from https://www.nasponline.org/Documents/Standards%20and%20Certification/Standards/2_Credentialing_Standards.pdf

National Association of School Psychologists. (2011). *Alternative careers and additional training for school psychologists.* Retrieved from http:// sbs.mnsu.edu/psych/psyd/sps/resources/altcareers_training.pdf

National Association of School Psychologists. (n.d.-a). *NCSP eligibility.* Retrieved from https://www.nasponline.org/standards-and-certification/national-certification/ncsp-eligibility

National Association of School Psychologists. (n.d.-b). *Salaries in school psychology: Results from the 2009–2010 NASP membership survey.* Retrieved from http://www.nasponline.org/assets/documents/About%20School %20Psychology/nasp_salaries_09_10.pdf

National Association of School Psychologists. (n.d.-c). *Who are school psychologists?* Retrieved from http://www.nasponline.org/about-school-psychology/who-are-school-psychologists

National Association of School Psychologists. (n.d.-d). *Why become an NCSP?* Retrieved from https://www.nasponline.org/standards-and-certification/national-certification/why-become-an-ncsp

Schwarz, S. W. (2009). Facts for policymakers: Adolescent mental health in the United States. *National Center for Children in Poverty.* Retrieved from http://nccp.org/publications/pdf/text_878.pdf

U.S. Department of Education, National Center for Education Statistics. (2015). *Digest of education statistics, 2013 (NCES 2015-011), Chapter 2.* Retrieved from https://nces.ed.gov/fastfacts/display.asp?id=64

Walker, H. M., & Shinn, M. R. (2002). Structuring school-based interventions to achieve integrated primary, secondary, and tertiary prevention goals for safe and effective schools. In M. R. Shinn, H. M. Walker, & G. Stoner (Eds.), *Interventions for academic and behavior problems: Vol. 2. Preventive and remedial approaches* (pp. 1–26). Bethesda, MD: National Association of School Psychologists Publications.

Wier, K. (2012). School psychologists feel the squeeze: As school budgets shrink, school-based mental-health services are losing resources and support. *Monitor on Psychology, 43,* 34. Retrieved from http://www.apa.org/monitor/2012/09/squeeze.aspx

Worrell, T. G., Skaggs, G. E., & Brown, M. B. (2006). School psychologists' job satisfaction: A 22-year perspective in the USA. *School Psychology International, 27,* 131–145. http://dx.doi.org/10.1177/ 0143034306064540

Youth.gov. (n.d.). *Risk and protective factors.* Retrieved from http://youth. gov/youth-topics/youth-mental-health/risk-and-protective-factors-youth

*Marc H. Bornstein*

# Psychologists Pursuing Scientific Research in Government Service

30

Many agencies in the federal government of the United States employ and rely on psychological scientists. The military, for example, has a long history of utilizing psychologists in a wide array of roles from intelligence analysis to the study of ergonomics to the treatment of posttraumatic stress disorder. Likewise, many civilian areas of the federal government hire psychologists to work on an equally diverse range of problems from basic biomedical research through applied research (e.g., traffic safety).

Marc H. Bornstein is senior investigator and head of child and family research at the *Eunice Kennedy Shriver* National Institute of Child Health and Human Development. He holds a BA from Columbia College, MS and PhD degrees from Yale University, and an honorary doctorate from the University of Padua. Bornstein is president-elect of the Society for Research in Child Development. He was named to the Top 20 Authors for Productivity in Developmental Science by the American Educational Research Association and has published widely. Bornstein is editor emeritus of *Child Development* and founding editor of *Parenting: Science and Practice*.

http://dx.doi.org/10.1037/15960-031
*Career Paths in Psychology: Where Your Degree Can Take You, Third Edition*,
R. J. Sternberg (Editor)

Psychologists are found in the Departments of Defense, Homeland Security, Veterans Affairs, and Transportation, as well as in the Department of Health and Human Services (DHHS). In several agencies of the DHHS—for example, the National Science Foundation (NSF), the Centers for Disease Control and Prevention (CDC), and the National Institutes of Health (NIH)—psychologists play important roles in administrative sectors as well as in both basic and applied research. In this chapter, I describe scientific psychology within one agency of the DHHS, the NIH, and specifically in the Division of Intramural Research in the *Eunice Kennedy Shriver* National Institute of Child Health and Human Development (NICHD).

## Agencies of the Department of Health and Human Services

The Department of Health and Human Services (DHHS) oversees several agencies that sponsor biomedical research in the public interest. Many offer career paths for psychologists. One such agency, which is concerned in part with basic and applied psychological research, is the NIH. The NIH, located on its own campus in Bethesda, MD, is the nation's, and perhaps the world's, foremost biomedical research facility. The NIH consists of almost 30 institutes and centers ranging in size from the National Cancer Institute (large) to the National Institute for Nursing Research (small).

One institute that offers diverse opportunities for psychologists is the *Eunice Kennedy Shriver* National Institute of Child Health and Human Development (NICHD). Established by the U.S. Congress and President John F. Kennedy in 1962, the NICHD supports and conducts research concerned broadly with human development. The NICHD is headed by a director, under whom two major divisions bifurcate. The Division of Extramural Research (DER), accounting for approximately 90% of the NICHD budget, is devoted to funding investigations that are investigator initiated or requested by the agency and arranged by contract awarded to institutions outside the NIH. Psychologists who work in the DER often contribute to decisions about, and oversee grants and contracts awarded to, institutions outside the federal government.

The Division of Intramural Research (DIR), to which approximately 10% of funds are allotted, houses approximately 80 principal investigators and their laboratories on the greater NIH Bethesda campus. Within the DIR, active protocols are devoted to clinical intervention and basic and applied research on topics related to the health of children, adults, families, and populations. The mission of the NICHD DIR is to seek fundamental knowledge about the nature, development, and behavior of living systems through basic and clinical research and to determine how to apply such knowledge to help ensure that women and men have good reproductive health, that children are born healthy, and that people develop to live healthy and productive lives. One laboratory within the DIR is Child and Family Research (CFR).

The mission of CFR is to investigate dispositional, experiential, and environmental factors that contribute to physical, mental, emotional, and social development in human beings across the first decades of life. The research goals of the CFR are to describe, analyze, and assess the capabilities and proclivities of developing children, including their biological characteristics, physiological functioning, and perceptual and cognitive abilities; emotional, social, and interactional styles; the nature and consequences of interactions within the family and social world for children and their parents; and influences of children's exposure to and interactions with the natural and designed environments on their development. Laboratory and home-based studies in the CFR use a variety of approaches, including psychophysiological recordings, experimental techniques, behavioral observations, standardized assessments, rating scales, interviews, and demographic and census records in both longitudinal and cross-sectional designs.

More specifically, research topics of the CFR concern the origins, status, and development of biopsychological constructs, structures, functions, and processes in human beings; effects of child characteristics and activities on parents; and the meaning of variations in parenting and in the family across different sociodemographic and cultural groups. Examples of sociodemographic comparisons under investigation include family socioeconomic status, maternal age and employment status, and child parity and childcare experience. Study sites include, among others, Argentina, Belgium, Brazil, Cameroon, Chile, England, France, Israel, Italy, Japan, Kenya, Peru, and the Republic of Korea as well as the United States; intracultural as well as cross-cultural comparisons of human development are pursued. In addition, the CFR studies three samples of families acculturating in the United States: Japanese Americans, South Americans, and Korean Americans.

Psychologists in CFR also conduct a broad program of research in neuroscience and behavioral pediatrics that investigates diverse questions at the interface of child development, biological growth, and physical health and attempt to build bridges to more directly applied areas, including the following:

- fetal assessment and its developmental sequelae;
- the roles of cardiac function, electroencephalographic cortical potentials, and eye movements in early development;

- deafness in child development and family life, including hearing children with hearing parents, deaf children with hearing parents, hearing children with deaf parents, and deaf children with deaf parents;
- development in children with autism spectrum disorder (ASD) and Down syndrome;
- cancer and major surgery in infancy and their developmental outcomes; and
- research in child development and early health care, including studies of children's knowledge, implementation, and evaluation of strategies for coping with stressful medical experiences; the development of children's understanding of health and health care; and relations among children's own health histories, pediatric health care utilization, and maternal health beliefs; and maternal depression and child development.

For more information, visit CFR online (CFR, 2016).

Within government laboratories (like the CFR), a number of possible positions are available for bachelor's level, master's level, and PhD-trained psychologists. At all levels, psychologists in government service collaborate in, supervise, or engage in research; conduct literature reviews; and publish research articles on knowledge and practice in particular problem areas. Normally, senior investigators hold a PhD, control funding, and are responsible for the nature and design of scientific investigations conducted within their research program; they also supervise other investigators and contractors who carry out all phases of research projects. Government researchers enjoy some degree of freedom, but program research must be consistent with the basic mission of the larger scientific unit of which they are a part and be approved by laboratory and scientific directors. The support and endorsement of site visitors (described later in this chapter) to a laboratory are essential.

## Comparing Government Research With Academic and Business Research

To gain insight into a government research career, it is beneficial to compare it with other similar situations, such as academia or business and industry. As in academia, senior investigators in government service often carry out research that they conceive, but many questions that occupy government researchers are also assigned to them, a situation that is more common in business and industry. Normally, too, government work includes both basic research that follows avenues into understanding new areas and applied research devoted to addressing practical questions and those related to policy. Research in business or industry often is concerned with the development of marketable products. Government research projects are also aimed at providing the public with information geared to solve problems. Government researchers conduct studies in laboratory settings; because it frequently applies to matters of public policy, government research often involves fieldwork.

Like academics, government researchers may belong to scholarly societies, attend scientific conferences and present their research, write journal articles and reviews, and sit on journal editorial boards. Unlike academics, they do not teach or (normally) write grants to support their research (although this situation is changing). The implementation of a government research plan more often than not is carried out by a team of researchers consisting of specialists from several different disciplines. Unlike academia, but similar to business and industry, becoming a specialist in alternative areas of psychology often proves difficult once one is on the job in a government research setting. Although opportunities for interagency collaborations may present themselves from time to time, in practice, they are rather difficult to effect in the government. By contrast, establishing collaborations with investigators outside government is comparatively easy and can be rewarding.

Unlike extramural scientists, intramural scientists at the NIH typically do not write grants or respond to requests for applications to support their research. Rather, the scientific director in an institute draws on the expertise of a consultant board of scientific counselors to recruit other senior extramural scientists from around the nation—who are experts in the research fields of each intramural laboratory—to conduct a site visit of that laboratory and to prepare a critical appraisal about the past, current, and future activity of the laboratory. It is on the basis of these site-visit reviews that intramural investigators compete for sources of support and personnel within the funding constraints of the DIR. Such site visits take place every 4 years, on average. Although a meritocracy should guide decisions, in practice, in the government (as possible in all settings) factors other than merit, such as disciplinary favoritism and prejudice, come into play. Additionally, intramural scientists are encouraged to apply for non-federal sources of support (e.g., foundations) to support their research.

## My Career and Basic Science Work

Government service attracts and retains psychologists who want to do research full time as well as play other roles in public service. I am senior investigator and head of CFR. I received a BA from Columbia College in New York City and a PhD from Yale University, both in psychology. Before coming to the NICHD, I held positions at the Max Planck Institute in Germany as a visiting scientist, at Princeton University, and at New York University. While at New York University, I also trained as a child clinical fellow at the Institute for Behavior Therapy. I have been in government service for nearly 25 years.

Before joining the government, I received support for my research from the J. S. Guggenheim Foundation, the William T. Grant Foundation, and the Spencer Foundation as well as the NSF and the NIH. I have written or edited dozens of books, including *Development in Infancy* (Bornstein, Arterberry, & Lamb, 2014), *Handbook of Cultural Developmental Science* (Bornstein, 2010), and the multivolume *Handbook of Parenting* (Bornstein, 2002), and authored hundreds of peer-reviewed scientific articles and chapters in scholarly collections and encyclopedias on experimental, methodological, comparative, developmental, cross-cultural, neuroscientific, pediatric, and aesthetic topics.

Within the NICHD CFR, my research has followed two intertwined directions. One concerns children's physical, cognitive, and socioemotional development, and the second concerns aspects of children's experiences with parents, family life, and culture. For example, results of my early work led to revelations about what infants know and the observation that measures of information processing in infancy predict competencies in later childhood. These findings challenged views about infancy and about human cognitive development as immeasurable, unstable, and not predictive. My approach to the study of child development, parenting, and family process incorporates three major avenues. First, my observations are based in the naturally occurring interactions of parents and children during the daily routines of family life as well as in laboratory-based experimental studies. Second, I take a longitudinal, ecological, relational dynamic systems approach to understanding phenomena in human development. Finally, I have extended my observations of child development, parenting, and family process to diverse cultures within and outside the United States, thereby advancing knowledge of culture-common and culture-specific aspects of each.

I also have geared my efforts to disseminate research on child development, parenting, and family process to multiple interested communities, including researchers, practitioners, policymakers, educators, and parents themselves. These efforts are organized to make child development and parenting flourishing areas of scientific inquiry. For example, I was principal scientist for parenting and child well-being at the Center for Child Well-Being, an organization dedicated to promoting the positive growth and development of children from birth to age 5 years by supporting those most responsible for children—their parents.

Federal officials, policymakers, educators, practitioners, and parents alike increasingly are turning to developmental scientists to provide evidence-based research on how to promote positive development in children and on how society might best support positive parenting and positive development. This research directly addresses socially relevant issues, and my efforts to disseminate work on child development and parenting are intended to bridge the gap between basic research and application.

## Advantages of Government Service

Longitudinal developmental investigations are those in which children and their parents are studied repeatedly across development. They are labor intensive and time consuming, yet they are unmatched in terms of the information they can provide and the questions they can address. Longitudinal studies document life histories of parent–child relationships, thereby enabling researchers to identify the antecedents and later consequences of experience and child behavior.

Much of my developmental research has been longitudinal. I have attempted to trace stability, change, and mutual influence in parent–child interactions from before birth and in the earliest months of infancy through childhood into adolescence and early adulthood. I have also extended my longitudinal research on families to well over a dozen societies. These longitudinal cross-cultural studies have produced an extensive archival database on child development, parenting, and family process, and they offer the field of developmental science a detailed portrayal of how broader cultural ideologies and customs suffuse everyday parenting cognitions and practices and styles to shape the course of human development.

Because funding depends on performance, past and promised, consistently productive and successful scientists within the DIR usually can count on a continuous (but not magnanimous) stream of funding, which permits their undertaking some kinds of research that are not well supported in academia or business and industry. For example, from the perspective of developmental science, longitudinal research, and especially cross-cultural longitudinal research, is unique for its potential yield; because of multiple and diverse impediments, normally it is rare as well. The nature of the funding stream within the NICHD DIR can support this kind of high-risk, high-payoff approach. Almost no institution outside the federal government is in a position to promise continuing support of this kind. So, for example, at the time of this writing, I am undertaking the 23-year follow-up to a longitudinal research program begun when the infants in participating families were 5 months of age. Similarly, I have been able to engage in multiple collaborations to conduct parallel (at least short-term) longitudinal studies with colleagues in a variety of different cultures worldwide.

Other benefits are associated with a position of responsibility in a government agency, such as the NICHD. For example, each year a small amount of available funding is set aside for travel to national and international scientific meetings and even for intramural research scientists themselves to organize workshops and conferences on relevant scientific topics. I have competed successfully for such funds and, through NICHD sponsorship, have organized research conferences on topics of my choosing.

## Disadvantages of Government Service

While a position as a federal scientist has the aforementioned advantages, it also has distinct disadvantages. The degree of academic and personal freedom that normally attends a tenured appointment within a university setting, for example, does not exist within the hierarchically structured and regimented federal bureaucracy. Despite the good will and efforts of succeeding executive administrations interested in streamlining government agencies, the functioning of the U.S. government remains mired in a tightening bundle of red-tape rules and regulations that sometimes thwart action, ingenuity, and enterprise to the detriment of progress in science, personal careers, functioning of research laboratories, and efficient use of taxpayer dollars.

For example, for most psychological scientists, research communications take place in one of two fora—journal publications and scientific conferences. Unfortunately, journal papers are normally years out of date. Hence, travel to conferences is vital for a variety of reasons, including career advancement, staying abreast of developments in one's field, having ample opportunity to engage counterparts outside of the federal government, sharing best practices, and enhancing overall ability to deliver breakthrough advancements in science. Furthermore, travel is often necessary for licensing, to attend refresher courses, and to earn continuing education credits. Despite these mission-critical reasons, severe travel restrictions and conference budgets for federal scientists in 2015 remain at 30% of their 2010 level (cemented in place by the 2013 U.S. government sequestration; to be discussed). In consequence of these restrictions on spending for travel and conferences ordered by the

Office of Management and Budget, the Science and Technology Council's April 2014 survey found that federal scientists have been disadvantaged because they rely on presenting research to their peers for professional advancement and recognition, while the spending restrictions paradoxically spawn new costs, voluminous paperwork, and multiple levels of staff review. As a result, departments now find themselves concerned about recruiting talent and keeping scientists from leaving for academia, business, and industry. Even considering the extraordinary productivity of research staff within the NIH, scientific progress could be increased several fold if scientists were released (to the degree possible) from the bonds of such red tape.

The NIH and other similar government research agencies do not (normally) grant degrees, so there are no students—undergraduate or graduate—to mentor, collaborate with, and teach. The NIH, however, does train young people in internships following their bachelor's degree and sponsor postdoctoral training.

One particular disadvantage for social and behavioral scientists is the lack of recognition within the executive administration or general scientific staff that major afflictions in the population of the United States (and the world) have distinct and identifiable social and behavioral causes and are not solely or wholly genetic or biological in origin or cure. For example, cancer, obesity, AIDS, traffic accidents, binge drinking, and lack of exercise all have high morbidity and mortality and often reflect fundamental behavioral choices and decision making. According to the American Cancer Society, in 2015 an estimated 1,658,370 new cancer cases will be diagnosed and 589,430 deaths in the United States will be attributable to cancer (American Cancer Society, 2015). Breast cancers are the most common form of cancer in the United States and are expected to rise by 50% by 2030. According to the National Cancer Institute, the rise in breast cancers will be attributable to three main causes: increasing numbers of older women in the population, increasing life expectancy, and an increase in tumors that are receptive to the hormone estrogen, the last of which is probably the result of changes in "circumstances and lifestyles" (Bernstein, 2015). Many cancer deaths are related to poor nutrition, physical inactivity, body mass index, smoking, and other circumstances and lifestyle factors, which means that many cancer deaths could be prevented if people stopped smoking, exercised more, ate healthier food, and so forth. These healthy and positive behavioral choices are learned in childhood and practiced throughout life and are not reducible to DNA. This argument alone ought to motivate more support for the social and behavior sciences, but on the NIH campus, for example, there are some 2,200 principal investigators (senior scientific staff), but only 1.44% are identified as social and behavioral scientists (and most of them do not self-identify as such).

The arrow of reductionism (*reductionism* is the philosophy that high-order phenomena can be reduced to biology) is strong within the currents of thinking and funding in the NIH and the U.S. government at large. For example, within the DIR of the Child Health Institute, most laboratories are concerned with cellular, molecular, or genetic function or theory. Only one laboratory in the DIR is concerned with basic social and behavioral research of the whole-organism human child (i.e., CFR). At the naval hospital in Camp Pendleton near San Diego, CA, only physicians are approved to attend annual conferences. In short, on the contemporary federal scene, social and behavioral science research is ill esteemed and poorly supported.

Government employment often is perceived as being secure and stable (like tenure in academia) relative to business and industry. Scientists in academia, however, have much freer access to remunerative opportunities outside of work than does the typical government researcher; academic psychologists can write books, act as expert witnesses in court, and consult. Scientists in business and industry normally are remunerated for their work at substantially higher levels than those in government service. For scientists who are civil servants in the government, supplementary employment is possible, but approval to do so is required at multiple bureaucratic levels because of the potential for conflict of interest between outside employment and government work. Often, the process of securing such permissions is onerous (i.e., justifications, oaths, and numerous signatures of various executives). Consequently, most government researchers simply give up doing outside work or severely limit the amount of outside work they do. Unlike in academia and business or industry, federal service for many is a nine-to-five job and has no sabbatical opportunities.

Finally, federal budgetary woes affect not only the conduct of science but also personal welfare. For instance, even federal employee-friendly executive administrations can arbitrarily freeze wages, as happened during the 3-year period 2011–2014. Separate from issues of how government functions are questions of whether, at times, it functions at all, as in recent government shutdowns and threats thereto over congressional disagreements about annual budgets disrupt scientific progress as does "sequestration," the governmental process of implementing automatic across-the-board cuts in spending for departments and agencies. One sequestration took effect in 2013, during which time seven agencies furloughed (unpaid days) more than 770,000 employees for 1–7 days. At present, Congress is entertaining bills to require federal employees to contribute more toward their retirement (Thrift Savings

Plan) plan with no increase in benefits, effectively constituting a pay cut of about 6%.

Of course, it is desirable for government to be more efficient, effective, and accountable, and it is critical for government to root out waste, but reductions in the federal workforce and all these other measures make for a government that is a less desirable place to work.

## Conclusion

Combining science and government service can be rewarding but at the same time frustrating. It is possible for researchers who are employed by the federal government to obtain a steady stream of funding for research, to engage in basic and applied science, and to have their findings affect policy. It is also possible that their science will be hampered by rules and regulations beyond their control. Many psychologists have been employed directly or indirectly by the federal government; famously, psychologist B. F. Skinner once conditioned pigeons to peck at targets in the nose cones of bombs to increase missile precision, and infamously two psychologists were responsible for the development of torture protocols used by the Central Intelligence Agency. Since World War II, the federal government has supported psychological research at federal installations (such as the NIH) as well as through grants and contracts to psychological scientists in the nation and around the world through their academic institutions. In his *Foundation* series, polymath Isaac Asimov cast psychologists (actually *psychohistorians*, scientific practitioners of predicting the future, developed by the Foundation's fictional founder, Hari Seldon) as the rulers of government to the benefit of all humankind. Would that governments in the 21st century were so far-thinking.

## References

American Cancer Society. (2015). *Cancer facts & figures 2015*. Atlanta, GA: Author. Retrieved from http://www.cancer.org/acs/groups/content/@editorial/documents/document/acspc-044552.pdf

Bernstein, L. (2015, April 20). Breast cancers predicted to rise by 50 percent by 2030. *The Washington Post*. Retrieved from https://

www.washingtonpost.com/news/to-your-health/wp/2015/04/20/breast-cancers-predicted-to-rise-by-50-percent-by-2030/

Bornstein, M. H. (2002). *Handbook of parenting.* Mahwah, NJ: Erlbaum.

Bornstein, M. H. (2010). *Handbook of cultural developmental science.* New York, NY: Psychology Press.

Bornstein, M. H., Arterberry, M. E., & Lamb, M. E. (2014). *Development in infancy* (5th ed.). New York, NY: Psychological Press.

Child and Family Research. (2016). Retrieved from http://www.cfr.nichd.nih.gov

*Robert J. Sternberg*

# Epilogue
## *Preparing for a Career in Psychology*

Many of the readers of this book are college students contemplating a career in psychology, whereas others are people who already are employed and considering switching fields, either from a field other than psychology or from one area of psychology to another. This chapter is addressed primarily to those who are not already in the field of psychology, but who are considering entering it.

As you have seen from the chapters of this book, different fields of specialization within psychology require slightly different preparation. But there is a common core of college coursework that will prepare you for just about any career in psychology.

Ideally, you will choose to major in either psychology or a closely related discipline, such as cognitive science, biology, or child development. The psychology major generally will give you the most flexibility for whatever career in psychology you might want to pursue. But for those who know the particular

http://dx.doi.org/10.1037/15960-032
*Career Paths in Psychology: Where Your Degree Can Take You, Third Edition,*
R. J. Sternberg (Editor)

subfield in which they want to specialize, other majors may work just fine. For example, someone who wants to be a behavioral neuroscientist would probably do quite well majoring in biology.

Whatever your major, a solid and broad background in psychology will be a definite plus if you want to go on to graduate school. Most graduate schools do not want their graduate students to have to take undergraduate psychology courses, nor do they want to repeat, at the graduate level, training that students are presumed to have had as undergraduates. Moreover, some graduate programs require for admission the Graduate Record Examination (GRE) in psychology, an advanced test that is difficult to master without a solid background in psychology.

At the very least, potential candidates for graduate school should have taken the introductory psychology course, a course in statistics, and courses in most or all of the traditional basic areas of psychology, such as biological (or physiological) psychology, clinical (or abnormal) psychology, cognitive psychology, developmental psychology, social psychology, and personality. Most students also should have some advanced courses, such as learning, experimental design, thinking, adult development, or social cognition. Success in advanced courses shows that you will be able to handle the more rigorous challenges of the graduate school curriculum.

If you do not major in psychology, consider minoring in it. In this way, you will at least have the fundamentals of the field. And whether or not you major in psychology, many graduate schools consider a broad background outside psychology to be important. Courses in the natural sciences, mathematics, and computer science are especially highly regarded. In addition, courses in sociology, anthropology, linguistics, and other social sciences will give you a broader perspective on the nature of human beings.

I strongly urge college students to get as much training and experience in writing and effective speaking as they can. It is difficult to overstate the importance of communication in psychology. Psychologists frequently find themselves writing case reports, articles for publication, grant proposals, and even books. Strong writing skills are essential. Psychologists also frequently find themselves speaking in front of audiences of other psychologists, students, parents, educators, businesspeople, and others. Public-speaking skills are thus a big plus for psychologists to have.

Many professors at the graduate level strongly urge college students to get research experience beyond that provided in lab-based courses. Such research experience can be had by working in a professor's laboratory, on an independent project supervised by a professor or advanced graduate student, or for a nonuniversity organization that conducts psychological research. Many applicants to graduate school have good credentials. Research experience, perhaps more than any other single attribute, is what often separates the most successful applicants to graduate school.

Research experience has another advantage. When you apply to graduate school, you typically need three letters of recommendation, preferably from psychologists. Working with someone in a laboratory provides an excellent way to get to know one or more psychologists, who then will be in a better position to write letters for you. One of the saddest things I encounter as a professor is when a student reaches the senior year, has not gotten to know any psychology faculty members well, and then is scrounging at the last minute for people to write letters.

Research experience is not the only way to get to know faculty well, of course. Taking small seminars from them or working with them on student-faculty committees provides another opportunity to get to know faculty. But coursework and committee participation often do not give faculty members the same level of insight into your research skills as does research experience, and many graduate schools are particularly eager to attract students with such skills and experience.

Many graduate programs require applicants to take the GRE for admission. One session (the general test) assesses verbal, quantitative, and analytical skills, and another session (the subject test) tests for subject matter knowledge. In some schools, the general test is required and the subject test is optional. It is best to prepare for this test over the long term by getting an excellent broad education. The Educational Testing Service provides information about the test, and books and courses are available that help one prepare for the examinations. The preparation materials may or may not raise scores, but they may give you the confidence you need to do your best on the tests.

Admissions offices seeking a diverse and interesting student body sometimes value extracurricular activities, but such activities typically count much less at the graduate level, unless they are related in some way to the graduate education for which you are preparing yourself. Examples include work in a psychological clinic or hospital, participation in psychological research, and membership in a psychology club. Occasionally, however, other kinds of life experiences are valued for their contributions to students' maturity. Many psychologists believe, for example, that successful work experience of almost any kind can bestow a kind of maturity that one cannot obtain merely from being a student. Some students take a year or two off to get such experience. This experience can be helpful, especially if it relates to one's career orientation, such as being a research assistant for a psychologist.

You should remember one other thing: When you fill out the application for graduate school, the essay you write will be considered seriously.

Graduate school admissions committees look for signs of understanding of, commitment to, and purpose in the field. Thus, merely saying you want to study psychology because you are interested in human nature is more likely to hurt you than to help you. Showing an understanding of what a particular program has to offer and of what the faculty members in a particular program do can help you gain admission to the program of your choice. No one expects you to know exactly what you want to do in graduate school. Admissions committees, however, do expect you to have formed at least some tentative interests.

Perhaps the single most important thing you can do is to get advice from faculty members, especially those working in the area of psychology you are interested in pursuing. College students are often shy about seeking advice. They shouldn't be: That's what faculty are there for. Seek out advice, and you will find that a lot of your preparations will go much more smoothly than you might have thought possible.

When you consider going to graduate school, remember that graduate school is not a continuation of the same kinds of activities you engaged in as an undergraduate. Coursework generally will be less emphasized, especially after the first or second year. At that point, research, teaching, and in some cases clinical experience typically are emphasized more. In graduate school, you make the transition from being merely a consumer of psychological knowledge to being a producer or a user of psychological knowledge.

Some people who enter careers in psychology majored in a field other than psychology as undergraduates and then decided, whether immediately on completing college or some years thereafter, that psychology was the field that truly interested them. Students can be and regularly are admitted to graduate programs whose main undergraduate concentration was in another field. The field need not even be a closely allied one, such as biology, sociology, or anthropology. Our program, from time to time, accepts students who majored in English literature, French, or mathematics.

If you are switching fields, however, you should make sure to complete coursework that gives you the equivalent of a college minor or, preferably, a college major in psychology. Graduate schools generally assume that enrolled students have undergraduate training in psychology, and their programs cannot repeat all the material of the undergraduate program. Many local colleges offer returning students opportunities to pick up the courses they need through part-time, summer, or other special programs. You may even be able to achieve much of the training on your own through independent reading.

A high score on the GRE Advanced Test in Psychology may convince some programs that you have mastered the basic material of psychology, regardless of course preparation. Moreover, some graduate programs admit students for a master's degree who majored in other fields, despite the students' minimal background in psychology, and decide later whether the students are qualified to pursue the doctorate. Again, gaining some research experience, such as by working as a research assistant, can also be invaluable.

Remember, however, that graduate schools differ widely in what they view as acceptable background for entrance into their programs. Some schools, for example, may view an undergraduate major in computer science or biology as being every bit as useful as an undergraduate major in psychology. Other schools may view relevant work experience as a decided advantage. You need to discuss the issue of your background with the appropriate official (usually a director of graduate studies) in each program to ascertain the program's expectations for admission.

You can start preparing for a career in psychology at almost any time. I hope you do seek out a career in psychology and that you are as happy with such a career as I am. But whatever you decide to do, good luck!

# Index

# About the Editor

**Robert J. Sternberg, PhD,** received his BA from Yale and his PhD from Stanford. He also is the recipient of 13 honorary doctorates. He is professor of human development at Cornell University and honorary professor of psychology at the University of Heidelberg, Germany. Prior to that, he served as a university dean, provost, and president. Earlier, he was IBM Professor of Psychology and Education in the Department of Psychology at Yale University and director of the Yale Center for the Psychology of Abilities, Competencies, and Expertise (PACE Center). He was also the 2003 president of the American Psychological Association and the 2012–2013 president of the Federation of Associations in Behavioral and Brain Sciences. He is editor of *Perspectives on Psychological Science* and previously was editor of *The APA Review of Books: Contemporary Psychology* and *Psychological Bulletin*. He has won many awards, including the James McKeen Cattell Award of the Association for Psychological Science. He is a member of the American Academy of Arts and Sciences and the National Academy of Education and a fellow of the American Psychological Association, Association for Psychological Science, American Educational Research Association, and American Association for the Advancement of Science.